THE NEW MIDDLE AGES

BONNIE WHEELER, *Series Editor*

The New Middle Ages presents transdisciplinary studies of medieval cultures. It includes both scholarly monographs and essay collections.

PUBLISHED BY PALGRAVE:

Women in the Medieval Islamic World: Power, Patronage, and Piety
    edited by Gavin R. G. Hambly

The Ethics of Nature in the Middle Ages: On Boccaccio's Poetaphysics
    by Gregory B. Stone

Presence and Presentation: Women in the Chinese Literati Tradition
    by Sherry J. Mou

The Lost Love Letters of Heloise and Abelard: Perceptions of Dialogue in Twelfth-Century France
    by Constant J. Mews

Understanding Scholastic Thought with Foucault
    by Philipp W. Rosemann

For Her Good Estate: The Life of Elizabeth de Burgh
    by Frances A. Underhill

Constructions of Widowhood and Virginity in the Middle Ages
    edited by Cindy L. Carlson and Angela Jane Weisl

Motherhood and Mothering in Anglo-Saxon England
    by Mary Dockray-Miller

Listening to Heloise: The Voice of a Twelfth-Century Woman
    edited by Bonnie Wheeler

The Postcolonial Middle Ages
    edited by Jeffrey Jerome Cohen

Chaucer's Pardoner and Gender Theory
    by Robert S. Sturges

Crossing the Bridge: Comparative Essays on Medieval European and Heian Japanese Women Writers
    edited by Barbara Stevenson and Cynthia Ho

Engaging Words: The Culture of Reading in the Later Middle Ages
    by Laurel Amtower

Robes and Honor: The Medieval World of Investiture
    edited by Stewart Gordon

Representing Rape in Medieval and Early Modern Literature
    edited by Elizabeth Robertson and Christine M. Rose

Same Sex Love and Desire Among Women in the Middle Ages
    edited by Francesca Canadé Sautman and Pamela Sheingorn

Listen Daughter: The Speculum virginum and the Formation of Religious Women in the Middle Ages
    edited by Constant J. Mews

Science, the Singular, and the Question of Theology
    by Richard A. Lee, Jr.

Gender in Debate from the Early Middle Ages to the Renaissance
    edited by Thelma S. Fenster and Clare A. Lees

Malory's Morte Darthur: *Remaking Arthurian Tradition*
    by Catherine Batt

THE PERSISTENCE OF MEDIEVALISM: NARRATIVE ADVENTURES IN CONTEMPORARY CULTURE

Angela Jane Weisl

THE PERSISTENCE OF MEDIEVALISM
© Angela Jane Weisl, 2003.

First published 2003 by
PALGRAVE MACMILLAN™
175 Fifth Avenue, New York, N.Y. 10010 and
Houndmills, Basingstoke, Hampshire, England RG21 6XS.
Companies and representatives throughout the world.

PALGRAVE MACMILLAN is the global academic imprint of the
Palgrave Macmillan division of St. Martin's Press, LLC and of
Palgrave Macmillan Ltd. Macmillan® is a registered trademark in the
United States, United Kingdom and other countries. Palgrave
is a registered trademark in the European Union and other countries.

ISBN 0–312–23968–8 hardback

Library of Congress Cataloging-in-Publication Data

Weisl, Angela Jane, 1963–
    The persistence of medievalism : narrative adventures in
contemporary culture / Angela Jane Weisl.
        p. cm.—(The New Middle Ages)
    Includes bibliographical references and index.
    ISBN 0–312–23968–8
        1. Popular culture—United States. 2. Medievalism—United States.
3. United States—Civilization—Medieval influences. 4. United States—
Civilization—1945– I. Title. II. New Middle Ages (Palgrave Macmillan
(Firm))

E169.12.W413 2003
306'.0973—dc21   2003045771

A catalogue record for this book is available from the British Library.

Design by Newgen Imaging Systems (P) Ltd., Chennai, India.

First edition: October, 2003
10 9 8 7 6 5 4 3 2 1

Printed in the United States of America.

CONTENTS

The Persistence of Medievalism

ACKNOWLEDGMENTS

From this book's conception to its realization, I've been given a great deal of help from a large number of people.

Sections of this work benefited enormously from being presented to a number of audiences whose different perspectives raised challenging and useful questions; I am grateful to the Society for American Baseball Research, especially Neal Traven for encouraging my attendance at the Boson Convention, and Cy Morong and Andy Moye who provided valuable comments on my paper; the New England Medieval Conference, in particular Monika Otter, for inviting me to speak to such an insightful audience; and the New Jersey College English Association for providing several opportunities to explore the ideas found here. Each of these presentations resulted in invaluable critiques that have shaped this project in profound ways. I am also grateful to Anne Clark Bartlett for setting the project in motion on a 1997 panel on autobiographical criticism at the International Congress on Medieval Studies in Kalamazoo. While the project has taken on a very different shape since then, its origins lie there. Of course, it is also necessary to thank the College of Arts and Sciences at Seton Hall University, in particular Deans James Van Oosting and Gregory A. Burton (no, Pete Rose should not be in the Hall of Fame), for providing financial support for these conferences.

This book would never have been completed without an impressive staff of research assistants at Seton Hall who deserve my boundless thanks. Kevin Burton was the project's starting pitcher; the bullpen continued his one-hit shut-out. Reliever Thomas LoGiudice did vital legwork at the library, and his handwriting appears on countless key articles from newspapers and journals that demonstrate the breadth of his contribution to the project, while left-hander Jonathan Stout provided back issues of *Sports Illustrated* and *ESPN: The Magazine* while simultaneously finding out more about Mark McGwire than he ever expected to know, all the while engaging me in stimulating conversations about baseball in contemporary culture. Kristina Dzwonczyk made my work during the 2001–02 academic year possible with her research support and willingness to work on several projects at once, while Maura Harrington came in at the bottom of the ninth inning to close out the game, checking notes, editing, preparing the index, and doing final bits of research.

Many others provided advice and encouragement as I imagined, constructed, and refigured this project. Friends, students, and colleagues from Seton Hall University, the Park Slope Jewish Center, Wittenberg University, and elsewhere answered peculiar questions in my unofficial surveys. Jim Gilson, Seton Hall's compliance officer, offered the insights of a "lay" reader. Elinor Nauen and Roberta Newman, both baseball scholars, encouraged me and provided guidance. Liz Milliken gave me many useful suggestions for historical research on American culture along with her valuable critiques, and she also introduced me to the strange world of Internet fan sights, which proved extremely important to parts of this project. My surviving parents, Edwin L. Weisl, Jr. and Barbara Weisl proved themselves once again thoughtful and insightful critics with distinct perspectives, and they, along with Fredrica Brooks, read versions of chapters and pointed out sections that needed clarification for audiences skilled in popular culture without equally full medieval backgrounds. They also offered suggestions and examples to enrich my discussion.

Two readers, in particular, have been instrumental in seeing this project to frutition. Bonnie Wheeler, editor of the New Middle Ages Series at Palgrave, has supported this book since it was a table of contents, and her belief in its contribution has brought it to life. Sharon Kinoshita's help extended well beyond the expected duties of a reader, for which I am enormously grateful. Her insights, suggestions, and questions have made this a stronger work, and her vast knowledge of popular culture is matched only by her expertise in medieval literature. Her suggestions for further reading have helped build the theoretical underpinnings of this work.

The patience and help of Matthew Ashford and Ian Steinberg at Palgrave and Mukesh V. S. at Newgen were invaluable to the production of this book. Many thanks, too, to the sharp-eyed and unnamed copy editor who helped make this a clean and clear text. Daniel Abraham provided the perfect cover image at short notice. Thanks to all of them, *The Persistence of Medievalism* exists in concrete form.

I have been the recipient of a great deal of help from several libraries; the National Baseball Hall of Fame and Museum provided access to their clippings files, while the Brooklyn and New York Public Libraries provided me with endless rolls of microfilm. New York University's Bobst Library gave me access to their impressive collections. However, the greatest and most hands-on support came from the library at Seton Hall University, whose commitment to new technology made available a wide range of necessary, and often difficult to locate, information. Barbara Ward tracked down countless Inter-Library Loan requests and let me exceed repeatedly my article and due date limits with unfailing good humor. While not librarians, other friends were great sources of information, oral and written; Beth and Marcia Baugh sent me the San Francisco coverage of everything from the 1996 World Series to Barry Bonds's six-hundredth home run; Cristina Ramundo lent me her copies of the *Star Wars* scripts that proved invaluable in writing about the first trilogy; Til Dallavalle and Jason Solomon contributed their expertise and insight on those same films, while Rabbi Carie Carter gave first-hand sense of the commitment of St. Louis fans.

Among all this help the contributions of two readers stand out. Mary McAleer Balkun and Robert Squillace have read every chapter in countless drafts, provided countless insights, suggested readings and examples, provided support during rough times, and shared the experience of researching and writing this project so intimately that their presence informs every page of the book. To them, carrot and stick, this work is dedicated.

INTRODUCTION

THE PERSISTENCE OF MEDIEVALISM

Are there any connections between the Heroic Fantasy of Frank Frazetta, the new Satanism, Excalibur, the Avalon sagas, and Jacques LeGoff? If they met aboard some unidentified flying object near Montaillou, would Darth Vader, Jacques Fournier, and Parsifal speak the same language? If so, would it be a galactic pidgin or the Latin of the Gospel according to St. Luke Skywalker?

—Umberto Eco, *Travels in Hyperreality*, 1986

It was the great Barbara Tuchman who pointed out the capital difficulties of writing about the Middle Ages: that medieval chronology is very hard to pin down, that contradictory facts are perpetually turning up in the sources and that there are frequent and frustrating gaps in the available information. But there is also the matter of reworking old ground that is unlikely to yield anything unknown before. Except in the rarest cases, the medieval historian can offer only a fresh way of looking at things.

—Geoffrey Moorhouse, "The Patron Saint of Greenies"*

It's really digging into what people thought, in a time when their thinking was a muddle of religion and folk belief and rags of misunderstood classical learning, instead of being what it is today, which I suppose you'd have to call a muddle of materialism, and folk-belief, and misunderstood scientific learning.

—Robertson Davies, *The Rebel Angels*, 1980

Imagine Umberto Eco's figurative UFO. First, chaos. Then, in the usual "point and smile" method of communication, the passengers would admire Le Roy Ladurie's pens and paper (or laptop computer), test the various merits of the light-saber versus the sword and puzzle a bit over each other's vestments, admiring the potential of Darth Vader's helmet as jousting-wear and teasing Parsifal about his operatic get-up. Once they worked out some oral means of communication, they would discover, however, their great connection. They all know the same stories. Parsifal and Luke Skywalker's exploits would ring familiar to each other as they compared tales about Yoda and Merlin, Han Solo and Lancelot; Jacques Fournier (the medieval one), despite finding certain objections, would certainly know the drill, while Jack Fournier's[1] (the ballplayer) experiences as a member of many old-time baseball teams would add his own tales of heroic victory and defeat into the mix. Darth Vader might well wheeze, but he would see his own type in various dark figures of the past.

This tension between history and story, between what is real, what is historically determined to be real, and what is fully the stuff of narrative essentially defines Eco's understanding of the Middle Ages and its relevance to the present; indeed, in a sense, for him the Middle Ages are both past and present, and he continues to explore this fascination in the novel *Baudolino*, echoing in fiction many of the same themes he explores in *Travels in Hyperreality*. At the end of the novel, the historian Niketas tries to find out how to incorporate Baudolino's story into his history of the last days of Byzantium. Also tied up in his concerns is whether to tell the story of the Genoese, who fabricated relics. Recognizing that this revelation will cause readers to lose their faith, Paphnutius tells Niketas, "It won't cost you much to alter events slightly. . . . Yes, I know it's not the truth, but in a great history little truths can be altered so that the greater truth emerges." This means leaving out the wonderous history of Prester John's kingdom, and Niketas notes, "It was a beautiful story. Too bad no one will find out about it." Paphnutius responds, "You surely don't believe you're the only writer of stories in this world. Sooner or later, someone—a greater liar than Baudolino—will tell it."[2] The story of Prester John does, indeed, get told in the Middle Ages, making Paphnutius's observation true, yet he makes it in a novel, the past thus postdating the present while predating the past. This intersection of times defines the use of medievalism in popular culture, both in its intersections of narrative and often fictional meanings imposed on and thus shaping what is true, and in its drawing together of past and present to make "history" take on a more fully transcendent meaning. A fuller analysis of Eco's theoretical New Middle Ages will enlighten this essential relationship.

Eco notes an "avalanche of pseudo-medieval pulp," which he calls "wash and wear sorcery and Holy Grail frappe,"[3] a phenomenon he ties in loose relationship—not cause and effect but a kind of parallel interlocutory course—to "tens of thousands of readers discovering Barbara Tuchman" and a uniquely American desire to devour "the Real Past,"[4] creating a tension he calls "a curious oscillation between fantastic neomedievalism and responsible philological examination."[5]

It is this oscillation that *The Persistence of Medievalism* engages. Eco's sense that the neomedieval state of the contemporary world represents a new

Middle Ages is as much political as aesthetic; he sees:

> a great peace that is breaking down, a great international power has unified
> the world in language, customs, ideologies, religions, art, and technology,
> and then at a certain point, thanks to its own ungovernable complexity,
> collapses. . .[because] barbarians are pressing at its borders; these barbarians
> are not necessarily uncultivated, but they are bringing new customs, new
> views of the world. These barbarians may burst with violence, because they
> want to seize a wealth that has been denied them, or they may steal into the
> social and cultural body of the reigning Pax, spreading new faiths and new
> perspectives of life.[6]

Considering the rhetoric that followed the events of September 11, 2001,
it is all too easy to see Eco's vision being enacted; with Osama Bin Laden's
deputies claiming that they "would not allow the tragedy of Al-Andalus to
be repeated," and George W. Bush claiming that the United States was on
a "new Crusade," Eco's sense of broken peace and violence seem very
much a part of contemporary life.[7] Medieval images are used to construct
new conflicts as old ones, reclaiming a past to incite the present to certain
reductionist modes of thought and behavior.

The contemporary presence of medievalism has the surprising result of
questioning the assumption that between now and the Middle Ages lies
an "unpassable abyss,"[8] a divide of time, distance, and often language.
Catherine Brown claims that "everyone who has ever read a medieval book
cold or taught one cold to undergraduates has felt this foreignness intimately in his or her suddenly awkward flesh. All those quotations, all
that Catholicism, all those arguments and counterarguments; not to mention those old words, weird verb forms, erratic spelling, and all that damn
Latin."[9] This familiar and humorous formulation may speak for the
medieval text; however, her concomitant assumption that "there is no
question that the Middle Ages is an other, perhaps even a foreign place,
someplace, as the etymology indicates, beyond our own doors" may not
seem so cut and dried in the face of the prominent persistence of medievalism in contemporary culture. A series of questions arise for Brown in her
reading of the Middle Ages: "What are we doing when we go there? What
happens to 'here' and 'there' when we go? The question isn't whether
medieval people did things differently than we do now; the question is what
we as putative nonmedievals are going to do with the difference. What stories do we tell ourselves about it? What do they do to and for us?"[10] Her
Middle Ages is constructed primarily from literary texts, and her relationship to the past is as a reader or audience, and she attempts to get at the
medieval experience by understanding their methods of reading and consuming texts. The value of her discussion for understanding contemporary

expressions of medievalism is its focus on text and audience, for it is in these two loci that this medievalism occurs. If contemporary medievalism often blurs the difference between then and now, it suggests one method of dealing with that difference. Medievalism in popular culture is found in the appropriation of medieval narrative assumptions and modes of storytelling, yet it is also present in the relationships of audience and culture, in its nostalgia for a culture more popularly than mass produced and more actively than passively consumed. In a sense, as Brown again notes, "the Middle Ages is less a foreign country than 'a living past with claims upon the present.'[11] And those claims call us to. . .learn to live in the middle, between familiar categories of past and present, subject and object, 'self' and 'other.'"[12] Indeed, it is this efflorescence of medievalism in popular assumption that makes that call, showing the Middle Ages not just with us but with significant claims upon what we think is inherently modern, on the time we think most different from the past.

In light of Brown's questions, it is valuable to examine one of the recent stories told about the "Middle Ages." In it, it is possible to see Eco's "barbarian" group stealing into the "social and cultural body" proving a significant return to a medieval set of aesthetics. Consider *A Knight's Tale*,[13] in which the main character, a squire named William Thatcher, masquerades as a knight, Sir Ulrich von Lichtenstein. He befriends a gambling, oft naked poet, Geoffrey Chaucer, who joins his party to promote this unknown jouster in the tournaments and courts of a loosely defined geography of "medieval Europe." William/Ulrich falls in love with Lady Jocelyn, oddly dressed in a Fashion-Week cross between Edwardian and medieval costume; at a post-joust party they dance first to a medieval tune and then to rock and roll, Queen's "We Will Rock You" evidently heading the charts on the medieval "top 40" of 1378.[14] Ulrich's own fashion statement is his armor, forged by Kate the Scott; made of some new alloy, it is both light and strong (a medieval "performance fabric") and carries Kate's "mark": the Nike Swoosh.

The creators of this film seem to know their Middle Ages, although it is unclear how much of what they put on the screen is pastiche, mishearing, or mistake. While hardly as famous as Chaucer, the real Ulrich von Lichtenstein plied his trade as a poet in twelfth-century Germany. Chaucer's abundant life records don't suggest a very dissolute life, with the notable exception of his run-in with Cecilia Champagne; the film's Chaucer appears to be channeling another poet, François Villon, whose life did often involve gambling and running from the law, although he probably stayed dressed, unlike the film's naked Chaucer. Because these characters are either poets or are named for poets, the film covertly suggests that the real identity of the Middle Ages lies in its literature; the film's ridiculous anachronisms are hardly without precedent in the medieval romances that inform the whole text of the movie. If the real Geoffrey Chaucer can have Trojans and Greeks wearing medieval armor and practicing courtly love in *Troilus and Criseyde*, then why can't a tournament audience sing along with Jock Jams? Whatever Troilus and Criseyde listened to in the Temple in Book I of *Troilus and Criseyde*, it probably would have been just as foreign to Deiphoebus and Diomede as Queen would have been to the real Ulrich von Lichtenstein and Geoffrey Chaucer, and Criseyde's "widewes habit large of samyt broun"[15] would seem as unlikely to Helen of Troy as the Lady Jocelyn's flowerpot hat would seem to Phillipa Chaucer. And why isn't a tournament the functional equivalent of a baseball game as the film implies with its bohort-side concession stands, rock music, colorful announcers, and screaming fans?

Just as Chaucer's poem makes the ancients "modern" in the fourteenth century, so, too, does *A Knight's Tale* make the past look like the twenty-first century. If the film doesn't do much to maintain an accurate vision of medieval history, it effectively captures the spirit of its literature. The medieval romance, one of the period's most expansive genres, in many examples puts forth the same exuberant energy and fantastic story. The only truly non-medieval element of the movie's plot is Ulrich's class; because he is a lowly squire, once discovered he can't fight until he is knighted by Edward the Black Prince, essentially joining the nobility through conferred mobility. In an authentic medieval romance, he would turn out instead to be Edward's long-lost son. The film captures the ambiguous nature of *gentillesse* and the goofy qualities of love in much the same ways that Chaucer's romances, or indeed Chrétien's, do. Without Chaucer's anxiety about following his "auctor" and sources, the filmmakers pay homage to their predecessors in the blending of seemingly real events from the past (the Trojan War, the Middle Ages) with a set of contemporary fantasies (courtly love, social mobility). For the Middle Ages and for the present, a loosely defined history, created out of myth, legend, and a scattering of facts, sometimes distorted, can provide both a testing ground for what is new and a way to reproduce and affirm older ideologies.

Silly and anachronistic movies about the Middle Ages that still capture something of its spirit are nothing new; I often find myself repeating what I was told in graduate school by Joan Ferrante, that *Monty Python and the Holy Grail* is the most accurate film about the Middle Ages ever made.[16] Real chain mail, real medieval music, the dead cart, the Black Knight ("come back here you coward; I'll bite you to death!"), the French Castle—only a few coconuts get in the way of the depiction of history: that is, of the Middle Ages more or less as it literarily depicted itself. What distinguishes *A Knight's Tale* from other medieval comedies is the way it blends medieval and modern; intentionally or unintentionally, the film draws viewers' attention to an intersection between the world of the Middle Ages and our own. I refer to Kate the armourer's mark, the "Swoosh" with which she decorates Ulrich's new breastplate. The familiarity of this image serves as more than just a hilarious visual pun; it suggests a return to a symbolic visual culture in our own time, replicating the semiotic qualities of medieval art. There is much decrying of reduced literacy rates in contemporary America—both in a literal and literary sense—blamed on everything from MTV to video games to the failure of Public Education. Whatever is responsible, we are increasingly living in an iconic world of signs. As I write, the screen of my computer presents me with a series of meaningful images: a boxed W for Microsoft Word, an encircled e for Internet Explorer, a small group of stick figures in an oval for Lotus Notes Email. The image of a small book rests at the bottom of the screen; a pencil moving over it while I type, encoding the act of writing that I am nonetheless doing in a different form—keyboard and screen. A red, blue, and green IBM sits over a small set of symbols that indicate battery, power, Caps Lock, Number Lock, and something I can't identify. A Globe and Chain take me to the World Wide Web (make of those images what you will).

The technological age presents a world of meaningful symbols; called "icons," they play their cards far from the chest, as they speak to a kind of religious devotion encoded in their pictorial selves. As a system of reading meaning into visual experience, iconography works both reductively and expansively. The Boxed W means Microsoft Word; the Swoosh means Nike; the cross means Christ; the dove means the Holy Ghost: this one-to-one equivalence sets limits around connections, producing a dictionary of prescriptive definitions. However, because each of these symbols also conjures up a series of stories or meanings, they enable a kind of mobility as well. Microsoft Word's W tells the story of corporate colonization and consolidation, perhaps a less transcendent narrative than the life of Christ, but nonetheless an important warning to its audience about the function of power in the world. Kate's Swoosh provides a more complex story and set of nonnarrative associations; readers will hear the echo of the Greek goddess and her swiftness, and while some might read the Nike symbol as another example of corporate greed, others are encouraged to see it as a sign of speed, freedom, and athleticism, a kind of fantasy of individual achievement or communal collectivity, depending on whether you wear your Nikes for running or basketball. Associated with celebrities and sports figures, it also encodes messages of desirability, popularity, and social acceptance. These qualities may or may not constitute a kind of contemporary religion; what is more interesting, however, is the style of visual reading they suggest. Eco writes, "the Middle Ages are the civilization of vision, where the cathedral is the great book in stone, and is indeed the advertisement, the TV screen, the mystic comic strip that must narrate and explain everything."[17] His anticipation of the Nike example is striking; included in the "everything" that these visual media explain are both "the episodes of sacred and profane history" and "the lives of the saints (great models of behavior, as superstars and pop singers are today, an elite without political power, but with great charismatic power)."[18] As cultural symbols, these anti-books construct a methodology of reading that is not strictly literate. Culture once again constructs itself out of a blending of "orature"[19] and literature, out of symbolic images that tell stories and convey meanings, and out of texts, past and present, in which those stories are preserved.

Eco locates his neomedievalism in both popular culture and a certain collage carried out "on the flotsam of past culture" in a more learned form.[20] However, his sense of the neomedieval aesthetic reveals a predominance of the former in constructing this relationship between the present and the past. The "taste for gaudy color and a notion of light" that he attributes to medieval society is echoed in the "multimedia orgy of the Electric Circus, with strobe lights and water effects" and the "indiscriminate reaction an astounded bourgeois feels when viewing a curious and precious object" is figured as a "young person seeing a poster of a dinosaur or motorcycle or transistorized box in which luminous beams rotate, a cross between a technological model and a science-fiction promise, with some elements of barbarian jewelry."[21] These comparisons hold far more firmly in the world of the popular than the world of high art. In contemporary society, an increasing division is taking place between the two worlds of art; movies and popular music make millions of dollars while museums and symphonies struggle, and there is rarely much overlap between their audiences, except when students are dragged off on cultural field trips. If Shakespeare's own audience was highly mixed, ranging from the nobility in the Lord's room to the peasant groundlings standing in front of the stage, the current audience for Shakespeare's plays consists of a cultural elite and elderly ladies with Public Television tote bags, although contemporary adaptations of the Bard on film have sought to bridge the divide by appealing to teenagers, the MTV generation.

Even superficial readings suggest that this cultural division is essentially a product of modernism, whose fragmented and obscurist program originated alongside a rise in new forms of media dissemination. Although the modernists were profoundly interested in the past, their use of it as a collage of references, combined with unfamiliar structural forms, helped to create a divide between high and popular art, to the point that Andreas Huyssen, in his examination of this phenomenon, calls it "the great divide."

Looking at this profound division, Huyssen suggests that "the culture of modernity has been characterized by a volatile relationship between high art and mass culture," adding that "Modernism constituted itself through a conscious strategy of exclusion, an anxiety of contamination by its other: an increasingly consuming and engulfing mass culture," which, "has appeared in the guise of an irreconcileable opposition."[22] Paying his debt to Adorno, Huyssen locates the bisection of culture in *l'art pour l'art* movements such as symbolism and abstract expressionism, but also in the worlds of experimental writing, literary criticism, and critical theory, whose exclusivity radically divides high culture from everyday life; historically, he ties this separation to the late nineteenth-century and post–World War II periods, as well as the contemporary academy.[23]

This phenomenon of cultural separation can be observed in the reading programs for children put forward in American literature pre- and post-dating the rise of modernism. In Maud Hart Lovelace's novels about the turn of the twentieth century, her Deep Valley, Minnesota characters are often shown reading for fun the literature now firmly consigned to the classroom; Carney Sibley, daughter of the town banker and Vassar student, is given a copy of *The Rubaiyat of Omar Khayyam* for her birthday, which she had wished for and which was making the rounds at college: " 'It's a book,' she thought to herself, and saw that it was a fine leather copy of the *Rubaiyat of Omar Khayyam*, illustrated with color pictures. 'Oh thank you!' she cried. 'I'm glad to own this.' "[24] While her status as a college student at an elite seven-sisters school makes her a more likely candidate than some others for this kind of reading (although how many Vassar students of 2002 wish to receive, say, Seamus Heaney's translation of *Beowulf* as a gift?), her friend Emily Webster, daughter of a quarry owner and unable to afford college, starts a Browning Club with her English teacher, the town librarian, and three other young women, one married.[25] Laura Ingalls Wilder, the most famous chronicler of farming life on the American Frontier, receives Tennyson's poems for Christmas and is captivated by "The Lotus Eaters."[26] Tennyson's poetry, for instance, sold incredibly well, ultimately making him a comfortable income, including £10,100 in 1892.[27] There are notable exceptions, but few of my students, who are all of Carney, Emily, and Laura's age, would find these kinds of books exciting holiday gifts; their exposure to Tennyson and Browning generally begins and ends inside the English classroom, nor do they embrace Don DeLillo or Adrienne Rich any more readily. This anecdotal assumption is borne out by Amazon.com's sales ranks; while Matthew Woodring Stover's 2002 novel *Traitor* (volume 13 in the *Star Wars: The New Jedi Order* series) ranks 52, Don DeLillo's 2002 novel *The Body Artist* ranks 52,735.[28] This suggests that while English majors might occasionally attend a Shakespeare play or a museum exhibit, most others content themselves with the consumption of mass culture through film, television, and music, even basing their reading on these genres.

Huyssen's sense of a cultural divide that profoundly separates the high from the popular is tied to the rise of mass production, a commodification of culture within industrial capitalism.[29] Indeed, in his view twentieth-century art has "reorganized the body of cultural meanings and symbolic significations to fit the logic of the commodity."[30] Mass production may lead to mass culture; however, the "mass" nature of this culture is not the sum total of its definition. Huyssen's sense that "monopoly culture has succeeded in swallowing up all forms of older popular cultures, in homogenizing all and any local and regional discourse, and in stifling by co-option any emerging resistances to the rule of commodity,"[31] while compelling, neglects the generative and truly popular aspects of popular culture—those impulses, I would argue, that are most overtly tied to medieval narrative.

The common line is that modernization "created not only a gap between popular culture and the upper social classes," but that it "tended to erase totally the motley and locally anchored 'little tradition,' " a folk culture that "was gradually replaced by a centrally produced mass culture which the authorities tried to control or use for their own purposes," as Ulf Boethius suggests.[32] Yet a careful look at popular culture reveals grassroots "fan culture" interacting with the mechanical productions of mass culture. Examples abound in the two worlds of particular consideration in this study. Within the sports world, stadiums such as Tropicana Field, PacBell Park, and the embarrassing Enron Field, which was rapidly renamed Minute Maid Field after the 2002 corporate scandal, are increasingly named for the commercial companies that own them; the twenty-five-year-old television program *This Week in Baseball* now intersperses rock videos with the plays of the week, essentially providing advertising space for record labels. On a recent trip to Yankee Stadium, I counted forty-nine advertising images visible from my seat in the Upper Deck. Products and indeed players are marketed through profitable licensing agreements. Many teams, for instance, have developed a variety of alternative uniforms in order to tempt fans to purchase more shirts and caps. Yet in contrast to those consumerist motivations, players' popularity is determined by often unexpected appeal. The example of Mark McGwire is prominent because media efforts to capitalize on the kind of popularity he enjoyed in 1998 have been unsuccessful; in the several seasons after McGwire's glory, attempts to market other players' successes in similar ways have ultimately failed, leaving McGwire as the promontory of living player enshrinement. McGwire's peak overshadowed his only contemporary rival—Cal Ripken, whose consecutive games played streak defined the 1996 season—significantly.

While Mark McGwire's status was preordained—he had hit 58 home runs in 1997 while changing leagues, and a great deal of sports writers assumed that he would contend for the home run record in 1998 before the season even began—Sammy Sosa's popularity in 1998 was both a product of his sudden emergence as a great home run hitter and his cheerful personality; although he never achieved the same vast international fan support that McGwire enjoyed, he was fervently adored in Santo Domingo, Dominican communities all over the United States, and in his team's home city of Chicago. Even though his story was part of a lager national narrative, Sosa's popularity is clearly a product of local, "folk" enthusiasms. Conversely, attempts to sell Barry Bonds, who broke McGwire's homerun record in 2001, have been significantly less successful; despite his enormous talent, his perceived grouchiness prevents him from gaining much love outside San Francisco. Clearly fan popularity and enthusiasm does not stem solely from the record itself; Roger Maris and Barry Bonds have both broken the home run record yet never achieved the support that McGwire and Sosa did, despite fairly aggressive marketing—Maris, for instance, appeared in two films, including *Safe At Home*,[33] also starring Mickey Mantle, his rival in the 1961 Home Run Race. While Roger Maris has recently become more popular, it is not because he has been marketed. On even more local levels, fan clubs spring up for unlikely heroes; in 1996, despite having former major-leaguers Darryl Strawberry and Jack Morris, the Saint Paul Saints of the Northern League's most popular player was Marty Neff, a somewhat chubby, somewhat lazy, somewhat choleric fellow, noted for annoying his teammates while pleasing the fans, whose talents were only impressive in the context of an independent league.[34] While there are always unlikely fan attachments at the individual level, equally unlikely ones develop within communities, and it is just as likely for the merchandising to follow these groundswells as to begin them. While a team might stock its stadium stores with jerseys bearing the names of its big stars, sudden enthusiasms for talented rookies and even grizzled journeymen may prompt sudden changes in stock. In a local example, while Derek Jeter, Bernie Williams, and Roger Clemens shirts are perennial bestsellers at Yankee Stadium, in 1999 and 2000, fan attachment to Luis Sojo, a veteran utility infielder with soft statistics who looked like he played in a weekend softball league became so popular that suddenly Sojo t-shirts were made available.

It is perhaps just this populist element in which the persistence of medievalism is found in contemporary culture. Separate from the cultural elitism created by modernism, yet at least partially resisting the mechanization of mass culture, this middle ground of popular culture is a place where a variety of assumptions and impulses meet. If modernity produces a divided audience for culture, with low culture "despised by society's arbiters of taste, not noted in the cultural pages of newspapers and not encountered in school,"[35] low culture must find its inspiration somewhere other than the culture of the elite. Since an imitation of "high" culture is untenable due to the unsettling difficulties of modernism (or postmodernism, for that matter), popular culture increasingly looks toward older forms and toward a period of less cultural exclusivity. In the Middle Ages, there was clearly more interaction between high and popular culture; within the church, clerics and theologians, despite their interest in philosophy and doctrine, still participated in the adoration of saints, the veneration of relics, and the journeys of pilgrimage, common vestiges of medieval popular religion. It is perhaps stating the obvious to note that within the literary world, high and low culture had to coexist, as no popular literature would have survived without being written down by the tiny elite population of the literate. The critical opinion of what constitutes medieval popular literature has changed—for instance, for a time the fabliaux were considered to be produced for a low audience, while it is now apparent that they were actually written in the courtly milieu—yet Aron Gurevich, in observing that "writings 'for everyone' took their themes not so much from the genres of high, literary culture as from those of folklore" indicates the preservation of popular oral material in written form, as he also notes the key mark that oral culture made on the "small island" of the written word.[36] The two binaries, "high and low" and "written and oral" cannot be directly mapped onto each other, although it is worth noting that there is little if any high oral culture after written culture takes hold in the medieval period. That said, in the Middle Ages, both halves of each pair are in interaction with each other; just as the cultural elite participates in popular culture and popular culture influences high culture, so too, do oral and written cultures interact within the body of medieval literature. Citing Bakhtin's culture of laughter, Boethius also observes this cultural intersection taking place in the Middle Ages: "the popular culture markedly diverged from the educated minority's grave, official culture but. . .the difference did not lead to any repudiation or dissociation on the part of the upper social classes. Priests and noblemen maintained the 'great' tradition, but they also had access to the 'little.' "[37] Thus unlike mass culture, commodified and confined to the masses, and elite culture that encodes its own exclusion, in its medievalizing aspects, the forms of popular culture I examine in this study provide a more level playing field than the two cultures that lie on either side of them.

In Huyssen's schema, modern high culture hides "its envy for the broad appeal of mass culture behind a screen of condescention and contempt" while "mass culture, saddled as it is with pangs of guilt, yearns for the dignity of serious culture which forever eludes it."[38] By reaching back for its inspiration to a less divided cultural milieu, medievalized popular culture reveals a potential to bridge Hyussen's divide. Indeed, that potential provides the lens through which it is possible to view the revivification of medieval narrative and ideology within popular culture. Attempts at academic legitimization of, or at least academic attention to, the particular examples considered in this book precede the growth of the cultural studies industry, thus demonstrating their nonprofessional appeal to an audience made up of both elite and mass elements. A baseball crowd may contain whole teams of little leaguers, families out for a pleasant afternoon or the beer-swilling, expletive-shouting louts who represent the cultural elite's biggest nightmare, but these groups have long been joined by prominent serious authors like Marianne Moore, Don DeLillo, and John Updike, and intellectuals such as Stephen Jay Gould and Doris Kearns Goodwin, or, most notably, A. Bartlett Giamatti, whose career took him from the Yale English Department to the University's Presidency to Commissioner of Baseball. Two annual academic conferences, the Cooperstown Convention, held at the National Baseball Hall of Fame, and the Society for American Baseball Research Conference, suggest a significant group of scholars working on this seemingly popular form. *Star Trek* and *Star Wars* also claim intellectual fans including Stephen Hawking and the Dalai Lama. And if they do not have their own conventions,[39] papers on both have been presented at the Modern Language Association and the number of books and articles on them in refereed journals is impressive enough again to suggest an inclusive form in which medieval cultural organizations of audience persist. These examples are by no means exclusive in this regard, yet they represent a raft of phenomena distinguishable from the mass "consume and excrete" psychology of much contemporary culture. It is the interaction of these disparate fan groups within these examples that separate them from other aspects of fan culture; while there is a good deal of cultural examination of Elvis obsession, for instance, few of those doing the work take part in the Graceland pilgrimages and rituals as anything more than sociological study.

The intersection of the intellectual and the popular provides an avenue into the contemporary appropriation of the narrative world of the Middle Ages. If these popular forms reiterate (often unwittingly) the narrative conventions of the premodern world, it is that which provides them with an interest different from that of strictly mass culture. Walter Benjamin views a work created in the age of mechanical reproduction as separate from earlier art that is defined by its cult and ritual value;[40] it is precisely these values that survive in medievalized popular culture. Inherently entwined in replication through both the technological means of their production and their appropriation of medieval genres, these cultural phenomena nevertheless search for the singular and authentic—be it an object, an individual, or an experience—with a cultish and ritualized devotion that echo Benjamin's definition of premodern art. He finds that "the unique-ness of a work of art is inseparable from its being imbedded in tradition," which these forms, tied to a tradition they do not necessarily overtly rec-ognize, display; his sense that "this tradition itself is thoroughly alive and extremely changeable" makes sense of the vividness and attraction of these cultural examples.[41] They take part in a tradition that is both old and con-stantly being remade; they are both mechanical (and thus mass) culture and art. A piece of sports memorabilia, such as Mark McGwire's seventieth home run ball, is mechanically reproduced (by the Rawlings factory in Costa Rica, which churns out thousands of similar balls a day) but becomes unique through its authenticity (the autograph or verifying mark that iden-tifies it) and its cult value. Its owner, "by owning the work of art, shares in its ritual power" as Benjamin notes; the object becomes extraordinarily valuable and conveys meaning on its owner who is, in the popular parlance of memorabilia, able to "own a piece of history" and thus becomes signif-icant. That this significance comes through the tradition that Benjamin ref-erences is clear; sports objects are made valuable through their connection to a tradition, often tied to records made or broken, within a continuum of measurable statistics, part of the history of the game. Thus they are part of an old tradition made new; having no inherent value in themselves, the meaning they acquire through that connection to an historical moment or individual—and the powers that the object is then afforded—are essentially those of medieval relics. That power assigned to the object turns back on the person who made it meaningful, turning athletes into heroes, both epic and saintly, creating pilgrimage sites out of stadia and halls of fame. Repre-senting modern obsessions, these cultural examples nevertheless recreate older forms of ritual understanding and practice.

While this tension between the modern and the traditional is easy to see in its objects, it also takes place in the more literary expressions of medievalism. Benjamin observes that in film, "mechanical reproduction is not, as with literature and painting, an external condition for mass distrib-ution. Mechanical reproduction is inherent in the very technique of film production. This technique not only permits in the most direct way but virtually causes mass distribution."[42] Indeed, it is hard to see science fiction as anything but tied to modernity and mass production, making it an unlikely locus for the persistence of medievalism. Yet even Abel Gance, in talking about his own films, noted the way that this most modern of genres resurrects premodern traditions: "all legends, all mythologies and all myths, all founders of religion, and the very religions. . .await their exposed resurrection, and the heroes crowd each other at the gate."[43]

Film is not just a good place to tell heroic stories, for Gance's religious language suggests the ritualized and cult potential of film. It is within this potential for cult and ritual response that medievalism becomes a part of culture, embedding it in a tradition while allowing that tradition to live and change within its new historical context. *Star Trek*, *Star Wars*, and their ilk enact old genres within new narrative contexts; as such they create a balance between old and new meanings at the same time. Within a futuristic context, they both tell medieval types of stories or at least reproduce medieval ideologies. Both have cult followings, and the texts themselves exist within a rich creative fan culture that does far more than passively receive this mass product. Benjamin believes that "reception in a state of distraction" finds "in the film its true means of exercise," and suggests that the "film makes the cult value recede into the background not only by putting the public in the position of the critic, but also by the fact that at the movies this position requires no attention."[44] It seems fair to assume that what is true for film is more so for television; although Benjamin does not discuss it directly, its more passive viewing qualities suggest an even more distracted reception. Most films and television shows embody Benjamin's assumptions; however, the examples that concern this book, while perhaps passively enjoyed by a part of their audiences, manage not to separate themselves from cult value, producing their own cults with their own rituals. As with the sports examples given earlier, popularity and attraction are determined not by the producers but by the fans, and their own elaborate role-playing games, literary efforts, physical creations, and artworks reflect desires often different from what the producers expect.[45] Hence the medievalist qualities of these works allow for both mass and truly popular response; imbedded in tradition, they still allow that tradition to live and change. Regardless of whether these popular reactions qualify the worlds that inspire them as art, they certainly reproduce a ritual culture.

The audience's sanction and sanctification of these cultural examples gives them a medieval flavor and context, yet there is a concomitant reversion within these forms, that the audience reacts to in these ways. It is the return to medieval generic conventions that cause these fan reactions. The rise of the Harlequin romance and other kinds of formula fiction fulfill Eco's sense that if our ideas of tragedy and beauty were acquired from ancient Greece and Rome, "from the Middle Ages we learned how to use them."[46] This use of medieval ideas is the flip side to audience response in what produces the persistence of medievalism, for the old forms themselves are exceptionally functional and flexible. Because of their premodern nature, medieval narrative genres are detached from the specifics of purely written forms; if high culture is primarily textual (of course including art within the body of texts), a medievalizing popular culture reflects the intersections of medieval literature and orature in its multiple manifestations. Just as much medieval literature shows an overt consciousness of its oral sources and backgrounds, so too, in contemporary popular culture do oral and "literary" interact; television and film are textual in that they are preserved in a single, set form, but also oral both in their form and in the conversation that rises around them and becomes a part of their overall effect. In some instances, popular works grow well beyond their own texts into other forms and manifestations, oral and written; for instance, the *Star Wars* films, of which there will soon be six, have spawned a huge range of objects and phenomena that are and are not part of the original text (the movies themselves). These include their shooting scripts, as well as films and books about them, not to mention novels that add new episodes, stories, and subplots to the Master narrative. Fan fiction creates further plots on a more local level. Furthermore, and most clearly an intersection of written with oral culture, the whole range of *Star Wars* toys, costumes, appurtenances, and action figures allows fans to act out their own versions of the story in infinite manifestations; my cousin Natty Horwitz has been spawning a vast, *Star Wars*–related narrative for several years in which he, Luke Skywalker, a number of droids, and some characters from *The Lord of the Rings* fight against the evil Glazier (apparently his own invention) and his minions.

It is no accident that much of this resurgent medievalism locates itself in narrative. As Susan Stewart notes, "Narrative is. . .a structure of desire, a structure that both invents and distances its object and thereby inscribes again and again the gap between signifier and signified that is the place of generation for the symbolic";[47] the medievalizing of contemporary culture, too, both invents and distances, constructing a present that, through reiterated stories, connects with the past and at once separates itself from that past through the strictly modern aspects of its media; in the gaps between the "real" Middle Ages and the received Middle Ages and between the seeming contemporaneity of reference and archaism of form, these narratives generate their symbolic meaning. Equally they are built on structures of desire—desire for a continuity with certain past forms and assumptions, desire to impose fixed structures of meaning on that which is elusive and ambiguous, desire for a transcendent liminality in a quotidian and often alienating world, and desire to reinforce comforting, if problematic, values of the past within the seemingly modern forms of the here and now. In her definitions of "longing," Stewart sees the continued story of the "generation of the subject." She comments, "I am particularly interested here in the capacity of narrative to generate significant objects and hence to both generate and engender a significant other."[48] The generated object is an essential part of the remedievalization of contemporary culture, as popular culture memorabilia takes on reliquary significance and function, first standing for the thing it represents and then creating its own narrative life through its "actions." These objects function to link past and present, both in their ability to tie history to the present and in their preservation of a medieval sense of objects; as Susan Pearce observes that souvenirs, as an actual part of a past experience, "possess the survival power of materiality not shared by words, actions, sights, or the other elements of experience, they alone have the power to carry the past into the present."[49] Tied up with desire, the longing for things that are a part of larger stories makes the objects first symbols and then independently operating stories in their own right, just as the saint's bones first participated in the hagiographies that sacralized them but then generated their own miracle narratives. These narratives in turn encode their possessors, as, in Baudrillard's terms, as "each individual and each group searches out his-her place in an order" through objects.[50] Thus, the narrative order of things provides meaning in multiple ways, for the thing itself and for those who are "characters" within the story, including the important "character" of audience. As others, these narratized objects exist outside ourselves, yet become, as Stewart also realizes, a "body which forms an attachment, transforming the very boundary, or outline, of the self."[51]

Nor do the desires negotiated by neomedieval narrative apply only to the individual. Danielle Régnier-Bohler comments "The representation of places and communities is governed by literary codes, and the ultimate secrets that appear to yield themselves up are actually subservient to metaphor."[52] Thus she explicates the relationship between narrative and history; "fiction can," she notes, "claim *narrative* verisimilitude, which is subject to laws of its own. Literature brings to life that which would otherwise be mere description. It fills the very gaps it seems to create. . .Even the most fantastic tales suggest finely wrought judgments of the relations between the individual and the collectivity; in literature, the fluctuating boundary between the one and the many is imagined, or. . .transformed."[53] Her description, which introduces a discussion explicitly of medieval literature, fits a contemporary cultural exploration equally well; in representing the modern or even the futuristic, contemporary culture in fact turns to those same literary codes and metaphors to yield the same ultimate secrets. Both the medieval and neomedieval forms establish relations between individual and community by revealing the boundary between them in essentially the same ways, ways that give identity and meaning to the individual "within the community and subject to its values" while still allowing him or her to "strike roots in a private territory" and discover "private truths." Although both show that the group seems to "be coming apart in the face of malevolent forces, yet in the end, the initial unity is restored, improved, and enriched."[54]

Our narrative culture responds to these same anxieties; medieval genres shape the ways we experience and define our public cultural discourse. Private and high culture remain profoundly tied to postmedieval genres, particularly the novel and post-renaissance drama, and to the assumptions of romanticism, modernism, and postmodernism; on the other hand, popular culture, created to be consumed and discussed, continually reproduces medieval generic assumptions. The world of popular culture now (television, journalism, the Internet) is less like an overtly written culture than it is like the rich narrative world of the Middle Ages, which supported an orature and a literature that interacted with each other to shape generic ideas and discursive production. Old literary assumptions persist in contemporary formula fiction, but they resonate well beyond the written text, manifesting themselves in the publicly experienced genres of sports, television, film, and, increasingly, the Internet. The epic impulses of the medieval world of war, once expressed in *Beowulf* and the *Song of Roland*, now echo in the sports world; the magical adventures and assumptions of romance persist in the liminal extra-terrestrial world of television and film science fiction. The Cult of Celebrity replaces the Cult of the Saints; Halls of Fame become pilgrimage sites of extraordinary power drawn from the ephemera celebrities left behind. That these contemporary productions are profoundly medieval is apparent in their specific connections to the genres they reflect; sports journalism produces a moralized epic in which good and evil are locked in a struggle for dominance (unlike the classical epic, in which both Greeks and Trojans are equally heroic), and while the scores of romance novels that grace bookstore and supermarket shelves replace the supernatural world of the medieval text with the heightened emotion of the sentimental novel, science fiction maintains liminality and magic by producing other planets and alien species. And one only need look to the frenzied bidding over Mark McGwire's home-run balls or Marilyn Monroe's personal effects to see the increasingly reliquary and saintly significance of popular celebrities. In this context, too, medieval generic ideas shape the way public culture is produced; they inform the way cultural stories are told; they create a renewed oral culture with a set of expectations that define character, plot, symbol, and meaning. A perusal of the sports pages, a night spent watching the sci-fi channel, or an exploration of the Internet reveal old ideas at work to shape what we think is uniquely contemporary.

The attraction of these themes and genres in a contemporary world shaped culturally by modernism while at the same time divided by it are multiple and often contradictory. There are certainly similarities between the disparate worlds of the Middle Ages and now; describing this resemblance, Ulf Boethius notes: "it [late modern culture] is both diverse and homogeneous, it is tolerant of 'love' culture; and its elite is multi-cultural—prone to participate also in the culture of the masses." Although he stresses the difference between medieval "pre-differentiated homogeneity" and contemporary "post-differentiated technological and secularized homogeneity (or uniformity)," conditions separated by the modernization of society, he suggests that "a dialectic may be sensed: our late modern culture comprises in a way a synthesis of medieval, pre-modern culture—which in principle was embraced by all—and subsequent modernity, with its sharp divisions between elite culture and popular culture."[55] The commonality of audience that such a medievalization of culture provides creates a potential for community and unification often lost within modern technological society, which strives for greater, globalizing assimilation while at the same time creating widening gulfs between groups. Within a mass culture increasingly commercial, these phenomena also provide space for the "homemade" or truly popular. The fan becomes meaningful within the creation of culture, rather than simply being constructed as a passive audience. In a sense, by looking backward to a period in which there was no mass production, medievalized culture activates those who are generally lost in the shuffle. While fan popularity is indeed often co-opted by the producers of mass culture—George Lucas licenses the Star Wars toys and Major League Baseball provides at least some of the pilgrimage sites— within this culture the fans ultimately write their own stories. Thus, the nexus of audience and form create a self-generated community of meaning.

The arranging of material into narrative units that reiterate medieval genres in modern contexts also generates a particular range of meanings. These meanings can fulfill desires no longer met in other institutions, such as religion, addressing impulses for sanctification, the preservation of relics, and the journeys of pilgrimage in ways that the church no longer can. Indeed, by providing these structures of meaning outside the confines of organized religion, they again serve to transcend categories that separate people and instead provide a shared community experience. Just as the fan's ability to create cultural foci is attractive for its construction of him or her as a vital (rather than merely receptive) audience, these sacred motivations also reflect importance back onto the fan, providing a personal, redemptive compensation for his or her adoration. Within the community of the faithful (of baseball fans, or Trekers, or even Elvis Worshippers) emphasis rests both on the shared group experience and on the potential for individual transformation. Within a techonologically advanced, anonymous mass culture, the power of the individual—both the object of veneration and the one who venerates and the objects that pass between them—within these structures cannot be emphasized enough. At the same time, through their inherently popular nature, these activities work against commercialization and mercantilization. The emphasis on things, on physical objects, does lead to their valuation in monetary terms, and indeed, the whole "sports-religion" memorabilia market generates a great deal of money; however, unlike culture created from the top down, these values are determined by and often materially benefit the fans themselves, again giving them a place and a meaning within a system that thus provides a kind of comfort and consolation through connections to an idealized history and past. The desire to own a piece of history, or at least to visit those pieces, to touch and observe them, leads to the possibility of transcendence. In the believer's moment of contact, time either moves from linear to connectedness, as past and present come together, or it appears to stand still, resonating in the moment. Both these time shifts echo the transfiguring qualities of medieval popular religion, and if the redemption provided by contemporary saints, relics, and pilgrimages do not gain the fan a place in heaven, they do provide him or her with certain kinds of redemption on earth.

If the attractive side of medievalized culture is its grassroots and "home-made" nature, its darker side is the reproduction of certain comfortable and often problematic values. By conforming to older genres, modern stories continue ideas and assumptions—such as those about race and gender—that can no longer be intellectually articulated. Thus these stories become compensatory retreats from *all* facets of modernity; while resisting the imposition of commercialization on the one hand, they resist strides toward human equality on the other. In the process they both preserve and distort the medieval. Although highly complex in their own right, for good or for ill, these phenomena often produce a reductive, stereotyped version of the medieval genres from which they draw. For instance, in the use of romance, both *Star Wars* and *Star Trek* project a more heteronormative idea of sexuality than they acknowledge, or than the medieval romance does, through their depiction of gender. In many ways, these phenomena, seemingly rad-ical in their popular generation and consumption, prove themselves to be surprisingly archaic and doctrinaire. However, that production itself pro-vides its own complexities ripe for examination. *The Persistence of Medieval-ism: Narrative Adventures in Contemporary Culture* seeks to examine specifically the ways medieval genre shapes contemporary public culture. By exploring several contemporary cultural phenomena, this study seeks to reveal the premodern underpinnings of public discourse, both through the narratives this discourse creates and the interaction of the audience with this discourse. An examination of these particular forms of storytelling shows the ways the Middle Ages shape our assumptions of how narrative works, what it is, and how we function as its creators and receivers, thus revealing the complex intrinsic ways medievalism persists in the modern world.

★★★★

Will and Ariel Durant entitled the medieval volume in their *Story of Civilization* series *The Age of Faith: A History of Medieval Civilization*.[56] Although the title provides a somewhat limited sense of the medieval world, this paradigm provides a useful point of departure for the examination of the persistence of medievalism in contemporary culture. Medieval popular culture often manifested itself in popular religion, a series of religious practices growing out of local worship that maintained a complex relationship to the official church. Despite a tendency to think of these as located firmly in the past, saints, relics, and pilgrimage remain a significant part of contemporary practice; separated from the church, they find their location in the cult of celebrity and the world of sports. Existing simultaneously with continued interest in religious pilgrimage, such as the Way of Saint James that draws thousands of visitors every summer, or the Church of Sainte Anne de Beaupré in Canada, these alternative pilgrimages encompass both secular fandom and a desire for sacred and transcendent experience. Notably, the remaining religious pilgrimages remain compelling in Catholic countries, rather than in the sphere of American religion, either Catholic or Protestant. While the most obvious examples include Elvis fans' attachment to Graceland as a sacred place, the vast crowds at the Metropolitan Museum of Arts' Jackie Kennedy show, and the auction of Marilyn Monroe's effects, these devotional forms mirror their medieval counterparts most closely in the practices of sport. Modern religion seeks to distance itself from mystical expression, turning toward a more rational understanding of the role of spirituality. From the adoption of the Vernacular Mass to the elimination of many popular saints from the calendar to the canonization of figures like Mother Elizabeth Ann Seton and Mother Catherine Drexell, who are noted for their charity and good works instead of their miracles, the Catholic Church has sought to exchange its premodern sensibility for a more contemporary model that will continue to attract parishioners in an increasingly skeptical world. These trends were followed equally by most Protestant groups and Modern Orthodox and non-Orthodox Judaism, serving to combat, at some level, increasing secularization. However, the removal of medieval forms of mystical practice from organized religion simply led to their reappearance elsewhere.

"From Big Mac to Saint Mark: Saints, Relics, and the Pilgrimage to Cooperstown" (chapter 1) considers the ways that medieval popular religion manifests itself in contemporary culture. A primary example of the persistence of medieval popular religion is the Mark McGwire story. Although the events are now firmly in the past, they stand to be revived when McGwire is elected to the National Baseball Hall of Fame in 2006; because he still continues to occupy the minds and energies of baseball fans despite his retirement, his story is still being written (or, perhaps, told).

It construes the athlete as a saintly figure destined for enshrinement, whose relics take on transcendent significance instantly without the need to wait for official canonization. While McGwire tells one story in his actions, his relics themselves tell another, both presentations offering a sacred alternative to modern organized religion. McGwire's heroic feats, such as hitting 70 home runs in the 1998 baseball season, function as miraculous occurrences, just as his hagiographic story draws from the medieval genre in its construction. Although much about McGwire and his situation is unique, at these levels he is just an effective current representative of a new cult of the saints.

Mark McGwire has not yet had any curative miracles attributed to him; however, his "good guy" reputation gives him an iconic significance that suggests a sanctified status. An examination of the Mark McGwire cult shows an intensely worshipful fan community that upholds him as an ideal well beyond the boundaries of his role as an athlete.

These aspects of McGwire's essential goodness, however, are not really the most important part of his sacred presentation, nor, in themselves, are the feats that established his stardom. McGwire may well be a role model, a good guy, someone whose importance to the people around him is determined as much by service as it is by baseball. He is often attributed with "saving baseball" after the 1994 strike that saw a drop in attendence and fan support, and is credited with helping the sport "reclaim America" after the Clinton/Lewinsky scandal. But his good character in itself does not produce the aura of saintliness; he was a good guy and a great home run hitter ten years ago, but no one ever talked about him as anything but another good ball player. His current saintliness is primarily determined by the value of the relics he produces.

During the 1998 home run race, the obsession with Mark McGwire paraphernalia reached a fever pitch; in some ways obsession with the stuff became more important than the games, particularly as McGwire and Sammy Sosa drew nearer the home run record, and the balls they hit became prized objects of enormous value. Thus things—whether balls, jerseys, or baseball cards—became semiotic objects that captured both the memory (of events themselves) and the imagination (what these events might mean beyond themselves). In other words, the object, because of its interpretability, becomes the speaking text; just as the saint's relics embody the story in medieval *inventios*, the objects themselves that make the hero immortal and incorrupt function the same ways as the pieces of the saint's body. The sale of false relics, parodied in Chaucer's "Pardoner's Tale" and many other places, played on the physical indistinguishability of one bone from the other, but becomes sinful because pigs' knuckles do not have the salutary value that the actual knuckles of a local saint would.

The connection between monetary value and transcendent meaning is again found in interpretability—and is no different from the value of relics in the medieval world. The narratives of *translatio* followed the relics themselves; their stories were produced as adjuncts to their possession. For all their sanctity, medieval pilgrimage sites were great loci of economic power; favorite concessions and memorabilia were sold at these sites; pilgrimage badges, like the scallop shell at Santiago de la Compostella, becoming the medieval equivalent of a Cardinal's cap or a McGwire jersey.

McGwire's home run balls are not saint's bones; their value is created out of a longing, a desire to interact with history and the transcendent that replaces the real physical object with a narrative that creates in its place a way of meaning or belonging. Similarly, the use of the Hall of Fame and Field of Dreams as pilgrimage sites produces narratives of meaning and resolution about the experience of visiting those places. Narrative must fill the affective gap; the story creates the place that then creates its own possibility as a site of transformation in a medieval sense. The thing, the new relic, is an "allegory" rather than an object; in itself, it may not perform miracles, but it functionally allows for a more modern kind of miracle of healing to take place. Thus, these objects cry out for locations; held privately they can only create a unitary discourse instead of a broader, shared one, more medieval in its ability to reach across space and time, to create a shared understanding that thus forms a community. Just as saints, relics, and pilgrimage helped to unify medieval Christians, so too do their contemporary equivalents unify sports fans, driving off the alienation inherent in the modern technological world.

The rhetorical and structural similarity to medieval saints' lives, relic stories, and pilgrimage narratives shows the continuing life of medieval popular religion in the contemporary sports world. The impulses that created these sacred aspects of the medieval world thus persist, in altered form, in the contemporary world; these examples—mere type texts of their own genres—reveal the essentially medieval underpinnings of the public discourse of sports. If contemporary religion no longer fulfills these desires, public culture provides a locus for them. Sports is merely one area for this preservation; as a particularly heroic world, it maintains several key aspects of medieval ritual and storytelling, yet it is not unique. By considering other aspects of public culture, it is possible to see the multiple ways that medievalism continues in the modern world, perpetuating archaic ideology and doctrine.

Even beyond its religious context, the sports world is a particularly fruitful place to consider the persistence of medievalism; as sports stars (such as Derek Jeter and Tiger Woods) become the rock stars of this yet-unnamed decade, they demonstrate the role of medieval narrative in constructing the culture that creates and defines them. The McGwire narrative is essentially hagiographic, drawing its inspiration from a connected series of medieval religious impulses that work together to form a continuous discourse (from saint to pilgrimage site), but the sports world is rich with other, disparate medieval genres that interact to produce other kinds of less unitary narratives. On the surface, sports, in and of itself, is inherently epic in its formulation, built on the stylized combat that replicates the world of war and conflict that shapes these kinds of stories. Combining fiction with truth, Troy Soos clearly expresses this connection in the opening of his second mystery novel about the exploits of Mickey Rawlings, early twentieth-century utility infielder:

> Ancient hostilities, rooted in tradition and nurtured by each generation, were once again about to explode into open warfare. And I was in foreign territory, about to serve as one of the combatants.
>
> I gave my uniform one last check. It was clean and pressed an needed no adjustment, but I rebuckled my belt a notch tighter anyway. The biting grip around my gut made me feel meaner, more primed for battle. Ready now, I hopped out of the visitors' dugout and onto the turf of Ebbets Field.[57]

Rawlings's sense of the ancient and traditional nature of the hostilities, in his case between the 1917 New York Giants and Brooklyn Dodgers, encapsulates the ways sports compensates for war—or at least the narrative of war. Constructed as conflict, the heroic home team either defends the city or goes forth to besiege the enemy in their enclosed park. Stadia prove themselves as penetrable as Troy, as the invading teams are as likely to vanquish the home teams as they are to be vanquished. Within the groups, heroes emerge—either the long-term heroes who become legends or the short-term heroes whose feats merely win one game instead of a season, the Rolands and the Olivers, Beowulfs, and Wiglafs. Replacing art as a communal public spectacle, sports provides emotional fulfillment of various kinds. As with narrative, it provides compelling characters and a fixed story with a given outcome—one team will win, providing order; it also offers action confined by time and set in a confined space (the field or park) that echoes the boundaries of narrative. With these boundaries, however, there is always potential for the impossible, the thrilling, and the miraculous—all experienced vicariously but immediately. The epic-heroic nature of this world shapes stories along two parallel lines: the knightly heroic, in which the athlete becomes a figure of supernatural prowess like *Beowulf*, able to perform superhuman feats, and the saintly heroic, in which the athlete's feats of strength take on religious and sanctifying powers that go beyond the elevation of the player him (or her)self to the elevation of others through association with him.

Because a sports hero's career is longer even than a medieval epic, they often require narratives to account for their falls and returns, particularly when those falls come through the interaction of their private lives with their public personae. While drug charges and felonies are often the causes of these falls, it is the sex scandal that plays out more overtly in a medieval narrative sense, drawing from the discourse of fabliau to make sense of the break in the previous epic story. The intrusion of women into an essentially masculinized narrative requires a genre that is capable of defining them and confining their influence to limit its power; as an "unambiguously male world,"[58] the contemporary social construction of sport provides no place for a feminine invasion. While the fabliau, then, can clarify the confusion of the hero's fall, it cannot tell the story of his return to prominence, a process that begins with another medieval narrative form, confession. In both an Augustinian and Foucauldian sense, confession serves as the bridge between the debased world of the sex scandal and heroic identity; it is the only possible narrative of return. These multiple genres, like those that define the path of saint from individual to object to place, string together to tell a single story, yet their very conflicting natures expose both the audience's interaction with the subject and the need for medieval structures in which to tell its tale, a way to turn life into art. Although this again represents a reduction of the complexity of medieval genre, its use is telling; as genre defines and confines the characters within the story, it impels readers' reactions, creating organized literary meaning out of messy truth. Thus this use of genre, through its imposition, provides a kind of comfort and security, by making a kind of sense.

In contrast to the image of the saintly hero embodied by Mark McGwire, the sports world presents another heroic model, the more knightly, epic figure whose extraordinary feats elevate him but do not sanctify him. "The Confessions of Wade Boggs; The Confessions of Saint Augustine: Sports, Sex Scandals, and Medieval Narrative Genres" (chapter 2) considers this model at work, while also examining what happens when that model is challenged by decidedly unheroic behavior. Because the perception of heroes is based on a narrative model, other narrative models—equally medieval in their origins and use—take over when the epic story is no longer tenable. In the 1980s, Wade Boggs achieved heroic status by winning five batting titles; his eighty-four superstitions, including eating chicken before every game, became part of his miraculous trappings; like Arthur's sword Excalibur, their ritualistic significance paralleled the epic ritual of the warrior arming for battle. All newspaper accounts suggested that Boggs was "destined for the Hall of Fame," itself an epic concept. However, the discovery of his fallibility, deviance, and immorality (instead of immortality) quickly reduced him to a fabliau figure—an object of ridicule rather than an object of admiration.

Boggs's heroic image was shattered when his extramarital, four-year affair with Margo Adams, a California Mortgage Broker, became public. When she sold their story to *Penthouse* magazine for $100,000, the descriptions of the affair read, as the details were revealed, like the old French fabliaux, like Boccaccio's and Chaucer's most spirited romps. The Boggs story became comic, bawdy, even slapstick; the focus shifted from superhuman achievement to subhuman (or all too human) frailty, providing the quick fix of fabliau in place of the epic's heroics.

The fallen hero angle causes the multiple genres of narrative employed in the public presentation of "news" to intersect. Just as the epic divides women, relegating them to the two supporting roles of the evil monster and the silent wife, so, too, does the hyper-masculine narrative of sport; when a woman intrudes on the foreground, the epic becomes nonfunctional, and the kinds of narratives that accommodate women must be used, finally, to write them out. These genres come into play to contain what are perceived as disruptive forces; they interrupt the epic but are finally subsumed by it; once they have separated out the feminized danger and restored the hero, the epic is allowed to reassert itself.

For Boggs to return from his fall from grace, it was essential to turn to yet another medieval narrative form, the confessional. Only then was restoration to anything like his previous status possible. Thus, Boggs's redemption occurs through his public remorse, his exit from the site of his sin. The "truth" of this story is as much a product of narrative as it is of reality; the genres that shape the different kinds of telling that take place also construct the ways we understand the characters and events within them. The constructive and moral qualities of the epic, fabliau, and romance encourage reactions in their audience that any "straight" recitation of the facts could not; basing themselves on a significant set of narrative precedents causes stories to shape life rather than the other way around.

If epic, fabliau, and confessional are genres that privilege men, the medieval courtly romance seems to allow more interactivity, both through its focus on love (taking two to tango) and its positing of liminal worlds of adventure in which the strict rules of courtly life are unbent through encounters with mysterious others. While this genre would seem to survive primarily in the formulaic romances, like Harlequins, that make up such a significant portion of the publishing industry,[59] a more authentically medieval form of this genre instead lives on in science fiction. "Where Many Have Gone Before: Gender and Genre in *Star Trek*" (chapter 3) shows how, in many of its incarnations, the television show replicates the world, the structure, and the assumptions of the romance, in particular in its relationship to gender. The two forms share an episodic nature that strings together a series of events loosely connected to each other in seemingly random order, the story developing around, rather than through, these events. However, the generic resemblance is a great deal closer than that. *Star Trek*'s famous description of the Starship Enterprise's continuing mission, "to explore strange new worlds, to seek out new life and new civilizations, to boldly go where no one has gone before"[60] locates the series firmly in the world of *avanture*; the strange new worlds, in the many ways that they resemble our world, continue the relationship between real and liminal worlds so central to courtly romance. In both, meaning is found by "setting forth," to echo the title of Erich Auerbach's defining piece on the romance genre;[61] a circular relationship of going out and coming back is the locus both for self-discovery and the reification of a set of values determined by the "real" world and tested in the liminal. While both these genres are, as Auerbach comments, "a hindrance to the full apprehension of reality as given,"[62] both still provide a kind of portrait of the cultures that produce them; Auerbach also points out that romance is "a self-portrayal of feudal knighthood with its mores and ideals,"[63] and *Star Trek* won a Screen Actors Guild Award for the portrayal of the American Scene in 1996.[64]

Auerbach writes of romance: "It not only contains a practically uninterrupted series of adventures; more specifically, it contains nothing but the requisites of adventure. Nothing is found in it which is not either accessory or preparatory to an adventure. It is a world specifically created and designed to give the knight opportunity to prove himself."[65] Once again, this description could work equally well in reference to *Star Trek*; with very few exceptions, every episode is another adventure, and nothing is found in them that is not an accessory to or preparation for another "voyage" of the Starship Enterprise. These adventurous encounters are also the proving grounds for the show's characters; it is through their responses that they are tested and proved worthy, whether they are making first contact with a new alien race or fighting each week's "giant ying-yang or creeping blorch."[66] The alien species that inhabit the liminal world of space echo the others, human and monstrous, of romance; they both show the knights or space crew what they are and serve to demonstrate the superiority of the systems by which the court or Starfleet works. Just as romance's heroes are proved in both prowess and courtesy by their encounters with other knights and creatures whose principles and talents are inferior to theirs, so, too, does the crew of the Starship Enterprise show itself repeatedly to be superior to the other species it encounters.

Both these genres engage gender issues in much the same ways as well. In the medieval romance, women are given a great deal of freedom and authority because of their power in love, and within the liminal worlds these texts construct, women on the narrative periphery may still occupy important positions, ranging from confidantes and go-betweens to judges and doctors. In *Star Trek*, each iteration contains lead female characters who occupy key positions in the crew, while the background is populated by female captains, admirals, leaders, and other powerful figures. The two lead women on *Star Trek: The Next Generation*, for instance, are the doctor and the ship's counselor. However, in both genres, this openness and opportunity have significant limits; what is permitted on the one hand is retracted on the other. Through its drive toward marriage and heteronormative relationships, romance ultimately takes away the power it provides its female characters; once they have consented to love the hero—or perhaps to consummate their love for the hero—all power relationships revert to convention, following the dictates of medieval public life. That *Star Trek* echoes this pattern is perhaps surprising to those who read it as a utopian vision of the future; however, even the episodes that seem to focus on female power ultimately drive to domesticate the female characters, repeatedly consigning them to conventional roles, focusing on them as objects of desire, and maintaining old ideas about women's irrational and emotional behavior. Thus *Star Trek* maintains the same balance of possibility and traditionalism as its medieval counterpart, making the future look a great deal like the past. The popularity of medieval romance in its time is echoed by the popularity of the contemporary science fiction that keeps the genre alive. Here, the doubling of the two primary medieval impulses is played out between the medieval qualities of its concrete productions and the force of fan popularity that creates an entire body of unauthorized or semi-authorized narratives surrounding the master (and mass produced) narrative. However, the powerful qualities of that audience response makes them attractive for incorporation by the producers of the original example. "Rexque Quondam [the foreseeable] Futurus: *Star Wars* and the Commerce of Arthurian Romance" (chapter 4) considers the persistence of medievalism in light of the equally persistent force of merchandising and mass commercialization. George Lucas's *Star Wars* films display many of the same features that make *Star Trek* an example of medieval romance—the liminal worlds, the alien others, the focus on adventure, the episodic narrative, and the affirmation of traditional, conservative values—and they also support a significant fan subculture. As a text, it resembles the Arthurian romance in both story and form. While Lucas likes to claim that *Star Wars* is a myth for modern times, it is striking that among the variety of mythic narratives he suggests, his strongest inspiration is clearly the medieval Arthurian romance. Featuring a love triangle that echoes the Arthur–Guenevere–Lancelot trio of Arthurian narrative, two avatars of Merlin, an Excalibur-like sword, and many other similar details, *Star Wars* clearly draws more overtly from medieval than classical narrative. However, something is missing; the *Star Wars* movies skirt all the issues the Arthurian romance engages; despite the love triangle, the films avoid the conflicts between love and loyalty faced by Arthur, Guenevere, and Lancelot by making the sterile and impotent Luke Leia's twin brother, snatching them away from each other before any difficult questions of incest might arise. The interplay of body and spirit also inherent in romance is avoided; *Star Wars* may have both repulsive and cute aliens, but it has no vital bodies. The central romance tension between individual desire and the state is obviated by the baggy nature of the "Rebel Alliance," which, for all its reference to the Old Republic, shows no evidence of any republican politics or values. Private desire does thus not really conflict with public duty.

However, the films do suggest a set of knightly values, put forward by the Jedi and their followers, and they, too, echo the romance genre's dual relationship to gender. Leia may carry a blaster and help fight the Imperial Stormtroopers, but even in the first film she needs to be rescued, and her later function is primarily that of a love interest. Thus, if *Star Wars* fails as a "myth for modern times," it is a romance for modern times; instead of engaging the difficulties and tensions that define the medieval genre, it escapes them, refashioning romance as theme park. In its attempt to imitate high culture by offering up a myth (for all its failure to do so), the wisdom of the past in light of which the audience is supposed to be awed, the *Star Wars* phenomenon produces a popular fan response that it then co-opts. Unlike the other examples of contemporary medievalism, the *Star Wars* enterprise works primarily from the top down, as much of the money that measures its success funnels back to the same place. In response to a product that offers a reductive version of the medieval genre and stories that inspire it, the popular response is simultaneously diluted. The films offer a purely escapist program, which its audience can be a part of if it buys the merchandise, learns the names of even the walk-on characters, and generally styles itself as fans in a modern, consumerist mode.

★★★★

Geoffrey Moorhouse quotes Barbara Tuchman as identifying numerous problems in writing about the Middle Ages: "that medieval chronology is very hard to pin down, that contradictory facts are perpetually turning up in the sources and that there are frequent and frustrating gaps in the available information. But there is also the matter of reworking old ground that is unlikely to yield anything unknown before. Except in the rarest cases, the medieval historian can offer only a fresh way of looking at things."[67] If staking out unknown ground within the period itself is challenging (although many medievalists since Tuchman have certainly managed to do so), the Middle Ages are exceptionally functional in enlightening the present. Although each of the examples this book considers can be seen as responding to particular political and aesthetic circumstances of its own time, the fact that they all respond by medievalizing suggests that this impulse is not just tied to particular events but to something inherent in the relationship between culture, its productions, and its audience in the modern world. Therefore, if the gender assumptions in *Star Trek* and *Star Wars* at some level reflect the backlash against feminism in the late 1970s and 1980s, or the sanctification of Mark McGwire attempts to counteract the embarrassment of a presidential sex scandal, the medievalizing that unifies them implies its effective role as a palliative to more general kinds of present concerns.

Whatever the factual difficulties of location the Middle Ages may then be, as an idea, the medieval period continues to inform contemporary culture in a variety of ways, both in the form of its productions and the audience's response. The Middle Ages that helps construct the culture of the present is essentially the received Middle Ages, a collection of ideas generated from what people think the Middle Ages may have been rather than what they actually were. However, the connections are neither loose nor tenuous; the relationship between the medieval past (real and imagined) and the cultural present plays itself out even at the level of the smallest detail. The National Baseball Hall of Fame creates its own origin narrative as a medieval *inventio* rather than a creation myth; depending on real places and people to give the story an aura of truth, its final authenticity comes from the relic that verifies it. Wade Boggs follows Augustine's tripartite journey to redemption (just as Augustine follows Aeneas's). Outer space echoes the forest of medieval romance. Indeed, it is this profound reiteration of the premodern within the modern that provides these popular genres with sufficient richness for study; if on the surface they seem to be taken entirely too seriously by their fans, beneath it they reveal a complex set of structures that makes literary analysis possible—and actually makes them more complex than they seem at first glance. Indeed, the function of the fans in relationship to this material is as medieval as the material itself. These cultural phenomena, in their structures and their interactions with their audiences, reveal some sense of themselves beyond formula, a reaching for meaning that echoes the medieval texts and world that structure them. Robertson Davies's explanation of the differences between the past and present is useful here; writing that medievalism is "really digging into what people thought, in a time when their thinking was a muddle of religion and folk belief and rags of misunderstood classical learning, instead of being what it is today, which I suppose you'd have to call a muddle of materialism, and folk-belief, and misunderstood scientific learning,"[68] he suggests the interlaced ways of thinking between the periods.

If the modes are different, the methods are the same; the process of digging into what people think reveals a similar nexus of systems, beliefs, and misunderstandings that shape the stories that define both cultural worlds.

It is impossible to know what relationship the creators of these modern texts (literary and otherwise) have to the Middle Ages; the producers of *Star Trek* and *Star Wars* show a distinct awareness of literary predecessors, although that understanding can be strangely flawed. For instance, an episode of *Star Trek: Voyager* ostensibly based on *Beowulf* suggested that a new, rather different variant manuscript must have turned up by the twenty-fourth century, one that gave astonishing subjectivity to Freawaru.[69] This flawed recollection of medieval narrative echoes Davies's sense of the flawed understanding of classical material that informed the Middle Ages, again showing patterns repeating themselves. If *Star Trek* gets *Beowulf* "wrong," in doing so, it mirrors the ways that Chaucer "misconstrues" his classical sources for *Troilus and Criseyde*; the intertextual connection extends beyond structures and forms a relationship similar to its own earlier sources.

What is striking are the ways medieval criticism, particularly some of its now "classic" works, illuminates contemporary culture. Medieval scholarship has recently brought to light many forgotten works and called attention to important trends, such as female spirituality, that were left out of traditional canonical study; however, it is just those canonical examinations that show the medieval nature of popular culture. Older criticism, such as Auerbach's examination of the structures of romance, may no longer speak to what is current in medieval studies, but it finds a new home in verifying the premodern nature of the here and now. This produces another symbiotic relationship; if contemporary theory can illuminate the past of the Middle Ages, so, too, can traditional medieval scholarship illuminate the present. In her evocatively titled *Getting Medieval*, an examination of sexualities and communities, pre- and postmodern, Carolyn Dinshaw notes that her work is linked to "postmodern historiography," and adds, "I turn next to postmodern discussions of writing history; looking particularly at Homi Bhabha's work, I demonstrate both its radical potential for contesting legitimating narratives of the past and its problematic totalizing of the distant past as well as essentializing of the present."[70] She also notes her debt to "Michel Foucault, the culture wars in the late twentieth century in the United States, and sodomy in the 1994 blockbuster *Pulp Fiction*," saying "exactly how these materials can be related to one another and exactly what we get by making them touch are among my principal concerns in this book."[71] *The Persistence of Medievalism* addresses Dinshaw's concerns in reverse; while indebted to Foucault, Baudrillard, and the discourse and assumptions of cultural studies in its examination of contemporary culture, more profoundly at work here are older understandings of the past that still bear on the production of the present and, that reveal the past, at least in its narrative forms, not to be very distant at all. If the "real" Middle Ages are divided from us by time, distance, and language, popular culture provides us a contemporary Middle Ages from which we are not separated, to which we respond in all the immediacy of the present. Thus "The New Middle Ages" may not be what or how we study, but where we live.

CHAPTER 1

FROM BIG MAC TO SAINT MARK: SAINTS, RELICS, AND THE PILGRIMAGE TO COOPERSTOWN

> *Connect* *with a hanging curve*
> *With a kindred spirit*
> *With the enemy*
> *With your heritage*
> *With the world*
> *With heaven*
>
> —Major League Baseball television advertisement, 2001
>
> *I believe in the Church of Baseball. . .*
>
> —Annie Savoy (Susan Sarandon), *Bull Durham*

One of my students, examining an arm-shaped reliquary box at the Cloisters,[1] commented that in the modern world, it seemed very peculiar to place such value on the remains of a person, even if that person was a saint. Clearly this student had never been to Cooperstown; while overt divine connection may no longer assure the preservation of someone's bones, extraordinary achievement in certain cultural arenas still assures a kind of enshrinement. How different, after all, are Ty Cobb's dentures (recently auctioned at Sothebys) from the arm of Saint Foy or the Head of John the Baptist? The relics of these contemporary saints show the medieval world to be very much with us; however, they are by no means the only examples of the ways the past inhabits our present. The very calendar remains organized around the medieval year; holidays and seasons control our thinking despite an almost complete alienation from the concerns with harvest and weather that inspire them. Why else decorate with snowmen and sleds in the dead of an Australian summer, or strew our urban homes with colored ears of corn for Thanksgiving? To replace the myriad saints' days between major holidays, we create new symbolic celebrations in much the same spirit: Arbor Day, Earth Day, Secretary's Day, Superbowl Sunday.

The sports world is a particularly fruitful place to consider the reiteration of medievalism; as athletes gain increasing celebrity beyond the limited communities of their sport, the conventions of medieval narrative begin to create and define them. As a world publicly experienced and publicly consumed, the sporting scene continually looks backward, reflecting medieval generic assumptions in its narrative production. Sports produces dual discourses, oral and written, that interact to shape generic ideas and discursive production. The profoundly medieval nature of the sports world is apparent in its specific connections to the narrative genre it reflects: the epic-heroic nature of this world works multiply to form the two kinds of stories told within it: the knightly heroic, in which the athlete becomes a figure of supernatural prowess like *Beowulf*, able to perform superhuman feats, and the saintly heroic, in which the athlete's feats of strength take on religious and sanctifying powers that go beyond the elevation of the player him (or her)self to the elevation of others through connections to him (or her).[2] This idolization produces both a literal and a literary culture. Literally, the sports hero is idolized by his or her fans; his or her equipment, uniforms, sports cards, and autographs become sought after and thus economically valuable; these objects are then collected and displayed; those same fans come to see them, bringing other fans; the heroes' reputations are thus perpetuated even to those who haven't seen them play in the first place. In a literary sense, this idolization produces its own hagiographies; the relics produced by these athlete-saints then become the locus for their own narratives, both through their private ownership and their public enshrinement in a Hall of Fame; the Hall of Fame then becomes a pilgrimage site, replete with its own creation narratives and historiographies (and even its own *inventios* and *translatios*). Pilgrim visitors then produce their own stories of miraculous transformation.

Saints, relics, and pilgrimage were essential parts of medieval popular religion, which was often less separate from "high" religion than might be assumed. As John Shinners notes,

> The everyday practices typically associated with popular religion—for instance, a preoccupation with miracles and prodigies, the enthusiastic veneration of saints, the recourse to quasi-magical prayers or charms, an acute concern for the dead—were indeed *popular* because they were common and widespread, as vital a part of the religious life of most educated elites, clergy, and lay alike, as they were the property of people at large.[3]

The practices Shinners notes are directly relevant to the modern world of sports in surprisingly specific ways: the "miracles and prodigies" can be seen in the obsession with extraordinary feats (in particular, hitting seventy home runs in a season) and the fascination with talented rookies (Mark McGwire in 1987 or Fernandomania over Fernando Valenzuela in 1981), the veneration of saints is reflected in obsessive fan favoritism, the "recourse to quasi-magical prayers or charms" in the vast currency of superstition (wearing the same underwear to every game will make the home team win), and the "acute concern for the dead," the continued interest in the careers of players long retired and even dead (Babe Ruth). Like much medieval popular religion, this adulation begins as a local devotion, whose groundswell causes it to take hold in "clerical circles,"[4] finally to be institutionalized by the church (the league itself; the Hall of Fame; the commissioner's office). Saints, in particular, were popularly produced in the Middle Ages, beginning essentially as grassroots local devotions and growing into the notable cults of worship; indeed, "local acclamation of a person's sanctity was always far more important for making saints and sustaining their cults than papal approval, even after 1234 when Pope Gregory IX officially claimed canonization of saints as the papacy's prerogative."[5] Baseball's Hall of Fame, too, teems with official immortals almost totally forgotten by actual fans: Ross Youngs, Addie Joss, and Mort Cooper (or is it his brother Walker?).

The local and personal character of medieval popular religion sought to "make tangible and effective the perceived link between this world and some higher reality," yet in so doing often sought "to render concrete what must remain mysterious."[6] This concretizing desire is, to some extent, behind the fascination with saints, relics, and pilgrimage; focusing on a literal part of a literal person in a literal place gives a physical body to that which is essentially transcendent. A relic can both encode its own history— the story of the saint's life and miracles, pre- and posthumous—and become a link to the essentially intangible world of divine grace; pilgrimage sites not only provide loci for these relics but also embody their own stories that are both literal and allegorical. Thus, the many medieval pieces of the true cross testify to both the need to make real what is mystical (putting a piece of the passion story into the worshipper's hand) and provide a site for prayers for future salvation and earthly prosperity; they constitute an intermediary between the earthly Christian, religious history, and a sacred future. That transcendence, however, is often couched in extremely functional terms; as Shinners notes, the "business-like, literal minded. . . attitude of medieval Christians toward their every day beliefs understandably arose from the simple human need to manifest nebulous ideas about the supernatural, life and death, and human celebration and tragedy in solid, understandable images and purposeful action." If much popular devotion of the period seems like gross superstition, it remains a way of coping with the world; "medieval people grabbed for whatever tools, natural or supernatural, seemed to work best under the circumstances."[7]

Lest medieval popular religion seem solely "preoccupied with marvels and wonders at the expense of genuine piety and conversion of life," it is important to remember the creative, generative character of its local and personal devotions. As such, it was "free from the academically narrow categories placed on something as encompassing, amorphous, and mysterious as religious belief."[8] While certainly functional in its almost exchange-based assumptions ("If I pray to X relic in Y way, I'll get Z"), much popular Christianity was profoundly affective, and as Shinners notes, "in their public and private devotions medieval people were often and deeply moved to pity, sorrow, joy, and terror. . . .Popular religion addressed feelings of genuine need, so it came from the heart, was emotionally focused, and intensely human."[9] Concrete in its actions, yet affective in its meaning, medieval popular Christianity addressed multiple, complex needs for a varied populace. To return to Shinners's opening point that "popular religion" was essentially everyone's religion, separate from the intellectual theology that also occupied monks, clerics, and some members of the upper classes, it becomes abundantly clear that in striving to "bridge the gap between the sacred and the profane"[10] this tradition functioned to connect the literal to the transcendent, this world of things and the next world of ideas. Trading in the physical world of relics and holy sites, popular religion also created a mode of narrative interpretability that allowed solid objects to become pathways to more divine experience. Specific similarities of medieval narrative production and ritual practice to contemporary sports culture will be examined in detail later; however, the tenor of the popular religious world of the Middle Ages provides a key background for understanding the points of contact between these two disparate worlds.

Or not. Major League Baseball's faith that the sport it markets can lead its fans to "connect. . .with heaven" implies transcendent possibilities in baseball's ability to bring people together and then take them beyond themselves. Indeed, these two worlds have often been imagined in contact, as Annie Savoy's declaration, "I believe in the Church of Baseball" from *Bull Durham* suggests. The website "The Worldwide Church of Baseball" is a popular example, while more scholarly discussions of religion and sport (both pro and con) are surprisingly common in both sociological and literary circles.[11] Russell Hollander's "The Religion of Baseball: Psychological Perspectives" suggests that religion may be a way to "make sense of the intensity of attachment that characterizes a segment of the baseball public. Baseball as religion offers us a way to understand its powerful hold on the psyche."[12] While Hollander's metaphoric understanding of religion is perhaps too simplified to make the religious dimensions of the presentation of baseball comprehensible, he does provide a series of examples of fans' and players' transcendent experiences, ranging from Jim Lefebvre's emotional response to playing in Yankee Stadium, which he compares to a temple, filled with the spirits of Babe Ruth and Lou Gehrig[13] to Philip Lowry's explanation of the title of his book, *Green Cathedrals:* "The more I have studied ballparks, the more they have begun to resemble mosques, or synagogues, or churches, or similar places of worship."[14] Lowry also notes the title is meant to convey "a quiet spiritual reverence" and celebrate ballparks' "mystical appeal."[15] If, as Hollander suggests, "Religious concerns and experiences are likely to change our notions of who we are and the ultimate meaning and purpose of our life," which he claims makes baseball unquestionably a religion, he also suggests that religion requires a transcendent dimension, defined in functional terms, which baseball provides.[16] Hollander also looks to Abraham Maslow, founder of humanistic psychology, for his definition of religion. Some of Maslow's points that Hollander feels are identifiable as the altered consciousness of "the realm of the sacred" include: "disorientation in space and time"; "the world seems pregnant with meaning"; "we surrender ourselves to the event with feelings of wonder, awe, reverence, worship"; and "the dichotomies, polarities, and conflicts of life are transcended or resolved."[17] Some of Hollander's sense of baseball as religion relies heavily on a post-Reformation idea of theology and a twentieth-century idea of transcendent experience; however, his use of Maslow reveals greater connections to religion in its medieval sense, just as it illustrates the ways in which baseball (and indeed many other contemporary cultural experiences in and outside the realm of sports) can be experienced in religious terms. Much of what Shinners says about the blending of the functional and transcendent qualities of medieval popular religion fits into these paradigms equally well.

One of the most fully developed analyses of the points of contact between these two worlds is put forward by A. Bartlett Giamatti, the late literature professor and Commissioner of Baseball, one of sports' most literary figures, who suggests that "sports are a series of rituals with distinct meanings."[18] He believes that sports "can be viewed as a kind of popular or debased religion" that mirrors Americans' most "sacred concerns";[19] arguing that "transcendent values arise in relation to [sport]. . .because people invest those activities or groups with those values."[20] The religious quality in sport, he claims, "lies first in the intensity of the devotion brought by the true believer, or fan."[21] Sports, "in all their obsessive, overemphasized, worshipped forms are an opiate to the masses."[22] While this narcotic metaphor drawn from Marx suggests a more postindustrial than medieval idea of religious function, in its attention to its mass quality, the aspect of sports that brings together people of different walks of life and different classes in a common pursuit, Giamatti's suggestion also echoes an important quality of the nontheological side of medieval religion. Indeed, he echoes Peter Brown's sense that the medieval church "was an artificial kin group. Its members were expected to project on the new community a fair measure of the sense of solidarity, of the loyalties, and of the obligations that had previously been directed to the physical family."[23] That "mass culture" and community are not far apart is clear from the fan experience, in which a group of seemingly disparate observers unite around a common goal, partaking in a series of experiences communally that create the same kind of solidarity and loyalty that Brown ascribes to the church.

Giamatti locates the importance of sports as "mass culture" in the shared nature of its rituals, by which the crowd becomes a community, partaking in "the common experience of being released to enjoy the moment."[24] While religion is not precisely about the same kind of enjoyment, it does create a shared, transcendent experience that has something to do with joy (and often with sorrow, frustration, or failure). Religion is also about ritual, just as "the game on the field enacts as well repetitive or ritualistic patterns. . . . The point is, sport is ceremony wherever you find it. It mimics the ritual quality of religious observances."[25] Indeed, Giamatti calls sport a "mimesis" of a religious experience, repeatedly engaged. Within this ritual, the fan plays the role of worshipper, who invests the players, or surrogates "with all his carefree hopes, his aspirations for freedom, his yearning for transmutation. . . .of effort into grace."[26] To take the dissolution of "work" into "free time"[27] that informs Giamatti's discussion one step further, this shift from "real" time into "immortal time" echoes that within the religious context, which occurs, for instance, during the ritual of the mass, or through the miraculous workings of a relic; the momentary act of "grace" creates a link between the profane world of the everyday and the sacred world. Thus, within this construct the athletes become the agents of transcendence; they become the source of hope and the locus of intense fan fixation. If, as Giamatti says, "All play aspires to the condition of paradise," a word that derives from the Avestan word for "enclosure," suggesting a "noble or special enclosure" (thus suggestive of the enclosed field of play as a simulacrum of Eden),[28] then it is the players who become the agents with the power to guide the worshipful fans to that state, the agents of grace.[29] In this agency, there rests an echo of Peter Brown's discussion of the rise of sainthood in medieval Europe, when "Mediteranean men and women. . .turned with increasing explicitness for friendship, inspiration and protection in this life and beyond the grave to invisible beings who were fellow humans and whom they could invest with the precise and palpable features of beloved and powerful figures in their own society."[30] The athletes aren't dead, but they still function much like Brown's saints; an examination of fan websites demonstrates the same turning for "friendship and inspiration" (if not protection) to "fellow humans" whom they have invested with palpable features of love and power.

A primary example of the persistence of medieval popular religion is the Mark McGwire story, still being written.[31] McGwire, one of baseball's greatest home run hitters, who broke Roger Maris's thirty-six-year-old record of sixty-one in the 1998 season, provides an example of the persistence of medieval popular religion in the stories written about him. They paint a picture of a saintly figure, destined for enshrinement, whose relics take on transcendent significance instantly without the need to wait for official canonization. While McGwire tells one story in his actions, his relics themselves tell another; both presentations construct a sacred alternative to modern organized religion. More than simply an inappropriate idolizing of athletes or a substitution for sacred experience, this sanctification of sports figures seems to address a question asked by an unnamed American Catholic theologian quoted in Kenneth Woodward's *Making Saints*: "What happens when formal canonization procedures no longer give us the saints we need?"[32] While making a religion out of sports is not without its comic and debased qualities, it is also possible to see the survival of the anti-institutional, local, and creative qualities of medieval popular religion in this world of public ritual.[33] While idolizing sports figures certainly involves hucksterism and commercialism, in its grassroots nature, it is also essentially subversive, presenting a challenge to official, authorized ideas in its popular nature. As organized religion becomes increasingly rational in its impulses, the need to establish links between the quotidian and the sacred finds a new venue. Though by no means a unique example, the public construction of Mark McGwire in 1998 shows these impulses profoundly at work. McGwire's heroic feats, such as hitting seventy home runs in a season, function as singular, miraculous occurrences, just as his story draws from medieval genre in its construction. Although much about McGwire and his situation is distinct, in this sense, he is just one effective current representative of a new cult of the saints.

Saints

In *Making Saints*, Kenneth L. Woodward notes:

> To make a saint, or to commune with saints already made, one must first know their stories. Indeed it is hardly an exaggeration to say that saints are their stories. In this view, making saints is a process whereby a life is transformed into a text.[34]

Thus, a discussion of this contemporary saint requires this transformation of "life into text," and must begin with a story.

The Legend of Saint Mark David McGwire

Mark, from *of mark*, means to take note or observe, for surely his actions were noted by many and led to great things. David, from the Hebrew, means *beloved*, as he was beloved by all for his redemptive acts and glorious feats, through which many were converted.

Mark McGwire was a most compassionate man, noted for his extraordinary hitting talents. As a child, he suffered from dim sight and great pains in his head, yet his troubles became clear to his physicians, who after many attempts were able to cure this malady. Thus he declared, "I was blind, but now I see." In his youth, he often gave away his clothes and shoes to the needy, and was thus forced to attend church in his bare feet. His talents were vast and his destiny clear even as a youth, yet his newfound sharpness of vision did not lead him along the straight and narrow path, and as a young man he was consumed by sin. After much torment, he sought the help of his confessors, and through their guidance and absolution, found the true way.

A native of California, he had been a citizen of the City of Oakland in his famed early years, and thus, he was so well thought of that he was traded to the Cardinals in the renowned baseball city of St. Louis in 1997. That winter, desiring to remain in that noble place, he sought a long-term contract and received the good wishes of all the members of that city by choosing to remain. Saying, "suffer the little children to come unto me," at the announcement of his contract, the saint revealed the donation of $1 million of his annual salary to the protection of abused and neglected children, at which point, he began to weep so profusely that business was halted for a long time. His support for these undesirables converted many, and many donations were made by the citizens of St. Louis, and of the country, to aid that cause.

Now, in 1994, there was a great schism within the Church of Baseball. Disputes between the players and syndics led to a players' strike that brought great strife between baseball and its fans. This raised much ill will, and many ceased to attend games and support their teams. The barons, consumed by greed, compelled their serfs to replace the players and do their work, but they were greatly enfeebled, and were unable to defend the sport. Finally, a truce was reached, but many followers had been lost, and in 1995 play resumed, greatly damaged and much reduced in the eyes of the people.

In the year of our lord, *anno domini* 1998, many astonishing events took place within the world of baseball. However, none were greater than those demonstrated by the saint, who did what none before him had achieved by hitting seventy home runs and passing the ancient and famed records of

Saint Babe Ruth and Roger Maris of blessed memory. In this pursuit, he was joined by Sammy Sosa, Sanctis Dominicanis; the Lord endowed them with such grace and power that not only did they achieve miraculous feats, but they drew many back to the fold, and many were converted.

Saint Mark McGwire's miracles were enacted around the league as he hit the longest home runs ever in many ballparks, all the while continuing to ease the pain of downtrodden children, saying "great is their mourning, and their misery, for the youth of our country is being lost to violence and despair." Each pronouncement caused great floods of tears, so that the face of the saint was often contorted in pain, while his incorrupt body remained great and powerful in its production of great blasts over outfield walls. The people loved him for his glorious feats, and they paid no attention to the things reporters said who sought to discredit the saint's actions, claiming they were enhanced by evil potions and thus acts of the devil. Thus did the saint's work continue and his redemptive power vanquish those who would destroy him.

Thousands came to see him, and through his actions, he elevated the poor, whose inexpensive seats became the most valuable in the park. His many relics elevated those who touched them, inspiring *caritas* as the fortunate ones returned them to him for public enshrinement in the Great Cathedral of Baseball, the Hall of Fame, in the Pilgrimage City of Cooperstown. In exchange, he provided many objects for private devotion to continue his postulants' worship of all that is great and beyond our seeing. Those relics that were not returned retained their ability to save their owners, as their sale changed lives and brought great support to the needy through the saint's inspired charity. Indeed, Philip Ozersky himself, who retrieved the seventieth relic, and his family, were brought out of poverty and thus gave many alms to the needy. These valuable relics aided many through their goodness and can be worshiped at the traveling shrine of Todd McFarlane. The image of the saint was much reproduced as an icon, for the mere sight of him can restore the weak and bring serenity to those in need.

As the record came near falling, the Syndics of Baseball became concerned about those Pardoners who might attempt to sell false relics and claim they were from the saint; the saint himself was also concerned and spoke out against these evil practices within the church. The Syndics began an authenticity campaign, identifying balls with a secret mark to prove their truth. Thus many were saved from buying false objects of devotion, and thus did not lose their souls along with their money.

During this time, the leader of the nation was found guilty of fornication, and the confidence of the community was lost. Yet Saints Mark and Sammy were able to redeem the country through their grace, and many were converted, returning to the Church of Baseball in great numbers. Thus they smote sin along with the ball. Their actions are said to have saved the sport, as it continues today as in days of old, when all postulants found its salutary balm each summer.

Later, the saint met with the Holy Father, Pope John Paul II, and bowed to kiss his ring. Thus his great humility was revealed to all who saw him there, and his devotion increased.

Many relics of the saint were brought to the Great Cathedral in Cooperstown and can be visited at the great hall there. All who set foot in the place where the saint's relics are kept find the devil driven from them and their faith in the power of the Church of Baseball restored and renewed. Yet the saint is also revered at many local shrines, both real and virtual. A pilgrimage through cyberspace provides many opportunities for palmers to worship at the many sites on the Saint Mark McGwire Fan Webring, while objects of private devotion adorn many homes in St. Louis and elsewhere.

While later years found the saint increasingly wounded and infirm, his presence still drew pilgrims to the ballpark, and his miracles continued to increase, as he became the first player to hit fifty home runs in three consecutive seasons and continued to produce relics and signs for those who came to see him. And all who observed him said, "Lord, thus you confer strength in weakness and bring success to his efforts. Let his prayers continue to give help to the infirm and his name be remembered in the Hall of Fame forever." And when his retirement came, all mourned his loss and prayed for him as he began to walk the path to his enshrinement in the Holy Church of Baseball.[35]

What is striking about this hagiography is not that it *can* be written, but that it *has* been written. While this version imposes much of the language of the *Legenda Aurea* on Mark McGwire's story, importing essential medieval features such as the explanation of McGwire's name and some of the specifically religious vocabulary, it is primarily drawn, in its ideas if not its language, from journalistic accounts from the 1998 baseball season and beyond. As the coverage of the McGwire/Sosa home run chase became increasingly public, moving beyond the sports pages into more general publications, its presentation became more and more religious in its content and form. Both athletes were quite well known before the race, yet a comparison between what was written about them before and after 1998 shows a profound change in the ways they are portrayed. This hagiographic treatment was not solely a product of sports writing; because of the Internet, the groundswell of fan sanctification was also preserved, showing its inherent work in establishing McGwire as saint.[36] By considering the key function of narrative in the transformation of local hero to saint, Woodward anticipates the process McGwire underwent from popular, good ball player to sacred figure; without the story that constructs the public figure within a definite set of terms, this transformation cannot take place. This set of terms is determined by the medieval saint's legends, themselves bound by formulae: "rather than attempting to display the workings of an individual soul, the saints and their biographers," Richard Kieckhefer notes in *Unquiet Souls*, "drew heavily, as in preceding centuries, on traditional types and models."[37] Sanctification is more a product of narration than of action; a noteworthy comparison is the fate of Barry Bonds, who in 2001 broke McGwire's record. A noted problem child, reportedly disliked by the media and his teammates alike, Bonds received little of the same treatment, despite his impressive feats. What distinguishes the current elevated presentation of Mark McGwire from the coverage of his earlier career, then, is its generic and linguistic approach. While his miraculous acts form the center around which the discussion is created, it is the story that ultimately makes the difference.

All the stories in Jacobus de Voragine's *Legenda Aurea* begin with a meditation on the saint's name; for instance, Saint Christopher (who shares an impressive size with Mark McGwire), "was called Christophoros, the Christ-bearer. He bore Christ in four ways, namely, on his shoulders when he carried him across the river, in his body by mortification, in his mind by devotion, and in his mouth by confessing Christ and preaching him."[38] McGwire's name, while dwelt on in less exalted terms, still remains an important part of his presentation, its syllables taking on symbolic meaning in the many article titles that bear it: "Mac sets the Mark";[39] "A Mark for the Ages";[40] "A Mac for All Seasons";[41] "The Mark of Excellence";[42] "Making his Mark."[43] "Mark" thus comes to designate far more than McGwire's first name, instead representing the elevated concept he embodies—the new record and its meaning, that which makes his mark on the sports world he inhabits. The signifier, thus, is made significant; the symbol and the thing it symbolizes can be seen to have a necessary relationship to each other. That some of this is merely good fortune seems obvious—the sports writers would have had a harder time of it had Maris's record been challenged by, say, Quilvio Veras or Omar Vizquel—yet the ubiquitous presence of these titles (and note the sacral echo in the reference to "A Man for All Seasons," about Saint Thomas More) suggests that he has the name for a purpose, as if his feats were thus predestined, written, in some sense, into his identity, his story.

Stories about McGwire's childhood again suggest an overdetermined sense of meaning and signification; his bad eyesight, his sinus problems, and his tendency to be easily scared despite his impressive size become wonders he overcame rather than fairly conventional problems. In *Mark McGwire: Home Run Hero*, written during the 1998 baseball season, Rob Raines documents these difficulties as if they were extraordinary, quoting McGwire as saying, for instance, "I have the worst eyes you could possibly have. No lie. Without contacts or glasses, I can't even see the big *E* on the eye chart"[44] and noting that when asked if he was nearsighted or far-sighted, he responded, "Blind."[45] He also comments that "wearing contacts didn't solve all of McGwire's problems as a youngster,"[46] building up the suggestion of greater afflictions than his sight may have been; by turning it into an important issue, Raines makes it a focus for McGwire's difference, and his special ability to overcome adversity, rather like Saint Bernard who as a child falls "seriously ill with pains in the head,"[47] which then lead him to God's mercy and allows him to be "graced both with a deeper sense of all that pertained to the Lord's birth and a more abundant eloquence in treating it."[48] More than adversity, however, it is McGwire's childhood acts that make his later saintly translation inevitable; Raines makes a great deal, for instance, of McGwire hitting a home run in his first official Little League at-bat at the age of ten, pointing out his separation from his peers: "Because he was taller and stronger than most kids his age, McGwire's nat-ural athletic ability separated him from most of the other youngsters."[49] While not quite the same as Saint Christopher's difference: "he was a man of prodigious size—he was twelve feet tall—and fearsome of visage,"[50] McGwire is still noted for his prodigious and miraculous acts (within con-text); at thirteen, while playing American Legion ball, "McGwire once hit a ball—literally—into the next county."[51] Indeed, even his father is struck by his son's distinction from his peers: "The surprising thing was that he had an innate sense of how to play. . . . He knew where to position players; he just knew. It was spine-tingling, his understanding of the game at such a young age."[52] While less elevated than Jesus preaching in the temple as a child, or Bernard's sudden "deeper sense of all that pertained to the Lord's birth," this uncanny understanding contributes to the presentation of McGwire as someone beyond average human attainment, graced with the special knowledge or abilities that lead to his final sanctification.

Miraculous acts alone don't make a saint, however. Mark McGwire's childhood is not that of a latter-day Hercules, a hero in the classical sense, as it would be if he were merely known for hitting childhood bombs over the outfield fences all over the state of California. Richard Kieckhefer's description of pre–fourteenth-century hagiographies clarifies this distinc-tion: "the vitae of the earlier Middle Ages commonly show the saints as epic heroes, bristling with heroic outward deeds; as commanding figures, intimate with God and exercising charismatic power before society; as bearers of virtus in the double sense of 'virtue' and 'power.' "[53] That this explication sounds almost identical to the descriptions of Mark McGwire in the newspapers is revealing. McGwire's power and his virtue thus combine to make the tale essentially moralized, turning medieval rather than classical in its essence; even in these early details, the story is as much about what McGwire is not and was not (a selfish player, obsessed with individual statistics, greedy, arrogant) than what he is (a father, a team player, a good guy, generous, charitable). His positive adult qualities must also be predetermined by his childhood activities; his early behavior, too, must anticipate his later acts of charity that play a significant role in his canonization. An article in *Sports Illustrated* reports:

> One day when Mark was a boy, Ginger and John [his parents] were trying to get him and his four brothers ready for church. Mark still wasn't dressed. "Where are your shoes?" Ginger asked.
>
> "I gave 'em to Stan," he said sheepishly. Stan was his friend. "He needed 'em."
>
> McGwire drove Ginger and John nuts with that kind of stuff. He'd give away his baseball gloves, his shirts, a sweater once.[54]

Rick Riley titles this article "The Good Father"; with its priestly overtones and its echo of "The Good Shepherd," he sets up a common trope in saints' lives, based on Christ's commandment to "sell all you have and give it to the poor": for instance, Saint Christina smashes her father's idols and gives the gold and silver to the poor, much to her father's horror.[55] That Mark McGwire, in his youth, gave his shoes to his friend Stan, who needed them for whatever reason, is nice enough, but what is striking are the details of his childhood that are considered essential parts of the story for an article in 1998. Because this hagiography is not primarily an Augustinian conversion narrative, any youthful high jinks are conveniently forgotten. We never hear, for instance, about the time he made Jimmy next door eat dirt or locked his little brother in the closet, events that may or may not have happened, but which would sully the image the reporters are trying to create. Just as with the saints, after all, the "elect could be identified. . .with absolute certainty,"[56] and McGwire's status as predestinate had to be constructed out of his past. These stories are only in part retroactive; that is, Raines's book was published during the 1998 season well before it was clear that McGwire was going to break Maris's record. This odor of sanctity, then, becomes part of the telling of the story as it happens. McGwire's potential to break the record caused the interest that brought the book to fruition, and made people interested enough to read the articles in sports magazines, but the sacral reading of him precedes the final acts that beatify him.[57]

What's past is prologue, in this sense; these details were irrelevant when Mark McGwire was just a really good ball player for the Oakland A's; his decision to join his wife for the birth of their first child and miss an opportunity to hit a fiftieth home run in the final game of his rookie season in 1987 was presented as a charming, if slightly daft, choice at the time, but it was related as an act of great sacrifice in the feature articles about him in 1998. Yet the story of McGwire's canonization really begins in 1997 with the signing of his long-term contract in St. Louis. Traded from Oakland in the middle of the 1997 season, he was expected to bolt to Southern California as a free agent at the end of the year; indeed, Oakland traded him in the first place because they thought they could not afford to keep him. As a result, his choice to stay with the Cardinals for what was considered, in its context, to be a fairly modest contract, was lauded as a great act of unselfish heroism: as Walt Jocketty, the Cardinals' general manager commented, "There's a lot of money being passed around. . .of people looking for the last dollar, I can assure you that Mark McGwire didn't do that. . . .He accepted less money to play in St. Louis. . . .I think that's an indication of the type of person we have here."[58] Indeed, one of the Cardinals' owners commented, "this was one of the most pleasant salary negotiations that any team has ever had with a player," a miraculous statement in itself, as anyone who follows the business of sports can immediately attest.[59] Having stepped into the semiotic world of hagiography, it is tempting to see the team's name as significant—McGwire's choice to remain a Cardinal, rather than the less religiously evocative Dodger, for instance, may be read as another coincidental signifier that wonderously becomes meaningful, just as his attending Damien High School, with its echoes of Saint Damien and Father Damien, the Leper Priest, adds to the predestined aura that surrounds him; while this particular signification is never considered in the newspaper coverage, repeated reading of it inspires one to think in such occult terms.

The headline of the *St. Louis Post-Dispatch* of September 20, 1997 reveals the key element in the change in Saint McGwire's status: "McGwire's Stature Rose as Tears Fell: 'I was Wanting So Much to Help Young Children.' "[60] In the press conference to announce the three-year contract, McGwire was supposed to discuss his newly discovered "love for St. Louis and his appreciation for St. Louis fans," yet the whole tenor shifted when he was asked about the charitable foundation he had established to help sexually abused children, to which he would be donating a million dollars a year:

> "It's going to be something new for me," he began, "I'm real excited. It's going to hopefully, deal with sexually and physically abused children, children. . ."
> And at that moment, as his emotions overcame him, as he lost his ability to speak and as the tears welled in his eyes, Mark McGwire went from being

popular to being loved. This was no greedy athlete, trying to sound sincere about championships and teamwork while inwardly gloating about his successful extraction of every possible cent from his bosses.

This was the baring of a man's soul. What followed was 33 seconds of silence.

. . .

There was more silence, more emotion, this time ended by applause from the Cardinals employees in the room. "It's a time in my life that I want to help them out. I'll do everything in my power. . .to help them out."[61]

Weeping is sanctioned in the sports world only under very specific circumstances: losing a championship, winning a championship, and retirement. And only retirement makes it permissible at a press conference. That McGwire's weeping was not only outside of the normal order of things, but that it significantly delayed the proceedings, and that it was over the fate of sexually and physically abused children made it a moral signifier that indeed altered his perceived status. The coverage in the *St. Louis Post-Dispatch* (and elsewhere) represents the transformative event that allows the later sanctification to take place; the profound difference between this and other contract signings—the turning of our attention away from baseball and onto greater matters—makes it a threshold through which the narrative passes from epic to saint's life. At this moment, multiple hagiographic themes intersect: weeping, compassion, charity, disadvantaged children (the contemporary functional equivalent of the lepers, widows, and orphans favored with medieval saints' charity), talent, and personality. Jeff Gordon's article, "McGwire's Mark on Community one for Ages," shows McGwire poised on the edge of multiple interpretations; the article begins "Hero worship is integral to our society. We need icons to rally around, beacons to lead us through the hum-drum grind of work, school, and keeping the litter box clean."[62] Noting that "St. Louis was starving for such a hero until Mark McGwire arrived," he asks, "Did anyone else leave you watching games with a childlike wonderment? Or inspire you to rehash great sports moments with co-workers around the coffee machine?" At this point, only the epic hero has apparently been discerned, yet Gordon's next line reveals Big Mac to be poised on the brink of something greater: "We were missing the most precious commodity. . .the megastar who transcends all boundaries to become part of our daily lives. . .How big will this guy be? Huge. Eclipse-like. Larger than the Arch."[63] McGwire's miraculous potential is prefigured in this article, as his home runs are described as "a wonderment" that leave people "marveling." His ability to make the ordinary extraordinary is summed up in the sentence, "This Cardinals' season, as forgettable as it has been, will have its place in baseball lore because of Mark."

Gordon not only distorts reality to fit McGwire into the humility topos, calling this son of a dentist, "working class," he also addresses the intersection of miraculousness and humility, pointing out, "McGwire hits tape-measure homers and simply trots around the bases, leaving the production numbers to more flamboyant sluggers. He isn't a whiner, cash hog, or prima donna, either. . . . McGwire is as accessible as they come, pleasant with the media, gracious with the fans, and respectful of his teammates." Finally, Gordon adds children to the mix: "A divorced father separated from his son, he laments the distance between them. A witness to the damages wrought by child abuse, he vows to spend millions helping kids. McGwire is not only the most accomplished athlete we've had in a long time, but the most human as well."[64] In retrospect, this article seems vastly overdetermined, as if McGwire's future records were encoded in the mere act of his choice to stay in St. Louis, yet it also shows fundamentally how the contract signing becomes the first step toward a larger narrative significance, that which turns McGwire's subsequent record-breaking feats into miraculous exempla rather than the merely heroic acts of a Roland or a Beowulf, just as Brown notes that the cult of the saints ideologically joined traditional heroes with a kind of moral perfection through which the saint was the "'friend of God'. . .he was an intercessor in a way which the hero could never have been."[65]

Indeed, Timmerman's earlier headline encodes two key aspects—tears and children—that are vital in McGwire's "rise in stature" to saintly hero. Weeping is a common feature of hagiography, an example of the extraordinary compassion the saints feel for the unfortunate and their suffering. For Margery Kempe, who is not canonized but whose *Book* reads like a saint's legend, the "gift of tears" occurs repeatedly throughout, "often in association with her meditations on the passion, sometimes in her reflections on sin." While Margery would "gladly have it stop while she was in public," her weeping often "aroused others to cry." She "insisted that her tears had salvific effect, and appealed to precedent in Christian tradition, such as the life of Mary of Oignies, for the gift of tears."[66] While Margery's general level of hysteria vastly exceeds McGwire's, their weeping has much in common, as both stem from thinking about others' pain (children's suffering, the passion) and the sin that causes it (abuse and neglect); their bouts of tears both arouse strong feelings in others, and in a sense, have a salvific effect, causing the "conversion" of others to the cause (as continued contributions from fans to the Mark McGwire Foundation for Children suggest). As a mystic and hysteric, Margery is a problematic source of comparison to a relatively composed ball player; however, she is not the only example of saintly tears.[67] In one of the first legends in the *Legenda Aurea*, Saint Andrew proves himself an avid weeper; hearing the tale of an old man named Nicholas who struggles with the sins of lust, but who is flung out of a brothel because he carries the gospel with him, Andrew "began to weep and remained in prayer for many hours; and then he refused to eat, saying: 'I will eat nothing until I know that the Lord will take pity on this old man.' "[68] While it's fairly safe to assume from the looks of him that Mark McGwire does not accompany his weeping with fasting, he echoes the saint in both response and action: his tears respond to suffering and lead him to work to end it.[69]

That McGwire's charity is focused on children also becomes a part of his iconic presentation. Because his goal is to "break the cycle of abuse and improve the lives of children who have been abused" in order to help them "be a better person, a better adult,"[70] he is figured as a savior in ways a charitable interest in adult literacy or amyotrophic lateral sclerosis might not. The common association of sexual abuse and neglect with poverty and disadvantage (accurate or not) also casts McGwire as an almsgiver; Timmermann's declaration that "his decision made it apparent that the most important thing to him in life is not money,"[71] is not quite "sell all you have and give it to the poor," but the attention paid to McGwire's decision to take a lower salary to stay in St. Louis and contribute a sizeable portion of that to helping children becomes the functional contemporary equivalent.

In fact, the equivalence has been in the making for quite some time. Children had already become the new ideal recipients of saintly *caritas* by the nineteenth century, and their intimate ties to the sports world—in which grown men play boys' games—is demonstrated from the earliest records of professional sports. Thus, they are intimate features of many sports sanctifications, of which the "Babe Ruth Miracle," while doubtless not the first, may be the most famous. In 1926, Ruth promised the sickly little Johnny Sylvester to "knock a homer for you"; the child's hero then went on to hit three in that night's game.[72] While game reports from that day use fairly restrained rhetoric, saying that this merely "cheered Sylvester up" and "while the doctors despaired for his life, he could think only of the world's series,"[73] the legend rapidly grew to include the child's miraculous recovery as a result of Ruth's feat. Indeed, the next day's paper quotes physicians convinced that "John owes his life to messages of encouragement which the boy received Wednesday from Babe Ruth and other world series players"[74] and adds, "physicians say that the boy's return to health began when he learned the news of Ruth's three homers in the fourth game of the series. His fever began to abate at once, and the favorable course was hastened today after he had listened to the radio returns, clutching the autographed baseballs which he received by air mail on Wednesday night."[75] Clearly this story joins heroics with relics; Johnny Sylvester's father, "thinking it might help, managed to get autographed baseballs from both the Yankees and the Cardinals and from that time on dated the boy's improvement, especially since Babe Ruth wrote promising a home run."[76] Thus the curative power extends from Ruth's actions and from his objects, as both play significant roles in little Johnny's resurrection from the dead. Although the accounts are varied and likely inaccurate, one report suggests that when Sylvester was taken to the hospital, he was given "thirty minutes of life,"[77] while others are more circumspect suggesting only "a dangerous condition with a high fever."[78]

In the tellingly titled *Babe: The Legend Comes to Life*, Robert Creamer reports, "The story of Johnny Sylvester is one of the most famous in Ruth lore. The simplest version says that Johnny, a young boy, lay dying in the hospital. Ruth came to visit him and promised him that he would hit a home run for him that afternoon. And he did, which so filled Johnny with the will to live that he miraculously recovered."[79] While Creamer's story is not in line with the newspaper's version (in which Babe Ruth actually visits Sylvester several days later, when Johnny is already on the mend), it retains the Babe's salutary image and curative powers. This "simple" version comes to replace the true account because of its increased dramatic and affective possibilities. In the egregious film, the *Babe Ruth Story*, starring William Bendix, Sylvester is actually taken to the game, where he rises from his bed from the point of death, or paralysis, or something, and walks again.[80]

The reporting of this event became an opportunity to dwell on Ruth's seemingly universal appeal; the *New York Times* used the Sylvester story to "account for the popularity of Ruth among the boys of America."[81] In a piece called "The Baseball Hero," the unnamed author examines Ruth's "subjects," who he claims

> range from the articulate child in knickerbockers to his grandsire. Fill in with all ages, classes and conditions of males, add the ladies who need to have baseball explained to them, and one has an idea of the empire of human hearts swayed by this specialist in home runs. His great value to the baseball industry is the coordination of eye and muscles enabling him to hit a ball so hard and far that thousands are attracted not so much to see the game won as to gaze upon Ruth in a supreme moment.

This charged rhetoric ends with a call to let detractors "consider how wholesome is the admiration he kindles." Describing the sport itself he notes, "baseball is universal. Its influence is beneficent. It makes sound and vigorous men."[82] That Ruth's heroics here extend beyond his miraculous cure of Johnny Sylvester, while not explicitly transcendent, produces an image of a perfected, public Ruth filled with an efficacious and salutary possibility.

Comparisons between Mark McGwire and Babe Ruth became increasingly prominent in 1998, as McGwire pursued Roger Maris's single-season home run record (comparisons of McGwire and Maris, who had one great season and several very good ones on either side of his record 1961 season, were more scarce). While Mark McGwire has not yet had any individual curative miracles attributed to him, he is credited with saving baseball, redeeming it from the crimes of the 1994 strike and even, in the midst of the Clinton/Lewinsky revelations, "lifting us out of the grubby mess that has become the daily news."[83] The 1994 Players Strike, which cancelled half a season, and the first cancelled World Series since 1904 (even two world wars hadn't prevented the World Series from being played) led to great acrimony in 1995 when most baseball owners brought in replacement players to attempt to start the season. These events were treated in the media as symptoms of the sport's terminal illness. Reduced attendance in 1995 did little to change those sentiments. A renewed basic agreement was not enough to return the game to its vaunted status as the National Pastime, and even the excitement of Cal Ripken breaking Lou Gehrig's consecutive games played record in 1995 and a compelling World Series in 1997, which featured the first wild card team to play in the Fall Classic and ended in a tight, intense, extra-innings seventh game, seemed insufficient to cure it. Ripken's Streak was given substantial credit at the time as a kind of tourniquet that staunched the sport's wound, yet, despite his popularity, he proved heroic without being salutary. Because his great feat was essentially human instead of miraculous—everyone can imagine going to work every day for thirteen years without an illness or injury, even if few of us manage it—he was insufficiently substantial to achieve the narrative identity as a saint/savior of what appeared to be a floundering sport. After a brief flurry of attention as Ripken passed Gehrig (one of the sport's martyr saints) and the legendary Japanese Leaguer Kinugasa (whose record of 2,215 topped Gehrig's 2,130 by 85), the woeful complaints about baseball's moribund condition resumed.

In 1998, Mark McGwire breathed "new life into a game that not long ago was presumed near death." According to Baseball Commissioner Bud Selig, "Mark McGwire deserves an enormous amount of credit for this wonderful renaissance. You can feel the electricity in the ballpark when he's there. It's hard to articulate how much he's meant."[84] And his influence was at times seen to be even greater, making up for the nation's woes brought on by the Clinton/Lewinsky scandal; a *Sports Illustrated* article quotes a fan begging opposing managers to "Please pitch to McGwire. . .This is what we need. This is what the country needs to help with the healing process and all the trouble that's going on in Washington. This will help cure the ills of the country."[85] Crowning the healing rhetoric, Daniel Okrent noted in *Time*, "We needed Mark McGwire in 1998, needed him desperately. He couldn't banish the stain of sleaze that leached through our public life this year, nor could he restore civility to our discourse. . .but what a balm he brought to the nation that seemed to spend the year flaying its flesh."[86] Perhaps the most humorous sense of McGwire's ability to affect diplomacy came during Vaclav Havel's visit to the United States in September 1998; when asked during a press conference what he thought of the Clinton/ Lewinsky scandal, the president of the Czech Republic responded, "I would like to offer congratulations to Mr. McGwire and to wish success to Mr. Sammy Sosa,"[87] shifting attention from the scandalous to the praiseworthy, a move that was greeted by "laughter and applause,"[88] including President Clinton's.[89]

Moreover, McGwire's salvation of baseball is cast as a conversion narrative, in which "lost" fans return in great numbers because of the miraculous acts performed by McGwire and Sosa, who receive credit, in part because "these are two people that everyone likes to see do well because they are good men."[90] (The many other impressive feats of the 1998 season, such as David Wells's Perfect Game, Kerry Woods's 20 strikeouts, and the Yankees' 114 American League record-breaking wins are rarely considered an essential part of this renewal.) In his history of the St. Louis Cardinals, Peter Golenbock simply titles his chapter on the 1998 home run chase "God";[91] in describing McGwire's reception in St. Louis, his former teammate, Jason Giambi, said, "He's like the Messiah there."[92] Mark McGwire is called "one of the few men in baseball no one can say a bad word about."[93] This rhetoric is then mimicked by actual in fan reactions: " 'I said I wouldn't go back,' says Rita Rybalski after showing up Wednesday at Wrigley Field in Chicago. . .'But how do you stay away when you see something like this? I couldn't stay away' "[94] and " 'I don't really know a Yankee player from a Giant (football player), but I know Mark McGwire and Sammy Sosa,' said Janice Aiello, a waitress who has never followed sports."[95] Peter Golenbock quotes a letter from an unnamed fan to Mark McGwire:

> . . .when the million-dollar prima donnas went on strike, I quit watching and going to the games. The league owners should put you on a pedestal. You made a fan out of thousands of people again. You have a love for the game and the fans. I wish we had people like you in Washington, D.C. God bless you and your family and bless Sammy also.[96]

More recently, "Joyce," a contributor to Gumby's Mark McGwire Message Board added, "When our country was at it's [sic] worst with disgusting judgement [sic] on the part of our President this was the only encouragement and enlightenment we had. It was a pleasant diversion from all the other things going on."[97] It is hard not to be reminded here of Peter Brown's discussion of the solemn drinking at the Festival of Saint Felix, which he notes was "one passing fleck of unalloyed joy [exactly why that's 'solemn', Brown doesn't explain] in the grim lives of the peasants and drovers of the Abruzzi";[98] while the public reaction to the Clinton/Lewinsky scandal seemed rather muted at the time, the tendency to read the 1998 home run chase as "unalloyed joy" in the face of "grim" reality recreates it as a kind of sacerdotal festival. Tom Verducci speaks of the "zealots who have turned Cardinals games into revival meetings, a chance to worship the almighty long ball and have their faith in baseball restored. The gospel according to Mark."[99] In a more comprehensive sense, Larry Doby is quoted as saying, "This has been a great moment for baseball. . . and a great moment for McGwire, I think the fans have appreciated the game of baseball in particular this year. If you look at the attendance, it's been great."[100] *Business Week* affirms this practical measure of salvation, noting, "a record 70.6 million people attended a major league baseball game [in 1998],. . . .Sosa's Chicago Cubs and McGwire's St. Louis Cardinals led the National League in road-game attendance—clear evidence that their homerun race sold tickets from coast to coast."[101] Calling the race a "quasi-miraculous conflation of events," the author wonders how this might be able to "transform the excitement. . .into enduring enthusiasm for the national pastime."[102]

Enhancing the religious aura of these conversions was McGwire's ability to help the meek inherit the earth, as the cheap bleacher seats, which make up in economy what they sacrifice in visibility, became the most desirable in the stadium. The Associated Press noted, "At Busch Stadium. . .thanks to Mark McGwire, the peanut gallery has become the shooting gallery." The left field stands became "standing room only," but the author notes, "the newfound enthusiasm for such seats—which has spilled over into ballparks in other cities McGwire visits—transcends mere excitement."[103] Because these seats were the final destination of many of McGwire's seventy home runs, as well as his batting practice dingers, they became the locus of "the rewards—cash or otherwise—that come from possessing a piece of baseball history."[104] That money is not the only reward—that some other kind of reward is an essential part of this experience—is key here; just as McGwire makes the undesirable (bleacher seats) desirable through his actions, he also makes the prize valuable beyond its monetary value, imbuing it with "history" in all its various meanings. Because "history" encoded in a baseball again links the present with eternity, making the ball a kind of relic that confers its value onto its holder, McGwire's presence becomes the essential means through which this elevation occurs. (A ball hit into the stands by the talented but human Ray

Lankford, St. Louis' next-best player in 1998, did not have the same rewards—cash or otherwise.) That the "otherwise" rewards were more valuable than the cash was evidenced by the charitability McGwire inspired; most of the fans who caught the significant home run balls returned them to McGwire in exchange for a brief meeting and a couple of autographs.[105]

If any questions remain about McGwire's uniquely sacral status, the unifying and salutary language with which he is described, which credits him with redeeming both the sport of baseball and the primary country in which it is played, certifies his elevated public presentation. Following Kieckhefer's description of the saint as hero and moral exemplum, McGwire's presentation assumes this double form. His feats—and their ability to galvanize a nation—make him heroic; in addition, his "good guy" reputation gives him an iconic significance that suggests a sanctified status, both in the official media and in the more grassroots world of the Internet. In a sense, this parallels Kieckhefer's observation that hagiographies work on multiple audiences: "to appeal to their lay audience, the vitae might contain evidence of charismatic or miraculous powers; to persuade the curia, they would relate in detail the saints' virtues."[106] Who, exactly, is "lay" and who is "curia" in this contemporary context is unclear, as in a sense, the "officials" of Major League Baseball are more likely to make their decisions about McGwire based on the numbers than the man himself, while the "lay" fans are more drawn to his personality. While it is McGwire's records that will gain him official canonization (his guaranteed future "enshrinement" in the Hall of Fame), it is the virtue that goes along with them that make him a locally (or nationally) venerated *beatus*.[107] Regardless of which part appeals to whom, all the accounts, paper and cyber, that construct McGwire, abide by this double presentation.

Although an examination of McGwire's statistics reveals an ability, rarely discussed, to contribute to his team in other ways as well, McGwire is justifiably known for his power—for hitting home runs. Jerry Izenberg, in a religiously infused rhetoric, sums this up: "small wonder the Oakland A's and God—not necessarily in that order. . .—sent Mark McGwire here [St. Louis] to punctuate the evening vespers with his bat. He has made a mighty weapon of it ever since he arrived,"[108] adding a reference to the "ecumenical power of the home run" to reinforce his point. McGwire is noted for hitting

> what are believed to be the longest bombs at Busch in St. Louis (545 feet, marked by a giant Band Aid), the Kingdome in Seattle (538, no designation) and Qualcomm in San Diego (458, a white seat with a giant red M). His batting practice dingers have done more harm to major league cities than urban decay. . . . He thumped one off a stairway railing on Waveland Avenue

[literally hitting the ball out of the park entirely], outside Wrigley Field in Chicago. He has cleared the roof at Tiger Stadium in Detroit. At Coors Field in Denver he hit one that ricocheted among the fully loaded Range Rovers in the players' parking lot. "That had to have gone 600 feet," says the man who threw him the supergopher, batting practice pitcher Dave McKay.[109]

All these epochal home runs, however, pale in comparison to his sixty-second hit in Chicago on September 8, 1998. Although number sixty-two was the "shortest, lamest homer of the year [only 341 feet]," it was also called "literally superhuman" by the Cardinals's manager.[110] Jerry Izenberg called the event "11 minutes of joy and relief, pride and adulation and the kind of foot-stomping, fist-shaking, throat-searing hysteria that only a collective date with history can generate."[111] He calls McGwire "the new spiritual mayor of St. Louis" and the event "baseball's countdown to Armageddon between the foul lines."[112] The transcendent nature of this event is made particularly clear as he says, "But when he [McGwire] started on this magnificent trip around the bases, fantasy and reality became interchangeable partners."[113] Vic Ziegel titled his article "You Can't Measure a Home Run this Big."[114] The miraculousness of the event is captured in the crowd's "ear-splitting roar that cut through the night, spilled out across the Mississippi River, and reached every corner of a nation that has been transfixed by McGwire's pursuit since the earliest hours of the season."[115] The commissioner of baseball's response, "It helped make people feel at peace and as one with the game again," puts the record once again in the context of conversion.[116]

When Joel Stein writes, "But once the chase became so big, we had to look for a deeper explanation, something greater than the obvious self-satisfaction of being able to say we witnessed history. . . . We have to look deep inside McGwire for the real drama," he reveals with special trenchance the essential connection between miracles and sanctification; that is, that the saint's great power is both an external and internal drama, a drama of action and of commitment.[117] Benedicta Ward points out that Augustine, in defining, "levels of wonder" wrote, "I call that miraculous which appears wonderful because it is either hard or impossible, beyond hope or ability."[118] McGwire's repeated comment "I'm in awe of myself" solidified the image of the miraculousness of his actions. In noting, "What makes this so gripping is that when the lights came up, McGwire glowed,"[119] Stein makes visible the wonder of McGwire's person and unwittingly echoes Gregory of Tours on Gregory of Langres's body: "His face was so filled with glory that it looked like a rose. It was deep rose red, and the rest of his body was glowing white like a lily."[120] That it is not the action that is significant but the one who acts becomes essential here; the glorious presence, in both cases, is revealed not in the event but in the body of the saint.

While McGwire breaking Roger Maris's record is in itself impressive, the miraculous nature of his doing so is further encoded in the way that all his home runs are taken out of the context of the game itself; ask almost anyone who won the game the night of McGwire's sixty-second homer, and they won't be able to answer you confidently.[121] In the context of the sport, the length of home runs is insignificant, yet this becomes a primary reportorial issue; in the *New York Daily News*, the "Road to the Record" chart, published the day after McGwire broke Maris's record, in declaring McGwire the "New Sultan of Swat," listed the distance for each blast, yet nowhere indicated the scores of any of the games in which they were hit.[122] When and how McGwire hit his home runs was insignificant; the reportage never addresses whether these were examples of clutch hitting with runners on base, whether they were game tiers or game winners, or indeed, whether they had any significance beyond themselves. As feats, they become meaningful in their own context, just as in hagiographies, the saints' miracles, rather than their consequences, are the narrative focus. Indeed, the only consequential result of saintly miracles is their ability to affect conversion, both within the story and for its readers; McGwire's function as an effective converter of lost souls has already been revealed at length. Thus, it is the attributes of the saint rather than the narrative itself—in this case, the narrative of the baseball game—that become significant. Bob Costas noted, "in a moment unblemished by any of the hype and contrivance that seems to be everywhere these days, McGwire connected the present and the past in a fashion so authentic and dramatic that it raises goosebumps to think of it even now."[123] The record itself, like any record, allows a kind of transcendence of time; it allows McGwire and the long-dead Ruth and Maris to commune with each other, in a sense to play with and against each other, in a present that will then become the past, the next player to make a run at the record in turn bringing McGwire back from the past.[124] (McGwire was interviewed a great deal during the 2001 season about Barry Bonds's successful march on his record.) It is this relationship to time and records that elevates McGwire beyond the ordinary. Costas's sense of the suspension of McGwire's alteration of everyday time echoes Woodward's comment: "in their [saints'] stories, history and faith, biography and ideas, time and the transcendent mix and meld."[125] By "mixing and melding" past and present, time and eternity, McGwire is brought out of the realm of the game and into the realm of the holy, in which his importance comes from his personal importance to others rather than his importance to the Cardinals in terms of their winning percentage. Indeed, it was often suggested that McGwire broke Maris's record and established the new single-season home run count instead of Sammy Sosa because Sosa's Cubs were in the middle of a pennant race, which required him to play for the team rather than the record.

As Kieckhefer notes, "it always had been one basic function of a saint, after all, to demonstrate in concrete detail what a life of virtue entails";[126] the presentation of Mark McGwire's person seems designed to demonstrate exactly this in modern, yet still strikingly medieval, terms. While the definition of what a "life of virtue entails" may have changed in the intervening 600 years, McGwire is no less saintly in his ability to demonstrate contemporary moral values in concrete detail. In senses both clichéd and complex, the representation of McGwire provides a tour of modern ideas about virtue. Noted for being unselfish as a ball player and a person, decidedly ungreedy (whatever that means in a profession where the league minimum salary is approximately $300,000), philanthropic, frankly unglamorous in a celebrity profession, and a devoted divorced parent, he embodies a series of ideals no less dear to the heart of contemporary America than the values of poverty, chastity, piety, and obedience were in medieval religious life. Readers of medieval saints, lives "had already accepted the values affirmed by these texts"; for them, as much as for contemporary followers of Mark McGwire, "the saints served as heroes whose extremism afforded a dramatic affirmation of shared values."[127] Equally, McGwire confirms a series of values through his very public enacting of them on a national stage. Because Mark McGwire has also suffered to get where he is—through divorce, injury, and failure—and continues to be afflicted by physical pain, his essential goodness becomes transcendent. The biblical model of Job's suffering in order to receive God's grace may be a less overt allegory for contemporary life, yet being tested by suffering is just as much a credential for sanctity now as it was for the medieval martyrs. The one criticism McGwire received throughout the 1998 season— for taking androstenedione, a muscle-building supplement banned by the International Olympic Committee and the National Football League, but not Major League Baseball—did little to affect fan perception and adulation; he was able to shrug off this one controversy without repercussions.[128] McGwire's afflictions are more quotidian than the "violent dismemberment and reintegration"[129] wrought on the early saints, yet they mark him as distinctly separate from other athletes who have achieved a kind of greatness without passing through this baptism of fire. Medieval hagiographies, in order to "edify the faithful as much as to exalt the saint. . .were laced with legends and marvelous anecdotes dramatizing the moral courage and spiritual power of the saint";[130] just so, the narratives of McGwire's suffering serve to reveal his perseverance in the face of difficulty, which makes his achievements and virtues all the greater. If these tales occasionally lean toward the absurd, for instance, exalting McGwire's willingness to contribute to the Animal Rescue Foundation by posing for their calendar with a Great Dane, to which he was extremely allergic, they still function to reveal his extraordinary qualities.[131]

Created, at least in part, by the print and television media, this idealization prevails even more strikingly in the local manifestations of fan culture. An examination of Mark McGwire websites includes the following examples: *The Mark McGwire Shrine*—"this is my tribute to the god that is Mark McGwire";[132] *Our Tribute to Mark McGwire*—"Just a nice tribute to Mark McGwire who we think is the greatest role model. . .in this generation";[133] *Mark McGwire Online*—"A gifted athlete, a caring father and good-hearted man, this gentle giant has truly lived up to the legend the world has spun around him."[134] Only *Mark McGwire Ate My Balls*[135] has anything negative to say, and that site's bulletin board is filled with praise for McGwire and opprobrium for the site's author. All these sites contain extensive links to McGwire's charitable organizations; those sites treat him like the next Mother Teresa. While the popular reporting in newspapers and magazines may be said to be in some sense authorized—that is, the reporters proceed from interviews with McGwire himself and his colleagues, and are at least to some extent based on factual information—these websites, of which there are eighty in the "Mark McGwire Fan Webring," put forward an essentially popular construction; based on the reportage itself, these "tributes" deviate from it in their more speculative, and thus more adulatory nature. If the newspapers are at least dimly aware of the sanctified myths they are making, the website owners are instead worshipping at the altar. The saint's miraculous feats cannot be equalled by the mere mortals who create and visit these sites; yet imitation and admiration are possible, thus, McGwire can lead others to uphold his virtues without actually doing similar deeds;[136] "[he] dramatizes the worth of workday values we want our kids to absorb: diligent attention to practice and homework, concentration, persistence, equanimity, teamwork."[137] All of those values can be achieved without hitting seventy home runs; therefore, McGwire's extraordinary accomplishments become symbolic of the virtues that produced them. This modeling is different from more standard hero worship other current star baseball players receive, although it is not unique; the rhetoric used to discuss McGwire's accomplishments and goodness and the projection of him as a result put him in an elite class of those (like Babe Ruth, for instance) who have transcended their time and place.

The virtues attributed to McGwire themselves testify to a nostalgia for premodern measures of success and worth. Instead of being known for his high salary and celebrity status, McGwire's charity, dedication, and achievement on the field suggest a loss of interest in the flash and glamor of fame in favor of more traditional virtues. McGwire's unwillingness to make endorsements leads him to be described as "a man with enormous values and enormous principles. . .Money is not his god."[138] A recent issue of *Baseball Weekly* featured McGwire on the cover, dressed as Santa Claus (who, despite our current associations, is actually a saint); the article called "The Spirit of Giving," once again profiles McGwire's efforts on behalf of sexually abused children—a group as charitably "unsafe" as Mother Teresa's lepers and indigents—revealing him in a sanctified light.[139] Another article calls him "A Powerhouse of Caring."[140] Charity is commonplace in the legends of the medieval saints; following the commandment that God makes to the rich man, "If thou wilt be perfect, sell all you have and give it to the poor, and come follow me and thou shalt have treasure in heaven,"[141] saints as diverse as Anthony, Martin of Tours, Radegund, and Francis contribute widely, distributing goods to the poor, giving the clothes off their backs (as McGwire did in his childhood), and shoring up decrepit shrines and churches. McGwire's choice to support sexually and physically abused children, even going so far as to film two public service announcements to encourage them to seek help,[142] echoes the medieval saints' propensity to serve those generally ignored. Saint Radegund, for instance, "turning her mind to further works of mercy. . .built a house at Athies where beds were elegantly made up for needy women gathered there. She would wash them herself in warm baths, tending to the putresecence of their diseases,"[143] while Saint Margaret, "when she went out of doors, either on foot or on horseback, crowds of poor people, orphans and widows flocked to her, as they would have done to a most loving mother, and none of them left her without being comforted."[144] None, it seems, leave Mark McGwire without being comforted either; the list of recipients of his charity is extensive: apart from the facilities funded by his foundation, in 1998 he also supported the Animal Rescue Foundation, the Sammy Sosa foundation (which helped victims of Hurricane Georges in the Dominican Republic), the Make-a-Wish Foundation, and a handful of other charities. More recent support includes the National Kidney Foundation (for bedwetters, another contemporary group of "lepers"), Reading is Fundamental, and the Arthritis Foundation. Saint Margaret's giving inspired others:"the rich who accompanied her or her own attendants used to hand to her their garments, or anything else they happened to have by them at the time, that she might give them to those who were in want. . .nor were her attendants at all offended but rather each strove who should first offer her what he had, since he knew for certain that she would pay it back two-fold";[145] just so, McGwire's foundation, stress the newspapers, has received "tons of unsolicited donations coming in by mail—some in $70 checks and some in $1 bills from young kids."[146]

McGwire's charity is combined with humility, another traditional virtue of the premodern world. In the process of his remarkable achievements, McGwire, besieged by reporters, was told "Hey Michael Jordan goes through this every day." His response, "Yeah,...but he's really good,"[147] rejects putting himself in the same category as the superstars, the same impulse that apparently governed his behavior as a child: "As a boy, McGwire would stash his trophies in the back of his closet, not on top of his dresser. They embarrassed him. On the form for the media guide at USC, he left the space next to ATHLETIC HONORS blank. . . . There's nothing baseball-related in [his house]. He has either given everything away, or it's in storage."[148] His common tendency to suggest that his own talents are modest in light of others', such as his former teammate and fellow Bash Brother, José Canseco, creates an image of someone singularly unimpressed with his own capabilities.[149] To the suggestions that McGwire belonged in the same category as Babe Ruth, he responded, "I'm about speechless when people put your name alongside his name. . . .He was obviously the most important sports figure in the world at the time."[150] Described as "almost embarrassed by his outstanding feats and clearly uncomfortable with his outside celebrity,"[151] McGwire remained humble in the face of victory, saying "I think I have amazed myself."[152] Humility is of course an essential saintly virtue, and like McGwire, Saint Martin, for instance, maintained his humble disposition while in the military, a masculine, public culture not unlike the world of sports. Saint Martin was

> content with only one servant as his attendant, and then, reversing roles, the master waited on the servant to such a degree that, for the most part, it was he who pulled off his boots. . . . For nearly three years before his baptism, he was a professional soldier, but he kept completely free from those vices in which that class of men became too frequently involved. He showed great kindness toward his fellow-soldiers, and wonderful affection, and his patience and humility surpassed what seemed possible to human nature. There is no need to praise the self-denial which he displayed: it was so great that, even at that date, he was regarded not so much as a soldier as a monk.[153]

In a similar display, Mark McGwire is noted for these same virtues; while he's likely to let the bat boy do his laundry, he is noted for great kindness toward teammates and colleagues, not to mention patience (with reporters, fans, and endless questions) and humility. Even his opponents take part in these sentiments; Scott Sullivan of the Cincinnati Reds, for instance, said, "It wouldn't bother me if he hits number 62 off me. . .I'd rather be associated with him than some jerk."[154] Ex-Oakland A teammate Scott Brosius notes, "He never really changed over the years, given his success, through the good times and through the hard times,. . .He would come up to you and talk to guys whether they had 10 years in the league or 10 days in the league. Never saw him look down on anybody at all."[155] Sammy Sosa's remark, "I think Mark is a great human being, and I think people could see the respect and admiration that developed between us and that while we were rivals, we were having fun,"[156] echoes the sentiments of Saint Martin's fellows. Favored with a vision, Saint Martin "was not puffed up with vain glory, but he acknowledged the goodness of God in his own action."[157] Likewise, Mark McGwire is willing to attribute his success to powers beyond himself: "The Man Upstairs know what's going to happen. I totally believe that, and that takes the pressure off,"[158] and "I really believe hitting home runs is a God-given talent."[159]

Whatever the strength of McGwire's characteristics, it is their representation in external signs that marks his elevated presentation. His profuse weeping—often seen and equally often reported—is upheld as an example of his extraordinary compassion and sensitivity to unfortunate children. The image of the teary McGwire is a popular one—both in response to questions about abused and neglected children and in response to his own achievements.[160] His devotion to his own son, which was very much a part of the narrative of 1998, is another potent symbol of a compassionate virtue that goes beyond the ordinary. In reference to some criticism she received for discussing McGwire's son's absence from the Cardinals's dugout in 2000, Joyce, a regular contributor to Gumby's Mark McGwire Message Board, noted "If you think this is women folk talk then why don't you open up an encyclopedia. You might be shocked to see a photo of Mark and Matt with the caption depicting a father's genuine love for his son and the game of baseball."[161] While I suspect anyone would be shocked to find McGwire in any reference work other than the *Baseball Encyclopedia*, the author's sense that he iconically represents the values of loving parenthood is accurate. When the Fox Family cable channel began running "Family Baseball" on Thursday nights in 2001, its promotional material all included the now famous picture of McGwire lifting his son in triumph after his sixty-second home run as the final shot, the representation of everything "family baseball" might mean.[162]

While personality and achievement combine to make Mark McGwire sanctifiable, no discussion of his iconic presence would be complete without a turn toward the physical body. Officially listed at either 6'5" tall and 225 lbs.,[163] or 6'5" and 250 by several Spring Preview Magazines[164] and the Official St. Louis Cardinals Website,[165] McGwire's impressive size is a key factor in the rhetoric of his construction. He is variously presented as "a 6'5", 250-pound duplex with pillars for forearms,"[166] "gifted with superhuman size and godlike strength,"[167] "a giant of a man,"[168] and "the guy with the awe-inspiring home-run swing and the league-leading biceps."[169] Indeed, few descriptions of him fail to remark on his awesome size; a recent fan post on Gumby's Mark McGwire Message Board marvelled in response to another fan seeing McGwire in Montreal, "the one thing I wonder is if with his mammoth size. . .I know people 6′5″. . . I know people that weigh 250 lbs.. . .I just can't imagine how HUGE he must seem in person. . .and can you imagine being a little kid, he must seem like a GIANT."[170] This discourse of giantism serves to separate McGwire from the quotidian and locate him within the realm of the superhuman and miraculous. Because his size goes beyond the statistical in its flexibility—he is listed at both 6′4″ and 6′5″, his weight ranging from 225 to 250 with various permutations in between; his biceps everything from 17 to 22 inches in girth—the attention shifts from actuality to a kind of nebulous vastness that becomes symbolic. The myth of immeasurability, which turns on a seemingly ordinary object's refusal to function by its worldly rules, thus allowing it to avoid a fixed, earthly definition, is a common medieval trope; one early example from Nennius shows the legend of Arthur moving from a story of war to something more mystical:

> There is another wonder in the region called Ercing. It is a tomb near a brook that is called the Mound of Anir, for Anir is the man buried there. He was the son of Arthur the soldier, who killed and buried him there. Men come to measure the mound, which is sometimes six feet long, sometimes nine or twelve of fifteen. However you measure it again and again, you will never get the same figure—and I have tried this myself.[171]

A more directly relevant example for this discussion is Saint Christopher, who is alternately called "a man of prodigious size—he was twelve feet tall—and fearsome of visage"[172] and "In his time there was no man anywhere so strong. / He was twenty-four feet tall, and thickset and broad."[173] Like Christopher, Mark McGwire's size is both representational and real; he inhabits an actual body that is 6′5″ tall and weighs somewhere between 225 and 250 lbs., yet in defying fixity while standing for enormity, he also becomes a cartoon, a superhero able to leap tall buildings in a single bound. A 1998 advertising feature in *Sports Illustrated* put this into overt language: "When he steps into the batter's box, St. Louis Cardinals slugger Mark McGwire, all bulging muscles and red-goateed scowl, looks like a superhero. And just as in a comic book, Big Mac once again vanquishes the hapless villain—in his case, an opposing pitcher."[174] It is this quality of mythical size, as much as anything else, that allows Daniel Okrent to call McGwire "a wonderful and beautiful beast who just happened to carry a nation on its back."[175] Combined with the human qualities of his suffering and weeping, McGwire becomes like the medieval giants who "conjoined absolute otherness with reassuring familiarity";[176] like the saints explored in detail earlier, McGwire is ultimately both human and inhuman; his hugeness is "displayed in an exaggerated relation to the social construction of identity."[177] He is us, but is greater than we are, as Melissa's Message Board post suggests; apparently unlike other people who are 6'5" and 250 lbs., McGwire is special; his size makes him "mammoth," "HUGE," and a "GIANT." Thus, as an object of admiration, imitation, and veneration, McGwire functions as a vast mirror reflecting back both human possibility and insignificance, as the saints do. Specifically, McGwire once again echoes Saint Christopher, who "having learned his lesson, humbly devotes his life to Christian service. He preaches the Gospel, but is especially an *athleta dei fortissima* who does battle against the armies of paganism."[178] Christopher, learning about Christianity from a hermit, balks at the requirements of fasting and prayer; instead, he is able to show his commitment through action, by using his size and strength to carry all who ask across the river. Eventually, Christopher must literally carry the weight of the world upon his shoulders, as he conveys Christ, in the guise of a child, through the rough waters. Christopher subsequently converts many through his actions. By enacting his devotion through his strength, Christopher becomes the *athleta*, or active saint, rather than the contemplative Christian proposed by the hermit. The striking Latin title refers equally effectively to the medieval saint and the modern ball player, who is also elevated by action; as an *athleta dei fortissima*, Mark McGwire's feats once again go beyond themselves, as home runs take on redemptive and vanquishing power, the "armies of paganism" being loosely identifiable as opposing pitchers, the Chicago Cubs, the failures of the presidency, and the decriers of baseball.

As various as McGwire's appeal may be, however, it is never constructed as sexual. In part, this stems from the dwelling on his impressive size; as Jeffrey Jerome Cohen notes, "his body an affront to natural proportion, the giant encodes an excess that places him outside the realm of the human, outside the possibility of desire."[179] In this statement, Cohen echoes Edmund Burke: "It is impossible to suppose a giant the object of love."[180] While many of McGwire's fellow players, such as New York Mets catcher Mike Piazza, have fan websites devoted to their sexual attractiveness,[181] the language that surrounds him is essentially devoid of desire. According to Cohen:

> A corpus caught within the process of its own coming into being, the giant is encountered in the performance of a masculinity as necessary as it is obscene. The giant's hybrid flesh is, however, not reducible to some pure state of male identity. Because he incorporates so much of the sensuous physicality with which medieval writers characterized women, and because his body functions as a disavowed point of origin, the giant shares more with the feminine, and specifically with the maternal, than his excessively male form might suggest.[182]

While Mark McGwire does not incorporate sensuous physicality or function as a disavowed point of origin, his hypermasculine, muscular body stands in contrast to his often feminized personality, providing the "problematic relationship between gender and embodment" that Cohen claims characterizes the medieval giant.[183] Joel Stein describes McGwire in these complicated terms: "Mark McGwire would be a robot, only who would make a robot that goes to therapy and cries during press conferences and *Driving Miss Daisy*? And who would give a robot red hair?"[184] If his steel-hard body suggests machine rather than human, the therapy, weeping, and "chick flick" are all feminine signifiers that complicate the presentation of McGwire as SuperMAN. In Stein's construction, McGwire is an "intensely physical guy who grew up in a household with four brothers and no sisters" who has "embraced a Jeffersonian rationality," both of which embody the medieval idea of masculinity that saw strength and reason as pillars of male perfection; yet McGwire also has "got this softness that also plays against type. . .he's deeply devoted to his son and his charity for sexually abused children. He's been going to a therapist every week since 1991."[185] Luke Cyphers notes "he posseses a bread-truck frame, 20-inch biceps and 17-inch forearms, yet he is as remarkable for his vulnerability as for his strengths."[186] Rick Reilly also engages this mixed presentation, beginning his article "Huge men don't cry, but the McGwires do"[187] and continuing, "Mark McGwire may be a 6'5", 250-pound duplex with pillars for forearms, but his lifestyle leans more toward branch librarian,"[188] the last word a signifier that, whatever its reality, is always identified with (old, undesirable) women. Reilly, and it seems McGwire himself, credits his "finding himself" to outpourings of emotion: "Then one day, tears streaming down his face, he found out [who the f— he was]":[189]

> "It took crying for me to realize, this is the *real* me. That day, when I cried, is when I realized I can open up. I can care. I can communicate. . . .It took crying for me to realize who I am now. I'm the Mark McGwire I'm supposed to be."
> And who's that?. . .Who are you?
> "Well, I'm—I'm an opinionated, understanding, communicative, sensitive. . . father"[190]

However naïve, this portrait—both self and externally constructed—may be, it does show Cohen's formulation at work; at once hugely physical and deeply emotional, tied to children and domestic life, Mark McGwire is figured "outside the possibility of desire."[191]

This feminization is part of a strategy to desexualize this big man with a big bat; his domestic side reduces the masculinity his extreme body projects. As a result, it removes the threat that a kind of physical hugeness implies because of its ability to overpower mere mortals and negates his gendered, and therefore sexual, form. The only reference to McGwire's beauty, Okrent's aforementioned "wonderful and beautiful beast who just happened to carry a nation on its back"[192] constructs him simultaneously as Beauty and the Beast, masculine and feminine, an ultimately androgynous form. By taking McGwire out of the sexual economy, he is once again made narratively sanctifiable. Woodward asks, "what is it about the passionate life of the body which the church finds unbecoming in a saint?";[193] while not answering his own question, he makes it clear that saintliness requires a kind of disembodiment or asexuality. A saint—particularly a female saint—may be desired, but only by the evil pagans whose desire is a mark of their perversion and rejection of truth and grace; a saint may desire, as Augustine does, but must reject the life of the body in order to achieve that same truth and grace. While virginity is not the same essential marker of saintliness in male hagiographies as it is in female ones, a final disassociation from the marriage market and the world of desire is an essential part of transcendence. One of Saint Christopher's final acts before his martyrdom replaces seduction with conversion; thrown into jail with two "shapely young women" being paid to entice him, Christopher instead "knelt to pray. When the two women tried to arouse him by stroking him and putting their arms around him, he stood up and said to them: 'What are you trying to do and for what reason were you sent here?' The two were frightened by the radiance of his face and said, 'Saint of God, pity us! Make us able to believe in the God whom you preach!'"[194] Saint Christopher may be more active in his rejection of sexuality, yet whatever Mark McGwire is doing in his free time behind closed doors, the public presentation of him embodies a kind of asexuality in a world where athletes are often treated as sex symbols.[195] While fan websites of several other athletes are a source of a great deal of licentious speculation, those devoted to Mark McGwire include very little dwelling on the body as an object of sexual fantasy; while some fans seem to want to marry him, their attachment seems more to his domesticity than to his desirability.[196]

After two difficult, injury-ridden seasons, Mark McGwire retired following the 2001 season, in which he was the most dangerous .187 hitter in the league, with twenty-nine home runs in ninety-seven games. Stating, "I believe I owe it to the Cardinals and the fans of St. Louis to step aside, so a talented free agent can be brought in as the final piece of what I expect can be a World Championship-caliber team," McGwire chose to leave a significant contract option "for the good of the team."[197] Nothing that "I am unable to perform at a level equal to the salary the organization would be paying me,"[198] McGwire again fulfilled the virtue of placing baseball as an institution above money and himself; "For years I have said my motivation for playing wasn't for fame and fortune but rather the love of competing. . . .Baseball is a team sport and I have been lucky enough to contribute to the success of some great teams."[199] While his focus remained on team achievement, revealing his essential humility, press coverage chose to focus on the often recounted milestones in his career, noting that he "retires with 583 home runs, fifth on the all time list" and that "he secured his place in baseball lore by slugging 70 homers in '98" and that he "captivated the nation."[200] Although his retirement ultimately came as a surprise to many fans and his manager, in the eyes of the press (who serve as the college of cardinals and canonize baseball's saints), its arguable prematurity has no effect on his future Hall of Fame induction. However, unless he chooses to return as a coach or manager, McGwire's retirement essentially functions as his death; many of his devoted fans on Gumby's Mark McGwire Discussion Board wonder if the site will close until his induction in 2006, or whether there will be anything for them to talk about. Until his miraculous reappearance and the resurgent interest that his induction will cause, he is essentially dead.

Despite an audience with Pope John Paul II in St. Louis on February 8, 1999, who praised him as an example of perseverance and devotion, urging young people to "train for their lives as Catholics the way the home run kings Mark McGwire and Sammy Sosa might train for the coming baseball season,"[201] Mark McGwire is unlikely to receive official canonization; however, within the baseball world he inhabits and perhaps beyond it, he is already beatified, merely awaiting official enshrinement in the National Baseball Hall of Fame. Richard Kieckhefer's sense that "the term 'saint' must thus be used in a broad sense, to include persons officially canonized as saints, those venerated as blessed but not canonized, and even a few who are represented in hagiographic fashion in the sources for their lives despite total absence of a cult,"[202] covers Mark McGwire nicely. So too, does Patrick Geary's sense that "canonization did not determine sainthood. If a dead person worked miracles that attracted an enthusiastic following, then that person was a saint with or without formal recognition."[203] Mark McGwire may not be dead, but his miracles attracted the same enthusiastic following and veneration, so producing the hagiographic sources for his cult. If his canonization in the baseball world is certain, he is also "venerated as blessed" even as his powers diminish, and his representation certainly takes place in hagiographic terms, however unintentional. Indeed, any examination of his fan websites makes clear that contemporary cults are no less avid than the medieval cults they follow. The value of his relics—the stuff he produced in the 1998 season and beyond—has proven to be extraordinary, and the objects themselves have inspired acts of public spirit that will be treated at length in the next section. Yet, if reading hagiography, as Mary-Ann Stouck notes, allows one "the opportunity to see many facets of a moment in history through the impact of a single important person upon the other people, events, and intellectual and spiritual movements that were drawn within his or her orbit,"[204] in examining Mark McGwire in 1998, it is possible to see the ways that a modern individual engaged the community in a most medieval way. If talking about saints is really talking about stories, as Stouck, Woodward, and Kieckhefer have suggested,[205] then it is also possible to see the role of sports writers and fans with websites in the sacral production of Mark McGwire. Their inscription of his past into the present and their choices of how to construct his identity show the selection process that turns the breaking of Roger Maris's home run record into a tale of virtuous triumph. If certain shady implications lurk around the edges (divorce, fornication, despair), all are removed through confession (McGwire's oft noted therapy), thus constructing the pure figure at the point at which the narrative begins to take on its sacred significance (the signing of his contract in St. Louis in 1997). The story of McGwire's early career, with its many ups and downs, is often told in the context of his frustrations with personal events such as his divorce, which distracted him from his on-field work. However, the tone changes (as do McGwire's statistics) after 1991. By his own account, "I just had to face the music. . .it was a turning point in my life, and it just happened to be a turning point in my career, too. No matter who you are in the world, sometimes you have to get slapped in the face." Having made up "his mind that he needed help, that he had to see a therapist," McGwire "rededicated [himself] to baseball."[206] Crediting therapy for his turnaround, McGwire noted, "I got my mind straight, and everything followed."[207] From that point forward, his story becomes one of salutary achievement, the negatives of the past merely obstacles overcome en route to a glorious future.

What made Mark McGwire and his home run chase sacred within the sports world was the construction of its salutary power, thus distinguishing it from the everyday, yet allowing it to continue to interact with it at the same time. McGwire and Sosa's race could lift the nation (or at least baseball) out of "the house of excrement"[208] (the Clinton/Lewinsky scandal; baseball's failure to attract fans after the 1994 strike) and carry it across the seas to the "holy city of Byzantium."[209] Because Mark McGwire's achievements "stand so far above the second place finisher that they seem to belong to another category altogether," he becomes the producer of grace "for the eerie and awesome quality of his particular excellence."[210] If McGwire is not a "real" saint, producing effective relics and healing miracles after his death, he is close enough; through his sanctified presentation, he fulfills the same needs and impulses that created the medieval cult of the saints. By providing a locus for devotion, an emotional affectivity, and an outlet and inspiration, Mark McGwire receives the cultic veneration that makes him sacred. If this is merely a simulacrum of religious experience in an emotional form, it still provides a kind of grace, if not real salvation; as Stephen Jay Gould notes:

> Mark McGwire has prevailed by creating, in his own person, the ultimate combination of the two great natural forces of luck and effort: the gift of an extraordinary body, with the steadfast dedication to training and study that can only merit the literal meaning of a wonderful word, enthusiasm, the intake of God.[211]

Take out "Mark McGwire" and substitute "grace" for luck, and this reads hagiographically. For what medieval saint does not possess these same gifts—the extraordinary body of the martyr, the dedication of the monk and confessor, and the God-given enthusiasm of all postulants to a transcendent world?

Relics

Bones may be the "pigges bones" of Chaucer's pardoner, those of an ordinary mortal, or the relics of a saint, according to the culturally induced perception of an individual. Moreover, . . .a relic cannot transmit this perception from one community to another, even if these communities share identical cultural and religious values. In order to effect this transmission, something essentially extraneous to the relic itself must be provided: a reliquary with an inscription or iconographic representation of the saint, a document attesting to its authenticity, or a tradition, oral or written, which identified that particular object with a specific individual or at least a specific type of individual.

—Patrick J. Geary, *Furta Sacra*

Baseball legend Ty Cobb is smiling somewhere—but there are a few gaps in his grin. Cobb went to the great ball field in the sky in 1961, leaving behind a slew of big-league records and one set of yellowed false teeth. His dentures eventually found their way to Barry Halper, a New Jersey collector who is to baseball memorabilia what Cobb was to center field. "My first reaction was: 'What am I going to do with a pair of dentures?' " recalls the fifty-nine-year-old Halper.

Now he knows. Cobb's teeth, and the rest of Halper's amazing collection, which includes such treasures as a ticket to the first World Series in 1903 and a lock of Babe Ruth's hair, are scheduled to be sold sometime this summer [1999] in live and on-line auctions run by

Sotheby's in New York. It may not have the snob appeal of the Jackie O auction, but Halper's collection is expected to attract a crowd as large and boisterous as Opening Day at Yankee Stadium.

"There is going to be a huge turnout of really passionate people," says David N. Redden, a Sotheby's executive vice-president. "I had a call from a partner in a well-known brokerage firm who's very interested. I said, 'The Halper Collection is the Holy Grail, isn't it?' "

—*Business Week,* February 22, 1999

Patrick Geary's contention that "as a physical object, divorced from a specific milieu, a relic is entirely without significance. Unlike other objects, the bare relic—a bone or a bit of dust—carries no fixed code or sign of its meaning"[212] helps to define relics in contrast to other commodities; he notes "any consideration of sacred relics as commodities in the Middle Ages may seem to be pushing to the extreme the definition of commodities as 'goods destined for circulation and exchange.' Can we reasonably describe a human body or portions thereof as *destined* for circulation?"[213] Although he notes that relics "*were* bought and sold, stolen and divided, much like any other commodity,"[214] relics remain essentially different from other objects of value, that difference being located in the source of their value. Devoid of any essential value of their own and without practical use, relics are "symbolic objects" of "the most arbitrary kind, passively reflecting so much meaning as they were given by a particular community,"[215] their value "a reflection of the values assigned by the society that honored [them]."[216] Indeed, Geary notes that the "most eagerly sought after relics of the medieval period—bodies or portions of bodies—were superficially similar to thousands of other corpses and skeletons universally available."[217]

Once assigned meaning, relics "provided the point of contact between mundane existence and the divine world. They were part of the sacred, the numinous; but incarnated in this world, as had been Christ, without losing their place in the other."[218] They were both affective and effective; as objects of devotion and piety, they provided focal points for worship and reintegration into authorized Christianity, as pilgrimage sites, such as Santiago de Compostela, became increasingly associated with sacred relics during the medieval period. Relics were also practically useful, providing, as Geary again notes, "the only recourse against the myriad ills, physical, mate-rial, and psychic, of a population defenseless before an incomprehensible and terrifying universe."[219] As a special kind of commodity, they are things with biographies, answering the questions that Igor Kopytoff asks about the "possibilities inherent in its [an object's] 'status' and in the period and culture";[220] like other commodities in their exchange value,[221] their difference comes from the source of that value. Rather than arising from the thing's aesthetic qualities, the worth of its materials, or its useful function, a relic derives its value from its ability to function beyond itself, to transcend its physical form and unite the realm of the physical with the realm of the transcendent. As such, it is both common and unique; as a physical object, it remains almost indistinguishable from others of its type—a bone is a bone, and a baseball is a baseball. Yet in its transcendent capability, it is distinguished from others of its type, unique in its value because of the presumed efficacy that determines it.

Modern relics may not address the "myriad ills, physical, material, and psychic" of contemporary society in the same direct way medieval relics did; however, they do salve a different kind of helplessness: the fear of anonymity, of falling through the cracks, created by the modern world. While some fears, such as death and disease, remain the same both in the medieval past and now, contemporary anxieties rest less in the natural world—wolves, failed harvests, mysterious plagues—than in the human world—losing one's job or means of support, being arrested, being destroyed by capricious machines. If contemporary relics address different kinds of ills, they still demonstrate the accounting of value disconnected from any actual use that Geary sees as the relic's defining characteristic. At the Barry Halper memorabilia auction, Ty Cobb's dentures, lot #1230, sold for $7,475; Babe Ruth's hair appears not to be listed specifically in the catalogue, although it may be included with another lot. The auction, while replete with baseballs, signed photographs, and baseball cards, also includes numerous personal items from many famous ballplayers: watches, handkerchiefs, wallets, shaving kits, hats, and other items of clothing. Ty Cobb's 1928 Philadelphia Athletics Signed Home Jersey, lot 767, brought in $332,500, while Lou Gehrig's 1927 Yankees Road Jersey sold for $305,000. A bargain at $189,500 was the 1920 Sale of Babe Ruth's (from the Red Sox to the Yankees) Signed Agreement,[222] suggesting that anything in contact with the greats has great theoretical value, derived, like medieval relics from Geary's "set of shared beliefs."[223] Like relics, these objects are "of no practical use. Once removed from their elaborate reliquaries or containers, they [are] not even decorative."[224] While one might argue that a jersey, framed and hung on a wall, is fairly decorative, it is again a kind of decoration based more on an ideological sense of "history" than an artistic aesthetic; Ty Cobb's dentures, despite coming with their original plastic holder, cannot even partake in this argument. Yet each object is distinguished by its rarity; signed items, made unique by the affixed autographs that separate them from any other of their type, generally fetch a higher price. As Mark Hyman notes, "demand for unusual items remains strong," quoting Tom Mortenson, the editor of *Sports Collectors Digest* as to the effect that "the prices being paid for some of these items are astounding."[225] Because this mark of the saint both authenticates and elevates the object, connecting it to a particular story and set of values, these relics become unique objects in a world of mass production, able to connect past and future, history and identity. Thus, if these relics can't heal the sick and help find lost objects, they can provide a recourse against the anonymity of contemporary society and the dislocation from history prominent in late twentieth- and early twenty-first-century culture.

In the sanctification of Mark McGwire, however important personal history, character, and size may be, they are not really the most vital part of his sacred presentation, nor, in themselves, are the feats that got him there. McGwire's beatification is similar to those of the saints from after the fourth century, after the end of the period of martyrdom: "almost all holy persons of the following centuries were those who lived heroic lives as friends of God rather than those who died heroic deaths,"[226] but his current saintliness is determined less by his heroic actions than by the value of the relics he produces. The fate of the home run balls was as essential a part of the story of the 1998 season as McGwire's and Sosa's race for the record: indeed, it was addressed early in the season as a concern that became prominent as soon as it became clear that breaking the record was likely. Of course, emphasis on relics is endemic to hero-worshipping in baseball; Mike Lupica's account of the 1998 baseball season begins in spring training with his son clutching his "McGwire card in his right hand."[227] Before entering the stadium to see the Cardinals play the Devil-Rays, Lupica continues, "we stopped to buy things."[228] While Mark McGwire's presence, in uniform, in person, "had done something to the place,"[229] he notes, "this is a time in sports when the obsession and fascination for the stuff—one that would turn into a national obsession about what would happen to the home run balls McGwire and Sosa would hit on the other side of the season, in September—had become more important than the games."[230] Sports, Lupica points out "is still about memory and imagination,"[231] and the stuff—balls, bats, cards—become semiotic objects that capture both the memory (of events themselves) and the imagination (what these events might mean beyond themselves). It is the imagination that creates the significance; as Tzvetan Todorov explains, "interpretation, in seeming to make the text speak, places fidelity in the other that is external. It seeks to capture the referents of literary discourse."[232] Geary notes, "although semiotic objects, [relics] are of the most arbitrary kind, passively reflecting so much meaning as they were given by a particular community";[233] as contemporary relics, memorabilia passively reflects a desire for community, for a shared set of symbols and meanings, across history and immune to time, that is so often missing in modern society. The objects' real value is in their interpretation, which creates a sense of coherence and meaning. Thus, the relics' stories encode a species of efficacy, producing a symbolic kind of redemption. In other words, the object, because of its interpretability, becomes the speaking text, just as the saints' relics embody their stories in medieval *inventios, translatios,* and hagiographies; the objects themselves that make the hero immortal and incorrupt function the same ways as the pieces of the saints' body.

Indeed, relics need not be actual body parts; as Eugene A. Dooley notes, "The second meaning of the word [relic] embraces all those things which the saint used when alive, or things which were sanctified by their contact with him."[234] Popular in the Middle Ages, and with resonance in contemporary memorabilia, were *brandea,* cloths lowered into the shrine, which were then drawn "up heavy with the blessing of the saint."[235] Woodward notes, "not only the saint's bodies but even their clothes and the instruments of their torture were venerated as sacred objects."[236] He tells a striking story of the funeral of Saint Ambrose, bishop of Milan, in 397: "crowds of men and women kept throwing their handkerchiefs and aprons at the body of the saint in the hope that he would touch it. Such *brandea,* as they were called, were prized as wonder-working relics."[237] This description cannot help evoking the commonly seen television footage of screaming fans trying to tear off shreds of Elvis's or the Beatles' clothing; current holy figures evoke a similar response. While these objects do not work wonders, they are certainly prized, displayed, and venerated, often enclosed in a frame or box that thus functions as the reliquary in which the sacred cloth or bones were stored.[238]

Not surprisingly, the McGwire saga provides as well documented an example of the modern relic's course as one is likely to find. That an entire book has been written about McGwire's seventieth home run ball suggests the essential importance of the object itself: a thing that in a moment acquires a story and a meaning that go well beyond its origin, taking a $9 baseball and making it suddenly enormously valuable. Just as with relics that acquire a value from their shared history rather than their intrinsic plastic qualities, the book's author notes, "In time, the tokens themselves—the game-used bats and balls and presumably washed undershirts—will carry more meaning when we rub up against them first hand, when the memories they hold are ours."[239] Meaning and value, in these senses, coincide: McGwire's ball sold at auction for $3.5 million; the Barry Halper memorabilia auction raised $22 million. That McGwire never actually touched the baseball himself, that with one whack of a stick he dispatched it far away over the outfield wall, shows the evanescence of significance— Saint Foy's arm looks much like another arm, yet false relics are not efficacious.

The sale of false relics, parodied in Chaucer's "Pardoner's Tale" and many other places, plays on the physical indistinguishability of one bone from the other, but becomes sinful because, within the believer's world, these pigs' knuckles do not have the salutary value that the actual knuckles of a local saint would. Major League Baseball's recent "memorabilia authentication" drive suggests a similar concern; the "fake" home run ball is of no value; the "real" one can make the fellow who caught it a millionaire. The industry's recent advertisement, in fact, reads "Thou Shalt Not Worship False Idols." The League promises that this program "combines the services of an impeccable third-party authenticator with a sate-of-the-art hologram, a serial numbering system and an online registration process," and thus establishing "standards by which authenticated autographs and game used memorabilia can easily be distinguished from other items in the market."[240] Official autograph signings and "the removal of all game used items" are to be observed by a "representative of the professional service firm Arthur Anderson,"[241] assuring their authenticity; then each item is to be affixed with "one of four tamper proof holograms."[242] These extraordinary measures echo the extended legislation in Canon Law on the authentication and approval of relics, the Church's official documentation, published collectively by Eugene Dooley in 1931, which requires that the Church produce authenticating documents: "The signature must be by hand, and not with a stamp, unless the prelate is notoriously prevented from paralysis or other bodily infirmity."[243] While the hologram may essentially be a stamp, individual observation seems to take the place of the handwritten signature. Calling Arthur Anderson "an impeccable third party,"[244] and including a quotation from an FBI Special Agent assuring that the program will "help protect consumers and assist law enforcement in detecting and prosecuting those who would sell fraudulent sports memorabilia,"[245] the descriptive "Authentication Program" pamphlet clearly casts the League Office in the role of the Church, assuring the value of relics and trapping false pardoners who attempt to pass off fraudulent material as the real thing. Because in the memorabilia business merchandise's "value is largely taken on faith,"[246] the suggestion has been made that "90% of the signed collectibles sold are fake."[247] Randall P. Hahn, who offers the one specifically McGwire-oriented authentication service, echoes church law even more overtly, saying of the autographs whose veracity he tests, "If I am not 100% sure of authenticity I would not put my name on it [sic]."[248] This concern is not a new one; Geary notes that, in the Middle Ages, while "the customers themselves were generally satisfied with their purchase," they were also "often justly concerned with the authenticity of the relics purchased from traveling relic-mongers."[249] The sale of medieval relics has much in common with contemporary memorabilia mongering; the most famous Carolingian supplier of relics, Deusdona "organized periodic caravans which crossed the Alps in the Spring and made the round of monastic fairs,"[250] anticipating the current proliferation of sports card shows and auctions. The similarity to "suppliers of objects of art in the twentieth" century that Geary suggests, and the ways that relics provided "an opportunity to make a profit,"[251] often from stealing, smuggling, or falsifying objects shows the tendency of shadiness to infiltrate the business of selling valuable things with thaumaturgic potential. The ability to verify these objects promises to assure both authenticity and value. A program (the Church's; Major League Baseball's) that seeks to alleviate forgery problems and reduce fraud thus assumes the inherent worth of authentic items and the complete inability of replicas to take their place. The difference between the true object and the false copy, then, is in desirability, value, and finally, in its ability to convey some kind of meaning.

On August 29, 1998, it had apparently become clear to Major League Baseball that either Mark McGwire or Sammy Sosa (if not both) was likely to break Roger Maris's single-season home run record; a meeting was called to decide how to authenticate home run balls and provide security in outfield seating areas. The security measures were responses to the assumed value of the balls. Because "people were talking like these baseballs could be worth as much as $1 million," Kevin Hallinan, Major League Baseball's security director, "wasn't about to see some little kid get trampled in the crush to get the ball";[252] as a result, he planned for "extraction teams" to remove "the ball and its new owner from the scene."[253] More vital, however, was the complex plan devised by Ruben Puente, an assistant to the director of Major League Baseball's security department who took charge of the McGwire/Sosa balls, to identify and authenticate the balls themselves:

> Puente quickly devised a way to mark all the balls to be pitched to McGwire sequentially, with a visible stamped number in footnote position atop the "s" of the Rawlings logo. In addition, he would mark the balls around the lacing with a distinct, invisible stamp, able to be seen under black or infrared light. His plan, once the leading home run hitter reached 59 home runs, was to put the first marked ball into play, and then the second, and the third, and so forth. If a ball left the field, the next in line took its place. If a ball was scuffed, or no longer suitable for game use, it was set aside for its succeeding number.[254]

Kept secret in order to "scuttle" the interference of "some con-man who doesn't have the goods,"[255] the elaborate nature of this plan bespeaks the concern for authenticity in relics. The Rawlings Sporting Goods Company hasn't changed the way they make baseballs since 1977, when it received its exclusive manufacturing contract from Major League Baseball; each ball, with an approximate wholesale cost of about $5,[256] is essentially identical. The ball hit into the stands at any given baseball game and dramatically wrestled for is the same as the ball sold to the public at sporting goods stores for approximately $9.[257] However, one of Puente's near misses shows how important the real thing is; when he acquired Sosa's sixty-fifth home run ball after it bounced back onto the field, he nearly managed to lose it. Noticing a group of fans trying to get autographs as he left the stadium, he saw one small child repeatedly pushed to the back. Calling the kid over, he handed him a baseball from his briefcase, saying "Here, son, I want you to have this. It's from Major League Baseball." Looking it over once before handing it to the child, he discovered he had almost given away Sosa's home run ball. Finding another, he handed it over; "the kid started smiling and hollering and going ballistic. Puente made sure to tell him it was just an ordinary baseball, but the kid didn't care. It was a brand-new official baseball, and it was the greatest thing in the world."[258] For all the charm of the kid's reaction, Puente himself was "shaken." "He explained to his colleagues how he'd almost given away Sosa's ball by mistake" and they all had a good laugh. "Reuben," one of them noted, "you're probably the only guy in the world, if you had given it to him, you could just go back to your hotel room and make another. No one would ever know."[259] This story is charming precisely because the ball would not have been authentic, valuable, or real had it been a recreation. Puente, like the Pardoner, could create a false relic, but it would ultimately be devoid of value, and the real ball, owned by an anonymous child somewhere in Milwaukee, would have joined the roster of lost treasures. The child's different interpretation of the object would have taken it outside the reliquary world, returning it to its status as "just a baseball"; instead of venerated, it might well have found its original use in a sandlot or backyard game, finally lost (like Ruth's sixtieth) over the fence or chewed by the neighbor's dog.

Concerns with authenticity did not rest solely in the home run balls. As McGwire items became increasingly popular, creating waiting lists for anything with his name on it, forgeries became commonplace. Signed baseball cards were particularly notable fakes, since McGwire never signed at card shows or events, only for children at games. Fake autographs appeared on bats, balls, jerseys, and possibly a jock strap as well.[260] Yi-Wyn Yen pointed out that "McGwire himself has challenged store owners in St. Louis and Denver about the validity of their merchandise."[261] His business manager is quoted as saying, "Mark was saddened that people had paid good money and didn't get something that was worth getting. . .There are a hundred stores and outlets selling bogus merchandise and you can't stop that. . .They're like ants—you spray the Raid, but they keep coming back."[262] It is authenticity, problematic as it may be, that again determines worth; a baseball with McGwire's signature on it is still a baseball, but instead of costing $9, its value increases with his popularity. At the beginning of the 1998 season, McGwire's rookie card sold for $25; in September, before Sixty-two, it cost $135, "and the value increases every day McGwire launches one over the fences, according to several owners of memorabilia stores and businesses."[263] Indeed, desire for McGwire objects led to a frenzy of desire similar to that for relics even before the record was broken, St. Louis Cardinal employees had "received requests for McGwire's under-wear and gum he had chewed during games" and there were waiting lists for anything with his name on it.[264] The rarity of authentic McGwire items also adds to their value; "the shortage of McGwire signed collectibles stems from his belief that autographs are for kids and his refusal to mass-sign merchandise";[265] thus, once again, these relics, through their distinc-tiveness, separate their owners from the anonymity of mass production and mass merchandising.[266] Like relics, "symbols of divine favor continuing to operate on behalf of men," these objects are also "reality symbolized, since they referred not beyond themselves but to themselves, as the saint residing among followers."[267] A "real" Mark McGwire autograph, home run ball, or rookie card may well tell the story of the whole 1998 season and its mirac-ulous events, but it is also reality, a tiny DNA sample of McGwire himself, a living piece of the man, fixed and eternal, time bound and timeless. In a world of copies, the authentic, the real moves into a whole new realm of value. Before it was hit, Barry Halper noted "the value of the 62nd home run ball could range anywhere from half a million to a million"—at the time, well above the highest price ever paid for an autographed baseball. As Walter Benjamin notes, "the whole sphere of authenticity is outside technical reproduction." The unique work of art has ritual and cultic power, and it is defined by "its presence in time and space, its unique exis-tence at the place where it happens to be." Within Benjamin's "Age of Mechanical Reproduction," McGwire's and Sosa's home run balls were, in their unique ability to encode time and space, unreproducible.[268] Unique in its ability to exist only once, such an object becomes the ultimate prize.

Before the prize itself was launched, however, its spirit was already working a kind of miracle. Starting on September 1, when Mark McGwire tied Hack Wilson's sixty-eight-year-old National League home run record with his fifty-sixth home run, fans catching the balls began to return them to McGwire, who had expressed an interest in giving them to the Hall of Fame, in exchange for some autographed items, and sometimes some game tickets.[269] Surprise at this inspired *caritas* was expressed widely at the time; Mike Vaccaro notes, "You wondered if the limits of human nature had been tested long enough, since for a week a parade of selfless, kind-hearted fans had marched into the Cardinals clubhouse, handed Mark McGwire his baseballs and walked away with some bats, a few signed balls and the fond best wishes of a public grown far too jaded and cynical."[270] Faced with temptation, they chose virtue: "They had walked right past the blood suckers and the con artists offering thousands of dollars. They'd resisted the temptation to cash in on a good thing and better fortune, trading a $9 baseball for the untold riches of memorabilia collectors. One after another, after the television cameras tracked them down, they pledged to hand the ball over to McGwire, all of them acting insulted at the prospect of redeeming their prize for profit."[271] If this language is insufficiently reminiscent of Augustine's Carthaginian fleshpots, consider Tom Verducci's comment after the sixty-first ball was caught and returned, which effectively locates this generosity in the realm of sanctity: "The spell of 62 has made Good Samaritans of would-be opportunists. Is that magic? You decide."[272] In this he echoes his colleague Gary Smith, who, in trying to account for the rash of returned balls, wrote, "maybe goodness gathers more goodness, like a snowball rolling downhill."[273] Verducci's sense of religious context informs the language of his whole article, each subheading building upon the baseball's reliquary significance: "The Ball has magnetic power"; "The Ball has healing power"; "The Ball has redemptive power"; "The Ball has magic power." To attribute so much power to an object is extraordinary; to attribute the kinds of power Verducci does, even jocularly, locates the baseball firmly in the world of efficacious things. Writing that the baseball "many believers would swear to you,. . .glows even under the brilliant sunshine of a scorching Saturday afternoon in the last great baseball city,"[274] and calling McGwire himself a "national treasure,"[275] he directly ties actions and reactions to objects. The magnetic power of the ball is what galvanizes America, making it a "Baseball Nation again";[276] McGwire's home run totals are "godly," and the balls with which he hits them "special" and identifiable "in perpetuity."[277] The ball's magnetism is matched by its curative powers, as Verducci reiterates McGwire's salvation of the country: "This is what the country needs to help with the healing process and all the trouble that's going on in Washington. This will help cure the ills of the country."[278] Finding McGwire's "ferocious cuts at history" soothing "like homemade chicken soup," he also notes, "It's all the easier to know he's worth rooting for, a gentle man who last Thursday spent his only off day in a month, from 11 in the morning until seven at night, filming a public-service announcement designed to help stop sexual abuse of children."[279] That this comment falls under the heading "The Ball has healing power" sharpens the link between McGwire and the things he produces; the saint and the relic, here, are essentially the same; the healing that takes place through his actions are encoded in the ball itself, and its enshrinement in the Hall of Fame, ensured by Deni Allen's return of #61 to McGwire, makes this curative power publicly and perpetually available.

Perhaps most interesting, despite its brevity, is the penultimate section of Verducci's piece, "The Ball has redemptive power." The healing of the nation is a kind of redemption, but McGwire's home run ball can apparently work in more personal and inside ways as well. By embodying the breaking of Roger Maris's record, McGwire's home run ball serves to elevate Maris to the status he never quite managed to achieve in life. Because Maris's achievement was deflated by baseball commissioner Ford Frick's decision to mark it with an asterisk because it was set in 162 games instead of Ruth's 154, it received less attention and unequivocal praise, at least from within the baseball establishment, than people now feel it deserved.[280] Jeff Idelson, a Hall of Fame official, brought the bat that Roger Maris used to hit his sixty-first home run to the September seventh game, sleeping with it in his hotel room the night before to protect this "national treasure." In 1961, no one paid much attention to Maris's bat, which was donated to the Hall of Fame in 1973; McGwire "included the children of Roger Maris [who were also at the game] in his public thoughts" holding the bat with which he hit his own home run and Maris's at the same time, saying "with genuine tears in his eyes": "I want the Maris family to know that they will always be in my heart. . .I can honestly say now that my bat will rest next to his in the Hall of Fame at Cooperstown"[281] while kissing each bat. That he treated them as relics himself reveals the same kind of sacral continuity shown in the many hagiographies in which saints are inspired by the relics of their predecessors. But, on the redemption front, McGwire's home run was able to redeem Maris, to bring him back into the public eye in a heroic light, and possibly reenergize the quest for his official canonization in the Hall of Fame. Thus, if McGwire's home run ball could heal the nation, it could also redeem an undervalued member of his own elevated community. The ball's magic power, with which Verducci ends, rests again on its reliquary significance; making "Good Samaritans out of would-be opportunists," it inspires charity and good works. But it also functions to create more relics: "from here on out every baseball thrown his way is a record waiting to happen. Every baseball glows."[282]

Indeed, some glowed before they even existed; well before #62 was hit, an anonymous doctor offered to arrange payments of approximately $1 million to the fan who caught the ball, in order to help in the continuing search for justice in the murders of three American nuns in El Salvador in 1980. Hoping to raise awareness, the doctor said, "what better way to publicize the cause than to tie it to the home run derby? I hope when sportscasters talk about the money, they will also talk about the cause."[283] The doctor planned to buy an annuity for the fan, and then resell the ball to raise money for the Lawyer's Committee on Human Rights, a New York organization that represents the families of the murdered nuns, as well as promoting human rights around the world. This desire, though unrealized, again links the ball especially firmly to salvation, this time in the context of human rights. Although this group and its cause have little relation to McGwire and his choice of charitable causes, the sense that the relic itself can be effective in the fight for human justice suggests a broad sense of its affective potential, casting the story as another kind of conversion narrative, in which many are saved by an act of charity tied to and inspired by the holy object itself.

If the sixty-first home run ball and the idea of the sixty-second could inspire so much, the actual ball that broke Maris's record and the seventieth ball that set the new one are even more significant. This home run, more than any of the others, made "time stand still; fifty thousand people, all of them having spent the summer waiting for this moment, praying for it, gasped for an instant tracing with their eyes the path of a baseball as is streaked like a laser beam off the bat of Mark McGwire."[284] If the moment itself becomes the conventional alteration of time essential for religious transcendence, the ball, by partaking in that moment, takes on that same transcendence, joining time and timelessness in its reliquary significance. Vaccaro calls the sixty-second ball "the holy grail of this home run chase, the one that soared into history."[285] As if its path were destined, Vacarro notes that "thankfully, in the end, the ball ended up exactly where it should have ended up, away from the bloodhounds, out of reach of the hucksters who would put a price tag on a priceless piece of history. Thankfully, there was a twenty-two-year-old kid named Tim Forneris, fresh out of St. Louis University, a part-time groundskeeper at Busch Stadium. A fresh-faced voice of innocence. That's how it should have been."[286] Forneris's "innocence," that quality so often associated with holiness, makes his act pure: "If there was a moment when the kid thought about keeping the ball, raffling it to the highest bidder, maybe trying to pay off some school loans, he didn't reveal them. Wouldn't. Giving the ball up was the most natural thing in the world."[287] Indeed, that Forneris managed to dispel anxiety about the ball ending up in the wrong hands smacks in this account of divine intervention: "perhaps the Good Lord himself grew unnerved by the human experiment He had hatched. Perhaps He touched the giant's bat and kept number 62 from reaching us."[288]

Not that the chosen one was indifferent to the relic's appeal. Forneris, who worked part-time as a groundskeeper for Busch Stadium and also as an analyst trainee for Anderson Consulting, making him "surrounded by money every day, big money, serious money," decided to give the ball up, because "Life is about experiences. . .nobody will ever be able to feel what I'm feeling right now. Nobody will ever be able to trade places with me. This is mine. This is mine forever."[289] Certainly he was aware of the power of the moment: "The young man's right hand went numb. His body trembled."[290] Gary Smith credits Forneris's religious training—"he had been an alter boy, a magna cum laude graduate of a Jesuit university, a volunteer at a homeless shelter"[291]—for his ability to feel the relic's power and surrender it at the same time, letting his conscience be his guide, allowing him to stretch "the limits of human nature," making him another symbol of saintly salvation: "remember it the next time you're convinced the world's gone all to hell. People still do the right thing once in a while. Thankfully."[292] Once again, the charged rhetoric that reveals the reliquary context of objects and their ability to work in mysterious ways. Within the context of gratitude (a religious emotion) that Vaccaro creates, Forneris is both inspired to his act of *caritas* (giving the ball to McGwire, who will then donate it to the Hall of Fame, making it publicly available and thus more widely salutary) by the ball itself and is also elevated as a result of that act, becoming himself a symbol for the values of generosity, selflessness, and kindness the relic comes to represent. Out of his hands, however, the relic continues to work its affective magic.

In an article titled "Generosity Still Pays Dividends in Forneris Saga," Tom Wheatly explores the life-changing results of Forneris's contact with #62. In August of 1999, Forneris and his family went to Cooperstown "to see Tim's relic at the baseball Hall of Fame," saying that he still "has no regrets about giving back his million-dollar ball."[293] Having "laughed off most snipers," including people who labeled him "the Idiot" and "the posterboy for financial misplanning," Forneris found himself rewarded for his act of kindness, receiving gifts of a Chrysler minivan in Cardinal red, sixty-two passes to a car wash, $450 from fans, a painting of a baseball and a rose from an Alabama Woman who "said [he] was in her prayers," invitations to meet President Clinton, a parade at Disney World, and a trip to the Players Choice Awards, where he finally met Mark McGwire and spent two hours visiting with him. Quoting Forneris's contention that all the fun he had as a result was "worth more than a million bucks," Wheatly concludes, "That's the Forneris Saga. Everything is unbelievable. Everything is the best part."[294] That the ball is the cause of both Forneris's actions and the actions of those who greeted his generosity with acts of their own is again explained through its medieval context: "the perception of the operation of relics on the part of most people, lay and clerical, seems to have been. . .immediate: relics were the saints, continuing to live among men. They were available sources of supernatural power for good or ill, and close contact with them or possession of them was a means of participating in that power."[295] Forneris's contact with and brief possession of the ball allows him to participate in its power, and like a medieval relic, the ball reveals its authenticity by continuing to perform miracles even in absence; not only is Forneris blessed with the experience of finding it, he continues to be blessed by its power some time after his inspired act of charity returned the ball to McGwire for its eventual enshrinement: "some days I think this whole thing has died out," he notes, "and then my dad will say, 'Rick Reilly called for you.' I'm like, 'the guy from *Sports Illustrated*? Are you kidding?' "[296]

Mark McGwire's final home run, hit on the last day of the 1998 baseball season, caused as much stir as his sixty-second, albeit less anticipated. Caught by Philip Ozersky, a research scientist at the Human Genome Project, it received more offers and more attention than #62 because it remained in circulation. Because the sixty-second ball was already on display at the Hall of Fame by the end of September, it was "presumably off the collectibles market forever";[297] according to Bill Connelly, a member of the American Society of Appraisers, "McGwire's 62nd held its value for what?—about 48 hours. . .After that, if it hadn't gone into the Hall, it would have dropped like a brick."[298] As Geary notes, "if a relic were willingly given away, one might conclude that the donor had not praised it highly";[299] while no one ever suggested that Forneris did not praise his find, the immediate removal of it from the economic market served to de-commoditize and resacralize it. Authorized and enshrined, its value was purely semiotic. The important relationship of circulation to value is clarified by Patrick Geary:

> From the perspective of the community in which the remains came to be venerated, the construction of value and the mode of circulation reflected the same assumptions as the production context: acquiring the relic gave it value because it was worth acquiring, and this acquisition (often in the face of grave or supernatural dangers) was itself evidence that the relics were genuine. Circulation thus created the commodity being circulated, although to survive as a commodity it had to continue to meet the high expectations raised by the mode of its creation.[300]

Rushed out of the stands by stadium security when he retrieved the ball from under his seat, Ozersky chose to take the ball home in order to make a decision about what to do with it. Hit first by the same extraordinary excitement that all the other fans describe, Ozersky's "own expression seems to want to explode in disbelief. He's not sure if he's speaking, or if maybe his thoughts are simply careening about in his head, but what he's thinking about saying is *Oh, my God. Oh, my God. Oh, my God.* Over and over."[301] While being led away by the cops, Ozersky was "clutching so tight to the ball it might hold a secret formula for world peace."[302] Certainly, he felt the magnitude of the situation: "his whole life, he doesn't even come close to a thing like this."[303] Unable to meet McGwire to exchange the ball in person, Ozersky decided that he really wanted "to hold onto it awhile,"[304] a decision that set the events of the rest of the story in motion.

That the ball had no value until it was hit and caught is clear; despite its authenticating markings, had it been hit out of the stadium and lost (probably an impossibility given the confines of St. Louis' Busch Stadium, but theoretically possible in other ballparks), it would be valuable only as a legend, the "Lost Ball of Mark McGwire." Once found, the legendary item would then acquire its monetary value, as a commodity can only have an actual value when it is actually there. The worth of acquiring the ball was set before Ozersky caught it, but his act then set into motion the valuation that resulted in the ball's sale at auction for a phenomenal price. The dangers that Ozersky faced—having it stolen, being trampled, being coerced into returning it to McGwire, or selling it in some unscrupulous way, fan opprobrium—may not have been supernatural, yet the experience itself, based on the descriptions in the press, seems to take on a supernatural quality that only contact with a valuable relic can provide. Thus, the ball's existence and presence makes it a circulable commodity, and Ozersky's choice not to give it to McGwire or the Hall of Fame allowed it to maintain its value in ways that Forneris's ball did not. The price it fetched matches Geary's assumption that the relic has to continue to meet the high expectations it sets; the seventieth home run ball, soon known only as "The Ball," through the speculation about what would happen to it, the hoopla of its final sale, the mystery of the buyer, and its final enshrinement, meets or perhaps exceeds the expectations set by its launching over the outfield wall on the last day of a storied season.

Geary's sense that a good "story increased the value of the relic" (*Furta* Sacra xii) is apparent in the history of #70. No matter what the circumstances were, as much money as #70 was sold for, instead of being constructed as a tale of modern capitalism, accounts of the sale still get turned into relic stories acting within a medieval context, and so revealing the powerful need for narrative to give an object its value.[305] Once Philip Ozersky decided to keep the ball, rejecting the offer to exchange it for other autographed items, the ball began to take on a significance that led him to say, "It's like I have two jobs. . .I have my work, and then there's the ball. . .this is a once-in-a-lifetime thing."[306] Already life-altering before it actually moved toward auction, Ozersky noted, "This baseball brought a nation together."[307] As with its medieval counterparts that were "perceived as the living saint,"[308] the ball took on the qualities of the slugger who launched it, gaining the same salutary qualities attributed to McGwire himself, standing for a kind of communal redemption, "the crowning moment in a year-long slugfest that captivated America."[309] Choosing the title "No. 70 Goes After Another Record," Douglas Martin casts the ball as a simulacrum of McGwire, a record-breaking object capable of the same actions as the record-breaking person.[310] Similarly, Daniel Paisner comments about some of the people to whom Ozersky showed his ball, "they want to rub up against Mark McGwire, even in this several-times-removed sort of way. They want to have a story to tell."[311]

As a relic, #70, like #62 and many of the other home runs balls before it, was able to change a life: bringing Ozersky $2.7 million dollars, it made him a "national celebrity."[312] Called "Auction's Holy Grail,"[313] the ball's authenticity as an affective object was made apparent in Ozersky's deliberations over what to do with it. Although tempted to give the ball to McGwire or the Hall of Fame, "the way he came to it left Ozersky thinking the money was meant for more than him."[314] Because his "coming up with the 70th home run ball placed him in a kind of spotlight," Ozersky felt "he should put the money to work in a public way, for the greater good."[315] Feeling that if he "kept control of the ball he could direct its impact," he imagined the

> benefits his ball could bring to any number of local charities, or to any number of underprivileged children. In his day-dreamings, he kept processing things in terms of children, and he wondered how much of this had to do with McGwire. He was well aware of McGwire's efforts on behalf of abused kids—more than anything else, it was the slugger's personal cause—and Ozersky supposed it was fitting to direct his proceeds from the ball in just this way. Plus, he always liked children, and it tore at his heart, some of the stories he'd hear, what kids were put through.[316]

The rhetorical closeness of this statement to many of McGwire's shows the ball working for "the greater good" through its own agency; in contemporary language, it essentially "channeled" the spirit of its saint in order to influence its postulants for good. By the time it went to auction, the ball had an even greater influence; Ozersky had decided that he wanted to "open a sports camp for abused children, with his sister Sharon," make a "sizeable donation to the Leukemia Society of America," to "give money to the American Cancer Society," and keep giving "to Cardinals Care, in honor of McGwire."[317] That the ball could make Ozersky a major philanthropist, along the lines of McGwire himself, shows the affective potential of the relics that embody their saints' qualities. Saints' lives are filled with stories of relics working in these ways. Because the power of the relic comes from that saint's thaumaturgic potential, the life-altering abilities of these home run balls manifest their authenticity as they prove their value.

The translation of the ball's value into overt monetary terms also showed reliquary tendencies. The division of saints' bodies into pieces to meet increasing need began as early as the eighth century, when, as R.W. Southern notes, "the incessant demand for relics caused the bodies of the early saints to be broken up, [because] they were the object of a huge commerce."[318] One of the first offers Ozersky received for the ball was from Jeff Becket, who, in the medieval spirit, wanted to take the cover off the ball, unravel the cotton windings that surrounded its rubber core, and encase each one in separate baseballs, which he would then sell for $29.95; the half-a-million balls that Becket imagined marketing certainly suggested a "huge commerce" along the lines of the distribution of relics in medieval Europe. He also proposed to resew the original covers around a new core and donate that to the Hall of Fame.[319] Whether this would make Becket akin to Chaucer's Pardoner or merely a modern version of Deusdona and the other "true" relic sellers of the Middle Ages is debatable; Daniel Paisner, author of *The Ball: Mark McGwire's 70th Home Run Ball and the Marketing of the American Dream*, sees Becket's scheme solely in monetary terms, writing that "what he [Becket] saw was green,"[320] yet it is possible to consider that in setting a price "that kids can afford for themselves,"[321] Beckett was merely reiterating an old reliquary convention. For, as Kieckhefer notes, "the translation and invention of bodies were accompanied by dismemberment and distribution of relics. Just as the soul was totally present in every part of the body, so. . .the spirit of the saint was powerfully present in each relic."[322] Beckett's plan would have allowed many more to partake in the relic's magic, and by placing the most visible portion of the Ball in the official shrine at the Hall of Fame ensure its canonization as an affective and official relic while simultaneously assuring its distribution, thus merely following a well-established and ancient pattern.

At this point, the relationship of authenticity to value reentered the equation; despite Major League Baseball's authentication campaign, Ozersky was urged—and indeed paid—by Professional Sports Authenticators to mark the ball with "an invisible DNA trace liquid that could be read with a special laser light,"[323] since "the Major League Baseball markings. . . would fade over time, and this would be especially so if the ball was placed under direct lighting, such as you might find in a museum display case. The DNA tag, however, would never fade. . .no matter what lighting or climate conditions the ball was subjected to."[324] Taking the idea of the cleric's official signature to new heights, this process serves to identify the relic as "authentic" for all time, seemingly to escape the fading value and popularity of medieval relics, whose authenticating documents were lost or whose saints went out of favor. Thus, should the ball lose immediate value (as was suggested it might when Barry Bonds broke McGwire's home run record in the 2001 season), it would still maintain its historic identity, should Saint Mark McGwire regain popularity after his death or enshrinement in the Hall of Fame, which will, at least briefly, bring him back to the height of popularity once again. Regardless of the game's future stars and record holders, these objects will remain to tell the story of this chapter of baseball's history, just as the sacred relics of saints no longer on the calendar remain parts of the reliquaries that house them, telling the story of their popular devotion. As a result, regardless of its current value on the memorabilia market, the ball itself continues overtly to fulfill Benjamin's description of the authentic work of art:

> This unique existence of the work of art determined the history to which it was subject throughout the time of its existence. This includes the changes which it may have suffered in physical condition over the years as well as the various changes in ownership. The traces of the first can be revealed only by chemical or physical analyses which it is impossible to perform on a reproduction; changes of ownership are subject to a tradition which must be traced from the situation of the original.[325]

Chemically and physically analyzable for their authenticity, and embodying both the history of their situation and their ownership, Mark McGwire's home run balls remain unique objects, bearers of their own time and place.

Lest one forget that "saints manifested their power not only through beneficial miracles like working cures and finding lost objects but also by punishing and afflicting people who have offended them,"[326] it is illustrative to see that the people who caught McGwire's home run balls and did not return them, for the most part, did not receive either the economic or personal rewards for which they hoped. Caught in an "anti-greed backlash,"[327] they became poster children for "money-hungry fandom."[328] With the exception of Ozersky, who made it clear from the start that he wished to donate a significant portion of his ball's earnings to his favorite charities, and the owner of the sixty-fourth ball, who was reunited with the older brother he did not know he had until four years prior and made it clear he didn't want to make money on the ball, because "just having it around is making me happy,"[329] many of the "lucky" fans received only minimum bids on their prizes and were generally reviled for their greed. Those who caught the balls and returned them seemed aware of the relics' dangerous power: "It would've burned a hole in my heart if I would've hung on to it," said Deni Allen, who caught the sixty-first ball.[330] Tim Forneris, when asked to consider before returning the ball the money it could bring him, responded "Dirty money. . . .it would brand you to sell it. It's sad to hoard things. Life is all about experience."[331] The large number who chose to return the balls all call their memories of the night "absolutely priceless," saying that they are "totally satisfied with their decision to return the ball to McGwire."[332] Those who did not, for the most part, all expressed a desire to be paid greatly for their prize, saying, in response to being asked what they wanted for them, "I'll know it when I hear it."[333] That they all expressed a certain disappointment—that they didn't get to meet McGwire; that they were bothered by the media; that they suddenly had anxiety about theft; that they couldn't sleep—suggests a kind of quiet punishment,[334] matched by the more overt punishment of receiving rather less money than they had hoped when their balls were put up at auction.

The bidding for #70 was not, perhaps, as excessive as Ozersky and Guernsey's Auction House had hoped; however, after a brief stall at $1.35 million—$35,000 beyond the minimum reserve—an avid bidding war between the necktie manufacturer Irwin Steinberg and an anonymous phone bidder eventually drove the price up to $2.7 million ($3.005 including the buyer's premium to the auction house). This remained, however, the greatest sum ever to be spent on a baseball, significantly more than the $126,000 paid for the previous record holder, the first home run ball Babe Ruth hit at Yankee Stadium.[335] The buyer, Todd McFarlane, creator of the comic book *Spawn*, bought several other baseballs from the auction, including Sammy Sosa's sixty-sixth and has since put them together into a traveling show, displaying them around the country. Making the balls public functions as a kind of act of charity; with no plans to charge admission to his collection, McFarlane commented, "I don't want them to be mine. . . . I want them to travel, to be out there,"[336] accepting that he would have to "enjoy the balls from a distance"[337] in his charitable desire to share his purchase with other fans. His urge to share parallels the medieval owners of relics, who "possessed the holy, in the form of portable relics," and "could show gratia by sharing these good things with others, and by bringing them from the places where they had once been exclusively available to communities scattered throughout" the medieval world.[338] Once again noting the salutary power of sports, McFarlane said, "Sports are one of the few things in the world that makes us [sic] forget about death, taxes, politics, and all the other garbage that sometimes goes on in our life. . .All the walls, all the barriers we have as individuals, as humans, go down,. . .But it just shuts us down and makes us forget the drudgery sometimes that's there."[339] Accepting the objects' magic, he even offered shock-jock Howard Stern and his staff the opportunity to hold some of his record home run balls "to see if maybe the thrill in owning such record-setting items would rub off on them."[340] Whether Stern was able to feel the power of the relics is not recorded, yet it is clear that for McFarlane, these items function well beyond themselves, providing yet another link to the world beyond mundane existence. Thus, like his medieval counterparts, he takes part in "the passing of relics from one community to another," which "heightened the special status of the members of the Christian elite by making them privileged agents, personally involved in administering the lovingkindness of God."[341] Because baseball "has rooted itself in the cultural firmament in a fixed, timeless manner that belies its own boundaries,"[342] its objects, too, take on meaning that belies their own boundaries; a sphere of leather with colored stitching can become more than an object of play entering a realm in which "the power of the unseen world was more accessible than anywhere else,"[343] with the balls' owners as agents of that unseen world, sharing their own special access with others.

The nexus of physicality, authenticity, affectivity, and value determines a relic's worth; if an object acquires tremendous value detached from its aesthetic value or function, and if it "works," its status is conferred. Yet, as Geary notes, "once relics had achieved recognition—had come to be perceived as genuine and efficacious—their continuing significance and value depended on their continued performance of miracles and on their relative value compared with other relics and sources of power. Studies of relics' value indicate considerable fluctuations in both the short and long term."[344] When Barry Bonds broke Mark McGwire's home run record on October 5, 2001, it was generally assumed that Todd McFarlane's investment was now worth considerably less than he paid for it, although McFarlane himself noted, "People will remember the home run race from 1998 more than they'll remember the one in 2001. . .Neil Armstrong was on the moon first and I guess you can say a couple guys tied him and some of them even broke his record for staying on the moon longer. . .so just because it's not the record, that doesn't mean it isn't part of a great story."[345] McFarlane's suggestion that he might just purchase Bonds's record breaking balls when they get out of court as well puts him firmly in the relics market; however, his contention that McGwire's importance will survive the breaking of his 1998 record suggests that however much the value of his relic fluctuates in the short term, it's long-term worth is assured.[346] In its ability to embody a story—the breaking of a thirty-seven-year-old record rather than a three-year-old one, the story of someone widely admired rather than widely reviled, the ability to create enthusiasm in the face of trouble (which Bonds's race could not after the September 11, 2001 terrorist attacks on New York and Washington)—preserves its value. Should McFarlane follow Barry Halper and put his collection up for auction, that gauge of the relic's value will reveal its staying power. While McFarlane might well not recover the same vast sums he spent for his prize, it seems likely that McGwire's historic home run ball will, like Babe Ruth's ball and Ty Cobb's false teeth, retain its transcendent meaning, speaking across time, and showing how "culturally induced and semipermeable" the boundaries between subject (both McGwire and the future buyer) and object really are.[347] If the ball no longer seems to have the thaumagurgic potential that brought people together in 1998, in its ability to fuse present and past, it maintains its efficacy and authenticity. However, the Bonds ball itself provides an interesting footnote; caught but dropped by one fan and stolen by another, its ownership and value are now being decided in court. This recalls Geary's *Furtae Sacrae*; he notes, "in the tenth and eleventh centuries, a new theme appeared in the justification of thefts: the spiritual and moral state of the individual perpetrator. Simply stated, the action of a good man was good."[348] That ownership and theft of relics are tied to morality again comes into play.

How can a baseball galvanize so much interest? Peter Brown notes, "how better to express the paradox of the linking of Heaven and Earth by an effect of 'inverted magnitudes,' by which the object around which boundless associations clustered should be so tiny and compact?"[349] Like the small bone chip of a saint, home run balls bring much attention to something so little; the "balls were simple game pieces, valuable more for what they represented than for what they actually were."[350] Indeed, Mike Gidwitz, a collector since the age of eight, was concerned when the focus in the home run balls' story turned to money "instead of the stories behind the objects."[351] When asked about their hobby, memorabilia collectors often note that they want to "own a piece of baseball history,"[352] or as Jeff Becket, who wanted to divide McGwire's seventieth home run ball into pieces, noted, "what happens in this country when we become interested by something? We want to own a piece of it."[353] Possession of the object conveys meaning upon the owner; rather than functioning simply as a souvenir of an event, these pieces of memorabilia make the possessor a part of the historical event, giving them a place and meaning within it. Or, as Walter Benjamin notes, for a collector, "and I mean a real collector, a collector as he ought to be—ownership is the most intimate relationship that one can have with objects. Not that they come alive in him; it is he who lives in them."[354] Thus the sense of alienation from history—or from the sacred—is eliminated by the object itself, which brings close the distant, bridging the inherent gap. To echo Southern, in relics "the power of the unseen world was more accessible than anywhere else" (30); the intangible becomes tangible; the evanescent becomes permanent. This desire to bring under control what is uncontrollable echoes the function of medieval relics, linking time and eternity and connecting their worshippers to the greater transcendence beyond the realities of their world. Or, as Douglas Martin notes,

> Arguably the home run ball is America's obsession, the objectified reflection of the country's simplest, perhaps, best dreams. In Don DeLillo's dark novel

"Underworld," the lost ball Bobby Thomson of the New York Giants hit to seize the pennant from the Brooklyn Dodgers in 1951 becomes a novelistic device, appearing at significant moments in the narrative. It ends up in the hands of the protagonist, who uses it to summon an unrecoverable past.[355]

That these objects hardly need the devices of a novel in order to "summon an unrecoverable past" is evident in the stories of McGwire's sixty-second and seventieth balls. It is Krysztof Pomian's contention that sacred objects played the role of mediation between this world and the next, the sacred and the secular, representing "not only the sacred but also the past, or more exactly, they represented the sacred because they were supposed to have come from a personage belonging to sacred history."[356] Both "intermediaries between those who look at and touched them and the invisible,"[357] Saint Mark's shin bone and Saint Mark McGwire's home run ball come equally from persons belonging to different kinds of sacred history; as such, they represent that history, while also drawing it together with eternity, either the eternity of God or the eternity of human memory. If medieval postulants and contemporary collectors feel separate and distant from what is greater than themselves, a concrete piece of the saint can tie them to it. Even without its overtly sacred context, it is possible to see the ways that memorabilia functions as a link between our own present and an idealized past, as a "go-between between those who gazed upon them and the invisible from whence they came";[358] within the context that creates their value, these objects are "resocialized," to use Philip Fisher's term; they move from the stage in which they are defined by their utility into the stage in which they are defined by their legends, which "summon and transmit" their spirit. This second life, the "second system of access" that Fisher calls "sacred," shifts the sign's recognition from one determined by its utile qualities to one determined by an outside system of value.[359] The object thus both defines the past (renamed as history) and exists in the present, mediating between the two. Whether a bone or a baseball, relics mediate between worlds that may go by different names—heaven, history—yet combine present and eternal ideas of time in the same way. In both cases, the objects' meaning comes from a kind of incarnation, encoded in the physical; the evanescent walks the earth, the word made flesh.

Pilgrimage

Thanne longen folk to goon on pilgrimages,
And palmers for to seken straunge strondes,

To ferne halwes, kowthe in sundry londes;
And specially from every shires ende
Of Englonde to Caunterbury they wende,
The hooly blissful martir for to seke,
That hem hath holpen whan that they were seeke.

—Geoffrey Chaucer, *"The General Prologue"*[360]

It was clearly a place with curative powers, a Medjugorge of the Middle West. Six years after the film Field of Dreams *was released, the movie's principal shooting location—a ballfield cut into a cornfield—continued to draw five hundred visitors every summer day. The figure is astonishing, because Dyersville is centrally located in the middle of nowhere.*[361]

—Steve Rushin, *Road Swing*

The foreword to *The Art of Pilgrimage* reminds us, "the object of pilgrimage is not rest and recreation—to get away from it all. To set out on a pilgrimage is to throw down a challenge to everyday life. Nothing matters now but this adventure. . .Specifics may differ, but the substance is always the same."[362] Subtitled "The Seeker's Guide to Making Travel Sacred," the book attempts to address the traveler's "longing for something more."[363] Suggesting that pilgrimage is "the kind of journeying that marks just this move from mindless to mindful, soulless to soulful,"[364] Phil Cousineau declares that "by definition it is life changing."[365] Citing medieval pilgrims' guidebooks like the *Marvels of Rome*, and Picaud's *The Pilgrim's Guide* with its descriptions of "sights, shrines, and people,"[366] he also notes their addition of "prayers for safe journeys, lists of relics, architectural wonders, commentaries both kind and caustic about those one might encounter along the route."[367] He sees his own project as a contemporary version, offering "those who have the deep desire to make a significant symbolic journey and need some inspiration and a few spiritual tools for the road."[368] "At the heart of this book," he writes, "is the belief that virtually every traveler can transform any journey into pilgrimage with a commitment to finding something personally sacred along the road."[369]

Cousineau's sense of the essential interaction between traveler and sacred space echoes the medieval sense of pilgrimage, travel undertaken for a spiritual purpose, with a sacred site as its goal, whatever more secular activities happened along the way. Seeking the "hooly blissful martyr," Chaucer's pilgrims travel from London to Canterbury, and the *Tales'* conclusion with the Parson's sermon suggests a final religious—if not so uplifting to a modern reader—moment of revelation. Pilgrimage sites' sanctity "did not come from where or what they were. It came from what was to be found there—what physical link with the divine sphere remained incarnate in the material world."[370] The exception was the pilgrimage to

Jerusalem, which drew its significance from the loci of the events of Christ's passion, but most European sites were defined by the miraculous objects—relics of saints—that were enshrined there available for the pilgrim's petitions and prayers for aid. From Santiago de Compostela, which held the relics of Saint James, to Canterbury's bones of Saint Thomas à Becket, travelers found opportunities for communing with the divine through what the holy had left behind. Patrick Geary notes that the original objects of veneration were the Christian martyrs, who in accordance with Roman law, were buried outside the walls of the city. He observes, "the suburban tombs of the martyrs became the sites of annual commemoration of the martyrs' passions. The faithful, led by the clergy of the city, would go out into the 'wilderness' to celebrate the memory of the martyrs."[371] The celebration of the memory rapidly became a celebration of the body itself, detaching the actual object from the site of its martyrdom, so that the transfer of relics conveyed holiness onto places rather than requiring the memory of the sacrificial event to confer holiness on the place. The function of the relic was transfigurative; "it was the cult of the saints that transformed cemeteries into shrines, shrines into cities, and prompted that robust form of social adventure and cohesion, the pilgrimage."[372]

Baseball's most famous pilgrimage site is the National Baseball Hall of Fame in Cooperstown, NY.[373] It is by no means the only one; another is the "Field of Dreams" in Dyersville, IA, with an equally national and international appeal. Less major sites—shrines to more local saints—include the Babe Ruth House in Baltimore; the Yogi Berra Museum and Learning Center in Montclair, NJ; Monument Park (situated between the outfield and the bullpen at Yankee Stadium in New York) and many ball parks themselves. Baseball is by no means unique either; shrines to sporting events and figures pepper the United States. In *Road Swing*, Steve Rushin, a reporter from *Sports Illustrated*, essentially goes on a pilgrimage worthy of the Wife of Bath, circling the country to visit sites as diverse as Jim Thorpe, PA, where the great athlete's bones are for the moment interred, to French Lick, IN, the birthplace of basketball legend Larry Bird. Sports is not the only producer of sites of pilgrimage, as other popular media produce sanctified figures who become represented (often after their death) by places, the most prominent among them being Graceland, the Elvis Presley home, museum, burial place, and shopping mall.[374] These sites, much like the various monastic pilgrimage sites that dotted medieval Europe, draw their importance both from what they represent and display.

Pilgrimage itself is two-fold, a journey coupled with its goal, the sacred location. Each one is potentially transformative; the journey itself, as a kind of literalized metaphor of the soul's journey to God, is the path by which the sacred space is reached. As Victor and Edith Turner note, "If mysticism is an interior pilgrimage, pilgrimage is an exterior mysticism."[375] Metaphorically, the medieval journey also represented Christ's journey into Jerusalem, or the saint's journey to heaven; in a more modern sense, then, the fans' journey replicates the athlete's, following, if not the same process, at least the same road to the Heavenly City. Both journey to Cooperstown, one through time (an impressive career), the other through space (the winding roads of upstate New York).

Alternatively, pilgrimage was penance, either imposed by ecclesiastical authority, or self-imposed as a "pure act of devotion."[376] Local and regional pilgrimages for ritual veneration of relics were combined with the more salvific, extended pilgrimages to shrines of international importance such as Jerusalem, Rome, Tours, and Compostela; the greater the journey, the greater the potential for redemption. Most pilgrims made "some concession to the principle that a pilgrimage should be accomplished in poverty."[377] To prepare their souls, it was customary for rich pilgrims to give alms to the poor before embarking; contributions were also made to monasteries and churches.[378] After making formal amends with those they had wronged in order to assure a sincere confession, pilgrims received formal blessings that reflected the feeling among pilgrims that they "belonged to an 'order' of the church, distinguished from other men by a uniform and by a solemn ritual of initiation."[379] The special dress—staff, scrip, broad-brimmed hat, and pilgrimage badge (on the return trip)—distinguished the pilgrim from other travelers along the road.

The difficulties of the pilgrimage journey in the Middle Ages were both practical and symbolic; a long journey during this period, as Jonathan Sumption notes, "was not a thing to be taken lightly"[380] as "the great sanctuaries were separated by hundreds of miles of unmade, ill-marked roads, many of them running through unpopulated tracts of Europe infested with bandits."[381] Pilgrimage blessings included a commonly conferred twelfth-century version that ran, "let the angels watch over thy servants. . . that they may reach their destination in safety,. . .that no enemy may attack them on the road, nor evil overcome them. Protect them from the perils of fast rivers, thieves, or wild beasts."[382] Other hazards included limited supplies of food and fodder, undrinkable water, lousy food, and natural catastrophes.[383] There was a "measure of protection against man-made hazards";[384] in 1096, the Archibishop of Lyon noted, "all those who travel to the shrines of the saints are protected against attack at all times, and not only in Lent. Those who disturb their journey will suffer the harshest penalties of the Church, so that the fear of God may remain for ever in their eyes."[385] Despite the inclusion of molesters of pilgrims in the annual bull *In Cena Domini* from 1303 on, pilgrims were still only marginally safer than other travelers, at the mercy of an international band of brigands and bandits.[386]

The difficult journey itself made saints of pilgrims, one of the most notable being Saint Bernard of Aosta, after whom the famed rescue dog is named.[387] Bovo of Provence, while defending alpine passes against Saracens, vowed to "lay down his arms, succor orphans and widows henceforth and visit the shrines of the Apostles Peter and Paul once a year, and more if he could, for the rest of his life."[388] Choosing austerity and humility over nobility, and a life of active service, Bovo found that "Pilgrimage fitted the mode of life he chose both as a form of penance and devotion and as an opportunity to display charity to those he encountered along the way."[389] After his death in Voghera on the way to Rome, "he was venerated there," becoming a site of pilgrimage himself.[390] Pilgrimage as a devotional form thus became a useful activity for men and women who chose to remain in the active life, although pilgrimages were also undertaken by monastics. For those not vowed to the life of perfect contemplation, pilgrimage was an opportunity for a turning to God in "a moderated style," which never required "abandoning the *vita activa* even while they took on certain monastic austerities."[391] The difficulty of the journey itself was often enhanced by the inaccessibility of the chief sites; for instance, the monastery of Conques, famous for its abduction of the body of Saint Foy, undertook its *furta sacra* because "its location placed Conques at a real disadvantage"[392] to the monastery of Figeac, "which was more favorably located to attract the devotion of the laity."[393] The "tortuous approach" to Conques needed to be offset by the importance of the saint who would convince pilgrims to undertake the dangerous trip.[394]

If the devotional aspects of the medieval journey seem lost in contemporary travel to pilgrimage sites, some of the conditions of journeying do remain the same. The route to the National Baseball Hall of Fame in Cooperstown, NY is perhaps not as arduous as that which medieval pilgrims traversed, yet by the standards of modern travel, the town is difficult to get to, being near no major city, and requires driving along winding roads which, in all seasons but summer, are subject to the relatively severe weather of upstate New York. Jonathan Yardley speaks for many when he calls the town "relatively inaccessible" and the winters "long and daunting."[395] It is this difficult travel to the "middle of nowhere" that leads Yardley to view Cooperstown as "authentic" and anticommercial instead of a presumably inauthentic tourist trap.[396] Indeed, in *Treasures of the Hall of Fame*, John Thorn notes, "dedicated souls make the pilgrimage to Cooperstown, New York, a picturesque village of 2,300 inhabitants that is served by no airport, no passenger train, no major highway. They don't get here by finding it on the way to there."[397] The Field of Dreams shares Cooperstown's remoteness enhanced by the American Midwest's sprawling distances; Steve Rushin describes the place as "centrally located in the middle of nowhere. . . . Townsfolk have to drive 175 miles just to get to Des Moines."[398] He elaborates:

> I left Austin after lunch, hope and Spamburger lodged in my heart. I steered south, toward Iowa and a landscape as flat as ballpark beer. Every twenty miles I passed through some tiny town, each one time-warped and almost too picturesque. The businesses all had names like Koster's Kar Korner, Kountry Kinfolk, Kum 'N' Go, and Kopper Kettle Kafe. With each mile, my pulse quickened. And is it any wonder? I was making for a cornfield near tiny Dyersville, Iowa. I was on my way to the Field of Dreams.[399]

Rushin's quickening pulse suggests—albeit sarcastically—the difference between Dyersville and any other small Iowa town; its Field of Dreams, the overtly sacred name belying its provincial identity, changes it from one kind of "time-warped town" to another—an image of the Middle Ages rather than an image of 1950s Middle America. Its distinction makes it meaningful, the process of getting there creating the desire and anticipation. It is tempting to note that modern travelers share with their medieval counterparts the danger of the road; brigandage and banditry in such forms as car-jacking are still possible, and contemporary pilgrims travel without the protection of the church. Indisputably, they are still subject to dreadful food (Cooperstown and Dyersville cuisine is pitched to the level of the fourteen-year-old boy) and uncomfortable conditions. However, more striking is the penitential and redemptive potential of such travel; as Rushin notes in his discussion of the Field of Dreams, the appeal of the place "has a lot to do with fathers and sons."[400] Indeed it furnishes a locus of male generational reconnection for travelers from countries such as "Australia, Japan, all over Europe. Places without baseball."[401] Thus its powers reach well beyond its mere connection with the American "National Pastime"; it has to offer something beyond a simple identification with a sport. Charles Fruehling Springwood also chronicles the redemptive potential of both sites at length, noting, "a visit to the Field of Dreams is viewed by many as a healthy, morally and physically purifying experience."[402] Thus, if these modern sites share both the arduous journey and the penitential possibility with their medieval counterparts, the journey to them is figured similarly—as the journey of the soul toward its redemptive meeting with the divine.

The second constituent of Pilgrimage, the sacred sites themselves, is created both by history and fiction; the sacred history of Rome and Jerusalem and the actual sites of martyrdom often establish what places become important, but the *inventios* and *translatios* that establish the power of these locations are no less vital in their authorization. These two genres, both intimately connected with relics, rely on a combination of object and place to gain their significance. The *inventio* is characterized by finding, by the locating of place in reference to what appears there; the *translatio*, on the other hand, brings the object to the place, and through that translation comes transformation.

Monika Otter offers a detailed account of *inventio*, defining it as "a liturgical term" that "refers to the discovery of a saint's relics. . .[in the] brief narratives about such findings of relics. . . .Most are connected to the story of the house's foundation. The connection may be direct or oblique, but *inventiones* are told, by and large, to explain a monastary's origin."[403] Using the *Revelation Sancti Stephani*, an influential text that spread throughout medieval Europe after its fifth-century production, as a model, Otter determines the type-narrative for the *inventio*:

> the relics are found either by coincidence, usually in connection with some construction or renovation project, or by divine guidance, through dreams or visions. The search for the right place and the digging itself are usually much emphasized; it is stressed that the community "earned" the relic through its intense desire and hard work. There must be an audience present, minimally represented by the bishop or other high clerics in charge, but often described as a large crowd of clergy and laity. There will be some confirmation that the relic is genuine: the body may be incorrupt, or at least emit a pleasing fragrance; sometimes there is an inscription or some identifying artifact. The *inventio* is followed by a *translatio*, that is, the body is brought to a more worthy shrine, and its authenticity is further confirmed by miracles.[404]

Although *inventiones* differ in "tone, style, and purpose," she suggests, this text is "clearly the narrative model for most of our texts."[405] The plot elements it provides remain constant, while the decoration around them changes in accordance with their varied locations and uses. Many writers of this kind of material found it adaptable "to contemporary affairs" and able to "reaffirm cultural and historical continuity,"[406] so that the genre could serve multiple political purposes along with validating the establishment of sacred places. Calling most medieval *inventiones* "foundation stories, both in a literal sense. . .and in a larger sense: *inventiones* serve, in many ways, as the foundation of a monastery's corporate identity and self-definition," Otter makes a key point for understanding both medieval and modern versions of the genre. Because these stories are "inspired by dreams and revelations but are also the result of a strenuous effort by the monks," they balance divine providence and grace with "human effort and initiative," which sets the stories "within the balance of the divine and the human."[407] As such, they both provide an origin for the community and a sense of its continuity over time.[408] The function of time in these stories is critical for understanding the connection between the medieval root texts and their modern counterparts; the balance of divine and human, historical and mythological echoes the relationships to time that bring something sacred or divine to the secular world's understanding of contemporary culture, transposing a medieval sense of that relationship onto the modern world subtracting only the doctrinal aspects of medieval popular religion. This balance locates the site both in time and out of it; providing its own beginnings and history, the *inventio* also locates the sacred place within a greater, more transcendent history that inherently borders on myth.

The varied examples that Otter provides, from Saint Edmund's head that speaks in response to his friends' shouting, to the story of the moving of Saint Aethelthryth of Ely to the new church, show the ways that these stories both identify sacred locations and demonstrate their continuing history, as the *inventiones* are generally written within the monasteries where their stories take place, establishing the uninterrupted connection from the saint's death to the contemporary moment. Purporting to be "factual historical accounts about the origins of religious houses," they nonetheless are often more psychologically or metaphorically apt than they are veracious, displaying a "patent artificiality and impossibility" that has "irritated modern historians, whose responses range from apologetics or mild derision to outright condemnation."[409] That said, Otter effectively considers the relationship between fictionality and history within the genre, noting:

> On the one-hand, they are almost always made-up history, either outright forgery or a bona fide reconstruction of what might have been. Like all etiological legends—stories that explore causes, that explain how a current state of affairs came about—they are necessarily retroactive: They are projected backward from a present end point to an imagined origin. . .On the other hand, *inventio* stories make specific, empirically verifiable truth claims about historical dates, places, people, and events; in many cases, indeed, they take on quasi-legal status, and it is of great practical importance that their accounts be understood and accepted as factually referential.[410]

Like the cult of relics to which they are tied, *inventiones* are "authenticating narratives"[411] that provide the same "truth" to a place that relic stories provide to the bones and teeth of the saints. If relics make saints present in time, while they concomitantly live in eternity, these stories provide the same kind of authentication for the places that house those relics. Indeed, they work reciprocally to authenticate each other. By the identifying of place through the agency of relics, the place itself becomes a kind of reliquary *en masse*, a vast equivalent of the decorative boxes and containers that held the venerated objects. As a site, then, it too becomes a kind of object of veneration, its name uttered in hushed and reverent tones as the embodiment of the transcendent experience it is supposed to provide. While the holy relics housed therein are essentially the point of the pilgrimage journey, the place itself becomes the goal—the voyage is made to Santiago, Rome, Walsingham, Jerusalem, or Cooperstown.

The origin narrative of the National Baseball Hall of Fame is essentially an *inventio*, taking part in both the literalizing and fictionalizing qualities of the genre that Otter considers. Standing in the place of Goselin or Walter Mapp, Albert Spalding, the cofounder of the National League and publisher of *Spalding's Official Baseball Guides*, initiated a journalistic debate that gave rise to an originary narrative of baseball's beginnings, rejecting the more evolutionary model proposed by Henry Chadwick, the English-born journalist, who suggested a development from British games like rounders and cricket, or perhaps an earlier form called Town Ball.[412] Despite references to baseball in Jane Austen's *Northanger Abbey* and a medieval manuscript illustration that shows a batter taking a swing with a stick at an inflated bladder that suggest an even older tradition,[413] Spalding preferred an "immaculate conception"[414] to Chadwick's continuous model. Stephen Jay Gould suggests that "too few people are comfortable with evolutionary modes of explanation in any form. . .and one reason must reside in our social and psychic attraction to creation myths in preference to evolutionary stories—for creation myths. . .identify heroes and sacred places, while evolutionary stories provide no palpable, particular thing as a symbol for reverence, worship, or patriotism."[415] Needing the "audience of laity and clerics" that Otter identifies in order to establish his *inventio*, Spalding formed the Mills Committee, consisting of two U.S. senators, the former president of the National League, and several ballplayers and businessmen, to create the necessary aura of authority. The division between the two interests represented on the committee—the game of baseball, which provided a kind of cultural authenticity, and the political and business worlds, representing both economic viability and social necessity—may well be seen as serving the same needs as the mixed audience of the *inventiones*; working from within, the former players and league president provide the same proximity to the action that the clergy do; working from outside, the businessmen and politicians take the place of the lay audience that authenticates the experience from a seemingly disinterested point of view, yet also provides the ultimate economic base for the monastery as a pilgrimage site. If baseball's "men of God" are those who play the sport, the nonathletes on the commission represent its congregation, its fans.

Drawing on "every possible shred of testimony, however tenuous, that might support an indigenous theory of baseball's origin," Spalding finally found something—a letter from Abner Graves, who claimed that baseball had been invented in Cooperstown, NY by one Abner Doubleday.[416] Graves claimed that in 1839, he saw Doubleday scrawl the diagram of his new game in the dirt while describing its rules to a group of boys playing marbles (or possibly Rounders) in back of the tailor shop (or Elihu Phinney's cow pasture).[417] Graves wrote:

> He went diligently among the boys in the town, and in several schools, explaining the plan, and inducing them to play Base Ball in lieu of other games. Doubleday's game was played in a good many places around town: sometimes in the old militia muster lot, or training ground, a couple of hundred yards southeasterly from the courthouse, where County Fairs were occasionally held; sometimes in Mr. Bennett's field south of Otsego Academy. . . .and other times over in the Miller's Bay neighborhood.[418]

The litany of places echoes Otter's sense that *inventiones* verify their legitimacy through reference to real locations; the variety of fields Graves lists serve to locate baseball firmly in Cooperstown through a kind of repetition. All these places are there in the town, and at all of them, the game was played; therefore, the occurrence becomes real because it is more than a one-time event. The rules are taken account of and used in places Spalding and his committee can seek out, presumably finding them still to be locations of pick-up baseball games. However, true to form, "truth" is combined with fictionality, as Spalding apparently did not know Graves, whose response seems to have come from an open call for information about the origins of American baseball. As another authenticating detail, Abner Doubleday provided the authority of his position; a Civil War general who returned fire at Fort Sumter, he gave weight to the story, locating it in American history. Being long dead, he was unable to testify, although his nephew, Robert Doubleday, did claim, when asked, that his uncle had "told him at length the story of how he invented baseball."[419] Researchers have concluded that Doubleday was not in Cooperstown in 1839, nor did he ever mention baseball in his extensive journals. Graves's age also problematizes the story, as he would have been five in that same year.[420] The Doubleday story, for all of its problems, still provided the impetus that turned Cooperstown into a pilgrimage site. On the basis of the myth, in 1917, a group of men "in Illion, New York. . .sat around a hot stove at Michael Fogarty's cigar store and agreed that there should be a monument to Doubleday in Cooperstown to honor his 'creation.' "[421] The men began a collection called the "Doubleday Memorial Fund." The enthusiasm generated by Sam Crane, a sportswriter for the *New York Journal*, brought the citizens of Cooperstown into the act; they purchased Phinney's Field, the ostensible site of the first game, made it into a baseball park, and eventually named it Doubleday Field. The bizarre nature of this commemoration becomes clear when one considers how few towns of 2,300 inhabitants have baseball fields that seat 10,000, a figure exceeding the capacity, for instance, of Keyspan Park, home of the Single-A League Brooklyn Cyclones, which seats 7,500. The population of Brooklyn, over 2,000,000, certainly couldn't fit into it once, let alone fit in three times over. Indeed, Cooperstown itself has no regular baseball team; the field hosts only the annual "Hall of Fame Game" and various exhibitions. In 1939, the community approached Major League Baseball with the idea of having a celebration of the hundredth anniversary of the game, which then provided the impetus for the museum itself.

What is obviously missing from this story is the presence of an authenticating relic, yet one appeared, found, as Otter asserts they must be, "by coincidence, usually in connection with some construction or renovation project, or by divine guidance, through dreams or visions."[422] Indeed, it is this relic—and the reliquary nature of the Hall of Fame itself—that confirms the identity of the Doubleday story as a medieval *inventio*. Stephen Clark, a local businessman who was one of the principal organizers of the Hall of Fame project, discovered "a dirty, misshapen ball, thought to be the first baseball, assumed to have been used by Doubleday and his friend Graves."[423] The ball was found by a farmer in an abandoned trunk in Fly Creek, NY and was determined to be that of Abner Graves, who had written the letter that began the origin narrative of Cooperstown. What Springwood calls "the serendipity of the find and the implied link between the ball, Graves, and ultimately, Doubleday" provided enough fodder for people to assume that this was the "original" baseball, soon called "The Doubleday baseball."[424] Clark then purchased the ball for $5 putting it on display in the local historical society until the official building of the Hall of Fame.

While many of Otter's principles of *inventio* narrative are missing here—the ball is not found with a particular audience present, nor does it perform particular miracles—there remain many aspects in common: the ball is authenticated and claimed to be genuine, although exactly how the trunk was determined to be Abner Graves's is uncertain, and value is rapidly established as an essential part of the narrative. As a physical representation of the miraculous origin, it provides authenticating truth. And while the ball is not an incorrupt body, being homemade, "battered and beaten, with the cover torn open,"[425] its clear antiquity, and its fortunate location can be seen as a *sportive* version of the "pleasing fragrance" that the unearthed

bodies of saints were said to give off. Taking it from its dark trunk and bearing it first to the historical society's exhibit room, and finally in a triumphal
procession to the new Hall of Fame building where it is enshrined in the
lobby, brings the "body to a more worthy shrine," in Otter's terms, in an
act of *translatio*, the other essential establishing narrative.[426] The ball's display echoes another medieval tradition; as Geary notes, "after the positive
recognition of the relics' authenticity came a public ritual known as the
'elevation,' in which the relics were formally offered to the public for
veneration."[427] The ball's placement, first in the historical society and then
with pride of place in the Hall of Fame itself introduces it to the public,
the authentication coming in the form of the document Graves sent to the
Mills Commission. Just as the "public, ritual discovery or invention and
examination of the relics publicized their existence and created or strengthened their cult"[428] in the medieval world, here the ball helps to publicize
the Hall of Fame movement and strengthens its support. The miracle that
thus confirms its authenticity may well be considered the founding of the
museum in the first place. As the object that legitimated Graves's claim,
the ball provided the seed for the collection that becomes the Hall of
Fame's attraction and the reason for its pilgrims to brave the twisting roads
that take them to Cooperstown.

Contending with criticism of the Doubleday myth in the 1980s, and
dealing with a group that wanted to move the Hall to Hoboken, Hall of
Fame executives stated that if baseball "was not actually first played here in
Cooperstown by Doubleday in 1839, it undoubtedly originated about that
time in a similar rural atmosphere. The Hall of Fame is in Cooperstown to
stay; at the very least, the village is certainly an acceptable symbolic site."[429]
Thorn's own reaction to this statement, "If baseball was not in fact invented
in Cooperstown, it ought to have been,"[430] shows the power of the
inventio to create history out of what is essentially fiction; "The National
Baseball Hall of Fame and Museum of Cooperstown, New York," Thorn
declares, "is not merely a monument that commemorates an historical
event, real or fanciful—it has a history of its own, in its own time, in its own
place." He continues, "Even though Cooperstown was not truly the home
base of baseball in 1839, it has been ever since. Like Mount Olympus,
it's where the legends live."[431] As a creation myth, this narrative identifies
"heroes and sacred places" providing "a symbol for reverence, worship, or
patriotism."[432] Indeed, the Hall of Fame itself encapsulates this essentializing narrative in its own caption, "In the hearts of those who love baseball,
he [Doubleday] is remembered as the lad in the pasture where the
game was invented. Only cynics would need to know more."[433] Locating
knowledge in the heart rather than the mind, the locus of faith rather than
reason, and separating true believers from heretics who would question the

tenets of the faith, the Hall of Fame turns its origin story into a test of the postulant's commitment; pilgrims pure of heart accept the relic narrative's authenticating truth, and only those of little faith do not.

Otter's sense that an *inventio* is "adaptable to contemporary affairs" and reaffirms "cultural and historical continuity" is also clearly at work in the establishing of the Doubleday legend; while Spalding's ostensible intention was to establish an "official" history of the popular game's origin, it is clear that he has a great deal more at stake in his insistence that baseball is indigenously American. Springwood suggests an "early predominance of a nostalgia for rural discourse," in which the game "has served as a terrain for the discursive struggle over the meanings of pastoral and urban metaphors."[434] By inventing tradition in this most medieval manner, both Spalding and the founders of the Hall itself "attempt to establish a continuity with a suitable historic past."[435] Springwood fittingly calls the development of the Hall "the story of a new, discursive spatial configuration that has been carved out of the 'history'—a utopian space of representation where imagery and real landscapes are conflated."[436] Thus Cooperstown as a place with a history reaffirms a cultural and historical continuity that links baseball with the pastoral landscape and America's agrarian traditional past. If this rural motif is not particularly medieval in a nostalgic sense, it still demonstrates the adaptability of the medieval narrative form to contemporary affairs, serving—if a different set of them—the same "multiple political purposes" along with the establishment of sacred places that Otter suggests. Creating both the Hall of Fame's "corporate identity and self-definition," this narrative provides the origin story for the community and establishes its importance over time.[437] Just as *inventios* function to create meaning attached to place, so, too, does this narrative provide an "indigenous origin" that provides the mythology of "a phenomenon that had become so quintessentially American" and locates that within the complex meanings of small-town, rural life, preserving a past within the present.[438] And if Graves's ball fails to speak as overtly as Saint Edmund's head, it still serves to identify the sacred location and demonstrate its continuing history, as its enshrinement in the Hall of Fame with many others of its kind projects both a past and a future; the trajectory from Graves' relic to Mark McGwire's sixty-second home run ball provides an uninterrupted connection from the sport's origins to the contemporary moment. This *inventio* may no longer purport to be a "factual historical account,"[439] yet it is clearly psychologically and metaphorically apt, as Thorn's earlier-quoted effusions reveal. Thus the Doubleday *inventio* is a kind of made-up history; as an etiological legend it creates a past from the vantage point of the present. Using certain verifiable truths, such as the location of baseball fields in Cooperstown and the Graves ball, carefully including real dates, places, and people (even if they weren't possibly in the same place at the point of the story's events), it blends its fiction with a kind of factually referential "reality" that reflects certain assumptions about its community's desires. With each further enshrinement, this linkage of the past and present, through a combination of real statistics, legends, emotions, and reliquary objects, continues. Tied to the objects and the building of the Hall of Fame, the Doubleday story then provides a double authentication, verifying the place just as the relics within it verify its sacred power. The Hall itself, then, becomes a giant reliquary; the origin story its hagiography.

The Hall of Fame's *inventio* allows it to claim pride of place in upstate New York and give meaning to an entire town whose only other industries are a museum of farm implements and the novelist James Fenimore Cooper. The Hall opened in 1939 with a dedication ceremony that included the "translation" of objects—signed balls, bats, jerseys, presentation silver, and the like—into the "Shrine of America's most beloved sport."[440] Ken Smith, former director of the museum, writes:

[A]s the Hall of Fame buries its roots deeper into the traditions of the United States and the game increases its scope of operation in the development of world brotherhood, pilgrims will beat a heavy path to its door. The pilgrims will not be let down,. . ., for the friendly red brick building emanates a peculiar kinship to all. There the irreplaceable relics of the diamond are stored. There priceless mementos. . .of all the mighty will eternally dwell in the hearts of all to whom the national game is a deep and sacred tradition.[441]

Smith's charged rhetoric (no page of his book is without the words "relic," "sacred," and "shrine") is still echoed in the experience of visiting the Hall of Fame. Springwood refers to the Hall of Fame as the "first-ever sports shrine of honor," noting that the gallery "contains the monumental plaques of the baseball players deemed immortal."[442] As well as the plaques, the Hall "displays memorabilia, ephemera, and artifacts of the game."[443] Smith's repeated referral to these objects as "relics" sets up his description of the Hall's pilgrims: "Hats come off instinctively as the travelers behold the simple grandeur of the Hall of Fame. Voices are muted. A low hum is heard as visitors make their way about the sunny room, reading inscriptions."[444] This response is, to an extent, overdetermined; a Hall of Fame pamphlet, which Springwood quotes, inscribes the visitors' experience: "Entering the majestic Hall of Fame Gallery you will find yourself in the very heart of the museum. Here over two-hundred greats are immortalized on bronze plaques. As you browse and read you will realize how these extraordinary individuals paved the way for all who follow them and you leave the gallery with a sense of awe and reverence."[445] That this response is religious, or quasi-religious, is evident in the language and tone that separate the Hall of Fame from more standard kinds of museums and attractions.

In an examination of medieval pilgrimage, Turner and Turner reveal a remarkably similarly constructed experience: "The pilgrim's new-found freedom from mundane or profane structures is increasingly circumscribed by symbolic structures: religious buildings, pictorial images, statuary, and sacralized features of topography, often described and designed in sacred tales and legend."[446] They further comment that "the pilgrim. . .is exposed to powerful religious sacra (shrines, images, liturgies, curative waters, ritual circumambulations of holy object, and so on), the beneficial effect of which depends upon the zeal and penitenacity of his quest."[447] That the two experiences are constructed the same way is evident; the visitor to the Hall of Fame, like his or her medieval counterpart, is invited on a journey through a site in which symbolic structures determine a response; the relationship of object, image, relic, and building creates a potential reverent reaction limited only by the visitor's eagerness for indoctrination. Earlier in this chapter, I have argued that baseball serves as a religion for its fans; Benjamin Rader's idea that the Cooperstown myth helps "establish baseball as a secular, peculiar American Religion"[448] is built on his sense that the Hall of Fame is a pilgrimage site akin to Mecca and Jerusalem.[449] Clifford Geertz's definition of religion as "a system of symbols which acts to establish powerful, pervasive, and long-lasting moods and motivations. . .by formulating conceptions of a general order of existence"[450] is Rader's overt basis for this claim; while offering "not a metaphysical scheme of the universe,"[451] baseball does offer all the trappings—origin myths, saints, relics, and sites of pilgrimage. Thus the Hall of Fame works much like Mecca or Jerusalem in the establishing of an authorized religious response; to return to the quotation that Gould calls to the reader's attention, the "cynic" who visits will fail to be awed, while the "true fan," whose "zeal and penitenacity" (or at least tenacity) are unrestrained by objective truth, will be. The Turners's sense that pilgrimages function "in order to intensify the pilgrim's attachment to his own religion"[452] is echoed here; the Hall of Fame authorizes the true fan, makes new ones, attempts to convert the cynic, and strengthens the fans' attachment to their beloved sport. If the source of that response is essentially inauthentic, a creation of myth rather than history, all the better; as a myth, it partakes in the creation of the sacred, forming a locus of consecration.

Just as a pilgrimage site cannot be separated from its story, it equally cannot be separated from the objects it displays. Indeed, the focus on objects led to early church-led protests against pilgrimage as a form of idolatry, for in the Middle Ages "there was voracious and uncritical consumption of relics and indulgences to be found at all levels of society."[453]

Because relics and the cult of the saints shifted the focus from Christ to his followers, from the spirit to the physical body, there was anxiety that this worship would lead to a return of paganism. It took time for these objects to be incorporated into medieval official religion; indeed in "the Tenth Century Bernard of Angers had had to work out in his own mind, after initial repugnance, that images of saints such as Gerald of Aurillac and Foy of Conques in fact performed a legitimate function."[454] The complex role of image and reliquary as intermediaries between the pilgrim and the saint, who then became an intermediary between the pilgrim and God, was what finally allowed the authorization of these popular modes. One primary way that these apparent idols were legitimated was in the understanding of the "superior efficacy of images in impressing holy truths upon men's minds";[455] because images were "seeable commemorative signs," they could "convey more information, more memorably, in a much shorter time. Books would never be able to achieve what one local pilgrimage might. Pilgrimage in this treatment becomes above all a mode of recourse and access to images and thereby a mode of instruction in religious truth, conveyed by the most effective means available."[456] As educative tools, images and relics work both to relate religious stories and truths; on pilgrimage their worth is doubled because "religious images strike him [the pilgrim], in these novel circumstances, as perhaps they have never done before, even though he may have seen very similar objects in his parish church almost every day of his life. The innocence of the eye is the whole point here, the 'cleansing of the doors of perception.'"[457] Thus, after an initial reluctance to endorse the cult of the saints and its concomitant religious travel, the medieval church found a useful tool in pilgrimage for relating and enhancing doctrine in the context of the goal of individual salvation or release from the sins and evils of the profane world.

Major League Baseball never put up any objections to relics and object worship, but it was slow to exploit their worth. Despite the early development of the Doubleday origin story, the full recognition of this material as valuable and efficacious develops slowly, essentially gaining ground after the 1922 Supreme Court decision that declared baseball, at least in the popular conception of the proceedings, something other than a business, the official "National Pastime" exempt from standard antitrust legislation.[458] Legal recognition made official the fan's sentiment that cast baseball as something more than a sport and a business, something akin to religion in the passionate feelings it evinced in its followers. This allowed baseball's legislating body to capitalize on these popular religious feelings for the game to sell their version of the game's true meaning and spirit. The Hall's powers of enshrinement created an official sense of what was valuable and important rather than merely locally popular; in its own self-authorization, it took over the creation of saints and regulated fame through the election rules that set specific criteria for induction. Just as in the Middle Ages, the production of the relic goes along with the saint and its pilgrimage site, Cooperstown assumes all three powers for itself: it determines the saints and transforms objects into relics, as it simultaneously becomes the pilgrimage site. The movement to build Doubleday Field and the Hall of Fame authorized itself in 1936 with its first induction, and the Hall itself opened shortly thereafter in 1939. This process became a model for a kind of co-option of popular sentiments of other sorts; for instance, the Hall of Fame produces the history of the Negro Leagues as another kind of sentimental nostalgia rather than confronting it as a simulacrum of racial discrimination in America. In its establishment of itself as an authorizing and governing body, in fact, Cooperstown became the model for all other Halls of Fame—the National Football Hall of Fame, the Rock and Roll Hall of Fame, even Graceland—that follow its lead.

Thus the Hall of Fame's establishment echoes the medieval development of pilgrimage in the tension between what is official and what is popular. If the fan's individual relationship to the game is often created by affection—thinking, for instance, that Chet Laabs (a "chunky, unremarkable outfielder, played for the [Detroit] Tigers from 1937 to 1939"[459]) was the greatest player ever—The Hall of Fame, along with the statistics industry, substitutes official greatness for personal attachment. As such, it uses its site of popular pilgrimage to create doctrine, subverting minor gods to the Great God of Baseball Success. For all its recognition of separate achievements, the Hall of Fame serves to define a singular test of what identifies that greatness; it attempts to claim an official value recognized by the official body that defines a set of values itself, placing certain talents and statistics over others, valorizing one set of "objective" criteria over other, more subjectively determined ones. And if, as Kenneth Woodward notes of the medieval period, "it was the cult of the saints that transformed cemeteries into shrines, shrines into cities, and prompted that robust form of social adventure and cohesion, the pilgrimage,"[460] so too does this official saint-making create and recreate Cooperstown's essential value: the removal of the game from the official economics of business into a more mystical realm in which the person who buys the $15 bleacher seat can go home with a $1 million baseball and then give it back to the (very rich) man who hit it. People's desire to "own a piece of history" or at least have visual access to it (which the Hall of Fame attempts to serve) creates a set of needs that are not the same impulses that make baseball commercially successful, just as popular manifestations in medieval religion did not always suit what the church regarded as theologically sound. But just as medieval official religion saw the value of incorporating popular sentiment and ritual into its purview, so too does official baseball seek to address both sides of fan desire. Not in conflict, but in collusion, the "business" of baseball and its identity as the "National Pastime" work together to authorize both sides of fan practice. All of the aspects of modern capitalism, such as advertising revenues and cable television contracts, matched with the attempt to create team identification in the fans, which draws people in specific locations to the ballpark (the ideal fan is the one willing to go see every single Milwaukee Brewers game regardless of who the players are; essentially, the man who roots for the uniform rather than whomever's wearing it), are clearly not the Hall of Fame's focus, as it pays homage to individual achievement over team success, and allies baseball with a rural, nostalgic, noncommercial mythos.

It is the function, thus, of the objects displayed within it that separates the Hall of Fame from a modern museum. Familiar as the "things in glass cases" method of display may be, the economic value of what we see in museums is an essential part of their worth. To return to the start of this chapter, the reliquary objects at the Cloisters are valuable because they are medieval, not because they produce transcendent religious experience. Their location in the museum's "Treasury" rather than in one of the reconstructed chapels enforces that separation of spheres of value. Benjamin delineates the difference between the cult and ritual value of art and its exhibition value, which are received on different planes, one economic and one ceremonial. For the latter, "what mattered with their existence, not their being on view," a valuation that included their magical and cultic properties far beyond any economic value they might have.[461] In Cooperstown, there are two essential modes of seeing, the images and the relics. The first are the oft-mentioned bronze plaques commemorating the Hall of Fame's annual inductees. These representations function much like sacred images or icons; speaking of the latter, Geary comments:

> these pictures were far more than simple artistic representations painted by human artists and intended to inspire the faithful or to educate the illiterate. Like the holy men, they enjoyed a special relationship with divine power. They participated directly in the existence and the being of the person they represented, so that the image brought the pilgrim into direct visual (that is to say in the traditional understanding of optics, tactical) contact with the person represented. To be in their presence was to look through a window into the other world and, correspondingly, to be seen by the person in the other world.[462]

If the images in the Hall of Fame do not exactly cause the visitor to feel that he or she is in the presence of Babe Ruth and Lou Gehrig, it is they that cause the hushed voices and awestruck response that Smith and

Springwood both describe. Educative and inspiring, these plaques do provide a tactile, iconic representation, as each one is both individualized (usually through some representation of physical features or at least a cap logo) but also essentially the same—from a fairly short distance, they are indistinguishable from each other, and thus provide the feeling of an over-whelming, unifying sanctity. In his description of the Hall of Fame, John Thorn rhetorically asks visitors, "Do you like to save the best for last?" then suggests "you go around the bases, then return here to baseball's real-life home plate."[463] Thorn tells visitors to "Step inside the Museum, your heart racing,"[464] again anticipating this passionate response; with his arrival at the plaque room, he declares, "The Hall of Fame Gallery is a shrine. Walk inside; people speak in hushed tones. The cool marble gives the feeling of an ancient temple, and it is indeed a holy place for those of us whose reli-gion is baseball. . . .to the fans, these bronze tablets are magical, like frag-ments from Mount Sinai."[465] He declares, "the dignity and solemnity of the tablets is in keeping with the celebration of a life now over" (even though many Hall of Famers are still alive and even active in the sport as coaches, managers, broadcasters, and scouts) and, calling the plaques of the first five inductees "The immortals" (Babe Ruth, Ty Cobb, Walter Johnson, Honus Wagner, and Christy Mathewson), continues, "we look on these five with awe and reverence, baseball's equivalent of Mount Rushmore."[466] In his more general introduction to this section, Thorn describes seeing an exhibit and "for a delicious moment, I was a part of that extended history. . .and I realized that the enormous pleasure of that moment—the reliving of history in a highly personal way—is what defines the Baseball Hall of Fame experience."[467] Thorn's rhetoric, for all its somewhat inflated style, identifies his experience entirely in keeping with what Geary describes; moved by the sanctity of the images before him, he experiences a shift in time that allows him the "I was there" experience, causing him to say "time stops in the Museum the same way it does at a baseball game. At the Museum it attaches itself to those things that make us halt in our tracks and reflect upon their essence and ours."[468] Once again, the experi-ence of shifting time sacralizes experience; the historical relics "connect us not only to our own childhood and to our parents but also to a national, collective past, one whose presence we sense but whose details have been lost."[469] The pleasure of play and remembrance, for Thorn, "bend time and elude it," while the "artifact recovers for us a lost bit of time."[470] If the plaques, then, do not strictly provide contact with the "saint" being repre-sented, they do let the viewer look through the window into the other world of the past in its most mystically constructed sense, a past that "halts us in our tracks" and causes us to reflect upon its essence. The early shrines "were not sanctified by the footsteps of Christ or the events of his passion.

Their sanctity did not come from where or what they were. It came from what was to be found there—what physical link with the divine sphere remained incarnate in the material world,"[471] so too does the Hall of Fame find its meaning not specifically in its location (for all its origin stories) or what may have taken place there, but in what it displays and the interaction of those displays with those who visit them.

While the plaques to inductees certainly get their due, the more pilgrim-crowded rooms are those filled with more efficacious objects—balls, bats, caps, and jerseys whose significance is conveyed by the moments they represent: Kenny Rogers's perfect game, Nolan Ryan's fifth no-hitter, Roger Clemens's first and second twenty-strike-out games, the 1998 home run chase. It is hardly necessary to point out that the caps look like what anyone can buy at the ballpark concession stands, only sweatier; the balls and bats much like what's available at a sporting goods store. They are not the same, or no one would come to look at them. Just as Mark McGwire's act of hitting the famed $9 baseball turns it into a $2.7 million dollar prize, so too are these essentially valueless objects transformed through the identity given to them by the authorized moments the Hall of Fame chooses to represent. Their treatment reveals their difference; if paintings in museums are merely hung, objects at the Hall of Fame are "enshrined." In *Road Swing*, Steve Rushin describes the Hall as "unbelievably captivating," "humanizing and awesome at the same time," and filled with "knee-buckling items."[472] Ken Smith echoes the ways that value is determined by that linkage of the present and the past, history and memory by saying of the Hall of Fame, "an unforgettable memory had been stored away" there.[473] In his chapter titled "The Shrine" he repeats that "the irreplaceable relics of the diamond are stored there" and adds, "there relics in the glass cases keep the interest hopping from era to era, from significance to nostalgia."[474] While the literature is "stored upstairs in the museum library" (because books are less efficacious than images, as Webb has noted), the "striking specimens are under glass with the relics."[475] Indeed, the whole movement to establish the Hall of Fame was driven by this impulse, calling its purpose the "collecting and preserving of pictures and relics reflecting the development of the National Game from the time of its inception, through the ingenuity of Major General Abner Doubleday, in 1939 to the present."[476]

While the testimony of pilgrims to the Hall of Fame doesn't usually contain the same tales of travel and hardship as medieval pilgrimage narratives, none (except the perpetually dissenting Bill James[477]) find fault with what they find. For many, Springwood notes, "The Hall of Fame is. . .a way to publicly consecrate their nostalgic, biographical experiences with baseball"; he adds that "many of the tourists with whom I spoke used words such as 'pilgrimage,' 'mecca,' 'sacred place,' 'shrine,' and 'journey' in describing their trip."[478] Thus, their understanding of their voyage as essentially sacred is in line with Cooperstown's official sense of itself as a pilgrimage site, an image repeatedly invoked by visitors who enact its ideas.[479] As such, they continually valorize its objects, which, as Brooke Hindle comments in her article "How Much is a Piece of the True Cross Worth?" suggest that "Man's need to touch the past has increased rather than decreased."[480] The objects turn the theoretical actual, while at the same time reinforcing myths.[481] If "like all sustained mass movements, pilgrimages tend to accrue rich superstructures of legend, myth, folklore, and literature,"[482] Cooperstown does the same; in its own advertising material, the National Baseball Hall of Fame claims to "Preserve history, honor excellence, and inspire generations,"[483] asking potential donors to "Join the Greatest Team Ever."[484] Creating historiography rather than history, the Hall of Fame produces an "authentic inauthenticity" to quote one of Springwood's interview subjects;[485] based on an *inventio* that emphasizes the word's root in invention, and engaging a discourse of a real "rural" America that has a great deal less to do with baseball than they imply, the Hall of Fame emphasizes an ideology over reality, but that ideology is fundamentally the source of the strong reactions the Hall invokes, far greater indeed than any real picture could induce.[486] And if strong reaction is essentially the stuff of pilgrimage, the Hall of Fame leads the way for other sites that elicit similarly strong reactions; Bob Costas, NBC's leading sports commentator, noted that the first time he visited the Monuments at Yankee Stadium, he burst into tears, thinking he was standing on the graves of Babe Ruth, Lou Gehrig, and Miller Huggins. When Springwood suggests that "nearly all the objects in the museum were, in a sense, living and breathing,"[487] he acknowledges their efficacious and reliquary power.

Even if this more personal, ritualized aspect of baseball seems separate from its corporate identity—as, in fact, the direction of the Hall is entirely separate from the ownership of Major League Baseball—it is by no means free from economics. As in Compostela and Canterbury before it, a whole industry has grown around the Cooperstown site itself to accommodate the contemporary pilgrims who come to worship there. Describing medieval pilgrimage sites, Turner and Turner note:

> A pilgrimage's foundation is typically marked by visions, miracles, or martyrdoms. The first pilgrims tend to arrive haphazardly, individually, and intermittently, though in great numbers, "voting with their feet"; their devotion is fresh and spontaneous. Later, there is progressive routinization and institutionalization of the sacred journey. Pilgrims now tend to come in organized groups, in sodalities, confraternities, and parish associations, on

specified feast days, or in accordance with a carefully planned calendar. Marketing facilities spring up close to the shrine and along the way. Secularized fiestas and fairs thrive near these. A whole system of licenses, permits, and ordinances, governing mercantile transactions, pilgrims' lodgings, and the conduct of fairs, develops as the number of pilgrims grows and their needs and wants proliferate. . . . To cater to the fired-up pilgrims' spiritual needs, the merchants of holy wares set up booths in the market, where they sell devotional statuettes and pictures, rosaries, missals, sacred tracts, and a variety of other sacramental objects and edifying literature.[488]

This is an almost uncanny description of Cooperstown, and it could be applied equally well to other modern pilgrimage sites, such as Graceland, or even those more obviously in the religious tradition, such as Sainte Anne de Beaupré in Québec. While Turner and Turner's description of the arrival of pilgrims does not exactly match the progress of travelers to Cooperstown, certainly travelers come today in organized groups (such as school classes, church groups, little-league teams, the Osaka [Japan] Old Kids Baseball Club) sharing a great deal in common with the confraternities of the past, at least in their unifying devotion to the site and its meaning. The Cooperstown calendar revolves around its own fair, Induction Weekend (at which new members of the Hall's roster of Saints are enshrined with great ceremony) in early August, which draws an enormous number of visitors for a single weekend of ritualized events—the autograph signing party for children, the induction itself, and the Hall of Fame Game. Other events, such as an annual conference on baseball and American culture, draw a somewhat different, if equally enthusiastic crowd. However, it is in the marketing facilities that the Turners's description is most apt; Cooperstown, a village of 2,300 inhabitants, boasts eighty-two Bed and Breakfasts, forty-six Hotels and Inns, fifty-six rentable cottages, and nine campgrounds. The Chamber of Commerce's official website lists thirty different places to eat, and eight museums and attractions to interest pilgrims (or perhaps the pilgrims' spouses) when they're not visiting the Hall of Fame itself. The village also offers services to visitors including financial, legal, medical, dental, and "writers, artists, and consultants." Under the section entitled "Way of Life," the website notes, "shopping in Cooperstown is a natural extension for the thousands of visitors who come to the Hall of Fame as they stroll down Main Street to Doubleday Field. Attractive shops line the streets of the shopping district offering a cornucopia of goods and services. It is estimated that every visitor spends an average of $50 during his or her stay in Otsego County."[489]

Cooperstown merchants follow their medieval counterparts, offering a huge variety of baseball objects for sale, quite apart from those available at the Hall of Fame's well-stocked gift shop. Springwood calls the village "a baseball carnival," counting "eighteen shops whose merchandise was either exclusively or primarily baseball-related. . .a brief sampling of these items [for sale in the eighteen stores] includes baseball cards, apparel, books, posters, miniature baseball figures, and souvenir bats."[490] The closeness of cards, books, posters and figurines to the "devotional statuettes and pictures, rosaries, missals, sacred tracts" that the Turners describe is evident, and the function of these as devotional objects can be observed in both the avid collection of memorabilia and the treatment of it. An examination of the objects shown in both the "Gumby's Collection" and "Randall's Collection" sections of Gumby's Mark McGwire Online shows them displayed and enshrined much as one would find them in the Hall of Fame itself. And while equating a bobblehead doll with a religious statue may seem debased, the current popularity of Jesus Sports Statuettes suggests that this conflation is once again being co-opted by the church for its own purposes.[491] Not that Cooperstown needs any help. A shop fittingly titled Baseball Nostalgia sells "museum-quality" items, primarily old-fashioned baseball equipment, at high prices, while other shops concern themselves more with an "overwhelming replication of signs and images."[492] The Cooperstown Ballcap Company and the Cooperstown Collection sell caps and other apparel, both of teams that did or do exist and of teams that exist only in the imagination—such as the New York Knights, featured in the Robert Redford film *The Natural*.[493] The Cooperstown Bat Company sells replica bats in various sizes, both for use and display. The focus of all this material for purchase is drawn from the Hall of Fame; Cooperstown would not sell these items, at least not to anything like this degree, without the presence of the Baseball Shrine to draw baseball pilgrims and their money thither.[494] Thus, this souvenir economy centers around the Hall of Fame and is produced by it. Geary observes that to "the community fortunate enough to have a saint's remains in its church, the benefits in revenue and status were enormous";[495] these benefits are also diffused to Cooperstown and its cousins.

Souvenirs are uniquely connected to pilgrimage, working in two directions—giving economic profit to the pilgrimage site and its environs, and providing "mementos of the out of ordinary experience."[496] In fulfilling both roles, they create tension between "material culture as either a commodity or sacred artifact."[497] This tension, however, is not unique to contemporary culture, but a product of a much older economy in which the sacred was both a source of material wealth and the transcendent. In the medieval period, the road to Compostela, for instance, grew into "a complex support system of refuges, hostels, hospitals and churches to provide both physical and spiritual sustenance for pilgrims traveling to

Santiago."[498] The medieval pilgrim had a great deal in common with the modern tourist: "Clearly, the medieval pilgrim had a passion for relics and special places. Equally, there is no doubt that today's tourist can achieve some level of intellectual self-improvement by visiting the relics of an historical past, be they temples, castles, stately homes or objects laid out in museums and art galleries."[499] Michael Houlihan distinguishes modern tourism from medieval pilgrimage, as he believes that "for the pilgrim, it was about the next life" and for the tourist "it is probably going to be more about this life, a rounded cultural experience";[500] he suggests that the ruins of churches, chapels, and the roads themselves have become a kind of vast, immobile souvenir that represents the historical past and in so doing "enjoy[s] the same or even greater cultural status as the shrine of St. James himself."[501] This separation, which makes the past something to be conserved rather than experienced, however, does not really apply to visitors at contemporary shrines like the Hall of Fame, who do not maintain the contemporary sense of distance from the objects on display that Houlihan suggests. The souvenirs of baseball, then, work more like the pilgrims' scallop shells, metal badges, and jet jewelry that provided them with a corporate identity and defined them as participants in an aspect of their own religion, just as the fans' collections mark them as a particular kind of baseball enthusiast. Thus, the shopping district of Cooperstown is a kind of "extension of the Hall of Fame and Museum gift shop, in which artifacts are transformed into commodities"[502] that, like the Compostela scallop shell, take on an authenticating function. They define pilgrims by proving that they have visited the shrine; they demonstrate their commitment to the shrine through their financial support, which allows the shrine's work to continue, and they become a devotional objects for the pilgrims who desire either to recall the events of the voyage or the religious feeling it created. If the objects in the Hall itself cause the sacral reactions that Thorn, Springwood, and Smith describe, then the souvenir can at least cause the pilgrim to recall that experience, if not reenact it completely. For most pilgrims, medieval and modern, "pilgrimage was a temporary hiatus in their normal lives. They abandoned their traditional milieus for a time in order to travel to a place where the power of God broke into mundane existence, and then they returned to their former lives,"[503] the souvenir stands for that moment "out of time" both as a marker of the trip and an articulation of their love—be it for the church or for baseball.

If the Hall of Fame provides a transcendent experience, it doesn't seem, at least, to perform overt miracles. In a sense this echoes the function of the larger medieval sites, for as Benedicta Ward notes, "the miracles do not seem to be the primary motive for pilgrimage to St. James' shrine at Compostela; the same may be said with even more assurance of the shrine of St. Peter in Rome."[504] The Turners echo Ward, noting that "even where the time of miraculous healings is reluctantly conceded to be past, believers firmly hold that faith is strengthened and salvation better secured by personal exposure to the beneficent unseen presence of the Blessed Virgin or the local saint, mediated through a cherished image or painting."[505] Thus, the Hall of Fame may well provide that strengthening of the faith and security of salvation through exposure to the beloved images therein without providing the actual miracles. Thus, if miracles were primarily the product of smaller, more local shrines, then that aspect of medieval pilgrimage experience is replicated by the Hall of Fame's counterpart in Dyersville, IA. While Cooperstown is far enough past its origin to be completely authorized, administered by an official body and thus putting forward its agenda, the Field of Dreams is still in the earlier stages of development as a sacred site, although plenty of pilgrims have "voted with their feet" and are even arriving in organized groups, including church groups. While the wholesale marketing of Dyersville has not yet begun, the Field per se has certainly turned itself into a successful shrine with its own economic rewards for Don Lansing, who owns most of it, and Al and Rita Ameskamp, who own part of left field. If the first pilgrims arrived "haphazardly, individually, though in great numbers. . .their devotion fresh and spontaneous,"[506] they have continued to seek out this remote location, looking for a kind of redemption or revivification less specifically tied to baseball than that which is sought at the Hall of Fame.

The Field of Dreams postdates the movie of the same name but has come to represent its essential *inventio*, a mystical apparition of old-time ballplayers appearing out of a cornfield and miraculously saving the farm-family from repossession and destitution. The movie, a version of W. P. Kinsella's novel *Shoeless Joe*, follows the story of an Iowa farmer, Ray Kinsella, who one summer evening hears a voice crying "If you build it, he will come" from the depths of his cornfield. Ray finally realizes that "it" is a baseball field (the voice provides no context for its message), which he proceeds to carve out of the same field; "he" turns out to be Shoeless Joe Jackson, of the 1919 Black Sox Scandal fame whom Kinsella's father had worshipped, always proclaiming Jackson's innocence in the bribery scandal despite Major League Baseball's official ban (Jackson, despite his prowess, is not enshrined in the Hall of Fame). One night, Shoeless Joe— later followed by several other dead baseball stars of the dim past—emerges out of the corn to play baseball. The "divine" voice also calls Ray to go search out Terrance Mann (in the novel, it is J. D. Salinger), a former political activist turned disillusioned writer, who will have his spirit renewed by viewing the field and its players. Because Ray's decision to build the field has required plowing under a significant portion of his crop, making him unable to keep up his mortgage payments, he is faced with foreclosure; however, Mann and Kinsella's daughter insist that if he maintains the field, "People will come!" Terrence Mann then delivers this monologue:

> Ray—people will come, Ray. They'll come to Iowa for reasons they can't even fathom. They will turn into your driveway, not knowing for sure why they're doing it. They'll arrive at your door as innocent children, longing for the past. Of course, "We won't mind if you look around," you'll say. "It's only twenty dollars per person." Any they'll pass over the money without even thinking about it, for it is money they have, and peace they like. And they'll walk out to the bleachers, sit in their shirtsleeves, on a perfect after-noon. And they'll find they have reserved seats somewhere along one of the baselines—where they sat when they were children, and cheered their heroes. And they'll watch the game, and it will be as if they dipped them-selves in magic waters. The memories will be so thick they'll have to brush them away from their faces.[507]

That for Mann, the field functions as a pilgrimage site is abundantly appar-ent. Rather than just a pleasant locus for baseball tourism (like Wrigley Field in Chicago or Fenway Park in Boston), the Field of Dreams provides a transcendent, mystical experience, bordering on the utopic, uniting the past and present in yet another echo of the medieval religious concept of time, while at the same time offering the metaphoric "mystical waters" that affect this transformative experience. Visitors are drawn for "reasons they can't even fathom," reasons far greater than the desire to see the ghosts of the Black Sox take a few pitches. Since this whole experience also serves an economic function, the admission price allowing Ray to pay off his debts, it becomes much like the pilgrimage sites of medieval Europe that became great centers of economic security. Mixing the sacred with the practical, Ray Kinsella's field in central Iowa takes on the double meaning of a Conques or a Compostela, and as the film closes with the road jammed with carloads of visitors, the crowds traversing the Way of St. James must spring to mind. The film also ends with a kind of personal redemption for Ray. Heeding the voice of the baseball gods and building the field also allows his reconciliation with his estranged, dead father, who appears out of the corn at night to play a game of catch with his son. The "he" who will ultimately come to the pilgrimage site is the father who is in heaven. Thus the site determines the kind of miracle it produces—a healing mira-cle for the modern age, salving the emotional pain of strained relationships, rather than giving sight to the blind or curing scrofula.

A film using baseball as a metaphor for something larger is nothing new. What is striking about this movie is not that it tells this somewhat sappy story, but that it becomes the *inventio* for a real pilgrimage site, a self-fulfilling prophecy for the Field of Dreams. Don Lansing, who provided most of the farmland and house for the film, and whose crop was plowed under to make the field, decided to maintain the field—although he made no claims to hear mystical voices, he "enjoyed having it. It was for him, in a sense, a large spatial souvenir."[508] However, fulfilling the prophecy of the film, people have come; as Stephen Mosher notes, "strangers from all corners of the country were arriving at his front door asking if they could play on his baseball field, rest on his bleachers, swing on his [Lansing's] porch, or even walk in his cornfield."[509] Al and Rita Ameskamp, who had provided a portion of left field, had replanted their field with corn after the filming in 1989, but "when they saw that people were coming to the ballfield, they decided to restore their portion to its original, complete dimensions by the following summer."[510] While the Field of Dreams has no identifying relic except the film itself (Shoeless Joe Jackson's bat has not been discovered in Don Lansing's basement, nor has an excavation under third base revealed Babe Ruth's head), yet the miracle story that creates it unites real places—Dyersville, IA; Don Lansing's Field—with the eternal and transcendent, giving them a meaning beyond their obvious significa- tion as exempla of small-town, corn-belt America. That these places repli- cate certain aspects of the Hall of Fame's rural nostalgia serves to show the pervasive, almost doctrinal function of baseball's mythology, which relocates to a pastoral world the "meaning" of a game played at its highest level (which both the Hall and the Field commemorate, as it's Major Leaguers, for the most part, who are remembered there) in urban, and occasionally suburban locales.

That the Field has become a pilgrimage site is clear by its popularity; there's no other reason to visit central Iowa, but during the summer it draws about 500 visitors every day, approximately 20,000 visitors annually from all over the world, the field having become a "pastoral vision of yearn- ing and faith."[511] And while the Field itself has no admission charge, both Don Lansing and the Ameskamps maintain souvenir trailers selling t-shirts, postcards, caps, posters, books, refreshments, and other items "so inexpress- ibly useless—decorative spoons, pewter corncobs—that one could only be listed as ORNAMENT: $2.50."[512] Just as medieval reliquary churches accepted alms from their visitors, both families keep lockboxes and solicit contributions to help maintain the site; "painted on the boxes is 'Help keep the dream alive.'"[513] Thus, like Cooperstown and medieval pilgrimage sites, the Field of Dreams conflates emotion and economy, drawing on abstract desires to produce concrete, monetary results. The amorphous quality of "the dream" (or of religious experience) is made physical through these sites, which then become the vehicle in the metaphor for which the dream is the tenor. What is intangible becomes tangible and commodified. The Field of Dreams offers "promises of nostalgic rejuvenation,"[514] although here "rejuvenation" is tied less explicitly to a historical past than it is to the messages of the film itself, producing a reflexive signification and reenactment; at the Field, baseball is less about baseball than it is a metaphor for other kinds of potential redemption. Both the film and the field represent "baseball as metaphor. The pilgrims to Dyersville seek the field because it has come to represent a magical passage to the realms of memory, imagination, and love."[515] For instance, Springwood was told by Ron Eberhard, a visitor to the Field of Dreams, that "People do not come to Dyersville and the 'Field of Dreams' for even close to similar reasons as the 'Baseball Hall of Fame.' The 'Field is for dreamers and visionaries. Cooperstown is for hero worshippers and those who want to live in the past."[516]

Springwood sees this distinction as "unconstrained, creative, and ludic" because "the signifier seems to have left behind the signified, as free-floating signs and images dominate to produce a cinematic utopia" at which "voices of resistance are practically nowhere to be heard."[517] His collected descriptions from visitors call the field "variously a site of myth, fantasy, religion, enchantment, magic, redemption, and dream-seeking,"[518] finding that "people's involvement with these sites is exceedingly meaningful, often ineffable, and nearly always *emotional*."[519] This variety of pilgrim desires comes together to produce a rhetoric of healing and redemption that counterbalances the reverentially sacred response to the Hall of Fame. Just as the film ultimately posits a reunification of Ray Kinsella and his father through Ray's building of the field, many of the experiential discourses that Springwood reveals through his anthropological study engage a narrative of miraculous filial redemption brought on by a visit to the field. For instance, Springwood tells the story of Jim Bohn whose twelve-year-old son Matt was killed in a plane crash outside Sioux City in 1989; Bohn and his son both loved *Field of Dreams* and baseball provided a link between them and Jim's father, another fan. The family visited the Field on the anniversary of the crash in order to, as Jim Bohn wrote in a letter to Don Lansing, "have the chance to talk with my son one more time."[520] The visit allowed the family to forge a "sort of poetic closure in understanding Matt's death," seeing him "through the heart" because of their profound belief (Springwood 114). Springwood's interviews revealed to him that "a common reason people cite for coming to the field concerns how the film's narrative, which deals with generation gaps, personal redemption and making peace with one's parents, speaks to their own life situations";[521] viewed by many as "a healthy, morally and physically purifying experience,"[522] it is also a place where, for example, men are suddenly able to express their love for their fathers and deal with the grief of their deaths through some kind of mystical intervention.[523] Medieval sites such as the Shrine of Saint James provided a more overt kind of healing, as the sermon attributed to Calixtus II attests: "From the time it was begun until today that church displays the glory of the miracles of St. James, for the sick are restored to health, the blind receive their sight, many tongues that were dumb are loosed, the deaf hear again, the lame are given the strength to walk, demoniacs are set free";[524] however, the miracle cures of the Field of Dreams are simply those of a modern kind, an emotional healing rather than a physical one, essentially steeped in the same discourse of redemption. If one set of miracles is cognitive, the other is affective, enacted on the mind instead of the body, a soothing of the modern plague of cross-generational tensions.

It is the desire to preserve this fleeting experience that once again creates the desire for souvenirs; the physical remains instrumental in this discourse of emotional redemption. Replicas are desirable, but a piece of the thing itself is even more so, just as vials of holy water and actual relics competed for pilgrims' attention with the scallop shells and statuettes available at medieval sites. Along with the souvenirs the Ameskamps provide, they make available a box of clear plastic vials filled with dirt from the field, each bearing the inscription "Dirt from LEFT 'FIELD of DREAMS' the Ameskamps" and during the appropriate season, offer ears of corn from the field itself for visitors to take as a souvenir. Just as "dust from tombs, particularly the Holy Sepulchre, was venerated from earliest times,"[525] so too is this dirt valuable as a relic of the place it represents. Because a piece of the thing itself might just contain some of the site's miraculous power, it becomes another desirable commodity in its potentiality. Unlike a souvenir, it might reenact certain aspects of the pilgrimage within the context of the traveler's real life, linking transcendent and real time. In order to authenticate the experience, "the search for the authentic object become[s] critical."[526] If, as Springwood suggests, "emotions have become commodities in the form of spectacles, or signifiers of experience,"[527] souvenirs become concrete authenticators of that experience, again making a literal commodity from one that is transcendent, abstract. And while he attributes this phenomenon to the modern age, a look at medieval popular religion shows this to be a much older relationship. Even if modern pilgrimage is enhanced by contemporary transportation and technology, it retains its "highly devotional tone" and "fervent personal piety," forming an "important part of the system of apologetic deployed against the secularization of the post-Darwinian world."[528] The Turners's choice of "post-Darwinian" brings into sharp relief the antievolutionary sense of the foundation narratives that characterize the Hall of Fame and, to some extent, the Field of Dreams, as both play against the evolutionary model inherent in contemporary scientific paradigms for history. Postmedieval in their time frame, contemporary pilgrimages remain "antimodern" in their redemptive, transcendent nature. After all, a definite point of origin provides transcendent meanings, the idea that things are as they were meant to be, in themselves, not contingent on outside circumstances so that there is no "real true game of baseball," only a series of evolutionary stages proceeding from some mysterious, swampy past. In a pragmatic sense, these kinds of meanings draw pilgrims, while evolutionary developments, because they provide no fixed locations, do not.

Religious tourism can take the form of sites like Sainte Anne de Beaupré, in Québec, which offers both the Church of Sainte Anne and Christorama, a religious theme park, or Graceland, where Elvists—true believers in "E"—have developed a ritual practice that strongly resembles an organized religion, with doctrine, priests, heretics, and relics.[529] Pilgrimage, in an official, church-sanctioned sense may have ended in the Reformation, but "old ideas have a habit of persisting," and a "major intellectual transformation may alter the climate of opinion,"[530] making this less an official or doctrinal act than a personal, popular quest, with all its assumptions essentially intact. Jonathan Sumption's sense that "if Christians have at times traveled long distances to venerate the remains of spiritual heroes, then it was because in doing so they satisfied an emotional need" applies equally well to modern visitors to the Field of Dreams and Hall of Fame. Whatever physical healings or literal miracles may have taken place, emotion is—and was—the essential focus of this kind of journey and is the locus for its fulfillment.[531] Nicholas Shrady echoes this suggestion, saying that "pilgrimage. . .seems to appeal to an instinctive movement of the human heart,"[532] and indeed, the desire for pilgrimage may well be at its core a desire for emotion itself, a kind of self-fulfilling need. Chaucer, as a poet of pilgrimage, clearly understands the "human frailties, the failures of vision, that affect every stage of the pilgrimage of man and render it at once ludicrous, touching, and sublime";[533] as a vision of pilgrimage, The Canterbury Tales shows that even within its fixed context, sacred travel means "diverse" things to "diverse folk." Using time rather than estates to separate individuals, pilgrimage emerges as a phenomenon at once personal and communal, giving the individual a place in a larger scheme. Uniting people across classes and countries, bringing together past and present, the real and the liminal, the mundane with the miraculous, created by participating in an overrarching shared discourse, pilgrimage at once unifies and allows for individual experiences and meanings.

The persistence of medieval popular religion in the contemporary world embodies a connection between monetary value and transcendent meaning that is found in interpretability—and is no different from the value of relics in the medieval world. Because "the boundaries between subject and object are culturally induced and semipermeable,"[534] relics can embody both an objective value and a subjective ability to touch people; all that has changed due to the cultural induction, which Geary indicates, by the actual objects themselves. While the images in both Cooperstown and Dyersville are at least in part manufactured, ready-made versions of a particular set of ideologies, they remain flexible in their ability to absorb multiple meanings from their visitors. By their difference from "real life," and by providing a hiatus from it, they offer something profoundly separate from the time frame and object relations of the quotidian. An object is sacred if it is somehow separate from the profane. The salutary aspects of the home run race separated it from the profane nature of the every day, making its physical products—the home run balls—perpetual preservers of that sacred moment in time. Yet that symbolic and miraculous possibility is not entirely distanced from the world, just as in the Middle Ages the relic functions both in the world of the transcendent and the world of the quotidian, both of which are expressed profoundly in its value. As a semiotic, interpretable object, the relic—bone or ball—is priceless; as a tradable commodity in the economy of exchange, its price may fluctuate, but it remains translatable into money. While it is hard to doubt the sincerity of their devotion to and belief in the power of the saint, the monks of the Monastery of Conques who sent an emissary to Agen to join the monastery there, break into the tomb, and make off with the saint's body[535] gained enormous economic advantage through their theft; their monastery became an important pilgrimage site despite the treacherous ascent required of its pilgrims, thus providing the monastery with political power as well as visitors' fees, gifts, and consumers for its products. The narratives of *inventio* and *translatio* followed the relics themselves; their stories were produced as adjuncts to their possession and served to build the sites of their worship. For all their sanctity, medieval pilgrimage sites were great loci of economic power; favorite concessions and memorabilia were sold at these sites, ranging from pilgrimage badges, like the scallop shell at Santiago de Compostela to powerful cakes and mystical waters, the medieval equivalent of Dodger Dogs.

The rhetorical and structural similarity of these baseball tales to medieval saints' lives, relic stories, and pilgrimage narratives shows the persistence of medieval popular religion in the contemporary world. The impulses that created these sacred aspects of the medieval world thus persist, in altered form, in the modern world; these examples—mere type texts of their own genres—reveal the essentially medieval underpinnings of the public discourse of sports. Saint Mark McGwire is assured of canonization in the Hall of Fame in 2006, five years after his 2001 retirement, likely by an overwhelming vote on his first ballot; once enshrined, his plaque and relics (some of which are already there) will be visited by postulants from across the United States. The question of what they hope to receive from this contemporary pilgrimage is hard to answer, yet the impetus for its undertaking seems profoundly tied to those impulses that led medieval pilgrims to their own sacred sites. Because contemporary religion no longer fulfills these desires, public culture provides a locus for them. In considering pilgrimage and drama in the York Cycle of mystery plays, Andrea R. Harbin discusses the ways that these plays draw the audience into liminal space, making York and Jerusalem one. This commingling establishes "the sort of *communitas* found in pilgrimage—the idea that souls are equal with regard to salvation. As in pilgrimage, this *communitas* is achieved through the display of the icons of the faith—not simply through holy relics, but through dramatic reenactment," which ultimately shows the citizens their place in the redemptive scheme.[536] In this same sense, the desires that produce these modern saints, relics, and pilgrimages also draw the audience into liminal space, uniting past, present, and future while establishing a community that, like pilgrimage, cuts across economic sectors, a community that offers, in Giamatti's terms, a fleeting glimpse of paradise. As a force both equalizing and hierarchical, this scheme gives its audience a place while maintaining both authoritative and popular impulses, using the former to justify the latter and vice versa. Sports is merely one locus for this preservation; as a particularly heroic world in which the popular audience plays a profound role, it maintains several key aspects of medieval ritual and storytelling, and as a place of complex yearning and hope, it receives a religious attention that many other aspects of culture do not. Yet it is not unique. Combined with other aspects of public culture, it is possible to see the multiple ways that medieval popular religion continues in the modern world, perpetuating archaic ideologies and doctrine.

CHAPTER 2

THE CONFESSIONS OF WADE BOGGS; THE CONFESSIONS OF SAINT AUGUSTINE: SPORTS, SEX SCANDALS, AND MEDIEVAL NARRATIVE GENRES

> *The Yankee pitcher went into his windup, threw a called strike, and against his will Wilson recalled that even Wade Boggs had been involved in a scandal with a woman. Boggs was the most methodical hitter in the majors, but for a while a few seasons back the scandal had affected his hitting. It involved a lawsuit, and his average had dipped. Sportswriters had used the opportunity to take jabs at him, and Wilson could remember thinking that what Boggs had done was despicable. But Boggs had struggled through it, and now Wilson realized he felt kinship with him, as if both of them had been wronged. Boggs tapped his cleats and singled into center field.*
>
> —Ethan Canin, *"City of Broken Hearts,"* 1994

Baseball plays an essential role in Ethan Canin's "City of Broken Hearts"; in a disordered and problematic life, it provides continuity, stability, and a kind of ritual for Wilson Kohler. To him, the sport is a ritual of order, a set of rules, behaviors, and figures. The story begins, "Wilson Kohler loved baseball. He thanked God for it, for the red basepath clay, for the green grass, for the trim and piping of the uniforms. Gorgeous was what it was. It took his breath away."[1] Yet as much as baseball is the partial subject of Canin's novella, Wilson Kolher himself reads the game before him like a story; without knowing Wade Boggs, Kohler "felt a kinship with him, as if both of them had been wronged";[2] he is like a fictional character: a figure with whom Wilson identifies, although Boggs's life situation barely matches his own. That Canin gets part of Boggs's story wrong (his average did not "dip" until several years after the "scandal with a woman"; it would have been dropping at about the time Kohler actually watches the game, in about 1992, when Boggs played the final year of his contract with the Red Sox and hit .259) merely heightens the fictionalization of the real subject. Kohler's "ritual of order" is ordered for Canin by the rules of narrative; to talk about baseball, he, just as Kohler does, must make it into a story, bound by its own set of structures. In this case, baseball is a subject for a novella, but in a larger sense, the sport is not a novel but a collection of other, older genres that draw on classical and medieval ideas of narrative that survive in the way the sport is presented and the way it is consumed.[3] The story through which Kohler identifies with Wade Boggs, in its "real" version reported in the newspapers, on television, and on radio, moves from an epic to a fabliau to a confessional to an epic again, each portion bound by its own particular narrative assumptions and conventions; these features that make the real into story are no doubt what cause Kohler's connection in the first place.

Life imitates art; the way we think about real events is determined by fictional narrative expectations. An obvious example is the way that biographies read like novels; the dull details of what the famous person ate for breakfast and did on a regular day are omitted in favor of dramatic events and psychological examination. "Real" figures, in biography, become compelling characters, whose lives unfold and develop along the same patterns that characters' lives in novels do. For instance, it's a rare biography that doesn't include some incidents from the subject's childhood, echoing the structures of the *bildungsroman*.[4] That the boundaries between the real and the novelistic breakdown is clear from the emergence of the biopic, a genre that purports to be "truth" yet often draws more heavily from fiction. The interplay of fiction, truth, and fact characterize these genres; the figure of the author or interpreter (even, as in an autobiography, when the author/interpreter is also the subject of the work) stands as an intermediary between the material and the audience, shaping the story into palatable and desirable forms.[5] The "true story" is still essentially a story. Without certain narrative assumptions in place (assumptions drawn from novelistic ideas of how a story should be told), no one would buy the book; the author is required to shape facts in order to make them interesting reading. More important for this chapter's purposes, however, are the immediate, public narratives found in the newspapers, on radio, and on television. Again, the imperatives of "story" control presentation; the way events are told shapes public perception and engages public interest. In contrast to the biography, which, like the novel, is part of an individual's private reading, and which involves extended private meditation, these modes of communication are experienced much more quickly, talked about with friends and colleagues, and abandoned. As Michiko Kakutani notes, "it's no surprise that sports has come to occupy an increasingly prominent place in the communal imagination. No longer does art supply the sort of public spectacle that can galvanize an entire community."[6] As a public function, sports replaces the oral, public, artistic performance that characterized classical and medieval artistic reception, and the written records of these public events follow the same narrative forms. Sports reporting is immediate, not extensive, and thus draws its narrative inspiration from more public genres.

Sports' deep ties to fiction are revealed in a number of ways. As Marie-Laure Ryan notes, "cultural norms and the values of the community are no less influential on the emplotting of baseball games than on the interpretation of literary texts."[7] This ability to read games as texts allows games to become texts; the process of transmission from action to page is essentially one of narration. As Jerry Klinkowitz observes, "the best baseball reporting adopts the conventions of fiction, such as characterization, development by dialogue, informing images, and attentiveness to the sound of language."[8] This is a process by which "the beat and wire service writers, columnists, and sports editors [are] transforming everything they see into a meta-narrative on the nature of the game."[9] Klinkowitz goes on to note, "for some, that nature is elevated into myth, the natural being fashioned to purpose, being made intentional, meaningful, even divine, in other words, made human."[10]

In particular, sports are invariably epic and heroic—or at least, the way they are reported is invariably epic and heroic. What sports are without the stories we tell about them is unclear; in a certain sense, there is no pure "sport"; children playing sandlot baseball or a sidewalk game of stickball imagine themselves winning the seventh game of the World Series and imitate their favorite players. It is impossible to find a sport free of the traditions and inventions from outside that mediate between athlete and audience, even when those are one and the same. Even the recreational athlete often sees him or herself in a cosmic struggle with time, terrain, or even the body that would rather be staying in bed than running in the park. Defined by the stories told about them, sports enact the "most basic narrative pattern: the fight of the hero and the antihero. The story of the game tells how one team overcame the other."[11] This trope is obvious to anyone who reads the sports pages; on any given day, the words "hero," "victory," and "conquest" appear in multiple articles. The heroic is reproduced at both the levels of language and narrative. Names of teams often follow this pattern—the recently popular Titans, Giants, Knights, and Eagles are all stock figures of epic and reflect the genre's pervasiveness in the sports world, while older, more totemic, names such as Lions, Tigers, or Bears show epic's ties to myth and ritual.[12] Given their history, these names more likely reflect epic assumptions rather than originate them, responding to the qualities of the sporting contest. Despite these obvious connections, little examination of sports reporting as storytelling has been undertaken, and the few studies available seem prone to overstate the mythological qualities of sport itself (often in Jungian terms) without examining the ways that these are a product of narrative expectation rather than some pure or essentialist connection to myth; that is, they neglect the importance of stories told about sports in favor of a kind of parallel origin to the myths themselves.[13] They do, however, recognize the relationship of sport to literary conventions; as Deeanne Westbrook notes in her introduction to *Ground Rules: Baseball and Myth*, "I had become aware that baseball literature has more coherence, more common themes and figures, more 'familiar' characters and acts, a greater tendency to approach the mysterious and the sacred, and more echoes of ancient myths than can be accounted for easily, given the secular topic and the modern setting."[14] Westbrook's study, which takes a structuralist look at baseball writing in order to show the ways the game fosters a "mythicity," begins with the essential connection between sport, particularly baseball, and narrative; this mythical mode creates typological characters in typological scenes, and her focus on the literature of baseball—poetry, fiction, and essays—demonstrates the generation of these types in the sport's transformation from "live" to narrated event. The sheer number of baseball novels, stories, and poems is a reflection of the interplay of the real and the fictional; just as the fictional provides a way of talking about the "real," so, too, does the real provide a subject decidedly well-suited to fiction. While Westbrook deals primarily with the way fiction makes use of the real to create myths, it is possible to turn the equation around—the myths provide ways of talking about, and thus understanding, the real. Peter Williams acknowledges the function of the press in "the deification of the American Athlete,"[15] which is less about the celebrity and wealth that contemporary athletes attain than it is about the agonic sports figures, mythical tools, and archetypal journeys that shape the American understanding of sports. While Williams's unwillingness to acknowledge the somewhat ridiculous qualities of this identification of Dionysus with Babe Ruth and Apollo with Walter Johnson makes his discussion seem overwrought, his basic assumption that athletics and mythic narrative are intimately connected, and that this connection is made in the way sports, particularly baseball, are "read," is vital.[16]

Both Westbrook and Williams work from a mythological perspective. But epic originates in myth, as a recollection of the *Iliad* and the *Odyssey* confirms. In an epic, the individual, often leading a group, drives back enemies and protects the community: although the point of the poem is hardly the final victory, in the *Iliad* Achilles nevertheless fronts the Greeks' triumph over the Trojans. In more medieval examples, Roland leads the French against the Saracens and finally defeats them; Guillaume d'Orange also drives off the Pagans; Beowulf saves Heorot from Grendel and the Geats from the Dragon. The basic model for sporting events, and as a result, sports reporting, is identical. While this mode is prevalent in individual sports,[17] it is even more closely allied to team sports, in which the "home" army, led by its superstar, fights off the marauding forces of the "other" team.[18] This metaphor can be played out in two ways, depending on the audience; the team can defend the city while playing at home and engage in a conquering siege while on the road, echoing either the pattern of the Guillaume d'Orange cycle or that of *Beowulf* and the *Chanson de Roland*.

Symbolically, however, the sports hero is able to lead his forces to drive back the other team, and one need only look to New York after the Yankees won the World Series in 1996 to see this restoration of the community taking place.[19] Fans are encouraged to identify with their heroes (just as the audience functions in an epic), to feel that "we did it," even though their only contribution to victory was yelling a lot. The mere act of talking about sport can lead to this identification, as Umberto Eco notes: "And since chatter about sport gives the illusion of interest in sport, the notion of *practicing sport* becomes confused with that of *talking sport*; the chatterer thinks himself an athlete and is no longer aware that he doesn't engage in sport."[20] Thus the fan enters into the action through the mere act of experiencing the events and their fictions. That advertisers and writers connect this pattern to the heroic is evident in a plethora of examples: the Mantle family's biography of Mickey Mantle is called *A Hero all His Life*, Yankee television advertisements encouraged viewers to watch "Your heroes in pinstripes."

What separates Achilles, Roland, and Beowulf from the ordinary warrior is the superhuman ability that enables them to take on seemingly unconquerable odds and triumph: Achilles is almost invulnerable and can thus slay more Trojans than anyone else; Roland's fighting abilities lead him to hold off the Saracens almost single-handedly until Charlemagne shows up to finish the job; and Beowulf, who has wrestled with sea serpents, and has the handgrip of thirty and the strength of ten, rips the invincible Grendel's arm from its socket, defeats his even more dangerous mother with a Giant's sword that no one else can lift, and finally kills a fire-breathing dragon. The sports equivalent requires the individual to do the seemingly impossible, to possess more ability, more talent, than others who are merely good. Like the narrative, which relies on action to distinguish the hero from his run-of-the-mill compatriots, sports "offers a primal drama whose depiction of characters and character requires no metaphors, no allegories, no purple prose; a drama in which perfection is not an abstract concept but a palpable goal—a goal as simple as the perfect hit, the perfect shot, the perfect game."[21] Narratized sports, like epic, elevate the performance into the inherent quality of the man; what he does becomes who he is. Sports heroism also demands a kind of invincibility; not only must athletes display astonishing feats of skill, they must continue to produce them.[22] The pitcher who achieves the "superhuman" by pitching a perfect game (of which there have been only 16 since 1900) still has to go out and face the next team five days later; if he's bad, or merely ordinary, he may find his heroic stature of the game before replaced by cries of "You suck!" The hero who cannot maintain his status has two choices: remain on the margins and sink into either obscurity or infamy, or find a channel through which to rise again.

This redemption requires some narrative structure other than the epic, however; the heroic model demands that the hero never fail until the end of the story. That is, the hero can fail to win, but he cannot fail to be heroic. While at the end of their stories, Achilles, Roland, and Beowulf all end up dead, they have accomplished all that is necessary or possible: the wars have been won, the monsters have been destroyed. And that is the END of the story. To continue their stories, fallen heroes must seek out other routes to the epic world. The prodigal son provides the type-narrative for this return; Dwight Gooden and Daryl Strawberry, who fell from grace through drug use and general substance-oriented depravity, returned, by "going straight" and bearing witness.[23]

In the story of the fallen hero, the multiple genres of narrative employed in the public presentation of "news" intersect. Combine sport with another favorite source of news, scandal—particularly sex scandal—and the full array of narrative imperatives come into play. It is even possible to view a scandal as its own genre, with its own narrative assumptions, built out of a combination of those particular medieval examples discussed here. Many of the same assumptions are in place, whether the scandal involves politicians, actors, athletes, or reporters themselves; however, the superhuman, epic qualities of sport provide a striking background against which these other, more humanizing genres stand out in sharp contrast.[24] Vital to a reading of sports scandals is the relentlessly masculine nature of the heroic genre that characterizes its telling; in epic, women are relegated to two supporting roles: the sexually rapacious monster and the silent wife, the whore and the madonna. Think of Calypso and Penelope, Grendel's Mother and Wealhtheow, Flohart and Guiborc, Dido and Lavinia. While there are counterexamples, and this reading can certainly be reductive when looking at premodern texts, it represents a strong pattern in the contemporary appropriation of medievalism, which, because of its ties to a culture at least partially mass produced, tends toward formulaic simplification. In literary epic, the formulae require the vanquishing of the first and the valorizing of the second, while relegating them both to the margins.[25] Christopher Baswell's explanation of medieval versions of the *Aeneid* story reveals that the "challenging" women the poems present must be "shunned, killed off, enclosed, or ultimately negotiated with";[26] episodes with women, "and the dangers they pose, are carefully delimited, even bracketed off from the imperial narrative, which is the first sign of their containment. What power these women do have centers on their eroticism."[27] So too in the hyper-male narrative of sport—when a woman intrudes on the story, the epic genre becomes nonfunctional, and the kinds of narratives that can accommodate women must be used, finally, to write them out. Because of their erotic power, women are inherently threatening to the epic mode, while at the same time, they are equally out of place within it. Other genres come into play to contain these disruptive forces; they interrupt the epic but are finally subsumed by it. By separating out the feminized danger, the epic mode is allowed to reassert itself. The hero is removed from his own story, yet, while the narrative mode changes, the alteration also functions to create its own final return to the heroic mode.

The current fascination with sports and sports figures may also reflect a kind of primal desire; because of the metaphoric battles that athletics play out, in which winning and losing and trying are more literalized than they are in politics, music or the movie industry, athletes fit more neatly into the mythical, narrative patterns at play. A. Bartlett Giamatti, former Shakespeare scholar at Yale and Commissioner of Baseball from 1986 until his death in 1989, one of sports' most literary figures, suggests for sports a more communal importance than politics or art;[28] he sees sports and fandom as a series of rituals with distinct meanings.[29] His suggestion that "sports can be viewed as a kind of popular or debased religion" that mirrors Americans' "sacred" concerns,[30] gets at the different hold that sports has on the public imagination. That the epic has a measure of sacred concern as well is clear; the heroes are on the side of God (or the gods), and the adversaries are not; as is so often reiterated in the *Song of Roland*, "Paien unt tort e chrestiens unt dreit" ["Pagans are wrong, and Christians right"].[31] The contemporary version might be, "The home team is right, the visitors wrong." As a result, the narrative patterns played out elsewhere take on a more overt, overblown dimension in this particular field.

This combination of patterns enacts the narrative paradigm of exile and redemption, and its connection to narrative forms and narrative expectations is most strikingly demonstrated through the example of Wade Boggs, then of the Boston Red Sox, whose heroic image was shattered in 1989 when it was revealed that for four years he had been carrying on an extramarital affair. This information became public when, after the relationship ended, his girlfriend, Margo Adams, sued him for breach of oral contract, claiming he had agreed to compensate her for the wages she lost while traveling with him on the road. When he refused to settle, and after the court reduced her claim from $5 million to a significantly smaller amount, she sold her story to *Penthouse* magazine for $100,000; the story revealed numerous prurient details of their sex life as well as quoting various uncomplimentary remarks Boggs allegedly made about his teammates and other players. The story was spread over two issues of the magazine; the second included seminude photographs of Margo Adams. Boggs's wife of 12 years, Debbie, decided to stay with him; Margo Adams lost her more modest claim, but later settled on appeal for an even smaller sum of money.

Prior to this incident, Wade Boggs had achieved heroic status by winning five batting titles and by producing extraordinary statistics; his 84 peculiar superstitions, which included the habit of eating chicken before every game became part of his miraculous trappings, like Achilles's shield or Arthur's sword Excalibur, their ritualistic aspects following the epic ritual of the warrior arming for battle.[32] All newspaper accounts before the incident suggest that he was "destined for the Hall of Fame," itself an essentially epic concept. For Doris Kearns Goodwin, well-known historian and baseball fanatic, "Stubborn determination and a shatterproof will have been the keys to Wade Boggs's success,"[33] his ability is a "gift from the gods" a "talent refined only through practice."[34] She described his sister's description of his superstitions and rituals: "They are the weapons he uses to maintain his control at the plate."[35] The language is striking here: "weapons" and "control" are the stuff of epic. The game becomes a battle, and the hitter the warrior. An article in the *Albany Times-Union*, written shortly before the whole scandal broke, suggests that a ceremonial visit to Cooperstown, where the Red Sox were playing in the annual Hall of Fame Game, was merely a foreshadowing of what was to come: "But even this trip to Cooperstown by Boggs was one to be acknowledged. This may have been a historic visit, one that could be recounted some 15 years from now when Boggs comes back as a full-fledged member of the prestigious club a few blocks down from Doubleday Field."[36] Indeed, this reporter's use of the term "historic" again echoes the concerns and language of epic criticism, if not epic itself.

However, the discovery of his fallibility, deviance, and immorality quickly reduced Boggs to a fabliau figure—an object of ridicule rather than an object of admiration. Like the ribald tales of the *Decameron* or the *Canterbury Tales*, the Boggs story became comic, bawdy, even slapstick; the focus shifted from superhuman achievement to subhuman (or perhaps all too human) behavior. The difference between fabliau and epic is overt; as R. Howard Bloch points out, "unlike the epic which is transcendent and cyclical. . .the fabliaux offer a quick fix. They are short and dirty; but they clean up their own mess, and they never leave any loose ends."[37] They put forward a vision of human nature "closer to a kind of grasping materialism than the idealism of courtly forms,"[38] of which epic is one; they are "scandalous" in the "excess of their sexual and scatological obscenity, their anticlericalism, antifeminism, anticourtliness, the consistency with which they indulge the senses, whet the appetites (erotic, gastronomic, economic), and affirm what Bakhtin identifies as the 'celebration of lower body parts.'"[39] Appropriately, "over half the fabliaux in our corpus narrate tales of marital infidelity";[40] the erotic world is treated in "direct, uneuphemistic, and vulgar language."[41] From the elevated heights of epic, the story descends into the debased world of scandal and gratuitous comedy.[42]

The fabliau, the genre of the sex joke, was partially determined by Margo Adams's choice to tell her story to *Penthouse*. While she and Boggs may well have had sincere feelings for each other, the locus required a kind of telling that reduced any elements of romance to "a lewd whistle."[43] The fundamental principles of ribaldry in the fabliau are that sex is money, sex is work, sex is humor, and redemption is impossible—though comeuppance essential. While Chaucer's fabliaux are atypical in many ways, in particular their little interest in the clergy, fabliau's favorite target, he still provides the most effective sense of the inner workings of the genre that comes from Chaucer's Miller as he introduces his own ribald tale: "An housbounde shall nat been inquisityf / Of Goddes pyvetee, nor of his wyf. / So he may fynde Goddes foyson there, / Of the remenant nedeth nat enquere" (MilT 3163–66). Finding "Goddes foyson" (God's bounty) within the genre is nearly impossible; at the end of the Miller's Tale, everyone "gets his":

> And every wight gan laughen at his [the
>   husband's] stryf
> Thus swyved was this carpenteris wyf,
> For al his kepyng and his jalousye,
> And Absolon hath kist her nether ye,
> And Nicholas is scalded in the towte.
> This tale is doon, and God save al the rowte!

(Miller's Tale 3850–54)

Margo Adams's Tale works on these same principles. Here, life doesn't imitate art; life imitates farce. Her case and her sale of the story both make the sex/money connection apparent; as the Wife of Bath, whose prologue is decidedly like a fabliau, points out, "al is for to selle" (Wife of Bath's Prologue 414). As Charles Muscatine also notes of the fabliaux, "one would expect a hedonistic culture to be interested in money, and the fabliaux do not disappoint us. . .money is valued as it gives access to pleasure, and also for its own sake. There is a persistent small rain of coins, a continual traffic of rewards, payments, and bribes."[44] However, salability has its limits; just as Chaucer's Cook's Tale stops at prostitution, breaking off after Perkyn Revelour meets his "comper of his owene sort" (Cook's Tale 4419) who "hadde a wyf that heeld for contenance / A shoppe, and swyved for hir sustenance" (Cook's Tale 4421–22) so too does this story restrain itself from making that final, narrative-destroying step (if Margo Adams is a prostitute, there's no case and no story): "Responding to the charge of payment for services, King (Boggs's lawyer) last night said, 'Obviously during this affair, Mr. Boggs also gave her some cash as a gift. It was not a payment. Again, I'm assuming Miss Adams is not calling herself a prostitute by saying they were payments for sexual services.' "[45] King adds "We can prove that she gets around, that she likes ballplayers, had made it a career, so to speak, and this is the end of her career, so to speak. She doesn't look so good anymore. Poor Wade is the last man on her train, so to speak. And he is a good target."[46] The repeated "so to speak"s create a suggestive filler for their own narrative space; Adams, King implies, is, if not a full-fledged whore, at least a golddigger, whose intent is financial not sexual; the case itself is her last hurrah.[47] Indeed, like an athlete, the goldigger has a limited career, tied to the body and its vicissitudes. The athlete is only good as long as his physical prowess holds up, while the baseball Annie is only popular as long as she maintains her youth and beauty. Adams, here, seems to be washing up before her lover; while she slips into obscurity, he goes on to play baseball for ten more years, winning a Gold Glove and a World Series. King's suggestion that Adams is washed up, at the end of her career, adds to the overall condemnatory tone of her presentation. By using interpretive language, by requiring the public to "read between the lines," King constructs her own language as narrative, as storytelling; readers are here exposed to her (and what she hopes will be their) version of the tale of Margo Adams.

In the newspaper accounts, Boggs, too, associates sex with economy, albeit in a rather more bizarre fashion. Since for him "Goddes foysen" is not only monetary but also statistical, he justifies the affair by pointing out that his batting average improved when Margo Adams traveled with him on the road: "When she [Adams] was with Mr. Boggs, he batted .341, as opposed to the anemic .221 he hit when accompanied by his wife."[48] In the process of telling all, Margo Adams notes, "One night I went to the game and he went 4 for 5. He found out that I hadn't worn panties underneath my dress. So for the next couple of months when he went into a slump, he'd ask me not to wear panties to the game. . . . It wasn't sexual—it was that he had gotten hits and wanted to be sure of the little things he had done to get those hits."[49] By joining sex and work, these statistical oddities hook into the conventions of fabliau, but they also add to the bizarre narrative of Boggs's superstitions.

Prostitution may be too far to go, but these kinds of sexual details apparently are not. This story, like Chaucer's and Boccaccio's fabliau, is populated by "low life" characters and turns on ribald humor. The medieval authors include tumescent monks, cheating Millers, revelers, and lusty wives; Wade Boggs and Margo Adams "[became] friends with a stripper in Cleveland"[50] who later takes part in one of the central sex jokes, named "Delta Force," (thus enhancing its silliness) in the story. Operation Delta Force, an elaborate prank, is another elaboration of preposterous and humorous carnality, another fabliau bed trick, which, in the moment before laughter, once again unifies sex and violence:

> [Bob] Stanley said Boggs and Crawford[51] got into his room by persuading a clerk to give them the key. Stanley said he was asleep when the two entered and pushed a woman [the stripper from Cleveland] into the room. Both were armed with cameras and took his picture, Stanley said.
>
> "All I know is that when I got up I was throwing punches," Stanley said.
>
> . . .
>
> "I laughed at it a lot later," Stanley said.[52]

Being the perpetrator of this sex joke does not prevent Wade Boggs from also being part of another, larger one himself. Popular items selling briskly outside Fenway Park before games in 1989 included t-shirts saying, ".356 Lifetime Average. And You Thought it was the Chicken."[53] Indeed, the sexual details in the *Penthouse* article, because of their prurience, start to seem too hilarious to be real:[54] Adams serving Boggs double-anchovy pizza while wearing sexy underwear is merely one example with deep ties to fabliaux; there are many stories in which women provide "menus along with sexual favors. Food, then, is a ready index of general pleasure in the fabliaux."[55]

In fabliau, sex is not tied to love or desire; it is more commonly connected to work, enhancing the sweaty, "lewd whistle" atmosphere of the stories by taking the culminating expression of romance love and making it into an effort. The Wife of Bath, in her fabliau-like prologue, comments of her first three husbands: "I set hem so a-werke, by my fey, / That many a nyght they songen 'Weilawey!'" (Wife of Bath's Prologue 215–16) and "As help me God, I laughe whan I thynke, / How pitously a-nyght I made hem swynke" (Wife of Bath's Prologue 201–02). In the Reeve's Tale, after the successful completion of the bed trick that lands Aleyn the clerk in bed with the Miller's daughter, and the Miller's wife in bed with his fellow, the Reeve notes: "Withinne a while this John the clerk up leep, / And on this goode wyf he leith on soore. / So myrie a fit ne hadde she nat fyl yoore; / He priketh harde and depe as he were mad" (Reeve's Tale 4228–31). Sex is not romantic or even sensual; it is hard, sweaty, and full of effort, treading the edge of violence. As reported, the Wade Boggs/Margo Adams version, while more direct, is no less about sex than hard work on the edge of violence, as Adams herself notes: "One time in Oakland, during a fit of passion, I began to scream—and I mean scream. I was heard all the way down the hall. Two players called security, thinking someone was being murdered."[56] Indeed, Bloch references the fabliau "*De Celle qui se fist foutre sur la fosse de son mari*," in which the Squire tells the lady he is trying to seduce that he is disconsolate because "I had placed all my love in a lady I know. She was beautiful, courteous, and wise; and I loved her more than myself. But I killed her by my excess.—You killed her? How was that, sinner?—By fucking, truly, dear lady."[57] That the lady then responds, "Noble man, come closer and deliver me from the world, kill me; make a little effort, and do to me worse than you did to your lady"[58] suggests that Margo Adams is in good literary company.[59]

By the end of the two-part article, Boggs's heroic reputation was completely destroyed. Reporters quickly expressed concern that "Boggs runs risk of losing Fame,"[60] suggesting that "Boggs could pay the biggest price of all for his admitted sins" because the requirements for the Hall of Fame include "integrity, sportsmanship, and character" along with "playing ability."[61] There was much talk of trading him to the Astros. Headlines like, "Battered image needs restoring"[62] and "Needed at Third, A Cold Shower"[63] display just how "fallen" the hero had become. The fabliau is a genre that allows no redemption—at their endings, the characters either get their comeuppance or get off scott free. Whether Boggs and Adams had it coming to them is a matter of debate; within the narrative context created for their relationship, however, they are both made to look ridiculous. While the events of the story stripped of the prurient detail and absurd statistics might allow one to feel some sympathy for either or both of them, the mode of its telling excludes that sympathy.

For Wade Boggs to return from this fall from grace, it was essential to turn to yet another narrative form, the confessional mode. Only then was restoration to anything like his previous status possible.

Boggs's first attempt to restore his status only served to further his descent. His claim that his affair with Margo Adams was the result of a disease—sex addiction—that he heard about while watching *Geraldo*[64] only furthered the ridicule. As one reporter noted, "If the Wade Boggs story weren't so funny, it would be sad. . .*A Sex Addict?* Come on, ladies and gentlemen. Let us climb aboard our spaceships and return from the Planet Zorg to something approximating an orbit within the sphere of reality. Nobody is a sex addict. A sex maniac maybe. . . ."[65] However hilarious, Boggs's confession of addiction suggests a move toward the confessional mode that would finally redeem him; all that is missing is an appropriate context. Indeed, it is Augustine who declares, shortly before his own conversion, "Lex enim peccati est uiolentia consuetudinis, qua trahitur et tenetur etiam inuitus animus eo merito, quo in eam uolens inlabitur" ["For the rule of sin is the force of habit, by which the mind is swept along and held fast even against its will, yet deservedly, because it fell into the habit of its own accord"].[66] The failure to acknowledge his "own accord" in the matter prevents Boggs's initial confession from succeeding; his shift to a more self-abnegating mode is the move necessary to assure redemption. Essentially, Boggs must perform a kind of penance to receive public absolution.[67]

Therefore, the story makes another narrative shift, this time to confession, a medieval form with numerous modern parallels. The "tell-all" autobiography has its roots in the confessional mode, as does the remorseful, post-scandal television or print "exclusive" interview (generally conducted by Barbara Walters).[68] As Michel Foucault observes, confession was established as an essential ritual for the "production of truth";[69] confession functions both as an acknowledgment of one's own actions and a guarantee of status and identity. Confession also authenticates the confessor by the "discourse of truth" he or she is "able or obliged to pronounce concerning himself."[70] Foucault also establishes confession's continuing widespread effects:

> It plays a part in justice, medicine, education, family relationships, and love relations, in the most ordinary affairs of everyday life, and in the most solemn rites; one confesses one's crimes, one's sins, one's thoughts and desires, one's illnesses and troubles; one goes about telling, with the greatest precision, whatever is most difficult to tell. One confesses in public and in private, to one's parents, one's educators, one's doctor, to those one loves;. . .One confesses—or is forced to confess.[71]

The specifics of Wade Boggs's confessions will be taken up shortly; however, this need to establish a combination of difficult truth and remorse to produce redemption is apparent. It is tied to the particulars of his sin, since "from the Christian penance to the present day, sex was a privileged theme of confession."[72] Confession transforms sex into discourse, action into words, and through that "produces intrinsic modifications in the person who articulates it; it exonerates, redeems, and purifies him; it unburdens him of his wrongs, liberates him, and promises him salvation. For centuries, the truth of sex was, at least for the most part, caught up in this discursive form."[73] Confession has subsequently taken multiple forms, oral and written, yet it is no longer just a question of "simply saying what was done—the sexual act—and how it was done; but of reconstructing, in and around the act, the thoughts that recapitulated it, the obsessions that accompanied it, the images, desires, modulations, and quality of the pleasure that animated it."[74] Confession may have changed in "Real life," but its narrative form remains unaltered; thus, the same details that previously were ridiculed as part of the fabliaux now become essential parts of the redemptive narrative; the acts, like the words, are transformed in meaning; the discourse that caused the fall can now help reverse it.

The prototype for this redemptive genre is Augustine's *Confessions*, the first spiritual autobiography, and the first narrative confession, which also models itself on a popular narrative, Virgil's *Aeneid*. The *Confessions'* extraordinary influence on medieval literature and thought, both as a metaphor for the individual religious journey and as a model for purification, provided the work with a status equaling the *Aeneid*'s secular influence. Just as Aeneas travels from Troy to Carthage to Rome, leaving his lover Dido in order to marry Lavinia and found Rome, so, too, does Augustine leave Hippo and travel to Carthage, where he is seduced by his lust (as well as various heretical philosophies); he then leaves for Rome and Milan, where his conversion to true Christianity and the "straight and narrow" path take place through the agency of a miracle. His mother, Monica, a Christian, plays a significant role in the story, as does her death. Aiding Augustine's conversion are his confessions of sin, usually accompanied by weeping and apology. As he fittingly notes, "plusque in me ualebat deterius inolitum, quam melius insolitum" [My lower instincts, which had taken firm hold of me, were stronger than the higher, which were untried].[75] While Augustine perceives his besetting sin to be fornication, his friends and mother are a great deal more worried about his manicheanism; he must reject both and embrace redemptive Christianity to allow his higher instincts to rule. In this move, Augustine gives up his wife and his mistress and marries the church, becoming a prelate and finally a bishop. Or, as John Baldwin notes, "when Augustine, the influential Church Father, for example, recounted his personal search for God in his *Confessions*, his adolescent sexual habits raised the first obstacle to his quest only to be last to be resolved before his soul could rest in peace with its Creator."[76] This narrative autobiography became the standard for the male saint's life in the medieval period, and Augustine's use of the *Aeneid* led to its allegorization; most strikingly, Dido (Aeneas's lover) came to stand for "delicto," or sin (as in "in flagrante delicto"), while Lavinia (Aeneas's wife) came to mean the "laboram viam" or the "straight and narrow path." Indeed, Dido's name is often glossed as "libido" or desire;[77] it is also read as "virago," or "man–woman," which points both to her powerful leadership and her lack of appropriate femininity, manifested in her lustful behavior.[78]

This pattern fits the Wade Boggs story in extraordinary, almost occult, detail. The choice of narrative controls the choice of details; otherwise, the story would not come off so similarly. While Boggs's besetting sin certainly is fornication, most of the sporting world was far more concerned with the nasty comments he was alleged to have made about his teammates, which were perceived to be an example of his selfishness, his failure to be a "team player," a kind of debased, secular parallel to Augustine's manicheanism.[79] In order to redeem himself, he undertakes Augustine's path. His move from Boston to New York, his abandoning of his mistress for his wife, and his repeated apologies form the basis for his redemption. *New York Post* reporter Joel Sherman (without reference to Augustine or Aeneas) shows the currency of Vergilian thinking within the Boggs's story: "Boggs left Boston under trying circumstances, not only on the heels of his worst season (.259 in 1992), but with his own teammates—more than ever—ripping him for being self-interested and the Fenway Park fans booing. As a Yankee, Boggs has been a near model citizen, fitting in without rancor."[80] While condemning Boggs for his behavior on one hand, a reporter notes, "his public confession reminded me again how correct the nuns were decades ago when they warned me about the dangers involved with pleasures of the flesh,"[81] a line virtually identical to many of Augustine's. An article in *Sports Illustrated* quotes Wade Boggs confessing to his wife:

> The best thing that ever happened to me was getting caught. It's made my marriage so much better. You realize, I could have thrown all this away for nothing. I remember when I came home to Debbie and confessed the whole thing. I thought, this is it. Now she'll pack up the bags and take the kids back to Tampa. But the first thing out of her mouth was, "No. We're going to fight this thing together." I went, "All right!" It was like a hundred tons was lifted off my back.[82]

This sense of the "fortunate fall" draws from thousands of years of literary history; the hero's flaw and descent function to bring him to insight and return (albeit sometimes in death), an experience of descent leading to transcendence, as with Augustine. Another article recognizes Boggs's confessional while bringing out its ludicrousness both in its title, "For Your Sins and Mine, Let me Say I'm Sorry," and its content:

> Every day at 5, 6, and 11 I watch the news to see another clip of Boggs telling another interviewer, "I'm sorry." He sits in the Florida sun, apologizing for everything he said, everything he did, everything she says he said, everything that ever happened, everywhere. He's sorry. . . .
>
> Wade, what about Jim Rice?
> I'm sorry.
> Wade, Bob Stanley?
> I'm sorry.

Dwight Evans?
I'm sorry.
The Hindenburg?
I'm sorry.[83]

While focusing on the confessional, this article also notes, "You'll be glad to know Boggs is all better now. Totally cured. It's like a miracle, isn't it?"[84] (It is also worth noting that the author, in the list of apologies, never mentions Margo Adams or Debbie Boggs; sex may be the besetting sin, but the redemption is most important in the masculine world of the epic, once again.) This conflict with his teammates that creates a quarrel between them is reminiscent of the focus on masculine relationships within the epic and the potentially dangerous results of such confrontations; for instance, the tension between Roland and Ganelon causes Ganelon's betrayal of the French and the destruction of Roland and the Rear Guard, and Palamon and Arcite's battle for Emelye's affections in Chaucer's Knight's Tale nearly destabilizes the whole narrative. Boggs's criticisms of his teammates made public by Margo Adams (almost a worse sin on her part than adultery) is clearly more damaging within the sports world than a little sexual indiscretion, as it threatens to undo the essential male bonds that make the whole system work (theoretically, at least, the team that can't get along in the locker room can't play well on the field). Despite the humor of the piece, it is clear that the goal of these confessions is to return to the epic mode, where the team (male) reigns supreme and the woman is written out. The apologies to his teammates are more important, at least on the sports pages, than Boggs's reconciliation with his wife, for instance. Articles abound with descriptions of the ballplayer's confessions and apologies to his teammates as well: "Boggs has tried to stem some of the damage himself. He said Rice accepted his apology. . .and issued several more apologies during an interview. . .on Channel 7."[85]

If the demonstrations of remorse, apologies, and confessions aren't sufficient to cast Boggs in a virtuous light, the "miracles" emphasized in the reported story create a saintly context that takes the tale from the quotidian into the supernatural. While Augustine hears a heavenly voice calling to him to "tolle lege, tolle lege" ["take it [the book] and read, take it and read"][86] opens his Bible and thus undertakes the final step on his road to conversion, Wade Boggs's miracles are less textually focused. Noteworthy, however, is the passage that Augustine actually reads, "non in comissationibus et ebreitatibus, non in cubilibus et inpudicitiis, non in contentione et aemulatione, sed induite dominum Iesum Christum et carnis prouidentiam ne feceritis in concupisentiis" ["Not in reveling or in drunkenness, not in lust and wantonness. Not in quarrels and rivalries, Rather, arm yourself with the Lord Jesus Christ; spend no more thought on nature and nature's appetites"][87] the exact approach required for Boggs's redemption. Augustine's first act, after his conversion, is to tell his mother, "indicamus: gaudet. Narramus quemadmodum gestuum sit: exulat et triumphat et benedicebat tibi" ["who was overjoyed, and when we went on to describe how it all had happened, she was jubilant with triumph"].[88]

Boggs's first miracle comes, symbolically, at his mother's funeral: his sister, who had been unable to speak for several years due to debilitating multiple sclerosis, was able to give a eulogy, which Boggs attributed to the divine intervention of his mother's spirit. While this event occurred several years prior to the events of his scandal, its inclusion in several articles during the scandal gives this part of the narrative a quasi-religious air. He also claims to have heard his mother talking to him from beyond the grave,[89] a kind of saintly visitation. The other miracles are even more like the kind found in medieval saint's lives; at the approximate time of the revelation of the Margo Adams affair, Boggs was attacked by a group of thugs attempting to steal his car: "Boggs figured it was all over. He escaped only because, as he told friends later, 'I willed myself invisible.'"[90] Although the line was quoted in several papers, it was never made clear how literally Boggs meant this. Even more pointed is a later example; Boggs managed to fall out of a pickup truck going twenty-five miles an hour, driven by his wife, and despite "radial-tire prints" on his elbow, emerged entirely unscathed. As the reporter of this article notes, "Boggs has really done it this time. He has pulled off a miracle."[91] Despite irresistible conjecture that his wife pushed him out of the car, we are still left with the inviolable, incorruptible body of the saint, surviving extraordinary torture on the way to glorious martyrdom. Once again, Boggs has been cast as a superhuman figure.

The problem with the conversion narrative is that most saints either end up bishops, hermits, or martyrs;[92] none of these models proves suitable for the baseball field. The saint's redemption is primarily personal, not public. Therefore, we need a redemptive model that is both personal and public, a narrative mode that provides both for redemption AND return. The path here is essentially a hybrid form—the epic narrative of the heroic combined with the more personal qualities of confession, a narrative of internal change that affects (and effects) a public role. The conversion implied by confession requires a change in the person; Saint Augustine is not the same person who began the narrative; so, too, is Wade Boggs both redeemed and changed by the circumstances of his story.

In *Sir Gawain and the Green Knight*, Gawain learns a lesson about truth, duty, and devotion; however, we last see him, not joining a monastery, but riding home on his horse to Arthur's court, a sadder and a wiser knight, but a knight nonetheless. He rejoins his old life, but wears the mark of his newfound humility and understanding:

> . . .and ferley he ells,
>
> Biknowez alle ðe costes of care ðat he hade,
>
> . . .
>
> Ðis ðe bende of ðis blame I bere in my nek.
> Ðis is ðe laðe and ðe losse ðat I laȝt have
> Of couardise and couetyse, ðat I am haf caȝt ðare;
> Ðis is ðe token of untrawðe ðat I am tan inne.
> And I mot nedez hit were wyle I may last;
> For mon may hyden his harme bot unhap ne may hit,
> For ðer hit onez is tached twynne wil hit neuer.
>
> [He]Confessed all his cares and discomfitures many,
>
> . . .
>
> This is the blazon of the blemish that I bear on my neck;
> This is the sign of sore loss that I have suffered there
> For the cowardice and coveting that I came to there;
> This is the badge of false faith that I was found in there,
> And I must bear it on my body till I breathe my last.
> For one may keep a deed dark, but undo it nowhit,
> Where a fault is made fast, it is fixed evermore.[93]

By permanently affixing a symbol of his sin on his body, Gawain creates a visual reminder of his change; he is now the perfect Christian knight, living the straight and narrow, eschewing the excesses and sins of Arthur's court, while still remaining within it. As a model, this is heroic, but in a different context from the epic; this example provides a heroic of vulnerability rather than invincibility, one that is both moral and essentially human. Gawain isn't the only example; saints have been known to wear their devotion into their bodies, either through self-flagellation or other mortifications of the flesh, or more literally, like Heinrich Susa, by carving IHP into the chest with a stylus.[94] Again, conversion narrative provides a striking model for reality: Wade Boggs recently had his wife's name, Debbie, tattooed on his left shoulder.[95] Not an anchor. Not a baseball. Not his lifetime batting average, nor a chicken. As a sign of a devotion to the straight and narrow, the moral life, Boggs's tattoo is a constant reminder of both what he almost lost and what he regained. This is, however, the opposite of Gawain's girdle, since the emphasis is on public return, not private redemption.

All evidence suggests that Wade Boggs has successfully returned to a kind of heroic status, no longer quite so superhuman, but admirable all the same. How completely his transgressions have been eliminated has been demonstrated in several ways: in discussing the general misdeeds of Albert

Belle during the 1996 season, Bobby Murcer, a Yankees broadcaster, commented that Belle is a terrible role model, "unlike Wade Boggs."[96] Current newspaper accounts of Boggs's career mention him as a certain future Hall of Famer. Also in 1996, a *New York Daily News* advertisement showed a picture of the third baseman batting next to a promotional for "Yankees Date Night. Five lucky couples will receive a copy of *Mighty Aphrodite.*"[97] In 1989, everyone would have found this hilariously ironic; in 1996, it went largely unnoticed.[98] Boggs's leap into the crowd when the team returned to New York after winning the 1996 American League Championship Series in Baltimore showed how fully he has regained status as a fan favorite; however, his enthusiasm for the fans, and his desire to share his pleasure with them physically, suggests a redeemed personality as well. No longer is he the distant and unreal hero; the superhuman machine has become human. The most powerful image of his redemption showed him on the back of a police horse, his arm raised in the triumphant salute of the conquering hero, after the final game of the 1996 World Series.[99] The resemblance of this image to similar medieval representations is striking; see, for instance, the image of the conquering William in the Bayeux Tapestry or the Green Knight (and indeed Gawain) in the *Gawain*-Manuscript (British Library; Cotton Nero A.x.). The Knight is himself again.

Striking, too, was Boggs's own celebration of his three-thousandth hit; rounding the bases, he blew a kiss to his dead mother in heaven (an Augustinian moment): "A few steps from home, Boggs again pointed up. He then got down on his knees and kissed the plate as his teammates and family waited to embrace him. . .Boggs's father, Win, his wife, Debbie, and his 12-year-old son, Brett came on the field to join the festivities."[100] His return is clearly complete. As the newspaper report notes, "Fireworks were set off when Boggs connected, the crowd of 39,512 gave him a standing ovation and a scramble developed for the historic ball."[101] Both an exaltation of the hero and a desire for a relic (the ball) combine to create the sainted figure Boggs has become, and his own language—"I finally put my flag in that mountain. So many guys have tried and come up short,. . .it was like the longest mile to walk up to the plate"[102] can be read as a pilgrim's progress, the conclusion of his path to the final return. That said, it also works in a more epic mode, echoing the military metaphor of raising the flag on conquered territory, an act often repeated by mountain climbers and even the astronauts who landed on the moon. The effect here is a combination of the redemption of confession and the return to epic as this image doubles itself. Again, this medieval sensibility is echoed in the reporter's diction: "Wade Boggs knelt down and kissed home plate. His trip was complete."[103] That Boggs retired at the end of the season is no surprise; like Augustine at the end of Book IX of the *Confessions*, he has run out of story. And since Boggs can't produce a three-book analysis of the rhetoric of *Genesis*, there is nothing left to say.

As compelling as these parallels between Wade Boggs's story and medieval narrative forms are, they are not, finally, intentional in any real sense. The issue is how stories get told. The narrative demands come not from inside—Boggs doesn't choose to be a figure in a fabliau or a new Saint Augustine—but from the outside. It is fans, readers, who cast public figures as fictional characters and thus impose expectations of behavior on them. Like Wilson Kohler, we want to find characters to revile and characters with whom to identify. Readers demand the way they want things told; Wade Boggs's story fits these narrative patterns, but it could also be narrated in other forms. His life with Margo Adams *wasn't* a fabliau—it just gets told that way. The details don't support this multi-generic scheme better than any other; the story could be a romance or a psychological novel. It is the telling that gives the details narrative; they don't have them on their own. When stories are told, what doesn't fit the pattern gets suppressed. There are issues, events, and concerns that are, by necessity, left out. They happened, but they aren't narrative.

The question, then, remains—if particular genres are used, and others are getting suppressed, why? Why are public scandals told through these generic types? What supports them and why are they privileged? In the sports arena, at least, there are some answers; these genres all erase women from any meaningful role in the story. They become marginal figures; they have no true subjectivity. Because she put up with the scandal and stayed with her husband, Debbie Boggs is the Madonna, the long-suffering wife, the desexualized figure whose primary function is to stand for the "laboram viam," the road of the redeemed; Margo Adams is the whore, the mistress, the bad girl, the sexual sin that must be left for the redemption to take place. The epic world excludes private concerns, and therefore women, who are confined to the domestic world. When they enter the story, the narrative has to find a way to get them out again. That epic and sports are both profoundly masculine worlds is undeniable; it is perhaps that which allies them so closely. And in both worlds, women are relegated to the sidelines. Ironically, both the confessional and fabliau have little room for women as subjects either; in the first, they are either the sainted influence for the act of contrition (such as Monica, Augustine's mother) or the sin that must be repented; in the latter, they are objects, like furniture, there for the sake of comedy, to be used and discarded. Although the woman requires the narrative form to change, the alternate forms do not allow her much greater place than the epic does.

So forceful are these narrative trends, that an examination of this story reveals the ways even Margo Adams writes herself out in her own telling;

by choosing to sell her story to *Penthouse*, by including prurient sexual details, and by agreeing to pose naked alongside her words, she casts herself into the very role she is trying to avoid. With no other roles provided, she makes herself into the stereotypical "other woman." No other narrative identities really exist through which to talk about her, and thus she constructs her own tale as a fabliau and then is bound by its restrictions. In doing so, Adams opens herself up to the male gaze; it is no accident that her story is accompanied by seminude, erotic pictures. Revealing the female body objectifies it while concomitantly concealing the male body from public view; she becomes the naked text, writable and controlled. Despite her attempt to tell her own story, the story succeeds in "writing" her into its desired place; by making her a visual object and clearly delineating her role as the adulterous woman, she is robbed of voice. Certainly the exposé places her desire for money at the root of the story, and Adams finally got that. Yet the *Penthouse* article shows her desire to tell her story from her point of view, which the writer/interviewer repeatedly co-opts by shifting the focus from any sincere feeling and sense of loss to objectifying ludicrous sexual detail. By avoiding that construction, Wade Boggs is able to return himself to subjectivity by speaking his own confession; the variety of narrative roles open to men allow him redemption and thus centrality, while Adams is perpetually relegated to the margins, reviled and essentially forgotten.

The imperatives of storytelling force the real into the fictional. Paul Ricoeur observes "A story should be more than an enumeration of events in a serial order, it should organize these events into a tangible totality, so as to make it always possible to ask: what is the theme of the story."[104] Or, as Ryan notes, "life is lived looking forward, but it is told looking backward. Narrative is essentially retrospective."[105] What the retellings of the Wade Boggs story reflect is a continuing connection to old modes of narration in the telling of contemporary events; when reality is transformed into story, it is constructed in narrative forms and abides by its assumptions. What does not fit those assumptions is cast aside, and details, characters, and patterns are made to fit the teller's mode. This narrative construction is essentially an interaction between readers and writers; while the genres of epic, fabliau, and confessional, and the assumptions they bring look backward to the Middle Ages, they are very much alive in the public consciousness. And because most news is provided through intermediaries who are as shaped by these narrative assumptions as their readers, "truth" is always tempered by the presence of fiction. As a result, readers bring the assumptions and narrative concerns of one to the other; we cast figures as characters in a set narrative; we make life imitate art.

CHAPTER 3

WHERE MANY HAVE GONE BEFORE: GENDER AND GENRE IN *STAR TREK**

Space—the final frontier. These are the voyages of the Starship Enterprise. Its continuing mission: to explore strange new worlds; to seek out new life and new civilizations; to boldly go where no one has gone before.

—Star Trek: The Next Generation, 1987–94

We redeth oft and findeth y-write—
And this clerkes wele it wite—
Layes that ben in harping
Ben y-founde of ferli thing.
Sum bethe of war and some of wo,
And sum of joye and mirthe also,
And sum of trecherie and of gile,
Of olde aventours that fel while;
And sum of bordes and ribaudry,
And many ther beth of fairy.

—"Lay le Freine," Middle English Verse Romances, 1986

The means by which they [courtly virtues] are proved and preserved is adventure, avanture, a very characteristic form of activity developed by courtly culture. Of course, fanciful depiction of the miracles and dangers awaiting those whom their destiny takes beyond the confines of the familiar world into distant and unexplored regions had long been known. . .

—Erich Auerbach, "The Knight Sets Forth," 1953

The medieval romance is the genre of movement, of transition. With origins in Celtic stories, classical and epic conventions, and lyric emotion, the romance displays sliding boundaries within its stories and within its own conventions. The anonymous writer of the Middle English "Lay le Freine," based on Marie de France's "Le Fresne," constitutes romance as a literary genre, yet notes at the same time its orality through its performance in music and song.[1] Lays, the author notes, are about many things: the violent and sorrowful aspects of battle and tragedy; the joy and mirth, deception, jokes, and sex of comic tales; old adventures; and, most of all, "fairies." An interesting introduction to a lay that contains no fairies and rather little of any of the other identifying characteristics it lists, it nonetheless presents a picture of the genre as one that is inherently flexible except in its necessary inclusion of what the opening to *Star Trek: The Next Generation* might call "new life and new civilizations" inhabiting "strange new worlds" that share a great deal with those of the Celtic romance tradition from which *Lai le Freine* draws.[2] Adventure, which the "Le Freine" author sees as a potential element of the lay, in Erich Auerbach's understanding becomes a function of movement, a "fanciful depiction of the miracles and dangers awaiting those whom their destiny takes beyond the confines of the familiar world into distant and unexplored regions," that inevitably creates physical transitions between these "fairy" worlds and the genre's own "real" world.[3] The movement out of the familiar world into these "distant and unexplored regions" closely echoes the voyages of the Starship Enterprise in its continuing mission as it boldly goes where no one has gone before. Rather than a "Wagon Train to the Stars," as Gene Roddenberry famously described his brainchild in an attempt to sell the first *Star Trek* series to television, the Enterprise's voyages prove it to be a form related to but much older than the western: a medieval romance with spaceships for horses and aliens in place of fairies.

In this revivification of medieval romance, *Star Trek* is not unique; however, it is the most fully articulated television science fiction drama, spawning six series and (by the time this book is being written) ten feature films. Its popularity may well have inspired the myriad of similar series that trade on many of the same assumptions: *Babylon 5*, *Stargate*, *Farscape*, and many less successful imitations, such as *Battlestar Galactica* and *Earth Two*. All these programs share a particular narrative form and a set of conventions that when laid bare show striking similarity to those of their medieval antecedent; in doing so, they assume a relationship explained by Frederic Jameson, as "social contracts between a writer and a specific public, whose function is to specify the proper use of a particular cultural artifact."[4] The audience, then, essentially specifies its own understanding of the genre of romance and its transference into science fiction, an understanding that draws heavily on a combination of both medieval and contemporary assumptions about the genre and its workings, yet equally heavily influenced by critical ideas of plot and movement rather than more contemporary readings of the genre's origins and function. Again, as Jameson notes, "the older generic categories do not. . .die out, but persist in the half-life of the subliterary genres of mass culture."[5] Including romances and gothic among these, he presages the revival of romance in outer space.

"Romance" has come to be associated with formulaic novels and films whose attention to love echoes the last line of the authorial opening to the "Lay le Freine": "Mest o love for sothe thei beth."[6] While most medieval romances involve love in some form, many do not; the so-called romance novels, which fill the shelves at Barnes and Noble, however, have made the exterior romance quest almost entirely interior, the truly other worlds of adventure being replaced by exotic but geographically identifiable locales and a liminality created solely by desire. Therefore, while a modern "romance" is more likely to take place in Paris than in Cleveland, it is unlikely to involve truly mystical encounters with fairies, giants, or aliens. Because of a shift in leisure readership in the eighteenth and nineteenth centuries that created a primarily female audience for the novel, the romantic focus moved from the knight's quest to the woman's more intimate, internal drive toward love; the obstacles she fights tend to be constituted by class or money rather than sword-bridges or dragons, and the masculine hero himself finds love an obstacle by which he is conquered and overcome. This domestication of the genre eliminates that essential adventuring that Auerbach and the "Le Freine" author call primary, which is why any association of science fiction and romance causes raised eyebrows. Viewers who remember Captain Kirk's tendency to love 'em and leave 'em might well hesitate to see a connection between the two forms; while there's plenty of "ribaudry," love doesn't really seem to be the narrative's driving force. A fuller consideration of medieval romance and its conventions, however, reveals this particular brand of television science fiction to be right in line with romance as understood in the Middle Ages; not only do *Star Trek* and its cousins reproduce this genre's forms, they reproduce its underlying assumptions as well. After an examination of its construction of gender roles, hierarchies, and codes of behavior, *Star Trek* looks a great deal like its medieval forebears; from the vantage point of the present, the future looks a great deal like the past.

Although contemporary critics often understand medieval romance "by its very name, 'romance' to exist more as a language (*lingua*) and a discourse (*sermo*) than a form"[7] it is still possible to identify generic characteristics that, if they don't define romance, certainly describe it. It is possible to say, in general, that medieval romance works in a loose, episodic way, which Auerbach characterizes by its additive style and lack of causal connections between events, paralleled in its "elastic and mobile" structure and its "hypotactically rich periodic syntax" and "consecutive constructions."[8] Thus, within any given romance, such as Chrétien de Troyes's *Yvain*, which Auerbach uses as his own type-text, the story's events are arranged loosely around a central narrative line and are almost interchangeable in their order, provided that the central movement remains intact. The key episodes of the second half of *Yvain*, the Castle of Infinite Misfortune, Yvain's run-in with the three unchivalrous devils, and his encounter with Harpin of the Mountain all serve to elevate his character and courtly virtue, and to help him regain his true identity, yet they remain only tangentially related and do not build one upon the other, merely adding to Yvain's list of accomplishments. Thus the order is made secondary to the events themselves, their function less determined by hypotactic relationships than by their amplification. Such a loose mode of construction motivates Patricia Parker to call the romance "inescapable," deferring "a particular end, objective, or object"; in her understanding, romance is "that mode or tendency which remains on the threshold before the promised end, still in the wilderness of wandering, 'error,' or 'trial,' " within which the Other is "the terminus of a fixed object."[9] Thus romance is "the liminal space before that object is fully named or revealed," a threshold "more precarious and more essential" that embodies the connection between "naming, identity, and closure or ending."[10] Thus, romance's narrative structure, by its very episodic nature, creates a distinct relationship to conclusion that produces two distinct spaces, the liminal and the real, its "romanceness" constructed within the liminal in relationship to the real. In Parker's and Auerbach's conception, the romance inheres in the wandering; it is the reintroduction of the "real," or the revelation of the name, that concludes it.

Indeed, the prevalent images of wandering within romance mimic the assumptions of the genre itself; first Calogrenant and then Yvain wander through the woods in search of the adventure of the Spring, and Gawain's drifting through the forest on route to the Green Chapel in *Sir Gawain and the Green Knight* is a paradigmatic image for the romance itself:

Mony klyf he ouerclambe in contreyez straunge.
Fer floten fro his frendez, fremedly he rydez.
At vche warþe oþer water þer þe wyȝe passed
He fonde a foo hym byfore, bot ferly hit were,
And þat so foule and so felle þat feȝt hym byhode.
So mony meruayl bi mount þer þe mon fyndez
Hit were to tore for to telle of þe tenþe dole.
Sumwhyle wyth wormez he werrez and wyth wolues als,
Sumwhyle wyth wodwos þat woned in þe knarrez,
Boþe wyth bullez and berez, and borez oþerquyle,
And etaynez þat hym anelede of þe heȝe felle.

. . .

Þus in peril and payne and plytes ful harde
Bi contray caryez þis knyȝt. . .

[Many a cliff must he climb in country wild;
Far off from all his friends, forlorn must he ride;
At each strand or stream where the stalwart passed
'Twere a marvel if he met not some monstrous foe,
And that so fierce and forbidding that fight he must.
So many were the wonders he wandered among
That to tell but the tenth part would tax my wits.
Now with serpents he wars, now with savage wolves,
Now with wild men of the woods, that watched from the rocks,
Both with bulls and with bears, and with boars besides,
And giants that came gibbering from the jagged steeps.

. . .

Thus in peril and pain and predicaments dire
He rides across the country. . . .][11]

The movement through space and time; the encounters with serpents, wolves, giants, and wodwos; Gawain's courage and the support of God; the mishaps and mortal harms and painful predicaments that beset him are all essential elements of romance. Gawain is moving toward a goal—the resolution to his conflict with the Green Knight at the Green Chapel—yet the process becomes as important as the product. His trip to Haut Desert is the paradigm for the romance journey, just as what takes place at Bertilak's castle is revealed at the poem's conclusion as part of the test. That the Green Knight's identity and purpose finally *are* revealed fits *Sir Gawain and the Green Knight* neatly into Parker's model; however, even more vital is the way the ending showcases the adventure in relationship to the poem's frame at Arthur's court. While the court and its values put boundaries on the poem, it is the meandering center in which the knight's true character and value are displayed.

Auerbach focuses on the function of *avanture*, calling it a "characteristic form of activity developed by courtly culture," and so tying together both the narrative movement and the social structure that dominates the romance.[12] Adventure, the "setting forth" of his title, he writes in a formulation worth quoting once again, involves "fanciful depiction of the miracles and dangers awaiting those whom their destiny takes beyond the confines of the familiar world into distant and unexplored regions," bringing both characters and readers into "narratives about the mysterious perils which also threaten man within the geographically familiar world, from the influence of gods, spirits, demons, and other magic powers"; within that world, "the fearless hero. . .by strength, virtue, cunning, and the help of God overcomes such dangers and frees others from them."[13] As a construction of romance, this definition also focuses on structure and liminality; the hero must encounter worlds different from his own, distant and unexplored, yet the structures of his own community are those that provide the strength, virtue, and help of God, if not the cunning, to ensure his victory. Auerbach notes the oddity of "an entire class, in the heyday of its flowering" regarding "the surmounting of such perils as its true mission—in the ideal conception of things as its exclusive mission," adding that whole cycles of romances are "taken over by it for the purpose of producing a chivalrous world of magic especially designed for the purpose" of surmounting such threats,[14] which thus becomes an act of reaffirming the social values of the culture that produces the romances. Thus the stories' "real" world is validated in the actions of the hero as he moves through the unreal worlds that both challenge and mirror his own; as the best representative of the values of the courtly system, the knight sets forth to triumph over the obstacles that ultimately allow his glorious return. Even though the poems' real world is in itself fictional, existing in a mythical past, they still espouse a set of values that in the twelfth century were particular to the courts themselves, but became increasingly available beyond them in the fourteenth century.[15] In *Yvain*, Calogrenant first undertakes the adventure of the Spring yet fails to defeat Esclados the Red because, as a minor player, he cannot embody the court's greatest values; Yvain is successful because he does represent courtly virtue. His failure to live up to those values, in turn, requires his second quest, in which he once again becomes "preu et cortois" [courteous and true][16] so regaining his status as the true representative of the courtly world. By saving ladies from slave labor and unfair estate distribution, killing giants, rescuing Lunette from her ordeal and the Lion from the Snake, he demonstrates both his strength and his courtesy and can finally receive Laudine's love. At the end of the romance:

> Or mes sire Yvains sa pes;
> Et poez croire c'onques mes
> Ne fu de nule rien si liez,
> Comant qu'il ait esté iriez.
> Molt an est a boen chief venuz
> Qu'il est amez et chier tenuz
> De sa dame, et ele de lui.
> Ne li sovient or de nelui
> Que par la joie l'antroblie
> Que il a de sa dolce amie.

> [And now Yvain had his peace,
> And surely, believe me, nothing
> Had ever pleased him better,
> However miserable he had been.
> It has all come right in the end.
> His lady loved him again,
> And cherished him, and he cherished her.

He'd forgotten all his worries,
Wiped away by the joy
He felt with his dear sweet love.][17]

Coming as a result of adventure, and confirming that Yvain has the virtues of prowess and courtesy with which he began the romance, the ending provides rewards for those who affirm the cultural values that the romance represents. While Chrétien seems to question those values at strategic points within the romance, stressing, for instance, the vast destruction and seemingly unnecessary qualities of the adventure at the Spring, most of his romances (the possible exceptions being the unfinished *Chevalier de la Charette* and *Conte de Graal*) conclude with courtly values firmly in place. The very public conclusion of *Erec and Enide*, which shows the couple's coronation and elevation, acts as a reward for the successful completion of their adventurous quests, just as Yvain's reunification with Laudine serves as his reward. All these characters finally assume their public roles within the chivalric system; Erec and Enide take over the governing of their lands, while Yvain remains to protect Laudine's spring.

Although they thereby remove themselves from the world of adventure and the unknown, that world has provided the test that proved their fitness for their place within the courtly hierarchy. Romances are thus clearly class determined, as only members of the court are permitted to undertake the adventures that allow them to have these elevating and confirming experiences. The few examples of poor ladies, such as Enide, are generally noble to begin with; and unknown knights, such as Perceval or Le Bel Inconnu, all turn out to be members of the right class after all; peasants, merchants, serfs, dwarves, and farmers are only admitted as accessories to the story, demonstrating by contrast the elevation and superiority of the higher caste. However, within the nobility, "noble behavior and refined manners" serve to distinguish the deserving from the undeserving.[18] Auerbach tends to associate these values primarily with unreality, arguing that "the relation of the courtly ideal to reality is determined by the fictitiousness and lack of practical purpose which, as we hope we have sufficiently shown, characterize it from the very first. Courtly culture gives rise to the ideal, which long remained a factor of considerable importance in Europe, that nobility, greatness, and intrinsic values have nothing in common with everyday reality,"[19] and indeed, the real courts of Europe from the twelfth to the fourteenth century may well not have abided by these in much more than symbolic ways. But even symbols count for something; the values of chivalric romance at the very least display a concern with maintaining hierarchy and status, determined by class, but within that limit they are judged by the performance of a set of behaviors embodied in the genre itself.

Although Eugene Vance understands the romance in more linguistic than formal terms, he still privileges this romance narrative purpose that gives the

> chivalric combat a new *telos*, in other words, to accelerate the transformation of twelfth-century chivalric conduct into a class emblem entitling its bearer to become a lover of noble women. In sort, the semantic function of metaphor, or *translatio* (understood as a generic term including all figures of thought) in the narrative discourse of chivalric romance is to "translate" warlike impulses into the impulse to love, that is, to subvert the *proprietas* of chivalric war by making it figurative.[20]

Thus romance doubles in language what it does in form; it reconstructs a set of values that replicate themselves literally and metaphorically, making the external violence inherent within the stories function as a figure for the more internal impulses and desires of the individual. Yet in doing so, this new telos constructs around itself a system that determines both values and value, both what is right and what is exchangeable. Valor is value, both of which are tied profoundly to class, status, and court. Indeed, the strategies of romance that reinforce courtly values both align with and seem to conflict with what goes on inside the genre's liminal worlds. The knightly ethos of bravery, courage, honor, and loyalty is often tested within the dimensions of the romance; when Yvain betrays his promise to Laudine and fails to return to her after a year, he must relearn ideals that seemed to be a part of his makeup in the first part of the romance. After going mad and running around the forest naked, being revived by several ladies, and rescuing the lion from the snake, Yvain undertakes a series of adventures that prove him courageous (he defeats three knights to rescue his friend Lunette; he fights Harpin of the Mountain on behalf of the knight whose castle the giant is harassing; he saves the ladies from the Castle of Infinite Misfortune, a medieval sweatshop), honorable (he refuses to continue the fight on behalf of the Lord of Blackthorn's younger daughter once he discovers that it's Gawain he's fighting, and even claims he has lost the fight), and (oddly enough) punctual (because he must arrive at several of these places on a rigid time schedule). Thus, in Yvain's case, the romance reaffirms the values of Arthur's court within its liminal world. Chivalric values are upheld; while a court may prove itself less chivalrous than one of its knights—as is the case with Arthur's court in both *Sir Gawain and the Green Knight* and Marie de France's "Lanval," in which the eponymous hero is treated shabbily twice, first being denied gifts for his service and then getting thrown into jail for a crime he didn't commit against a deceitful and lying queen— the principles that are supposed to govern the court are nevertheless affirmed by the knight's fuller embodiment of them. Gawain and Lanval (and indeed Yvain as well) are heroic because they fulfill the poem's moral plan: Gawain proves himself both more valiant and more humble, and thus more moral than the court, while Lanval certainly shows himself far more generous and truthful than Arthur and Guenevere do.

It is in the matter of courtesy where the two worlds of romance present conflicting sets of values, the liminal providing a world of possibility that the public world of the court denies. The generic conventions of romance both allow experimentation and limit difference; while the episodic structure provides endless possibility for encounters with the strange, the genre is ultimately coercive and confining. I have argued elsewhere that romance "is a dangerous formula which, while allowing poems' middles capacious range, determines their endings, imposing a closure which, finally, asserts—or demands—a set of expectations created by the audience but finally determined by the genre's representation of the society it inhabits"; these expectations are the very values that reaffirm a hierarchical status quo.[21] This status quo constructs traditional gender roles in the face of a great deal of ostensible gender freedom; romance's liminal worlds provide women and men with significant alternative relationships to power, mobility, and each other, yet, by insisting on the primacy of marriage, romance endings reverse that potential, thereby affirming the traditional hierarchies and structures that the sacrament requires. Romance's mutability makes it an ideal locus from which to explore gender, yet it also makes the genre a necessary place to constrict gender freedom. In the medieval romance, it is the love plot that creates this locus of conflict; because it ordains women's superiority within courtship, it allows them a kind of power; because of the way the conclusion of that plot is constructed, however, that power must be taken away once the lady is conquered by her lover. Within many medieval examples, a limited kind of public power and mobility is available to women, but only "if they are old, ugly, or dangerous, and thus prevented from playing the heroine."[22] In Chaucer's "Wife of Bath's Tale," a romance that plays out this duality in a particularly revealing and striking way, the Loathly Lady shows enormous power and self-determination while she is old and ugly, finding the knight herself and demanding his hand as the price for saving his life. In the face of his disgust at the thought of marrying the ugliest woman that ever could be imagined, the lady turns preacher, delivering a sermon on the values of "gentilesse": respect for elders, Christian poverty and charity, and faithfulness in marriage. A "literally repulsive text,"[23] according to Carolyn Dinshaw, the Loathly Lady still espouses romance values in a feminine voice—until she must finally become the heroine who fulfills all the knight's desires. Once she agrees to "obey him in everything / That myghte doon hym plesance or lyking,"[24] she has reconfirmed the conventional identity of the heroine in medieval culture—young, beautiful, and silent, a product of male desires. "The Wife of Bath's Tale" imagines a world of female power and authority, in which the queen and ladies are the knight's judge and jury, and in which his lesson is that "women desiren to have sovereynetee / As wel over her housbond as hir love, / And for to been in maistrie hym above," yet no lady with power can be the heroine, and no heroine can have power.[25]

Even within the less charged world of Yvain, Laudine's primary power over the hero comes from Yvain's attraction to her; she can "save" him by saying "yes," and destroy him by saying "no." Her political power as queen is significant, yet her awareness of her perpetual need to have a knight to defend her spring suggests ways in which female power is always compromised. In love she is his superior: Lunette tells Yvain that Laudine "qu'avoir vos vialt en sa prison, / et si i vialt avoir le cors / que nes li cuers n'an soit defors" [She wants you to be her prisoner, / She wishes to have your body / For herself, not even your heart / To be free].[26] Yvain has no objections; he agrees to put himself completely in her power, saying "Riennule a feire ne redot / que moi vos pleise a commander" [Nothing could make me hesitate / to do whatever you wish].[27] The power relationship reverses, however, as soon as they both consent, as "Mes sire Yvain n'en ot pas ire / ce vospuis bien conter et dire" [Yvain was more / the master than words could describe].[28] That this power relationship is played out within the same love relationship twice within a single romance serves to confirm the importance of both the lady's authority within love and the absolute necessity of her losing it once the relationship is established. Yvain, like the "Wife of Bath's Tale," provides multiple images of women with certain forms of authority: two ladies rescue Yvain from madness through the magic ointment provided by another woman, Morgan le Fay; Lunette warns Laudine that "N'en svex vos eü message / de la dameisele sauvage / qui letres vos en anvea?" [Our Lady Sauvage has long since / Sent word of his [King Arthur's] coming, sent a letter / with that news] suggesting that this mysterious, savage lady has access to privileged information;[29] Lunette herself shows great mobility within the romance, moving from place to place and coaxing Laudine into making the choice to love Yvain twice (Lunette nearly gets killed for her actions and needs a champion to defend her, though; her authority only goes so far). However, all these characters are peripheral; authoritative women may be permissible—even essential—in romance, but they are consigned to its margins. Thus, the poems reaffirm traditional medieval ideas of gender function, particularly within the secular world. In replicating this hierarchy, as well as the hierarchies of male authority, romance conclusions constrict the freedom of the genre's center, suggesting a drive toward fixed structures, unity, and the courtly tradition. The complexity and number of medieval romances make sweeping statements like these risk stereotyping, as there are examples that challenge, undercut, or test these conventions, and others still that provide alternative kinds of conclusions. That said, in many of these, the challenge to the texts' values is played out in the poem's body and swept away at its conclusion, or it lurks in the margins, providing a tension that, while not actually resolved, is contained in some manner by the poem's ending. As a genre, to the extent that it can be defined in these ways, romance functions as a kind of generic double bind, exploring new worlds while reconfirming old values.

Science fiction, on its surface, would seem to have little in common with the romance, preoccupied as it is with the future rather than the past. As a masculine genre, it also seems distant from the overtly feminine conception of the contemporary popular romance, its preoccupation with technology at the expense of emotion instead projecting the interior desires of romance onto exterior objects—spacecraft, blasters, and death stars. Science fiction claims its origins in the gothic novel, because of a shared fascination with the horrific unknown, and to the western, the genre of the old frontier of the American West as science fiction is the genre of the "new frontier" of Space. Gene Roddenberry's previously mentioned and often quoted description of his program as "Wagon Train to the Stars" is buttressed by the title of the fifth *Star Trek* film, *The Final Frontier*,[30] thus, the association between the two genres has some apparent basis. The often epic nature of the western is described by Frederick Goldin in his reading of George Armstrong Custer's attack on the Sioux and the *Song of Roland*, showing similar relationships to the past and the nation's crusading spirit.[31]

Compelling as Roddenberry and Goldin's assumptions are, a closer look contravenes their presumptions, as least in part, as the sci-fi future shares much more with the idealized past of romance than with the world of dime novels. The sixth film in the *Star Trek* series, for instance, requires a more complex reading of genre; called *The Undiscovered Country*, its obsession with Shakespeare[32] (General Chang notably observes "You have never truly understood Shakespeare until you have read him in the original Klingon") suggests that the outer voyage through the undiscovered reaches of Space echoes an interior journey, doubly symbolized by the reference to *Hamlet*, in which the "undiscovered country" is death, and the film's conclusion, in which intergalactic peace between the United Federation of Planets and the Klingon Empire requires a revised system of thinking.[33] However, a careful observer of *Star Trek* in all its generations does not need a dose of Shakespeare to make apparent the metaphoric nature of the science fiction quest, for a consideration of the workings of this influential series brings forward its medieval inspiration and romance origins.

Auerbach argues that "aventure," with which he begins his definition of the genre, has a dual function in romance; it is both the locus of the liminality that gives romance its distinctive flavor and the self-reflexive image of courtly society that the romance throws back to its reader. Romance, in effect, consists of a series of supernatural adventures that take place in supernatural space: "the landscape is the enchanted landscape of fairy tales; we are surrounded by mystery, by secret murmurings and whispers. All the numerous castles and places, the battles and adventures, of the courtly romances—are things of fairy land."[34] At the same time, a "self-portrayal of feudal knighthood with its mores and ideals is the fundamental purpose of courtly romance"; its exterior forms of life provide "salient pictures of contemporary conditions."[35] It takes no acrobatics to apply Auerbach's constructions to define *Star Trek*; compare the chapter's first epigraph to this revision: "the landscape is the mysterious landscape of space; we are surrounded by the unexplored, by secret murmurings and whispers. All the numerous planets and stars, the battles and adventures, of the *Star Trek* series—are things of outer space." At the same time, the series shows "a self-portrayal of Starfleet with its mores and ideals" as its fundamental purpose; its "exterior forms of life" provide "salient pictures of contemporary [both within and without the fictitious world of the series] conditions." Even a quick survey of the world of fairy tales and the world of Outer Space furnishes obvious parallels; obsessed with the other, romance offers both literal giants, dragons, and wizards as well as more human outsiders who challenge or reflect back the world of the hero; these two groups are well represented in science fiction, as the many alien species that inhabit *Star Trek*'s strange new worlds can be as supernatural as the romance monsters or as familiar as its other adversaries. As in romance, too, species can be deceiving; Yvain's lion appears first as a wild beast but then shows himself as loyal, gracious, and chivalrous in fighting as any knight Yvain encounters. On the other hand, the two sisters prove themselves far more disruptive to the story's social fabric. So too, in *Star Trek* in which the strangest looking aliens can turn out to be friends, while the most familiar can prove decidedly more problematic.

More crucially, the essential spaces of medieval romance, the court and the "outside," are replicated in the *Star Trek* series. Each generation of the show has its own court, either a starship or a space station, which is important both in itself and as a representative of a greater ideal. Although the political systems, feudal and futuristic, differ in significant detail, the fascination with these systems and the hierarchies they produce is a value that the two genres share. *Star Trek*'s ideal system is dually represented; in its mobile form, it is Starfleet, the military and exploratory arm of the static ideal, the United Federation of Planets, "an alliance of approximately 150 planetary governments and colonies, united for mutual trade, exploratory, scientific, cultural, diplomatic, and defensive endeavors. Founded in 2161. The Federation is governed by the Federation Council, composed of representatives from the various member planets, that meet in the city of San Francisco on Earth."[36] Starfleet, with a service academy and headquarters also located in San Francisco, is governed by the "Starfleet General Orders and Regulations," including the key "Prime Directive," which mandates that "Starfleet personnel and spacecraft are prohibited from interfering in the normal development of any society, and that any Starfleet vessel or crew member is expendable to prevent violation of this rule."[37] The expectations and values of the Federation, and indeed the prime directive, are often challenged, yet the function of the stories the series tells, like medieval romance in regard to the courtly ideals the *Trek* ethos resembles, is to show these mores and ideals triumphant in action. *Yvain* centers around the violation of the courtly "prime directive," as he breaks his promise to Laudine and does not return after his year away with Gawain; the overcoming of the consequences of that violation provide the second part of the action, causing Yvain's quest to regain his identity and status that finally reunites him with his lady and the responsibilities he once held lightly. As in romance, in science fiction, this action takes place primarily outside the court (or in interaction with those from outside it) in the liminal spaces of the variously constructed "M-Class" (inhabitable) planets and representatives thereof that the crews encounter.[38] As both enclosed spaces and mobile units, the starships (and their various shuttlecraft, probes, run-abouts, and pods) function both as the knight's horse and as an enclosed narrative space that can, depending on the particular story's needs, represent either the "real" or the "liminal" world.[39] This unwieldy pairing—the same ship representing both court and horse—may explain the prevalence of smaller space vehicles—is a consequence of the genre, yet the dual images of the ships acknowledge it. Externally, they are sleek, fast, and powerful, representing their function as objects of movement; inside, the bridge is womb-like, with rounded ceilings and curved furniture, all focusing on the central, elevated Captain's Chair, a figure of authority within a fixed space. Given its role as the show's most enduring example, this examination will focus on the Starship Enterprise in its various incarnations, but primarily NCC-17D, the ship manned by the crew of the most successful series, *The Next Generation*, though reference will be made to the original series and the films insofar as they establish and replicate the same assumptions.

The Starship Enterprise itself provides the physical space within which many of the series events occur, "but it also creates imaginative, political, and communal spaces that give shape to the fictional world of *The Next Generation*," creating a locus for both reality and unreality.[40] Serving as a structuring force within the text, the ship generates specifically "romance" narrative possibilities, cast as it is in the process of exploration, of necessity creating encounters between its crew and that which is outside. Sarah Hardy and Rebecca Kulka see the Enterprise as "an example illustrating the thesis that fictional spaces can constitute and control the forms of subjectivity and social practice that they contain."[41] As a concrete physical space, they argue, it can play "a central constitutive role in the dramas it contains," yet at the same time, "this very space is designed in such a way as to call into question its own boundaries and make any easy understanding of space as a simple container of action impossible."[42] Like the spaces of romance, the Enterprise has permeable boundaries; the transporter beam moves people in and out of the ship at the press of a button, and the holodecks permit the playing out of fantasies and adventures in an atmosphere simultaneously real and fabricated.

In one of many parallel examples from medieval romance, the Kingdom of Gorre in Chrétien's *Lancelot* exists within the same geographic landscape as Arthur's court, yet once we have crossed the sword bridge, a whole other system of expectations comes into play. Since this land is ruled by the law of love rather than chivalry, what appeared a wise decision outside the kingdom—Lancelot's hesitation to get into the dwarf's cart—becomes a harmful one, as it implied his hesitation to place love over duty, his lady (Guenevere, imprisoned in Gorre) over his lord (Arthur). Yet, even this court is still a court; ruled by a king who values honor and duty, Gorre provides a mirror image of Camelot. Thus the spaces are rendered in dialogic relation to each other, the transition between them revealing Bakhtin's threshold, a place where crisis, change, or fate takes place, where forbidden lines are crossed, and where renewal or death take place.[43] Just as the narrative of *Lancelot* is produced by the dialogue between Gorre and Camelot, so too are the narratives of *Star Trek* produced in the spaces between the ship and the strange new worlds it explores. Just as Lancelot as a subject changes between the two worlds that engage him in Chrétien's poem, so are the characters on board the Enterprise engaged in "mutually determining, dialogical relationships" with Space. The transporter beam makes the ship's boundaries flexible for the Enterprise crew, the bulkheads are permeable for some of the energy creatures they encounter, and even the membranes of the body are transgressible for certain aliens or forces who can meld with, enter, or possess the ship's humanoid inhabitants; thus, Inner and Outer Space slip into each other.

Perhaps because of the permeable spatial boundaries that inhabit the genre, romance fundamentally concerns itself with the relationship between the public and private, mixing physical, external action with interior feelings and the enclosed spaces of love; science fiction, too, creates an interaction between interior and exterior space on multiple levels. As Hardy and Kulka observe, "the hermeneutics of space and subjectivity are necessarily intertwined and must proceed together."[44] While it is possible to read all fictional spaces as being engaged in this way, the expectations of romance and its modes of self-constitution seem particularly determined by this dialogical relationship; even if space in romance is much less detailed than in other genres (and indeed, in *Star Trek*, many planets, created out of reusable paintings, models, and sets, suspiciously resemble each other), it plays key roles; the places of commencement and return are played against the spaces of wandering, of *aventure*. Auerbach's title for his chapter on romance, "The Knight Sets Forth" expresses this spatial necessity; "setting forth" must proceed from and must go to, thus constructing an essential, if vague, geography.

Most *Star Trek* episodes involve contact with some (often unfamiliar) alien species and a visit to an unexplored place, the interaction of the Enterprise character with his or her situation, and Space thus becomes the narrative through which change occurs. Equally often, episodes begin and end on the Enterprise, constituting it as the space from which the character sets forth and to which he or she returns. In "The Inner Light,"[45] for instance, the Enterprise, traveling between missions, encounters a mysterious space probe that penetrates the boundaries of the ship, locks on to Captain Picard, and renders him unconscious. He then awakens in what appears to be a dream, echoing the dream visions of the Middle Ages; he finds himself on the planet Kataan, an Iron worker named Kamin married to a woman called Eline. The planet is experiencing an extreme drought, for which Picard/Kamin attempts to produce relief through some creative technology; meanwhile, several years seem to pass, as Kamin and Eline have two children. They age; Eline dies; the drought worsens. Finally it becomes apparent that the planet's sun is going nova; with no means of survival, the planet's leaders launch their historical records in a probe. When the Enterprise's doctor finally breaks the link between the probe and the captain, he awakens, seeming to have lived approximately thirty years in the show's forty-eight minutes. Having assimilated the planet's culture, he is able to play their plaintive music on a wooden flute, thus bringing the liminal world into the real world of the Starship Enterprise.

Like most romances, this story begins and ends in the same place; through mystical means, Picard has set forth, encountered a magical "fairy-tale land," and, in a sense, preserved it. In place of monsters and black knights, Kamin fights the drought;[46] whereas the community at first finds his plans absurd, he eventually gains status within Kataan for his attempts. Picard's return to the Enterprise shows him changed; deeply moved by the experience, he ends the episode playing the Rekkesian flute music alone in his room. The overt dialogue between Picard and another planet's history, doubled by the probe's permeating the boundaries of the Enterprise, shows characters and spaces in discourse with each other. Picard/Kamin inhabits both identities at once; he is placed at the threshold between the two worlds, the "reality" of the Enterprise shown by the crew's attempts to break what they perceive to be a life-threatening link while the liminality of the experience created by the probe is played out. The story, if not the characters, moves between these two spatial frames, their connection only revealed at the conclusion of the narrative.

Despite the rather different dynamics between individual and group, this story's pattern echoes that of *Sir Gawain and the Green Knight*, in which the boundaries of Arthur's court are penetrated by the Green Knight, a representative of a liminal world that Gawain ultimately must enter. It is Gawain's own choice to take on the Green Knight's challenge, but like Picard, he is unaware of its meaning at the time it happens. His stay at Haut Desert and his deal with Sir Bertilak initially seem to fall outside the main story of beheading, leaving both Gawain (and the poem's audience) uncertain of their connection to his quest; however, at the Green Chapel, what seemed marginal becomes central, as Gawain is judged for his behavior at Haut Desert and is left with only a scratch. After a discussion with the Green Knight/Sir Bertilak that reveals the multiple meanings of his adventure, he returns to Camelot from where he began, wearing the Green Girdle as a symbol of his experience, just as Picard learns that the history of Kataan exists in the probe (and now in his mind) and retains the flute and its music as a memory of his life on another planet. Haut Desert and the Green Chapel provide commentary on Arthur's court in more overt ways than Kataan comments on the Enterprise, but both stories' conclusions draw our attention to the individual experiences of Gawain and Picard rather than the greater public meaning. While we're told that the population of Camelot adopts green girdles "with gay laughter and gracious intent" to "be worn with one accord for that worthy's sake,"[47] the lasting impression is of Gawain's stronger statement:

> Þis is þe bende of þis blame I bere in my nek.
> Þis is þe laþe and þe losse þat I la3t haue
> Of couardise and couetyse, þat I haf ca3t þare;
> Þis is þe token of untrawþe þat I am tan inne.
> And I mot nedez hit were wyle I may last;
> For mon may hyden his harme bot unhap ne may hit,
> For þer hit onez is tachched twynne wil hit neuer.
>
> [This is the blazon of the blemish that I bear on my neck;
> This is the sign of sore loss that I have suffered there

For the cowardice and coveting that I came to there;
This is the badge of false faith that I was found in there,
And I must bear it on my body till I breathe my last,
For one may keep a deed dark, but undo it no whit,
For where a fault is made fast, it is fixed ever more.][48]

Captain Picard does not give an equivalent speech to his crew; having been chosen, he has little direct tie to his action. He choses solitude instead; yet the final image of him playing the plaintive music of Kataan also puts the focus on the semiotic object of remembrance that encodes the experience that those who did not live it cannot truly understand.

Picard and Gawain are reintegrated into their communities, but they are both altered by their experiences in liminal space in ways that distinguish them from the others who have not moved from their original spots.[49] At the end of *The Next Generation* episode, the camera pulls away, leaving the ship in Space among the stars; at the end of *Sir Gawain and the Green Knight*, the narrative pulls away, moving back out into history: "Þus in Arthurus day þis aunter bitidde / Þe Brutus bokez þerof beres wyttenesse. / Syþen Brutus, þe bolde burne, boȝed hider fyrst, / After þe segge and þe asaute watz sesed at Troye, / Iwysse" [In the old days of Arthur this happening befell; / The Books of Brutus' deeds bear witness thereto / Since Brutus the bold knight, embarked for this land / After the siege of Troy and the city fared amiss].[50] Both stories "manage the potential dissonance of self and society, the familiar and the strange"[51] as both Picard and Gawain find themselves operating within unfamiliar societies that then influence their functions within their own societies. Having negotiated the strange, they encounter changed relationships to the familiar. While Gawain's is explicitly spelled out, the importance of Picard's adventure on Kataan is made manifest in the future when, a season later, he is still profoundly moved by the music and cannot share it with anyone until he meets Nella Darren, a potential love interest and pianist, in an episode entitled "Lessons."[52] The tying together of these two episodes, one reproducing the romance form and the other its central love narrative, show *Star Trek* as romance on multiple levels; within individual stories we find romance structures and themes, yet the overarching episodic structure also echoes romance in its loose connections that bring back almost-forgotten events in the past in ways that do not necessarily serve to conclude them.

The further workings of liminality are effectively described by Victor and Edith Turner:

It has become clear to us that liminality is not only *transition* but also *potentiality*, not only "going to be" but also "what may be," a formulable domain in which all that is not manifest in the normal day-to-day operation of social structures (whether on account of social repression or because it is rendered cognitively "invisible" by prestigious paradigmatic denial) can be studied objectively, despite the often bizarre and metaphorical character of its contents.[53]

Within liminal space, each adventure encodes both the change that comes as its result and also the possibilities it may offer. "What may be" in the Turners's terms is all that exists outside the everyday functioning of the generically constituted real world. Their sense that this liminality can be objectively studied despite its highly subjective and individual nature implies the ways that the "other worlds" reflect back upon the real worlds from which they seem separate. Many *Star Trek* episodes show liminality to work in this double way, as the "outside" experience is transformative within the confines of its own narrative, yet suggests a more systematic or fundamental change, a "what may be," that goes beyond the limits of the individual story.

One such episode is "Darmok,"[54] which creates multiple other worlds through the Enterprise's encounter with the Children of Tama, a peaceful, advanced species with whom they nonetheless cannot communicate. Captain Picard's firm belief that patience and good faith are enough to create dialogue is challenged as the Tamarians open their interaction with a series of mysterious phrases that seem to describe places and people but that, even when processed by the "universal translator," carry no comprehensible meaning. The Tamarians indeed look more alien than many humanoid species on *Star Trek*: mud-colored, hairless, and lizard-like. Both crews are clearly frustrated, but the alien captain, against the protests of his first officer, declares "Darmok and Jilad at Tenagra," and instantaneously he and Captain Picard are beamed down to a mysterious planet to fight a fierce and angry electromagnetic creature. Deanna Troi, the empathic ship's counselor, and Data, the android who has met "some 1,754 different races" in his twenty-six years in Starfleet, attempt to make some sense of the Tamarian language, while Riker, the Enterprise's first officer, dickers with his Tamarian counterpart over the captains' safety and almost starts a war after a foiled rescue attempt of Picard. In the process of fighting the creature, Picard begins to comprehend the Tamarian language, which is made of narrative images based in their mythology; "Darmok and Jilad at Tenagra" refers to understanding created through the facing of a common foe. However, the predatory beast that the two captains fight fatally wounds Dathon during the Enterprise's attempt to beam Picard out; in a very moving scene, Picard learns some of Dathon's cultural stories and then, pressed to tell one of his own, recites the ancient middle eastern tale of *Gilgamesh* as Dathon slowly expires. When a second rescue attempt returns Picard to the Enterprise, he prevents the Tamarians from firing by speaking to them in their own language, mystifying and impressing his own crew. This series of events then itself becomes part of the Tamarian language, the alien crew declaring "Picard and Dathon at El-Adrel" before they leave orbit.

The "going to be" of this narrative lies in what is obvious in its ending; some kind of communication will be established, and Picard and the Enterprise will survive the experience. However, the "what may be" is the possibility of fuller communication and understanding with a species so different from the "us" of the Enterprise that the structure of their language is fundamentally different from all others that the universal translator can understand. The future of Tamarian/Federation relations is not established at the end of the episode, yet, because of the final success of their contact, it is clear that they are "at least not a new enemy" if not "a new friend"; here transition and potentiality meet; the transition between incomprehensibility and comprehension has been enacted in the liminal space of El-Adrel, creating an unresolved potentiality for understanding on the literal level of interspecies relations and the more metaphoric level of interaction in general. Despite its epic references (presumably the story of "Darmok and Jilad" has more in common with *Gilgamesh* than it does with *Sir Gawain*), the structure and movement of "Darmok" nevertheless replicate those of the medieval romance. Picard's experience affects him; again, he is alone at the end of the episode, holding the Tamarian knife given to him by Dathon and staring at the stars, the *Star Trek* shorthand for profound thought. Uncertain whether he would be able to sacrifice himself for the sake of greater communication, yet aware that a culture's own stories are essential for self-understanding, Picard is once again transformed by his unique experience outside of the real world of his own ship.

Clearly, the liminal worlds of romance and science fiction have a great deal in common with each other. Jameson's description of the intersection of real and liminal contains charged language: "in contrast to realism, its [romance's] inner-worldly objects such as landscape or village, forest or mansion—mere temporary stopping places on the lumbering coach or express-train itinerary of realistic representation—are somehow transformed into folds in space, into discontinuous pockets of homogeneous time and heightened symbolic closure."[55] All he needs to do to include science fiction is to add a spaceship to his traveling units; the movement between the real world (court, starship) and these liminal localities are exactly the discontinuous space folds encountered in both manifestations of romance, and create the heightened meaning that Jameson's reading suggests, particularly in his assumption that "worldness" is essential. While Chrétien's Kingdom of Görre, Haut Desert, and the many strange new worlds that the Starship Enterprise encounters seem to present an unreality that plays by different sets of rules, these lands outside society rarely have the last word, while at the same time influencing what that last word is or means. They are bound by their own sets of rules and their own hierarchies that construct orders of behavior and power. Starfleet, no less than the courtly world, is ultimately confirmed by these stories; although it is repeatedly set in contrast to the liminal and imaginary worlds of adventure, it rarely ends up subservient to them. To again echo Jameson on the twelfth century, "social and spatial isolation was overcome, and the feudal nobility became conscious of itself as a universal class or 'subject of history,' newly endowed with codified ideology"; as a result, "romance in its original strong form may then be understood as an imaginary 'solution'" to a problem of conflicting ideologies; particulary in its projection of "evil" onto a figure (generally a hostile knight) who ultimately buys into the system and is "reinserted into the unity of social class," losing his "sinister unfamiliarity."[56] The internal, magical world of romance thus serves to confirm its society's values and indoctrinate those who would oppose it into its assumptions. Instead, liminal space (or Outer Space) becomes a place that confirms the assumptions of romance reality, showing the strength of its values and the importance of its ethical system. At many levels, *Star Trek* also presents a system in which possibilities are explored as a means to show the superiority and often supremacy of the ultimately conservative values the show embodies through Starfleet and the crew of the Enterprise.

Ilsa Bick calls this a "Master Narrative," suggesting that "not only is this 'master' template the mold from which all future texts surrounding *Star Trek* are formed, these texts must pay homage to these implicit constructions just as every new show must continually reference and revere Gene Roddenberry, the 'Great Bird of the Galaxy.'"[57] One of the Enterprise's many purposes in its rescue missions is to demonstrate the superior set of cultural codes that drive it by rescuing victims from untenable situations or liberating them from other dangerous powers.[58] Often ambiguous, these "cultural codes" generally value diplomacy over violence, freedom over constraint, in theory, democracy over totalitarian politics, although the profoundly hierarchical nature of Starfleet and its ships covertly challenges that assumption. While some of these reiterated values do include "choice" and "consent," particularly in the rape narratives that Sarah Projansky explores, the structure of the narratives repeatedly "naturalize his [Picard's] and the Federation's superiority over both women and other species. In short, *The Next Generation* renders choice, consent, and women's embodied voices ineffectual and silent and fills that silence with the voice of Federation superiority."[59] Rescue missions, as inherent plot elements of both romance and science fiction, allow for this kind of statement of values; if the values of Starfleet and those of courtly literature differ, their means of expression often do not. Within the course of his recuperation of his identity, Yvain rescues the ladies in the silk-making sweatshop from the Castle of Infinite Misfortune, defends the Lord of Blackthorn's younger daughter, liberates the castle from Harpin of the Mountain, saves Lunette from imprisonment and certain death, and snatches the lion from the jaws of the snake. And if Yvain's quests create a break from Arthur's court to which he does not return, he does take up residence as the protector of the Spring and thus leader of his own community whose own failings in chivalry (they cannot defend the Spring themselves) suggests the necessity for courtly order to be imposed to prevent their ultimate downfall.

These apparently selfless deeds, however, serve primarily as gestures that help Yvain restore his reputation for all the values the Arthurian court holds dear—prowess, courtesy, bravery, loyalty, and honor. Frederick Goldin views courtly literature as containing "a revealing picture of how the best educated and most powerful secular class in the Middle Ages regarded itself and justified its existence; for in this story it must have recognized its own ideal image."[60] In courtly lyric and narrative, love is the locus for the perfection of the values that define the courtier: "in longing and service he becomes more skillful at arms, more graceful in song, more generous, more decorous, more humble, more noble. Seen this way, courtly love was an ethical system, intended to perfect and justify the courtly class by depicting its ideal."[61] In these observations, Goldin echoes Auerbach, although Auerbach finds the confirmation of social values primarily in the adventures rather than the love plot of the romances.

In both romance and *Star Trek* an anxiety about chaos lurks in the background, informing the ultimate endorsement of courtly order. In romance, love is figured as both necessary and threatening to the social order; after marrying Enide, Erec becomes so enchanted with domestic life—or at least with lying around with his lady—that he neglects his knightly duty. The feminized Erec is a danger to the court, which forces the second quest that restores him to his "manly" self and allows him to become king of his ancestral lands. Chrétien attributes the motivation for the quest to Enide's need to learn her place and duty, and the emphasis on Enide's silence in the second part clearly consigns her to a secondary position that allows Erec to regain the prowess he lost in an excess of courtesy. In other romances, anxiety appears in the diverse forms of Green Knights, Dragons, Giants, and dangerous forests. Otherness is disruption—in the form of ladies and love, or in other projections of the unknown that are governed by systems different from those of the court—that poses a threat to the court's (often tenuous) order. In *Star Trek*, even the anarchy of individual wills poses a threat to the order established by the military hierarchy of Starfleet. In an early episode, "The Naked Now,"[62] an individual loss of control brought on by a virus (the same virus that caused chaos on the Enterprise in the original series episode "The Naked Time"), threatens the "efficiency, and thus the integrity, of the collective machine. More important, however, it shows a situation where absolute self-determination directly threatens *order*. Ideologically, 'free will' is encoded as 'death,'; 'rank and file' is encoded as 'life.'"[63] Much of that chaos was sexual, as the Captain and the Doctor nearly acted on a mutual attraction, and Tasha Yar, the Security Officer, had sex with Data the Android; everyone acted drunken and willful, upsetting the balance of power, professionalism, and collectivity. The casting aside of rank, implying a potential equality, posed the episode's principal threat; by the end of the hour, however, a treatment was found and everyone returned to their established positions. Order, then, provides the cure for chaos, the reestablishment of Starfleet's primary values being the positive "reality" against which the liminal chaos is played.

The Next Generation repeatedly finds confirmation of "Federation" values in its missions, although those values are not always what they seem to be on the surface. For all its apparent investment in liberal values, the

> celebration of difference that helps define the cultural vision of the Enterprise does not go along with a laissez-faire approach to normative and hierarchical structures. On the contrary, the liberal utopia of the Federation is enabled by the enforcement of such structures. The ship is designed to combine access to maximally diverse range of individual and communal pursuits with the rationalized separation of social roles, via both a precise division of labor and a respected chain of command.[64]

Much as in romance, in which the seeming openness and mobility are finally contained by courtly structures, in *Star Trek*, the Federation's seeming democratic and liberal sensibilities are actually confined within intense structures of restraint. In the face of other, problematic systems, the Enterprise and its crew must repeatedly demonstrate the superiority—and indeed the necessity—of these defining values. Indeed, this theme echoed throughout the show's first season. In the evocatively named "Code of Honor,"[65] the Enterprise crew pits its idea of "civilization" against that of the Ligonians. In one of its most grotesquely racist and orientalist portrayals,[66] the Ligonians, played entirely by African Americans in Arabian Nights get-ups, appear to be an advanced but tribal society who still decide disputes of honor by hand-to-hand combat—particularly between women for the right to be the Chief's "First One." As the Ligonian woman is able, through Dr. Crusher's tricks, both to die and survive combat with one of the Enterprise officers, her honor is served; however, this outcome is cast in negative comparison to the more diplomatic methods of the Enterprise crew. A few episodes later, in "The Last Outpost,"[67] a mystical figure, the Tkon Portal Guard, who bears an uncanny resemblance to the Green Knight, tests Commander Riker through a challenge, but lets him off in the end because he is impressed by Riker's wisdom and Federation ethics, which allows the rescue of the Enterprise and a Ferengi ship. In "Justice,"[68] Captain Picard argues ethics with a figure claiming to be the Edo people's God and finally convinces him that when laws are absolute, there can be no real justice, thus saving Wesley Crusher from punishment. And the list goes on. Noting that "fiction as a genre is not necessarily freer from the ideological imperatives of the culture it describes than more explicitly didactic textual forms," Lee Heller considers the utopian impulses at work in *Star Trek*.[69] Although she ascribes at least some of the show's didactic nature to the culture of television, it is also produced by its genre; as narrative forms that function to confirm the culture that produces them, or at least confirm the values it hopes to uphold, both romance and science fiction serve often to reproduce themselves, showing the superiority of their ethics in the face of dangerous alternatives.

The underlying rhetoric of alien races further suggests the projection of Starfleet values in contrast to the "otherness" of liminal encounters. Jeffrey Weinstock sees a division of *Star Trek* aliens into two groups that I will call the "primitive" and the "uptight"; the former (such as the Klingons) need to learn emotional restraint and the latter (such as the Vulcans) need to learn to "loosen up"; Weinstock notes, "through this universe of inadequate alien other travels controlled and duty bound Captain Picard, exemplifying the virtues of Aristotelian mean and, Christ-like, teaching the barbaric primitive races and the logical, emotionally frigid races he encounters the value of *mercy*."[70] This is not an uncommon trope in romance; for instance, throughout *Erec and Enide*, Erec educates the knights he defeats, showing them their uncourtly ways and sending them back to Queen Guenevere as prisoners. He also exhibits mercy in his reluctance to kill these knights, although the suggestion that they would quite happily kill him suffuses Chrétien's poem. When Erec defeats Ydier of Nutt, he lectures him:

> . . .tu sofris ton nain anrievre
> ferir la pucele ma dame;
> grant viltance est de ferir fame.
> Ed moi après referi il;
> Molt me tennis lors anpor vil:
> Trop grant oltrage asez feïs,
> Quant tu tel oltrage veïs,
> Si le sofris et sit e plot
> D'une tel fauture et d'un bot
> Qui feri la pucele et moi.

[. . .you let
Your haughty dwarf strike
My queen's maid. What a savage
Deed, striking a woman!
And then he did it to me.
You took me for some sort of serf:
What vile arrogance, to see
Such an outrage and, silent, allow
It to happen, and even take
Delight in watching that miserable
Midget insult the girl
And me].[71]

Showing him the error of his ways, Erec sends the knight, his lady, and his dwarf to Camelot—the place of true courtliness—as punishment; Ydier willingly goes and surrenders to the queen, bowing gracefully and saying "vaincu m'a d'armes et conquis" [I am vanquished], showing he has finally learned something about humility.[72] Erec later teaches the count the error of his ways, once again after defeating him in combat; revealing his own guilty attempt to abduct Enide, the count says, "sor moi en est venuz li max, / que fos feisoie et deslëax / et traits et forssenez. / Onques ne fu de mere nez / miaudres chevaliers de cestui" [I / was a traitor, disloyal, false, / Crazed by my wild treason. / No man born of woman / Is a better knight than this one].[73] While much more intrinsic to the feudal culture described here, the uncourtly knights and counts reiterate the superiority of the Arthurian court and the chivalric system it upholds; by acknowledging their bad behavior and the inherent superiority of Erec, its representative, they are assimilated into the system, their rebelliousness having been vanquished. When Weinstock says of *Star Trek*, "it is taken as self-evident that all alien cultures, if they do not already, will understand and recognize the obvious superiority of human parameters such as beliefs in the ideas of individual responsibility and equity, and the experiences of guilt and compassion,"[74] he could just as well be talking about Chrétien's romance. Even if the aliens are more distinctly other than Chrétien's rebel knights, they still reflect the Enterprise's status back on itself, and by accepting its superior principles, begin the process of integration, often made literal by their culture's eventual assimilation into the United Federation of Planets. The knights (and other less human creatures) that Erec encounters ultimately all accept his superiority on moral as well as militaristic terms, seeing the errors of their own ways and choosing his "Camelot" values (morality, kindness to ladies, guilt [for sinners] and compassion) instead. This submission to Erec's whole system is revealed most overtly after he defeats the giant and saves Cador, who declares:

> . . .Franz chevaliers,
> tu es mes sire droiuriers;
> mon seignor vuel feire de toi,
> et par reason faire le doi,
> que tu m'as sauvee la vie;
> l'ame me fust del cors partie
> a grief tormant et a maritre.
>
> . . .
>
> Sire, je te voel fere homage:
> Toz jors mez avoec vos irai,
> Con mon seignor vos servirai.
>
> [Good knight, you are now
> My lord, my master in everything
> By right and reason together,
> For my life belongs to you,
> Who saved it before they could snatch
> The soul right out of my body.
> . . .I wish
> To follow you the rest
> Of my life, go wherever
> You go, and serve you always.][75]

Since Cador is basically a good fellow but still submits to Erec's rule, the primacy of Camelot's way of doing things is clearly revealed. Erec's quest through Logres, defeating evil and educating knights in true chivalry thus prefigures Captain Picard saving alien races from themselves and educating them in the values and hierarchies of Starfleet.

Throughout romance, the hierarchies that love and adventure temporarily upset are reconfirmed. At the end of *Eric and Enide*, the couple returns from their second quest triumphant, ready to assume the mantle of official and public leadership. *Sir Gawain and the Green Knight* returns to Arthur's court, confirming its centrality, even while questioning it. Yvain returns to defend his spring, taking up his role as lord of Laudine's manor. In "Lay le Freine," the lovely orphan without status is revealed to be the daughter of a Lord, fit to marry her lover and play her public role. In this same sense, the duties and responsibilities of rank are always upheld on *Star Trek*; the captain may be shaken, abducted, or possessed, but in the end he is always the captain, and his crew is always at his command.[76] Although different in certain ways, the cultures of romance and *Star Trek* are both predicated on rigid systems of order and control, which, upturned by the events of their stories, are nevertheless reasserted at their conclusions.

This reproduction of external values further develops in the presentation of gender within both the romance and science fiction. Within the construct of the quest in medieval romance, the woman is that which is sought, both the narrative center and its goal. As a desired object she is very powerful, and this power is enacted "In multiple ways"; because she creates the hero's needs and thus controls them, she appears to control him, as evidenced by the common trope of the lady who can "save or spill" her lover by saying "yes" or "no." In discussing romance, Susan Crane finds that "gender and genre are not simply analogous but intersecting constructions," and that "Gender provides a way of reading aspects of the genre beyond courtship alone. Social hierarchies, magic, adventure, and less salient operations are unclear in isolation from it."[77] That social hierarchies, magic, and adventure are uniquely tied to science fiction as well only adds to the sense that in the later genre, the earlier lives again. An examination of gender in *Star Trek* shows a similar intertwined quality between the generic features of the narrative and the roles of men and women within it; in brief, they define each other. At first glance, *Star Trek* seems to provide more equal roles for women, in concert with its futuristic sensibility, just as at first glance, women in romance seem to enjoy greater freedom of movement, power, and voice than that offered to them in other medieval genres. A second glance, however, suggests a less optimistic picture, as these possibilities reveal themselves to be in the service of much more traditional and repressive conventions, coercing where they appear to emancipate. Romance is concerned with mutability, constructed out of slippery relationships between gender and power; women are given a voice, and even access to public and private authority; in the process, men's roles in relationship to women can slip and change within a dynamic genre. That dynamism, however, is still constrained within a set of conventions: female characters are both essential yet inherently marginalized; the power structures of love ordain women's superiority yet take it away as soon as they are "conquered" by their lovers; and public power is permissible for women only if they are not also the story's heroines. The counterexamples prove the pervasive nature of this pattern; Lanval's lady cannot exist in the "real" world of the court for all her power, and at the end, Lanval must leave Carleon for Avalun, riding behind her to echo the submissive place of the man in the liminal world, both that of romance narrative and that to which they are returning. As pure fairy, she—and the love in which she holds complete power—can only function in the mystical alternative world to that of the court. More strikingly, Chrétien's Guenevere wields enormous power over him in *Lancelot*, yet it becomes one of the poem's problems and potentially a reason that Chrétien left it unfinished (although this is pure conjecture). Not only their rarity, but the ways that they disrupt the usual romance pattern show how inherent the final submission of the heroine is to the genre. The heroine's status thus becomes "a kind of glass ceiling that defines roles, positions, and possibilities" creating a state of double confinement.[78] Because the genre produces limits on gender, gender limits the genre, affecting the kinds of stories it can tell. These two competing forces result in fixed narrative controls predicated by the narrative's gender expectations.

Women on *Star Trek: The Next Generation* appear to have transcended the roles made available to their counterparts on the original series; in place of the mini-skirted nurse and communications officer, the Enterprise D boasts of Dr. Beverly Crusher and Lt. Commander Deanna Troi, ship's counselor. This certainly seems a step upward; indeed, Marleen Barr takes an optimistic view of the situation, noting that in science fiction, "writers are not hindered by the constraints of patriarchal social reality, they can imagine presently impossible possibilities for women. Their genre is ideally suited for exploring the potential of women's changing roles."[79] However, when one explores those roles in the context of particular stories, it increasingly becomes clear that Barr's vision is not played out in *Star Trek*. The female doctor is really nothing new; the Enterprise women fulfill the same roles as many peripheral women in romance—indeed in *Yvain*, Lunette serves as confidante and counselor, while the combined medicinal efforts of Morgan le Fay and her ointment-bearing friends cure Yvain from his madness and put him on the path to redemption. *Tristan* also shows these same patterns; the first Isolde, queen of Ireland, is the only person who can heal Tristan of the wound he receives at Morold's hands, and the much-abused Brangane serves as confidante to both Isolde and Tristan throughout the different versions. In a sense, the traditionality of this role for women opens up one of the problems of Deanna Troi's and Beverly Crusher's presentation; both are more often treated as women than as doctors, as the stories about them often involve romance; Beverly's maternal concern for her son; or Deanna's intuition, either saving the day or going on overload.

The even more peripheral female characters on the Enterprise fulfill equally traditional roles: Keiko O'Brien, for all her botanical studies, serves primarily as the bride of Transporter Chief Miles O'Brien and the mother of their child, Molly (as a bridge character on the next series, *Star Trek: Deep Space 9*, Keiko produces another child and becomes a school teacher for the station's children); Guinan, played by Whoopi Goldberg, is another confidante, this time associated with nurturing through her role as ship's bartender. Donna Reid-Jeffrey characterizes the series' women without mincing words, "All crew women and most alien females are typified as irrational, emotional, subservient, disposable, and manipulated easily with sex. In contrast to the men, women are clearly defined in their roles. Emancipation does not seem to have come for the women of the future."[80]

Reid-Jeffrey is unwilling to give the show any credit for trying, yet her sense that the overarching progress that the show professes to demonstrate is highly gendered is clear. Susan Hines's description of *StarTrek*'s female characters overtly, if unconsciously, replicates the structures of romance: "Women characters are portrayed as empowered and self-assertive, but by the end of their respective episodes all have succumbed to or have been destroyed by the greater power of patriarchy and its constraints."[81] One of many examples is the episode entitled "Liaisons."[82] As part of a cultural exchange, Captain Picard welcomes two Iyaaran diplomats aboard the Enterprise and then heads off to their planet with one more diplomat to meet their leader. While Deanna Troi plays out her nurturing role by introducing the gentle Loquel to various indulgent chocolate desserts, Picard's shuttle crashes on a strange planet. He awakens to find himself rescued by Anna, an apparent survivor of another crash, who cares for him inside a crashed freighter. Sent to retrieve part of his shuttle, she destroys it instead and confesses that she loves Picard. After some sympathy, he discovers that her sophisticated medical care is actually holding him captive and that he's not really injured badly; she then disappears. The Iyaarian diplomat arrives, but before that Anna threatens to jump off a cliff. Picard then discovers that Voval the diplomat and Anna are the same; Voval has taken on her form to study the human emotion of love, which his people find an alien concept.

In this episode—admittedly not one of *The Next Generation*'s strongest—Anna appears to be the knight in shining armor who rescues Picard from danger, although she is also feminine, providing him with shelter and care. However, she increasingly shows herself to be irrational, emotional, and flaky, preventing man's movement (a kind of simulacrum of Dido) rather than allowing it to proceed, interfering with his attempt to contact the Enterprise. Starting out as the noble savior, she quickly proves to be a threat. Finally, the rationalism of man takes over, and Anna returns to her original form, the emotionally limited, male Voval, thus restoring order and allowing Picard to resume his place. The brief window of potentiality in which Anna appears as a self-motivated, active figure is rapidly closed when she becomes a problematic force that needs to be restrained. This narrative progress is replicated in "Silicon Avatar," an episode striking in gender terms for several reasons. In this story, Dr. Kila Marr, a scientist, is tracking a "Crystalline Entity" that has killed her son Renny. A powerful and chilly exemplum of the mad scientist feminized, Marr is angry at Data because his brother, the emotional android Lore, apparently lured the Entity to her son's home planet, but she rapidly becomes forgiving when Data proves to have all the colonists' memories stored in his databank and can even replicate her son's voice. Although Picard tries negotiating with the Entity through a tacheon pulse, and it seems to be working, Marr raises the frequency of the pulse and shatters the Entity. The Silicon Avatar is ultimately Marr herself; like the entity, she is cold, irrational, and kills without warning; at the end of the episode, Data suggests that her son would be sorry that her mother had ruined her career in this manner.

In "Silicon Avatar," two kinds of romance anxiety about women are revealed. As the scientist, Marr does occupy a position of intellectual power, a role usually offered only to men, such as the original series' Mr. Spock or *The Next Generation*'s Mr. Data. As a Vulcan and an Android, both are essentially emotionless, which Dr. Marr also first appears to be; however, hers turns out to be an aberration, a rejection of "rightful" femininity, brought on by revenge fantasies. In this respect she is like Morgan Le Fay, the ambiguous figure of many medieval romances; in *Yvain* she supplies the ointment that cures the hero's insanity, but in *Sir Gawain and the Green Knight*, Bertilak says of Morgan the Goddess: "Ho wayned me þis wonder your wyttez to reue, / For to haf greued Gaynour and gart hir to dyȝe" [She put this shape upon me to puzzle your wits / To afflict the fair queen, and frighten her to death].[83] In the latter case, Morgan is vengeful and spiteful, much like both Dr. Kila Marr and another narrative figure of twisted femininity, Grendel's mother. Furthermore, Bertilak's description follows on Gawain's speech defining women as temptresses and destroyers of men. Dr. Marr, then, becomes a dark figure, seemingly calm but ruled by thwarted concern and emotion, endangering men in her own revenge plot. The most striking aspect of this episode, however, is the idea of dangerous femininity projected through the doubling of Marr and the Crystalline Entity itself. As cold yet irrational destroyers, both suggest a profound anxiety about female power that must be tamed, and if not tamed, then destroyed. Although the official account of the title suggests that "avatar" was understood as "the appearance on earth of a god in bodily form," or "a repository of knowledge," referring to Data,[84] clearly the Crystalline Entity and Dr. Marr are avatars of each other; Marr an earthbound example of dangerous womanhood who, in destroying her enemy, destroys herself, so allowing masculine rationality to reign supreme.

Indeed, this anxiety about rapacious femininity lurks in the backgrounds—and often the foregrounds—of several episodes, appearing in various guises. In the episode "Devil's Due,"[85] the Enterprise encounters Ardra, the shape-shifting devil of the planet Ventax II, who has made a pact with the planet's inhabitants—1,000 years of peace and health in return for eternal slavery. After Picard eschews her sexual advances, she makes the Enterprise disappear. Although the planet's leaders are impressed by her illusions and agree to submit to her judgment, the Enterprise crew locates the concealed ship that produces her special effects and exposes her as a con-artist. As in "Silicon Avatar," femininity is linked to destruction and violence, although here it is sexualized, turned into a product of rapacious desire that masculine logic again overcomes.

That the individual episodes of *The Next Generation* are filled with problematic women confirms a prevailing, overarching anxiety about female power; the stories can seem to allow for women's autonomy in multiple ways, but ultimately they return to their more traditional masculinist vision. For instance, "The Drumhead,"[86] one of the program's most watched episodes, creates a powerful woman who seems to be a force for good, Admiral Norah Satie, a noted investigator who comes out of retirement to conduct a probe following an explosion in the Enterprise's dilithium chamber. In her position, she echoes the many female legal figures in romance, most notably the queen and ladies in Chaucer's "Wife of Bath's Tale" or the Lady in Marie de France's "Lanval." Although the story begins by stressing Satie's judicial abilities, she quickly loses control and turns the investigation into a witch-hunt reminiscent of the McCarthy hearings or the Salem Trials, going so far with her inquisition as to accuse Picard himself. Needless to say, her irrational fury, unleashed in an impressive diatribe, shocks everyone, disgusts her superior admiral (a man, of course), and breaks up the trial. "The Drumhead" provides another example of the story giving and taking away female power in true romance form. Like the Queen and ladies who serve as judge and jury in the "Wife of Bath's Tale," the episode postulates a world with women in legal power; however, that power is quickly shown to be too dangerous in a woman's irrational hands and must be taken away. That Satie's true horror reveals itself through uncontrolled speech puts her in a long context of male anxiety regarding women; writing about the Middle Ages, Lee Patterson notes, "anti-feminist literature presents woman as an inveterate and interminable talker, wagging her tongue like the clapper on a bell. And for much of this literature a woman's voice is not merely part of her weaponry but the very mode of her existence, the substance from which she is constituted as well as the means through which she is made manifest."[87] The focus in "The Drumhead" on Satie's angry manipulation of language shows a continuing anxiety about women's speech; true to Patterson's words, Satie's voice is her weapon, her greatest threat, but in the end, it proves her downfall. In the "Wife of Bath's Tale," by comparison, women's speech is at least educative and salvific rather than condemnatory. In some senses, *The Next Generation* is thus shown to be less radical than Chaucer and 1400 C.E. more enlightened than "Stardate 44769.2"; in the "Wife of Bath's Tale," the queen and ladies judge the knight's case fairly and allow him to go free, having learned what women most desire; if the Loathy Lady, his wise counsel, fares less well, at least the structures of power that Chaucer allows endure throughout the length of the tale. In the Federation's universe, even such recurring characters as the evil half-Romulan general Sela, played by Denise Crosby, and the sexually predatory yet comic Lwaxana Troi, mother of the ship's counselor, though less overtly detailed, represent versions of this anxiety about the various kinds of feminine power.

It is impossible to consider the issue of gender and romance in *The Next Generation* without discussion of "The Perfect Mate,"[88] perhaps the series' most problematic portrayal of femininity, in relation to the "Wife of Bath's Tale." At the end of that narrative, the Loathly Lady, having heard the knight's complaints about her age, ugliness, and poverty and having rebutted them at length, asks the knight to choose what he would have her be, foul and faithful or fair and faithless. The knight, unable to select between the two distinct but apparently equal forms of humiliation, answers, "Cheseth yourself which may be moost pleasance / And moost honour to yow and me also,"[89] thus seeming to give her the *maistrye*—the thing that women most desire. However, his apparent yielding of power actually ends hers; she becomes both fair and faithful, the tale noting that she will thus "obey him in everything / that myghte doon hym plesaunce and lyking."[90] There are many readings of the "Wife of Bath's Tale" that view this outcome as a kind of equality;[91] however, the silencing of the lady and her transformation from "Loathy" to "Lovely" in such charged language suggest that she finally becomes the ideal heroine, a projection of masculine desire, confined to her subservient role by the expectations of romance. Women who are old, ugly, and smart cannot be the heroines of romance and cannot reap its rewards; beautiful romance heroines cannot by the same token be self-determined, authoritative, and noisy. Thus, the heroine cannot ultimately be a force within "her" tale; she must be defined by the role to which she is consigned.

This romance coercion is brutally apparent in "The Perfect Mate." The episode opens with the Kriosian ambassador arriving on board the Enterprise with a peace-gift for the people of Volt, with whom they have long been at war. When the Enterprise rescues a pair of Ferengi, a greedy, commerce-obsessed race, trouble ensues, as they attempt to steal the gift, stored in a large, glowing egg. From it emerges Kamala, a beautiful woman in full evening dress, who declares to Captain Picard, "I am for you, Alric of Volt." Kamala turns out to be an "empathic mesomorph," a genetic anomaly born only rarely; the result of her mutation is that she can become whatever any man wants her to be. Bred and educated to be a *Beowulf*-style *frearu-webbe*, or peace weaver, she is prepared to marry Volt's ruler to cement the treaty between the two nations. The ambassador confines her to quarters; however, Dr. Crusher's concern that her exchange for peace is either a form of slavery or prostitution, both of which violate the prime directive, causes Picard to insist that Kamala has freedom to roam around the ship. Her visit to Ten-Forward, the ship's bar, nearly causes chaos; she is alternatively a dance-hall floozie for a group of miners and a rapacious, growling Klingon, acting as each man would have her, playing out a variety of gender and class stereotypes. Finally, Picard requests that Kamala return to her quarters. Finding himself drawn to her because, in his presence, she quotes Shakespeare and discusses Archeology, he tries to avoid her but is stuck attending her after the ambassador is injured in a brawl with the Ferengi. Indeed, Picard must perform key parts of the Kriosian ritual of peace and marriage in the ambassador's place. Although Kamala tells Picard that he is the first man to suggest that she has value in herself, it is unclear whether that statement, too, merely represents another way that she morphs to please him, particularly as she has just said, "But you know me better than you realize. I am independent, forceful, brilliant, and adventurous—exactly as you would have me be, Captain."[92] Alric of Volt finally arrives and confesses that he's more interested in the treaty than the marriage; Kamala tells Picard that she has "bonded" to the starship captain, but because she has thus learned his sense of duty and responsibility, she will go ahead with the marriage to Alric and will still be able to sense and fulfill his desires. The episode ends with the marriage, Kamala repeating her opening line, "I am yours, Alric of Volt."

This episode fails the Gloria Steinam test spectacularly—that if one can't reverse the genders and have the story make sense, it's problematic. It is impossible to imagine a story in which a male "empathic mesomorph" comes aboard the Enterprise, declares, "I am for you, Alricia of Volt," and falls for Deanna Troi—impossible because the whole story requires the prior assumption that women are secondary and exist to fulfill male desire. The episode also fails to understand its own tragedy; instead of dwelling on Kamala's sacrifice in marrying Alric (who is presented as an unattractive little toad), the episode concludes with meditative shots of the sad Picard, making the tragedy his own, in giving up his Perfect Mate. Despite lip service given to the problems of Kamala's enslavement or prostitution, the story finally endorses her sacrifice, claiming that it is, at some level, her choice. As Lee Haller observes, "Kamala quite clearly appears as the male ideal of female subordination through self-transformation,"[93] a statement that sounds equally at home in relation to the ending of the "Wife of Bath's Tale" as it does of the "The Perfect Mate." The male desire for the selfless woman ultimately wins out; Picard may mouth the "necessity that Kamala have an autonomous subjectivity, but nevertheless falls in love with her precisely insofar as she does not."[94] While Kamala does exert a certain sexual power over men, much as the women in medieval romance do, ultimately her "biologically determined 'sense' renders her essentially powerless; she is fundamentally subservient to a man's desire because she is physically unable to form any identity of her own."[95] Like the many medieval heroines she resembles, Kamala must ultimately choose duty, whatever its relationship to desire. Because the romance drives toward marriage—the social integration and control of love—heroines are forced from their world of power, which is predicated on desire, to one in which they function essentially as property. Kamala's marriage is no different; she is suppressed because she is ultimately perilous. Underneath her subservience and lack of self-definintion rest a potential threat to male order and male ideology. The ambassador argues when Picard requests her shipboard freedom, "It's too dangerous. She must remain in her quarters," and later explains, "She's at the height of her sexual allure. Every man on the ship will be fighting over her";[96] as such, she "represents the potential chaos that would result from breaking of institutionalized male bonds; she threatens to undermine the Enterprise's esprit de corps. Like Helen of Troy, to whom she is compared, Kamala undermines relationships between men."[97] Because her presence causes men to act out of desire rather than out of duty, and because those desires may then come into conflict with each other, causing friction and ultimately chaos, Kamala must be confined, first to her quarters, and finally in marriage. She is only safe as an object of exchange; as "the figure of threatening and alluring woman,"[98] she is most easily contained as a valuable, exchangeable commodity. At the moment she attains an autonomous self (at which she is given *maistrye*), she must be married to the other man—duty is safe, desire is not.

"The Perfect Mate" replicates one other quality of courtly literature that shows the ways the genre serves to replicate its own ideologies and desires. In one scene, Kamala speaks to Picard framed in a mirror, where the audience sees her as she views herself. Like the endless mirrors that populate medieval lyric and romance, this is a Mirror of Narcissus; in that sense, the episode suggests that the seductress figure is the creation of men, a reflection of them projected back from a blank, silvered surface. Frederick Goldin, in *The Mirror of Narcissus*, notes, "the lady is a mirror in which everything else is seen."[99] He goes on to argue, "It is for us that she exists. She is to be consulted, like a mirror, by every courtly person. She reflects our future condition, the goal of our striving. She makes visible for us what would otherwise be mere concepts disassociated from experience: *ricor, pretz, cortesia, digz belhs, grans onors*. . . ."[100] Goldin's language reflects his own imbrication in the courtly mentality; by "us" he clearly means men, who, seeing themselves reflected in the lady, find their own prowess, courtesy, beautiful words, and great honor. While the theme of masculine amelioration is not fully explored in "The Perfect Mate," the sense of the woman as mirror of man defines the episode; as a projection of man's desires, she is "the lover's image of his own perfection" in the form of "an honored lady in whom the ideal is considered to be realized."[101] This point is driven home at the end of the episode; serving the captain his favorite "tea, Earl Grey, hot," Dr. Crusher proves herself to be his mirror too. Attempting to explain his unhappiness about Kamala, Picard says, "Who she is changes when the next man comes in the room. And I keep hoping he won't. But of course he does." Wishing that the mirror will always reflect him— he is, after all, reflecting on his own feelings rather than her fate—Picard wishes to keep Kamala for himself but knows he can't. However, it is clear that he doesn't need the Perfect Mate to be reflected back on himself. Giving up on explaining he tells the Doctor, "Perhaps I just needed a shoulder." Beverly responds, "It's always there, Jean-Luc."[102] Goldin quotes Jeanroy's remark, "one is tempted to believe that all the poets loved the same lady";[103] in this episode it is possible to see that, as mirrors of men, all women ultimately are the same lady.

Indeed, the reproduction of romance gender ideology does not confine itself to women from outside the Enterprise. As noted earlier, Beverly Crusher and Deanna Troi fulfill roles traditionally given to women in romance. As these roles are generally peripheral, however, their contexts need to be changed in those episodes that make them heroines. In one striking example, "Sub Rosa,"[104] Beverly is romanced by a ghost who lives in a candle and has seduced female members of her family for over 800 years. This story clearly has a great deal in common with the gothic novel, yet what is most telling about the story is that in order to remain with this ghost, Beverly chooses to resign from Starfleet and take up residence on her grandmother's planet, Caldos IV. Although usually seen in her uniform, Crusher appears in this episode in an odd collection of garments ranging from a tartan floor-length dress to a sexy nightgown and robe. All of this transformation occurs because Beverly experiences "odd nighttime sensations of pleasure";[105] a little romance (including finding her quarters strewn with three hundred camellias) and she's ready to give up her career and autonomy to live in some futuristic nostalgic vision of Auld Scotland. Finally, the ghost is revealed to be an anaphasic plasma being that has used her family as hosts to stay alive and corporeal for generations; he blasts Picard, Data, and Geordi, before Beverly finally decides she has no choice but to destroy the candle and return to her duties. The key point in this silly episode for the present discussion is Beverly's tranformation, which clearly signals that she cannot be a doctor and a romance heroine at the same time. Once again, the coercion of the genre is at work, constraining gender to a specific set of terms. These defining ideas of gender are broached from the opposite direction in an earlier episode; when astrophysicist Nella Darren refuses to give up her (dangerous) job to become Picard's lover, she no longer serves any narrative necessity and must request a transfer from the Enterprise. Her autonomy and talents, which made her attractive to Picard in the first place (as a desirable potential heroine) become problematic when they refuse to be sacrificed to the genre's expectations.[106] Beverly also takes part in one of *The Next Generation's* heteronormative episodes; having fallen in love with Odan, a Trill mediator, she discovers that he has a parasite living inside him. It ultimately turns out that this parasite in fact is Odan; his body is simply a host, and is ailing. After moving the parasite/ Odan into Riker for a while, the Trills send a new body—a woman's. Crusher, claiming she can't adjust to this constant changing, breaks off the relationship.[107] While it might be possible to consider this episode in light of the gender slippage so common in medieval romance, it fundamentally serves to underline the show's compulsory heterosexuality. Just as marriage clears up any gender confusion within the medieval text, here Beverly's choice puts the kibosh on any alternative sexualities. Once again, romance expectations clash with the story's liberal and utopian assumptions, suggesting that the future may well look a great deal like the past.

In fact, Dr. Crusher's role seems primarily to be found in confirming the values *The Next Generation* ostensibly likes to deny. In the final episode, "All Good Things. . .,"[108] Crusher replicates this romance gender pattern completely. In the future that the final episode projects, Beverly is "Captain Picard," having married and divorced Jean-Luc in the interim. Picard himself is infirm and unwell, possibly suffering from hallucinations brought on by an advancing disease. As in romance, the woman is given access to power and authority, and with it, she scolds her former captain and husband. However, she is commanding a ship in trouble; her small medical vessel is literally about to explode. Couching this in comic-book terms, Marleen Barr notes, "Beverly immediately goes from commanding to becoming Lois Lane rescued by Superman (in the form of the Enterprise commanded by Admiral Riker). Beverly was Superman for one brief shining moment. But her exploding ship burns far brighter than her time as captain."[109] If Beverly can, for one moment, question patriarchal power and become a self-authorizing figure, so too must she ultimately be confined; the romance can give women power, but it cannot continue to depict the women who wield it.

The Next Generation's more overtly feminized character, Deanna Troi, is provided even less access to power than Dr. Crusher; as the empathic Betazoid counselor, Troi's abilities are located in an exaggerated form of "female intution." In fact, Lynne Joyrich feels that Deanna "personifies the professionalization of femininity itself. Valued for her ability simply to sense feelings and incite them in others [rather] than for anything she might do. . ., Deanna is employed for her pure emotive capabilities: she embodies rather than performs work per se."[110] Exemplifying the traditionally feminine traits of empathy, intuition, and emotion, she is all that is womanly, rarely even carrying a phaser on away missions. For the first five and a half seasons of the show, Troi's femininity was further feminized—and indeed eroticized—through her costume; instead of wearing the standard Starfleet uniform, she alternated between several brightly colored, low-cut jumpsuits that emphasized her figure and drew attention to her difference from the more asexually dressed remainder of the crew, a distinction furthered when, midway through the series, several dresses were added to her wardrobe. She is further stereotyped throughout the series by her obsession with chocolate; this is oddly doubly suggestive, figuring both a bodily sensuality and a childish attachment to sweets. Both associations serve to undermine her power, on the one hand making her physical rather than intellectual, and on the other hand infantilizing her. The connection to food also domesticates her, albeit not so overtly as an interest in cooking would. Her difference from the others "illustrates a double meaning of her species and her gender,"[111] drawing attention away from her as a member of the group and highlighting her contrast to them. As in the romance, the woman is constructed as other, different, and separate, something to be desired and conquered. She may be a mirror or a projection of the knight's desires, but she is also that off which they bounce and therefore distinct from the male hero.

As a result of her difference, the stories about Troi more frequently cast her as an object of desire and work staunchly to neutralize her power. Sarah Projansky notes that "the show undermines Troi's authority and her voice, both of which are located specifically—and only—in a bioessentially feminine body"[112] by making her the focal character in a series of rape narratives: in "The Child,"[113] she is impregnated in her sleep by a mysterious force (a glowing white light); in "Violations"[114] and "Man of the People,"[115] she is put into a coma by two distinct varieties of mental probe. In "The Child," despite concerns about security and the nature of the invader, Troi announces that she's having the baby; in one particular shot, the captain is called to Sick Bay to see her, and she stares mutely at him, her rounded belly turning her body into a speaking text. Her easy birth—an odd version of the nativity—produces a seemingly harmless child who ages eight years in a day. Unfortunately, this life force who has assumed a human body just to learn more about humans (which includes playing with puppies) causes a plague sample to grow and nearly burst its container, threatening the crew; the child reverts to his real, incorporeal form, as a tearful Deanna watches him leave. Throughout the story, she is entirely defined by her pregnancy; until the final moment, she makes what Projansky calls the "maternal, bodily choice"[116] over the "Starfleet Officer" choice, risking her crewmates and herself.

In "Man of the People," Troi serves both as a silent body and as a projection of masculine anxiety, becoming one of the "Femme Sauvage" figures previously considered. In the episode, an ambassador joins the Enterprise to be taken to peace talks aimed at halting an interplanetary war. After the woman with him, who he claims is his mother, dies, Troi begins aging rapidly and acting with amorous abandon. The woman has accused Troi of having designs on Alkar, the ambassador; however, upset at her outburst, Troi aids Alkar in his planet's funeral ritual. She is left feeling somewhat off-kilter, with her libido running out of control. Seducing a young ensign after Riker and Alker refuse her advances, she eventually stabs Captain Picard. After some medical investigation, it appears that Alkar has imposed a process on Troi that deposited all his negative thoughts and feelings into her in order to clear his mind for negotiations; his "mother" was, in fact, his previous victim. Picard fakes the now aged and hysterical Troi's death to break her "link" with Alkar, leaving him to die in agony, and Troi is restored to youth, health, and control. Troi's silence in her "death" speaks again of the dangerous woman, whose rapacious sexuality is destructive to others but ultimately to herself. The show seems quite unconscious of the overdetermined nature of this production; as the repository for a man's "darker thoughts and unwanted emotions," women become sex-crazed monsters, quickly turning old and ugly (like Dorian Gray's picture) before they can do any real harm. Deanna reverses the pattern of the "Wife of Bath's Tale," changing from the young and beautiful heroine to the Loathly Lady, a figure who turns out to be just as impotent as her lovely counterpart. As an old, shriveled thing, Deanna can't kill Picard when she stabs him; only he can "kill" and silence her. Adding to the monstrous sense of this portrayal of femininity gone mad is a "Bride of Frankenstein" hairdo, replete with white stripe, which Deanna sports in the process of her aging. Identifying her with a creature from classic horror shows her to be a creation of man run amok, the ultimate avatar of the sexual and controlling Morgan le Fay.

Deanna's romance function reaches its apex in the show's last season and a half; in "Chain of Command,"[117] under the temporary command of another captain, Deanna is asked to wear her uniform like the rest of the crew. Her role during the episode does seem less overtly feminized, particularly as Captain Jellico addresses her as "Commander" (her official rank is Lieutenant Commander). However, when Picard returns, he calls her "Counselor Troi," indicating his assumption of her place on the Enterprise, "marked not in terms of military designation but rather in terms of a 'feminized' profession."[118] However, this costume change does lead in subsequent shows to greater vacillation between feminized and authoritative positions; although Troi's degeneration into a sexual harpie in "Man of the

People" does follow "Chain of Command," and she still is cast in several romances, she also takes the Bridge Test in "Thine Own Self,"[119] elevating her rank to Commander and giving her increased responsibilities, including night watch. Troi gains the most authority in "Face of the Enemy,"[120] in which she wakes up to find herself kidnapped and on board a Romulan ship, disguised as a Tal Shiar (CIA) special intelligence officer. She is being used by an underground resistance group to help smuggle out three defectors to the Federation. Forced to play a tough, cold, militaristic leader, Troi successfully hatches a plan to beam the defectors to the Enterprise. After several battles of wills with the ship's equally tough (yet female) Captain, Troi manages to carry out the plot until the final moment, when she is beamed back to the Enterprise just in time. Interestingly enough, this story was planned for Dr. Crusher, until the writers decided that Troi's empathic powers would add to the plot.[121] Marina Sirtis, who played Troi, claimed that this episode was her favorite, since she was kidnapped because she was an empath, not a woman,[122] and noted her own impatience with her perpetual casting as the "chick." For all the force of this episode, the last two seasons continued a tense balance, giving Troi more to do, but putting much of that increased attention in the context of love plots. After an episode-long affair with Will Riker's long-lost double,[123] she began a relationship with the Klingon security officer, Lt. Worf. The various images of this relationship included domestic scenes of their marriage (in a parallel universe) with Troi first flirting with and then soothing an anxious, phase-shifting Worf,[124] a jealous Deanna nearly killing herself (in another phase shift) because of an empathic imprint,[125] a genetically reverting Worf-as-Giant-Bug attempting to mate with the Deanna-as-Fish by biting her, and finally scenes of their courtship in the series' final episode. Once again, the series offers women power yet then takes it away, offering domesticity in its place; Commander Deanna Troi, Romulan Double-Agent, is once again returned to her conventional role.

Calling Troi's significant fashion changes "a result of an incident somehow indicative of war—war, at least between an individual and a collective identity,"[126] Amelia Hastie reveals the role of women in romance—constructed individually within love plots, they are ultimately assumed into the collective feudal (or Starfleet) identity through marriage (or incorporation), a kind of assimilation brought on by the movement of an ostensible individual freedom leading toward a corporate goal. As Hastie points out, through wearing her uniform, "the extreme imbalances in Troi's fashions—the excessive sexual garb that precedes it [in 'Man of the People'] and the butch costume that follows it [in 'Face of the Enemy']—seem to reach an equilibrium or find 'an exchangeable truth' in her wearing of the standard Starfleet uniform. In other words, after her body has been ravaged as a 'receptacle' in 'Man of the People' and later as a Romulan in 'Face of the Enemy,' we hardly notice that Troi has been successfully assimilated into the uniform Enterprise 'collective.'"[127] As the rapacious sexual 'virago' and the hypermasculine commander, Troi's space wanderings have invited her to play out complex relationships to power in her feminine form, yet at the same time, they return her to defined, fixed positions within the greater system; with clothing marking her as a member of Starfleet, and her title "Counselor" firmly in place to determine her function, she has been brought back into the world of hierarchized gender authority. Her earlier eroticized costume figured her mainly in sexual terms, stemming from a "collection of necessary conventions"[128] to cast her as the romance heroine; her later outfit, in turn, shows the ways that her gender identity has been co-opted. For all the options she was able to explore in the final seasons, many of which gave her access to increased power and authority, in the final episode, the roles she plays reveal a continued assertion of gender conventions. In the episode's future, Captain Beverly Picard's ship may blow up, but Deanna Troi has died, causing a rift between Riker and Worf who were competing for her love; in its present, she is at the center of the ill-fated love triangle, the episode opening with her on a date with the Klingon, whom she is continuing in her attempt to civilize. In the final scene, the entire cast plays a game of poker, joined by the Captain for the first time; although in the last line he declares, "The sky's the limit," this is clearly not so for the female crew. Deanna may be a member of the group, but she's there to listen, to console, and to be desired. As much as she stands out on the Enterprise, she is "placed within its collective control."[129] In the end, she is Lunette and Laudine (although perhaps less clever than either), heroine and confidante, consigned to the roles she has been playing since the twelfth century.[130]

Star Trek seems destined to repeat the patterns of a medieval genre in multiple ways. Set in a world of adventure and liminal space, it follows its antecedent in its structures and conventions, playing with romance's mutability while confirming its constraints. Central to the romance world are the self's encounters with the other, itself a kind of liminal territory between worlds, as is further figured by setting these encounters outside the "real" world. Matilda Tomaryn Bruckner notes that "much has been said in recent years about the alterity of the Middle English romance,"[131] and while it is dangerous to suggest that medieval and contemporary culture are the same, a close examination of *Star Trek* suggests that "then" and "now" are rather closer than Bruckner suggests. The "lessons" and "profound delights" of romance that engage Bruckner evidently continue to engage contemporary viewers in an only superficially altered form. Indeed, her brief reference to the *Star Wars* films, which she compares to the Vulgate cycle, shows her own sense of the relationship between medieval and modern manifestations of the same genre.[132] If Jameson is correct that the underlying impulse of all contemporary works of art comprehends "our deepest fantasies about the nature of social life, both as we live it now and as we feel in our bones it ought to be lived,"[133] Star Trek, through the construction of its ideals, echoes contemporary values and reiterates them in ways meant to make realizing their potential possible. Reading this as a kind of "fantasy bribe" that promises people what they desire without necessarily ever providing it, Jameson suggests:

> To rewrite the concept of a management of desire in social terms now allows us to think repression and wish fulfillment together within the unity of a single mechanism, which gives and takes alike in a kind of psychic compromise or horse-trading, which strategically arouses fantasy content within careful symbolic containment structures which defuse it, gratifying intolerable, unrealizable, properly imperishable desires only to the degree to which they can again be laid to rest.[134]

This formulation describes the contemporary art of Star Trek and the medieval art of romance equally well. As wish-fulfillment fantasies, both manage desire within a single text, offering possibilities and reinforcing repressive structures at the same time. Liminality provides the spaces for fantasy, in contrast to the real worlds of containment that surround it; in liminal space, there is room for the exploration of potential, but the real world co-opts it, putting it to rest. In the strange new worlds of Star Trek and the dark forests of romance, the dialogue between potential and restraint takes place, propagating adventure while retaining very traditional values. The vitality of the modern genre, as the medieval, rests on the consent of its audience to accept such restraint; as we shall see in regard to the Star Wars trilogy, even the liminal potentiality of StarTrek may be compromised without breaking the deal.

CHAPTER 4

REXQUE QUONDAM [THE FORESEEABLE] FUTURUS: *STAR WARS* AND THE COMMERCE OF ARTHURIAN ROMANCE

With Star Wars *I consciously set out to re-create myths and the classic mythological motifs. I wanted to use those motifs to deal with issues that exist today. The more research I did, the more I realized that the issues are the same ones that existed 3,000 years ago. That we haven't come very far emotionally.*

—George Lucas, *Time*, 1999

There is no Arthurian "now." At every stage of the Arthurian tradition, the narrative moment, the moment of the tale's telling, hesitates between a past irrevocably lost and a future return forever awaited. As in almost every story, the Arthurian narrator speaks of a finite moment that has ended; yet this same narrator also lives before a vaguely predicted messianic return of the king. Such narration hovers then between its historic past and its apocalyptic future.

—Christopher Baswell and William Sharpe, *The Passing of Arthur*, 1986

HIC IACET ARTHURUS REX QUONDAM REXQUE FUTURUS.

—Sir Thomas Malory, *Works*, 1971

One of the most popular and prolific movie franchises of the last thirty years, George Lucas's *Star Wars* at first appears to be a political and aesthetic response to the particular landscape of the late 1970s and early 1980s. The aftermath of the monetary and oil crises, defeat in Vietnam, the disillusions of Watergate, and their concomitant uncertainty accompanied a trend in filmmaking designed to puncture illusions and disenchant their audiences. At first, Lucas' films' success seemed to be a reassertion of illusions in a particularly anxious time; however the success of the franchise despite the films getting worse and worse reviews suggests that the films respond to something general to the last thirty years rather than a specific cultural moment. The opening line of the first film, *Star Wars Episode IV: A New Hope*, the now famous "A long time ago in a Galaxy far, far away," offers a kind of answer; the films provide a carefully constructed fairy tale that may have begun in 1977 but continues to grow; indeed, in the words of John Seabrook, *Star Wars* may be "the most carefully tended secular story on Earth."[1] It is a single story, "a finite expanding universe,"[2] but, far more than just the five films (and the sixth that's on the way), it includes novels, stories, comic books, CD-Roms, Nintendo games, role-playing games, toys, action figures, and ornaments, appearing in all the ever-multiplying media of the contemporary era. More than a series of movies, *Star Wars* is an entire cultural universe. As a product that mixes the literary imperatives of character, plot, and theme with the essentially cinematic qualities of special effects and driving motion, it has shown itself to be a relentless part of American culture since its first release in 1977. Credited with ushering in "the soulless action flick and the kind of merchandising that brings us R2-D2 beverage coolers," it has also been called "An American Myth," and "an international phenomenon."[3] One of its many striking qualities is its refusal to go away; even in the bare period between the release of *Return of the Jedi* in 1983 and *The Phantom Menace* in 1999, the *Star Wars* universe continued to expand; during this time Bantam began its series of novels, and *Star Wars* products continued to show strong sales, eventually spawning the biannual Star Wars Summit Meeting of its licensees. Its extraordinary appeal is difficult to define; asked to explain it, George Sorensen, the president of LucasArts, a subsidiary of George Lucas's vast empire, commented, "I'm as perplexed by this as anyone, and I'm right in the midst of it," adding,

> I don't really think this is caused by some evil master plan of merchandisers and marketers. The demand is already out there, and we're just meeting it— it would exist without us. I don't know if I want to say this in print, but I feel like Star Wars is the mythology of a nonsectarian world. It describes how people want to live. People all view politics as corrupt, much more so in Europe than here, and yet people are not cynical underneath—they want to believe in something pure, noble. That's Star Wars.[4]

Sorenson's description of *Star Wars* as "non-sectarian myth" shows his indoctrination in the assumptions of the project's mastermind; anyone familiar with the whole business of *Star Wars* is well aware of George Lucas's attempt to claim his films as a myth for modern times. Steeped in the terminology of Joseph Campbell's successful popularizations of mythology, Lucas believes himself to be "taking these old stories and putting them into the most modern of idioms, the cinema."[5] Expressing decidedly Jungian sentiments when asked about creating the character Darth Maul for the *Phantom Menace*, Lucas noted, "if you're trying to build an icon of evil, you have to go down into the subconscious of the human race over a period of *time* and pull out the images that equate to the emotion you're trying to project." Asked about what he found in his exploration, Lucas responded, "A lot of evil characters have horns."[6] He frequently expresses an overwhelming belief that he is "telling an old myth in a new way," adding, "Myths tell us these old stories in a way that doesn't threaten us. They're an imaginary land where you can be safe. But they deal with real truths that need to be told."[7]

Perhaps even more striking than Lucas's vision of his own project is his ability to convince others of its mythological status. The travelling exhibit that began at the Smithsonian Museum of Air and Space in 1997–98 and is currently touring the country, evocatively called *Star Wars: The Magic of Myth*, suggests a wholesale acceptance of these assumptions; as Daniel McKay comments in regard to the exhibition, "we are instructed that these films have cultural capital; they are relevant to a 'timeless' audience because of their mythological themes."[8] At the Brooklyn Museum, the exhibit began in an ante-room with examples of classical art demonstrating early manifestations of *Star Wars'* mythic concepts such as the hero and monsters; the audience then entered the exhibit itself, which showed artifacts (costumes, background paintings, one of the original Yoda puppets) and film clips alongside extremely reductive explanations of the mythological themes the movies are supposed to explore. Andrew Gordon adds a more recent source of influence: "In the absence of any shared contemporary myths, Lucas has constructed out of the useable past, of out bits of American pop culture, a new mythology which can satisfy both children and adults."[9] However, it is decidedly more accurate to consider Lucas, as Armand Singer and Michael Lastinger do, to be a "bricoleur," piecing together fragments from earlier sources than movie serials of the 1930s.[10] Noting that "certain events, real or imagined, have proved transcendent for Western civilization, fertile sources for endless myth, legend, narrative: the Trojan War; the advent of Christianity; King Arthur, Merlin, and the Round Table Knights, The Crusades"[11]—they show *Star Wars* to be a piecing together of earlier materials (which they define, mistakenly, as essentially "epic") that end up as "essentially a retelling of the 'dragon-slayer' tale."[12] Indeed, interviews with Lucas himself suggest a somewhat vague understanding of myth both on his own part and that of his acolytes; in Orville Schell's evaluation of Lucas written shortly before *Episode I: The Phantom Menace* was released, he calls *Star Wars* both a "fairy tale" and a "morality play,"[13] two genres that differ distinctly from the mythology that Lucas thinks he's producing. In the same article, Lucas ennumerates the "myths" from which he draws; naming "Homer, Jason, Jesus, King Arthur, Siegfried and Huck Finn with the Viking Sagas, Grimm's fairy tales, Hans Christian

Andersen's stories, Flash Gordon movies and J. R. R. Tolkein's fantasies," Schell and Lucas seem unaware that this "new all-purpose amalgamation" is drawn primarily from non-mythic, postclassical sources.[14] In effect echoing the unconsciously medieval foundation of Lucas's imagination, Schell notes, "Skywalker Ranch," where much of George Lucas's business empire is housed "is an attempt to recreate a kind of village idyll, with happy figurative peasants working under the tutelage of a benevolent seigneur."[15] This feudal manor is certainly not the Athenian Forum; taking the product as more than just a series of movies, the whole business seems steeped in a world rather more specifically medieval than the general mythological one Lucas claims.

Noting that "all mythology is grounded in the particulars of a society and culture, in a people's way of life, in the *praxis*—the practice—of living in a specific time and place,"[16] MacKay reveals the problems with reading the films as modern myth; located outside of time and place, detached from their own culture's space and time, they inhabit a far more liminal space than myth provides. Calling these films in particular and films in general "a two-hour liminal experience that excites the passions and nerves of the audience,"[17] MacKay effectively locates *Star Wars* generically by courtesy of its medium. Beyond this critique of Lucas's assumptions about his own project, one can offer a different understanding of the film's generic assumptions and, as a result, its effects. Perhaps the relationship of *Star Wars* projects to myth—not in itself a genre, as Lucas seems to regard it—can best be described in Bulfinch's terms; "If no other knowledge deserves to be called useful but that which helps to enlarge our possessions or to raise our station in society, then Mythology has no claim to the appellation. But if that which tends to make us happier and better can be called useful, then we claim that epithet for our subject. For Mythology is the handmaid of literature; and literature is one of the best allies of virtue and promoters of happiness."[18] For Bulfinch, the best reason to study and read myth is to understand literature; this idea is illustrative in understanding the relationship of myth to *Star Wars*. For, generically, *Star Wars* follows the medieval conventions of comedy. Although "comedy" in the film industry means a movie full of yucks, taken in its more traditional sense, *Star Wars* qualifies; it may not end with a wedding (although the union of Han Solo and Leia is certainly projected), but all three of the first series of films end with some kind of conclusion that restores order, allows a rebel victory, and anticipates the final triumph. As comedy, it is designed to promote virtue and happiness, to use Bulfinch's terms again. It is literature, not myth, that provides such narrative models, while myth is simply that which literature references, as Bulfinch comments: "without a knowledge of mythology much of the elegant literature of our own language cannot be understood and appreciated."[19] His examples—references from such poets as Byron and Milton—suggest that myth is that which lurks in allusion, not that which defines any contemporary literary product. While more complex definitions of mythology abound, this one provides a useful understanding of what *Star Wars* is and what it's not.

For all George Lucas's (self)mythologizing, his inspirations are much narrower than his sweeping characterizations acknowledge, drawing heavily from medieval, in particular Arthurian, romance. Calling King Arthur "the best-known character from medieval literature," and adding that "most readers of English are familiar with some stories about him," Edward Donald Kennedy suggests a useful parallel between the Arthurian and *Star Wars* corpi—their ubiquity.[20] Quite apart from the obvious narrative connections between them, the two products share their narrative structures; both are single, overarching narratives with a main plot to which numerous tangential stories have been attached. If the largest versions of Arthurian production, either the French Vulgate Cycle or Malory's *Le Morte Darthur*, function much like the *Star Wars* films, offering up the "authorized" version, the many sideline romances, tales, ballads, and other Arthurian material produced in the Middle Ages echo the novels, role-playing games, CD-Roms, and other subsidiary *Star Wars* narratives that are a part of the sum-total of what *Star Wars* is. While it is certainly possible to see elements of classical and non-western stories within the *Star Wars* narrative, particularly in the first two films of the second trilogy, which seem to draw on the early twenty-first century fascination with zen and yoga, none of those examples have produced the same volume or variety of offshoots and versions that the Arthurian romance and *Star Wars* story have. The borrowings are not just thematic or narrative, they are structural as well; if the Arthurian romance "franchise" was less controlled than Lucas's project, both produce main stories with countless offshoots, sideline narratives, and alternative stories. Perhaps most revealingly, like the Arthurian romance, *Star Wars* draws from a variety of myths and legends while creating its own essentially medieval world. Whatever narrative fragments Lucas draws from the broad stream of world mythology, the framework of the society he envisions, the basic elements that define the relations of the characters to each other are inspired almost entirely by a popular conception of the feudal world.

The figure of Arthur, who "usually enjoys a popular reputation as a great king,"[21] clearly comes from an historical antecedent, as the chronicles of Gildas and Nenius suggest; he has also been examined by comparative mythologists during their flowering, receiving a great deal of attention from both Jessie L. Weston in numerous works and James Frazer in *The Golden Bough*, in which he was figured as a "Brythonic god" and "Culture Hero." This mythologizing of Arthur, whose primary medieval function was literary, once again calls to mind the mythologizing of Lucas's characters and story; however, the Arthurian readings are largely extratextual, relating to the story's origins but not its actual product, just as the Joseph Campbell mythologizing lurks in the background of the *Star Wars* films without defining them, despite what George Lucas declares. Christopher Baswell and William Sharpe note that "no Arthurian story is experienced without some foreknowledge of its end, an awareness that the text at once acknowledges and avoids through any of a complex range of methods: echo, deferral, revisionism."[22] This, too, is true for *Star Wars*; the new series of films, the "prequels," by necessity encode the previous stories; with knowledge of the end of the story, these versions can only add detail and background, which the *Phantom Menace*, *Attack of the Clones*, and presumably the final film in this trilogy, both acknowledge and avoid. All the extant films echo each other; the prequel series holds off the inevitability of the earlier (in production) trilogy by constantly deferring it. We know Anakin Skywalker will become Darth Vader, and that Princess Amidala will give birth to the twins Luke and Leia Skywalker; the twins will, of course, be separated, while Luke is sent to his uncle and aunt to be raised in secret obscurity. Watching the original trilogy, viewers know from the start that the Empire will be conquered and the Rebels will emerge triumphant, and that Luke, Leia, and Han Solo will be instrumental in that victory; however, by telling only a part of the story, each film continually defers the ending to increase the desire. This kind of storytelling finds significant inspiration in the medieval romance, the genre of Arthur; as in the medieval king's story, the "narrator and reader live in the empty if long moment between loss and return."[23] (As, indeed, the first trilogy ends after the destruction of the Empire but before the restoration of the Republic.)

Despite its absence from most, if not all, discussions of both Arthurian and Medieval Cinema,[24] *Star Wars* is a product deeply medieval and Arthurian, transferred to a futuristic context. Norris J. Lacy's contention that "few legends have been recast more often or in more forms than that of Arthur. . . .Arthur has been familiar to may centuries and in numerous languages and media,"[25] would reserve a place for *Star Wars* in the Arthurian canon. If, as he suggests, "the Arthurian tradition is rich and complex, with every generation, indeed every writer and artist, reinterpreting the material in light of contemporary conceptions of the King or current, artistic, ideological, or even political views. In part, it is this 'transposability' of the legend that explains, or at least permits, its popularity,"[26] it is easy to see *Star Wars* as yet another addition to this tradition. Even if it is unlike Tennyson's *Idylls of the King* or even Marion Zimmer Bradley's *Mists of Avalon* because it does not directly retell the Arthurian story, *Star Wars* nevertheless seems a reinterpretation of Arthur's story to fit present concerns; despite the blasters and spaceships, in its generic form and narrative direction, the whole *Star Wars* business is an intensely medieval enterprise. Put simply, Luke Skywalker may not be Arthur, but he (and his story) are certainly Arthurian.

Umberto Eco usefully distinguishes the return of the Middle Ages from a returning classical heritage by separating the medieval "utilitarian brico-lage" from the early modern/Renaissance "philological reconstruction."[27] Noting that the many Middle Ages don't always fit the same archetype (striking language given Lucas's attachment to unitary, archetypal readings of Campbell's and his own work), Eco suggests that while the classical period is reconstructed of uncontemplated remains—that is, fragments accepted as authoritative in their original forms—the Middle Ages is always "mended and patched. . ., as something in which we still live"; he suggests that even "when we live with Aristotle or Plato, we deal with them in the same terms suggested by our medieval ancestors" in order to connect them with everyday life.[28] Naming ten types of "Middle Ages," ranging from "the Middle ages as a *pretext*" to the "Middle Ages as *Romanticism*," Eco writes that choosing among them indicates "who we are and what we dream of, if we are simply practicing a more or less honest form of divertissement, if we are wondering about our basic problems or if we are supporting, perhaps with-out realizing it, some new reactionary plot."[29] *Star Wars* falls comfortably into Eco's varied assumptions about the Middle Ages; insofar as it engages classical myth, it creates a story-quilt out of a patchwork of the past, read-ing its mythology through the more medieval paradigm of moral response. Lucas's sense that "the issues are the same ones that existed 3,000 years ago. That we haven't come very far emotionally,"[30] further shows the ways that this medieval bricolage claims a connection with everyday life, engaging a similar set of problems and experiences. The films are indeed a "more-or-less honest form of divertissement"; Jessica Tiffin observes that "profound, the films are apparently not. The root of their appeal, however, seems to lie in a far from simplistic rehashing of genre, cliché, and narrative expectation, to produce something which cuts through apparent nativity [*sic*] of content to a profound level of mass appeal."[31]

Lucas addresses the ways in which the films deal with "our basic prob-lems" in his discussion of the films' themes: "*Star Wars* is made up of many themes. It's not one little simple parable. One is our relationship to machines, which are fearful, but also benign. Then there is the lesson of friendship and symbiotic relationships, of your obligations to your fellow-man, to other people that are around you."[32] Include the films' obvious themes of growing up (both Luke Skywalker, and in the new series, his father Anakin, come of age, for better or worse), family (in the course of the first three films Luke acquires real and symbolic fathers, a sister, and various pets), and social place (Luke's search for his ideal career leads him from irrigation to piloting to Jedi knight), and the concern with our "basic problems" becomes apparent, while at the same time echoing the medieval nature of these problems, as the Arthurian saga is essentially concerned with many of the same issues.[33] The films also encode a "new reactionary plot," revealed also in their connection to their medieval antecedents, as they, like all romances, finally serve to reaffirm the status quo at many levels, such as hierarchy, social convention, and gender. Viewers may well note that while it's the Rebel Alliance (although the function of monarchy within that rebellion is raised by the presence of her highness, Princess Leia) that seeks to overthrow the Evil Empire (with all its anticipation of Ronald Reagan and the Eastern Bloc), the Alliance's political program is essentially a quasi-liberal reflection of American democracy without a rebellious impulse in sight. Just as strongly, the capitalistic motive that produces scores of *Star Wars* action figures, spin-off novels, toys, costumes, and life-sized cardboard cut-outs is a reactionary plot in itself.

Following Eco's understanding of the new Middle Ages, what essentially makes Lucas's project more medieval than classical are the moral clichés within which the *Star Wars* narratives deal; within them "all morals are absolute," and they show a reductive "clarity of moral vision."[34] John Seabrook suggests the way these stories and images seem to be "replacing lessons people used to get from religion," saying, "the lessons of Star Wars— that good is stronger than evil, that human values can triumph over superior technology, that even the lowliest of us can be redeemed, and that all this is relatively free of moral ambiguity—is a very powerful force indeed."[35] Noting that the "*Star Wars* trilogy exhibits a Manichean pattern of black-and-white morality in which the metaphors of 'light' as good and 'dark' as evil are realized not only in the 'dark' and (presumably) light sides of 'the Force,' but also in the corporeal divisions of 'clean white' rebels and non-white alien scum,"[36] Jeffrey Weinstock reveals the overtly moralized nature of the films as well as uncovering another reactionary plot. Adding that "Jabba's engorged size and repulsive appearance correlate directly with his unrestrained appetite for wealth and power [and I would add, sex]. In opposition to Jabba's excess, the white, human heroes demonstrate the (American) virtues of self-government, control, and discipline,"[37] he further elaborates the problematic and overly easy moral equations that the films establish. Despite their seeming appeal to rebelliousness, John Rieder notes, "their rebellion is entirely specious, because it takes place within the confines of a totalizing morality that excludes the possibility of a genuine Other appearing in any guise but that of merely another 'mythic' representative of good or evil. And the moral choice between good and evil is as irrelevant as the rebellion."[38] Thus, the nature of the conflict within the story is so externalized as to have no internal content; because there is no real possibility of rebellion, given the absolute projection of evil within the story, the choice is not really there to make. Once again, the films choose to reduce in order to totalize, rather than engage the potential complexities of the issues they raise. It is not hard to recall one's Ovid in order to recognize the significantly more ambiguous nature of good and evil in classical mythology; while figures like the Cyclops, with his one eye and voracious appetite are clearly "bad," in Jabba-like terms, what is "good" is significantly harder to define, as the "hero" of many classical stories is a profoundly mixed figure. Indeed, in his maladroit courtship of Galatea, even Polyphemus evokes some sympathy. If Luke Skywalker is all that is virtuous and good, Odysseus is not.

Noting that "the generic roots of Lucas's are very old indeed," Jessica Tiffin addresses the medievalizing nature of the *Star Wars* myth, saying, "most fundamentally, *Star Wars* is fairy tale, fantasy, romance; and to return to my original theme, it goes deeper than these, to participate in the underlying impulses and structures of myth."[39] As a "popular galactic fairy tale. . .the classic saga of charming princesses and brave knights,"[40] *Star Wars* is unadulterated romance; yet Tiffin's assumptions that romance, in itself, is insufficiently profound to explain the more complex nature of the films is shortsighted. In their projection of the hero and his journey, the films reflect Northrop Frye's discussion of the depth of this aspect of the genre:

> The hero of romance moves in a world in which the ordinary laws of nature are slightly suspended: prodigies of courage and endurance, unnatural to us, are natural to him, and enchanted weapons, talking animals, terrifying ogres and witches, and talismans of miraculous power violate no rules of probability once the postulates of romance have been established.[41]

The ease of applying Frye's definition to *Star Wars* shows how fittingly it defines the films' genre; Luke is quite comfortable with antigravity vehicles, droids, and spaceships, which defy our current laws of natural and scientific possibility; he wields an enchanted light saber, makes friends with various "talking" animals (Chewbaca, the Ewoks), meets terrifying ogres like Jabba the Hut and Darth Vader, and if he's missing a talisman of miraculous power, doubtless one of the next *Star Wars* films will provide one. Within the context of the *Star Wars* universe, all of this is perfectly expected; as Lucas notes, "I'm localizing it [his myth] for the planet."[42]

Characterizing the medieval nature of *Star Wars* is intimately tied up with genre; the many romance assumptions it displays suggest that its ultimate inability to be a "myth for modern times" comes in its failure to be modern at all. John Rieder comments that "what most typifies the films' exploitation of that generic history is their overriding nostalgia: in this case, an active nostalgia that not only distorts its memories but then actually creates new object in their idealized form."[43] The films' nostalgia is drawn directly from romance; while Rieder's focus is to remove *Star Wars* from the science fiction camp, he reveals its ties to much older genres through its need to look backward into an idealized past. Its projection of itself into the past, a "Long time ago, in a galaxy far, far away" reflects the same idealized past in which the Arthurian romances are inevitably set; they all take place in a nonexistent Golden Age of chivalry and virtue that has now receded from view. The opening of Chaucer's Wife of Bath's Tale provides a striking contrast with the fourteenth-century present, opening "In th'olde dayes of the Kyng Arthour, / Of which that Britons speken greet honour."[44] The Wife then reminds us that back then, "Al was this land fulfilled of fayerye. / The elf-queene, with her joly compaignye, / Daunced ful ofte in many a grene mede."[45] The introduction of nonhuman players echoes *Star Wars'* cast of beeping droids, talking Wookies, and the other strange creatures that inhabit the films; Chaucer again firmly locates this world in the past, reiterating, "I speke of manye hundred yeres ago."[46] For all the reflecting back on contemporary society that both texts do—the galaxy far, far away is still us, just as the Wife of Bath's magical Arthurian world is her own audience—they create themselves firmly in a liminal past. David Wyatt observes, "desire and loss station us in time, and *Star Wars* begins. . .as a massive retreat from time into a fantasy of space. Space permits the illusion of detachment and distance."[47] This "Space" in its liminal qualities reproduces the spaces of the medieval romance, providing a world in which many of the conventions of our own are no longer in place, for all their echoing around the edges. Cars can fly and machines can talk; yet the ultimate values of the film—family, order, and loyalty—seem perfectly conventional, if hard to achieve, in contemporary society.

The perpetual and repetitive nature of the story, as well as its episodic qualities are also indicative of romance. Suggesting that "repetition assures us that a story can recover itself, that its themes are all interconnected," Wyatt shows the ways that the films create comfort through familiarity; locating themselves within old narrative patterns, they provide the certainties of resolution and comedy that romances do and myths do not. Thus the films manage to avoid anxiety; in their assumptions about relationships, the films are profoundly pre-Freudian; Darth Vader may be Luke's father but Luke doesn't kill him; Luke and Leia are siblings but the specter of incest never rears its head. In a sense, in place of the originality of myth we are given the "same old story" in newish clothes. As in romance, any challenges to the system are contained; the carnival of liminal space allows for rebel fighters who strive for an equally hierarchical and orderly republic with its own policing force, the Jedi Knights. Rieder notes the romance quality of this conflict as well: "there is no indication of any historical, economic, or political background to the war; it simply puts light against dark, good against evil."[48] If the Arthurian story/history begins as an attempt by native British to hold off the Saxon invasions, by the twelfth century when Chrétien de Troyes writes his Arthurian romances, those specific political elements are absent in favor of more liminal sorts of conflict. Arthur's dispute with Meleogant and the Kingdom of Görre, or the more internal battle with Mordred, replace the geopolitical issues that provided the impulse for earlier Arthur stories. Similarly, in *Star Wars*, for all the political talk, the conflict is not over any particular territory or even really between conflicting ideologies but between moral manifestations played out on a (literally) cosmic stage. The films' two main figures of evil, the Emperor and Darth Vader echo the conflicts in the Arthurian romance; the Emperor, with his almost mystical appearance and magic powers, is a liminal figure, and Vader, like Mordred, is an internal problem, a member of the "good side" gone wrong.

Princess Leia Organa may pick up a blaster in the first film, but as with the heroines of romance, who are ultimately confined to their feminine and domestic roles, she ends up in iron underwear, rescued by her own Sir Lancelot. The gender assumptions of Arthurian romance play out in *Star Wars*; in this as in most romances, as Roberta Krueger notes, "the lady is neither the principal protagonist—the subject of the narrative's action— nor the narrator, the subject who speaks. Within the adventure, she is typ- ically an object of exchange of an object of desire."[49] Having been an object of exchange as a prisoner in the first film, Leia increasingly becomes the object of desire, the primary question surrounding her being which man will get her. Like her medieval counterparts, she "observes the con- flicts between knights and valorizes the knights' honor with her approving presence."[50] A striking example of this function comes in at the end of the first movie; in the Main Throne Room at the Massai Outpost, Han Solo, Luke, and Chewbaca parade into the main temple between rows of troops:

> At the far end stands a vision in white, the beautiful, young Senator Leia. Luke and the others solemnly march up the long aisle and kneel before Senator Leia. . . .Leia is dressed in a long white dress and is staggeringly beautiful. She rises and places a gold medallion around Han's neck. He winks at her. She rises and then repeats the ceremony with Luke, who is moved by the event. They turn and face the assembled troops, who all bow before them.[51]

The focus on Leia's beauty and purity (the white dress), and her presence as observer in this scene make her increasingly static and feminized; by hanging the medals around Han's and Luke's necks, she valorizes them for their work without acknowledging her own essential part in the victory over the empire. Thus the story enforces the dominant structure of masculine desire and female passivity, which continues in the next two films. That Krueger is describing Guenevere in Chrétien's *Le Chevalier de la Charette* in her observation on the lady's role in romance strengthens the alliance of the films both with romance in general and Arthurian romance in particular. Leia is further subverted within the romance mode; because female desire is both enigmatic and problematic, it can serve as a destabilizing force within masculine society, disrupting masculine bonds; because of the danger of the desiring woman, the *Star Wars* films prevent her from choosing between her suitors; by making Luke her brother, Lucas prevents any interruption of the necessary friendship between Luke Skywalker and Han Solo.

Dan Ruby echoes the masculine structures of romance in his understanding of the way this relationship plays out, saying *Star Wars'* "world of romantic combat is structured around male relationships and male-oriented viewpoints. Women exist primarily to provide motivations for male activity."[52] Like Morgan le Fay in *Sir Gawain and the Green* Knight, who is pushed aside "because her marginalization is central to its own revision of Arthurian history,"[53] Leia may begin the whole adventure with her message stored inside R2D2, but she is ultimately relegated to the margins; she can be sought and repeatedly rescued, but she only has a few active moments, strangling Jabba the Hutt with the chain he has used to enslave her, and rescuing Luke at the end of the *Empire Strikes Back* (although she needs Lando Calrissian and Chewbaca to help her). In discussing the ways that *Sir Gawain and the Green Knight* marginalizes both Guenevere and Morgan, Sheila Fisher draws a connection between them that elucidates Princess Leia Organa in her double role. Although the poem's "erasure of women. . .is uneasy and incomplete,"[54] she writes, it is essential in an attempt to stave off the destruction of Camelot through women's agency and desire. The removal of Leia to the margins, and the casting of her at the end as dutiful sister and lover, defined by her relationship to men, works equally well to prevent her from being a threat within the entirely masculine and patriarchal resolution of the story.

The collage nature of Lucas's inspiration, even within the Arthurian program, is shown through the duplications and doublings of characters, yet the encapsulation of various Arthurian examples within the films also shows the breadth of this material's influence. The different stories that make up the Arthurian corpus invest different parts of the films; for instance, Luke Skywalker begins as an avatar of one Arthurian figure and ends up a projection of another. Luke himself is both Arthur and Perceval; he may fulfill the former's story in a number of ways, but like Perceval, he essentially goes from hunting rabbits in the forest to being a knight of the round table. Perceval begins as "a rustic *Dümmling*: guileless and ingenuous, he knows nothing of knowledge or restraint."[55] Luke begins as a rustic, sharing Perceval's "forest values and lack of formal education" which like his predecessor's, "cause clumsy, humorous ineptitude in all courtly pursuits."[56] Apt to make mistakes (he nearly gets himself killed several times in the first film), inept with the light saber, and tongue-tied around the princess, he manages to get the rescue party nearly crushed in a garbage compactor, where he is almost eaten by a snake. However, like Perceval, he receives an education; in place of Gornemant de Gohort and his mother, Luke has Obi-Wan Kenobi to guide him out of youth and "through periods of deliberate instruction."[57] As in the Perceval romances, there are many scenes of instruction; once Obi-Wan is no longer available, Yoda takes over. Like Percival also, Luke ends up a figure of asexual purity, despite the display of his potential to be the courtly hero in the first film. Luke's process of development, thus, echoes another Arthurian hero when it is not echoing the King's.

The *Star Wars* text certainly finds elements of romance outside of the development of its main characters and plot; indeed, romance assumptions inform much of the film. The exotic settings and alien life forms that replace the overt others, the dragons and giants of romance, are much the same as those discussed in the previous chapter, identifying the world of *Star Wars* as essentially liminal. Although some places, such as the bar at Mos Eisley, are stranger than others, there is no world outside the magical one against which it is played off. For all the dirty reality of garbage shutes, spaceship repair, and imperial bureaucracy, the only world of different rules is that of the Force, which allows Luke to "see" his mentors after they are dead, "feel" where he's supposed to shoot the Death Star, and find Darth Vader. As with his medieval counterparts, even Luke's internal quest is set within a publicly romance world; Chewbaca the Wookie echoes the wild figures of romance: Yvain's Lion, the Green Knight, Sir Gromer Somer Jour. Talking animals and robots mirror their medieval counterparts; it is not terribly hard to imagine the cute, gabbly Ewoks populating the margins of medieval manuscripts. Within this romance context, the characters are consigned to playing romance roles. Although in the final film, Luke wears black and treads along the edge of becoming a tragic hero, unemotional and withdrawn, he is ultimately reintegrated into the romance program, fighting the final battle that leads to the happy, redemptive (and thus, in medieval generic terms, non-epic) ending.

A further take on the specifically Arthurian character of *Star Wars* is delineated rather forcefully by Marilyn R. Sherman:

> The parallels to the Authurian [*sic*] cycle are obvious and numerous. For example, Luke gets his knowledge of the Jedi Knights and their noble values for the wise, mystical, and Merlin-like character, Obi-Wan Kenobi. These knights are custodians of peace and justice in this galactical civilization, and they are armed with appropriate weapons. Luke Skywalkers's Excalibur is a light saber, not a clumsy storm trooper blaster that kills at random, but a clean clear ray that dispatches its deserving victim with finality.[58]

These obvious references proliferate, as Sara Boyle notes, commenting that "what intrigued me the most was how much that galaxy far, far away was like Sir Thomas Malory's realm of Logres. Arthur Pendragon and Luke Skywalker have a good deal in common."[59] Luke, like Arthur, is ignorant of his real parentage, and his discovery of the truth is equally striking: "when Arthur drew the sword from the stone, a symbol of his royal lineage, he was shocked. He assumed Sir Ector was his natural father and was dismayed to learn otherwise. Luke learned to his horror that his real father was not a worthy Jedi Knight murdered by the evil Darth Vader, but Vader himself."[60] Both Luke and Arthur have secluded and anonymous childhoods, Arthur with Ector and Kay and Luke with Uncle Owen and Aunt Beru. After Arthur removes the sword in Malory's text, he is told by Sir Ector, "I was never your fader not of your blood, but I wote wel ye are of an hyher blood than I wende ye were," to which "Arthur made grete doole when he undersood that syre Ector was not his fader."[61] Similarly, in *The Empire Strikes Back*, near the end of the film, when Darth Vader tells Luke, "I am your Father," Luke responds, "No, no, That's not true. That's impossible."[62] His anxiety continues through the end of the film and leads to the final redemption of Vader in the *Return of the Jedi*. While other heroes of non-medieval myth and legend may also grow up ignorant of their parentage (such as Moses), the aura of knighthood surrounding Luke makes the Arthurian connection primary, as the comments of Sherman and Boyle confirm.

One of the most obvious parallels between the two narratives is the role of mentors; in the Arthur story, "Merlin, the prophet and enchanter, knew the truth about Arthur's birth and cast his fate, protecting him and planning for the future. He provided Arthur with the weapon that symbolized his destiny, brought him to the throne, and advised him on policy and welfare."[63] Luke Skywalker's two Merlins, Obi-Wan Kenobi and Yoda, provide much of the same function in the *Star Wars* saga. Kenobi gives Lunke his first light saber and teaches him how to use it, while Yoda provides his training in the use of the Force. All three mentors are quasi-mystical figures;

if Merlin gives plenty of prosaic advice about whom Arthur should have as an ally and whom he shouldn't trust, he is also responsible for the illusion that begot Arthur, the masking of Uther Pendragon as Gorlois that allowed him to lie with Igreyne in the first place. As David Wyatt notes, "when Yoda plays Merlin to Luke's Arthur—*Star Wars* cannot help assume its place in an imaginative line."[64] In this case, the line is the Arthurian romance.

The similarities continue. The two knights each have two swords; Arthur pulls one out of the stone and then acquires Excalibur from the Lady of the Lake, while Luke first uses his father's light saber (given by Kenobi) and then makes his own. Arthur's two acquisitions are more mystical—indeed, in the second he and Merlin "rode tyll they com to a laake that was a fayre water and borde. And in the myddis Arthure was ware of an arme clothed in whyght Samyte, that helde a fayre swerde in that hond"[65]—while Luke's are more prosaic: once Obi-Wan Kenobi tells Luke that he knew his father and who he was, Kenobi pulls the light saber out of a chest, saying "I have something here for you. Your father wanted you to have this when you were old enough, but your uncle wouldn't allow it. He feared you might follow old Obi-Wan on some damned-fool idealistic crusade like your father did," then adding, "Your father's light sabre. This is the weapon of a Jedi Knight. Not as clumsy or as random as a blaster. An elegant weapon for a more civilized time."[66] Despite these differences, the role of both mentors is equally important, and both Luke and Arthur prove to be particularly talented at wielding the weapons their mentors provide. Of Arthur, Malory says, "kynge Arthure dud so mervaylesly in armys that all mean had wondir,"[67] whereas in *Star Wars* Luke finally proves himself a talented saber fighter in various scenes. As Boyle notes, "in both cases, the weapons were symbolic as well as functional, marking a special position within a society and a special responsibility to that society. He who bore such swift and deadly weapons had to be one who would use them only in the cause of right."[68] Luke's light saber marks him as a Jedi; while other characters use various kinds of weapons, only Jedi, future Jedi, or past Jedi make use of these laser swords. Arthur's swords make him the king, and with them come the responsibilities of governance and leadership that separate him from his former life and family. Of course, the sword symbolism—as a marker of masculinity, violence, and power, for instance—has more complex implications, for the moment, it is sufficient to take both on their sunny, surface terms.

Boyle also suggests a similarity between the Jedi code and the chivalric code that governs the Arthurian romances: "inherent in the chivalric code were similar responsibilities to strive for good, to seek the ideal. Power should be used honorably for the greater good. Skill at arms should bring glory, not shame or tragedy. Arthur always sought to bear these responsibilities, to rule wisely, to be a merciful and just king. Mordred used the privileges of chivalry to take a kingdom by treachery and died destroying it."[69] For Luke Skywalker, it was the "Force" and its concomitant power that the Jedi were able to use to enhance their abilities and influence others that served the same role. Like chivalry, Boyle comments, the "Force" was "a grave responsibility to be used only for good, to insure peace and freedom" and should be "wielded only by those with the discipline of mind not to abuse it. But the Force could be abused. Turned to selfish ends, the power could be used to dominate and enslave."[70] If the Chivalric Code is not quite the overt player in the medieval romances that the "Force" is in the *Star Wars* films, it remains in the background influencing the behaviors of the characters and the assumptions of the texts, from Chrétien de Troyes to Malory. It is also one of the most commonly held misconceptions about medieval romance (and medieval culture) that knights rode around, each with his own carefully scripted copy of Andreas Capellanus's code of courtly behavior tucked into his armor. Indeed, Lucas's Force represents a common misunderstanding of chivalry, if not the source material itself. Thus for both works, similar codes of behavior inform both the works and are affirmed by them, with chivalry and the "Force" serving as parallel ideologies for good, the characters trying to live by these codes of virtue, while the very fact that they do so certifies the values the codes represent. While both are certainly forces for good, as Boyle notes, they, too, are also problematic; since both the Jedi and the Arthurian Knights are deeply tied to violence, both codes are essentially hierarchical and anti-individualistic, and both groups serve as a kind of police force that imposes their ideologies on others, these "forces" both liberate and repress at the same time.

Boyle occupies herself little with the love triangles that inform both works, although these reveal some of the two works' most striking connections. Arthur Pendragon is married to Gwenyver, daughter of Leodegrauns, who falls in love with Lancelot, ultimately destroying Camelot and the Round Table. Arthur is delighted with Gwenyver when Leodegrauns brings her to Camelot: Malory notes that Arthur "made grete joy for hir commynge" and said, "Thys fayre lady ys passyngly wellcom to me, for I have loved hir longe, and therefore there ys nothynge so leeff to me."[71] Although Gwenyver is selected as Arthur's wife, which makes his relationship to what he sees different from the situation in *Star Wars*, the female's primary function in both works is to be seen and rated accordingly. Both heroic, masculine gazes fix the woman as an object of admiration and desire. Arthur's ownership of Gwenyver is what Luke's longing look quests for; he is only able to give up his wish to possess Leia (and then with some regret) when her true identity is made known to him in the second film. Right from the start, Luke's admiration for Leia is apparent when he sees her video message implanted into R2D2, as he instantly says, "Who is she? She's beautiful."[72] Her beauty becomes her identity. The directions in the facsimile script echo his enchantment, repeating commentary like "Luke becomes intrigued by the beautiful young girl," "Luke gazes at the beautiful young princess for a few moments," and "Luke looks longingly at the lovely little princess."[73] After various squabbles, rescues, and battles, at the end of the first film, Luke stares longingly at Princess Leia as he and Han Solo are rewarded and decorated for their roles in the destruction of the Death Star. Neither Arthur's nor Luke's desires are ultimately fulfilled; we find out relatively soon in the Arthurian story that "Sir Launcelot loved queen Gwenyver paramour and she hym agayne,"[74] while Leia and Han Solo are winking and making eyes at each other in the same aforementioned scene at the end of the first movie, and by the second, are declaring their love for each other even as Han is frozen in punishment for helping the Rebel Alliance. In one of *Star Wars'* most genuine, if least recognized, Arthurian moments, Luke matches his medieval counterpart in impotence; although they can both desire the girl, ultimately, neither one can have her. Arthur and Guenevere remain childless, and Guenevere's indiscretion with Lancelot finally destroys Camelot, in part because it is left without an obvious successor to Arthur. In *Star Wars*, Luke must also remain impotent, the duties of sexual desire passed on to Han Solo, although Lucas makes the situation less complex and ambiguous by making Luke and Leia twin siblings. Andrew Gordon comments that "throughout, the fantasy balances contradictory desires and meticulously covers its tracks so that Luke is always guilt-free and sexually innocent."[75] Thus Leia becomes both Guenevere and Morgan, yet neither, because she eschews the problematic qualities of either one, while Han Solo, the Lancelot figure torn between lover and friend, finally gets the girl without having to betray his king in the process. Gordon's sense of this dynamic echoes the function of Lancelot within the Arthurian narrative: "he [Solo]. . .is a sexual surrogate for Luke, acting out Luke's passion for Leia, the forbidden sister/mother figure, to allow Luke to remain apparently asexual and guilt-free throughout the trilogy. Solo is punished for Luke's forbidden passion by being frozen and later suffering temporary blindness."[76] Like Lancelot, Solo is punished, but unlike Lancelot, he also ultimately wins the prize. And if Gordon's Freudian language seems obsessed with guilt, it parallels certain qualities of Arthur's sexual presentation, which frees him from guilt for everything but letting the affair between his wife and his friend continue. At the end of the last film, as the Death Star explodes, Han and Leia stand in Endor Forest looking up at the sky, Han with an anxious expression on his face. Gordon reads this climactic detonation as "a substitute for the orgasm Luke and Leia can never experience,"[77] a somewhat humorous suggestion that nonetheless recognizes the ultimately symbolic nature of their relationship.[78] Assuring Leia "I'm sure Luke wasn't on that thing when it blew," Solo asks, "You love him, don't you?" Leia apprises him of something the audience has known since the second movie, "It's not like that at all. He's my brother." They grin cheerfully and embrace.[79] Lancelot and Guenevere never had it so good.

The familial nature of the drama also reflects the Arthurian program demonstrating again the vitality of medievalized narrative in Lucas's supposedly pan-mythic approach. Ostensibly a conflict of a rebel group against an oppressive imperial regime, *Star Wars* is really about Luke Skywalker finding himself in the shadow of multiple fathers; his real father, who appears in two guises—the evil Darth Vader, and the valiant Jedi Anakin Skywalker—and his substitute fathers Yoda and Obi-Wan Kenobi, all of whom appear in the sky, smiling down in approval at the end of the final film. During the ultimate battle in which the Death Star is finally destroyed, Luke again meets Vader who tries to lure him over to the Dark Side; Luke resists, and when Vader threatens to try to lure Leia away in his place, Luke pulls out his light saber and charges his father. The battle is described in the script:

> Luke ignites his lightsaber and screams in anger, rushing at his father with a frenzy we have not seen before. Sparks fly as Luke and Vader fight in the cramped area. Luke's hatred forces Vader to retreat out of the low area and across a bridge overlooking a vast elevator shaft. Each stroke of Luke's sword drives his father further toward defeat.
>
> The Dark Lord is knocked to his knees, and as he raises his sword to block another onslaught, Luke slashes Vader's right hand off at the wrist, causing metal and electronic parts to fly from the mechanical stump. Vader's sword clatters uselessly away, over the edge of the platform and into the bottomless shaft below. Luke moves over to Vader and holds the blade of his sword to the Dark Lord's throat.[80]

The Arthurian story is equally a familial battle, if one with fewer parents. At the end of Malory's tale, Arthur "toke his horse and seyde, 'Alas, this unhappy day!' and so rode to hys party and Sir Mordred in lyke wyse."[81] Despite the structural asymmetry, since Arthur is father, not son, the climax of the intergenerational battle has many similarities to the *Star Wars* version:

> And nevere syns was there seyne a more dolefuller batayle in no Crysten londe, for there was but rysshynge and rydynge, foynynge and strykynge, and many a grym worde was there spokyn of aythir to other, and many a deadly stroke. But ever kynge Arthure rode thorowoute the batayle of sir Mordred many tymys and ded full nobely, as a noble kynge shulde do, and at all tymes

he fainted never. And sir Mordred ded hys devoure that day and put
hymselffe in grete perell.

. . .

And whan Sir Mordred saw kynge Arthur he ran untyll hym with hys swerde
drawn in hys honed, and there kung Arthur smote sir Mordred undir the
shylde, with a foyne of his speare, thorowoute the body more than a fadom.
And whan sir Mordred felte that he had hys dethys wounde he threste hym-
selff with the might that he had upp to the burre of kyng Arthurs speare, and
rygt so he smote hys fadir, kynge Arthure, with hys swerde holdynge in both
hys hondys, upon the side of the hede, that the swerde peced the helmet and
the tay of the brayne. And therewith Mordred daysshed downe starke dede
to the erthe.[82]

In both these familial battles, father and son struggle, fighting with swords
(or sabers) against the backdrop of a larger conflict. Arthur is, indeed,
encouraged to give up the battle when it is clear his troops have defeated
a significant portion of Mordred's and have won the day; while Luke's battle is only symbolically important within the larger struggle between the
Empire and the Rebels, since it is not the fight that blows up the Death
Star and ultimately ends the war. Yet both conflicts are what become primarily significant within their narratives; Luke's choice not to kill Vader to
save both of them from the Dark Side is as vital as Arthur's and Mordred's
mutual deaths. The two endings are simply reverse images of each other.
Arthur and Mordred mutually defeat each other, destroying Camelot, and
Arthur is carried on his funeral barge to Avalon. Luke and Vader make the
mutual choice not to kill each other and instead destroy the Emperor at the
end of the film; although Vader essentially dies in the process, he dies as
"Anakin Skywalker," the Jedi hero and is given a hero's burial on a pyre
that echoes medieval antecedents like *Beowulf*. The unmasking of Vader
reveals his true self, the good father, who ultimately redeems his own dark
past. Lucas, again, is not telling the Arthurian story verbatim, yet the amalgamation of its themes asserts the profound nature of Arthurian inspiration
within his overall narrative. Even when the players are reversed, many of
the very specific qualities of these themes remain in place. Both Arthur and
Vader die in acts of redemption, their fatal wounds a result of a family conflict played out in opposition, bad son versus good son. At the end of both
narratives, good has triumphed over evil, although in the *Le Morte Darthur*
both the "good" and the "triumph" are rather more ambiguous, since they
require Arthur's death and thus the abandonment of the ideals of Camelot.
While Luke, Leia, Han, and the Ewoks rejoice, the inhabitants of Camelot
grieve, the most redemptive feature of the Arthurian ending being
Guenevere's joining a convent and living out her last days there sadly: "and

never creature coude make her myry, but ever she lyved in fastynge, prayers, and almes-dedis, that all maner of people mervayled how virtuously she was chaunged."[83] Virtue, one should note, still triumphs, but pre-consumerist virtue can wear the face of sorrow.

At the end of Malory's text, we are told "som men say in many partys of Ingelonde that kynge Arthure ys nat dede, but had by the wyll of oure Lorde Jesu into another place, and men say that he shall com agayne, and he shall wynne the Holy Crosse. Yet I wol nat say that hit shall be so, but rather I wolde sey: here in thys worlde he chaunged hys lyff. And many men say that there ys written upon the tumbe thys: HIC IACET ARTHURUS, REX QUONDAM REXQUE FUTURUS."[84] The perpetuating quality of this ending is echoed at the end of *Return of the Jedi*, when the beatific faces of Obi-Wan Kenobi, Yoda, and Anakin Skywalker float above the celebrating crowds below. In another sense, the whole *Star Wars* enterprise is engaged with this return; the original films were rereleased in theaters in anticipation of the beginning of the "Prequel" series that started with the 1999 *Phantom Menace*, and within this next series, Anakin Skywalker, Obi-Wan Kenobi, and Yoda all do return. Even if these films inhabit a previous narrative time to the original ones, they still bring back that which was effectively "dead" at the end of the first series. Although the Arthur figure himself has not yet returned (although it seems likely that he will in the third of the prequel films, if only as a fetus), the romance world that contains him seems destined to repeat itself into the foreseeable future. If the films do not resurrect him, the paraphernalia will; a quick visual survey of two New York shops, Comics Plus in Brooklyn and Forbidden Planet in Manhattan,[85] suggests that even when *Star Wars* films are not on the big screen, the concomitant merchandise maintains its hold on the popular imagination. Even if the sequel trilogy of *Star Wars VII-IX* is never made, the variety and availability of *Star Wars* toys, displays, action figures, comic books, and even novels suggests that Lucas's project is indeed *Rex Quondam Rexque Futurus*.

For all its similarities to the Arthurian program, in *Star Wars*, a great deal is missing; the movies skirt the issues that the medieval, and particularly the Arthurian romances engage. One often forgotten factor of the Arthurian story is Arthur's cheerful pre-marital procreation, which breeds both Sir Borre, the son of Lyonors, who becomes a knight of the Round Table, and Mordred, via Arthur's indiscretion with his aunt: "for she was a passynge fayre lady, Wherefore the kynge caste grete love unto hir and desired to ly by her. And so they were agreed, and begate upon hir sir Mordred."[86] Luke, by contrast, remains virginal throughout; indeed, it apparently goes with the Jedi territory.

In declaring that "in *Star Wars* this ambiguity of mankind is resolved. All the heroes are good, and evil is externalized and defeated,"[87] Sherman (unconsciously) reveals *Star Wars*' essential rejection of complexity and disjunction, which cleans up the anxieties of the Arthurian story. For all her delineation of the parallels between them, she ultimately points directly to their differences. Although she suggests that this "craving for a resolution of ambiguities" is a function of "mass audience. . .eagerly reapplying the structure of ancient myths and fairy tales to achieve some degree of psychic order,"[88] she shows both a profound understanding of the films' inner workings and a misunderstanding of the function of classical myth—and at some level, fairy tale as well—in attributing such simplicity to them. Lucas makes no distinction between the different myths on which he draws, yet a significant portion of the material to which he oft refers, the Greek and Latin tradition, works very differently from the Arthurian corpus that shapes the films' narratives. Since classical myth informs the genre of tragedy, in which everybody carries his or her own fate internally, making the same person both hero and villain in the one skin and heroism finally a frustrated or inconsequential virtue, it does not externalize evil in order to defeat it. Indeed, classical heroism is tied up with failure; rather than a story of triumph, it explores the realm of courage in the face of its own defeat. In the whole Trojan War cycle, as well as the Theban Cycle of tragedies, this theme is quite obvious, but even in a work that seems to present a more triumphant or successful heroism, *The Odyssey*, the picture of goodness remains deeply contingent. While Odysseus does get home, resolving the narrative, in the underworld, he still must face the prophecy of his own death and Achilles's desire to be the lowest slave on earth rather than the most famous of the dead. The Phaiakian Idyll calls Odysseus's brand of heroics into question, suggesting that it propagates a cycle of destruction that can only be stopped by the gods' interference. Classical notions of fame read it as fleeting and localized; heroism is always linked to humans' incapacity to shape their own destiny. The production of an evil force that resides outside the hero to be defeated by him, which is more commonly found within medieval narrative, ranging from the Saracens in the *Song of Roland* to Mordred in many versions of the Arthurian story, separates the conflicting forces found within the classical hero into two discrete figures, making an internal battle an external one. Yet while the medieval material is more sanguine, ending the Arthurian story with the possibility of Arthur's ultimate return, it does not provide a totalizing heroism either. If the medieval *imitatio Christi* allows for a complete resolution, it can only work within its own religious context, not promising an end to suffering in *this* world; it provides a simple moral compass of good and evil (such as in the *Psychomachia*), but those assumptions do not really migrate into the secular material. The totalizing, moral potential always lurks in the background (such as in *Sir Gawain and the Green Knight*), yet the romances themselves always show human failure to achieve this complete resolution. While the Arthurian texts do provide some examples of externalized evil in dragons, giants, Morgan le Fay (sometimes), and Mordred, they also recognize that people are by nature unresolved, making characters such as Gawain, Lancelot, Guenevere, and even Arthur himself profoundly ambiguous. Thus, Steven Galipeau's suggestion that "the entire *Star Wars* saga can be approached as a cultural dream"[89] sheds light on the way we might read and understand it.

What the *Star Wars* films finally leave us with is more a romance than a myth for modern times. Even Lucas himself suggests the diminution of form that the films embody: "I see *Star Wars* as taking all the issues that religion represents and trying to distill them down into a more modern and easily accessible construct—that there is a greater mystery out there."[90] In Lucas's understanding, what is modern is that which is reduced, simplified, and packaged; religion becomes an aphorism, as, he suggests, "religion no longer occupies that central place in our culture today. Young people in particular are turning to the movies for their inspiration, not organized religion."[91] Returning to some of Umberto Eco's medieval dreams, we have Romance as theme park like the castles of Disneyland, as a complete escape from the issues it traditionally engages (such as those the contemporary romance production of *Star Trek* contends with). *Star Wars* is a representation of Eco's medievalized (but to that very extent not medieval) art "not systematic but additive and compositive," an example of the "great enterprise of popularization, with interchanges and borrowings, reciprocal and continuous."[92] In his portrait of Skywalker Ranch (with its suggestive theme park-like name), John Seabrook notes, "the most exciting things in the house are to be found in the two glass cases in the front hall, where the holiest relics are stored. The 'real' lightsaber that Luke uses in 'Star Wars' is here, and so are Indy's [Indiana Jones's] bullwhip and the diary that leads Indy to the Holy Grail. The Holy Grail itself is stored in the Archives Building."[93] Seabrook's language ("holiest relics") to describe the ephemera from Lucas's movies reveals both the premodern and contemporary ways in which the project casts itself; choosing a fundamentally medieval and sacral term to define these objects shows their most immediate cultural context. Casting the "Holy Grail" as film prop, locatable not in Glastonbury or Avalon but in the Archives Building, makes the past into plastic.

In this phenomenon, medievalism interacts with the modern as mass production and popularity come together. In *An All-Consuming Century: Why Commercialism Won in Modern America*, Gary Cross calls *Star Wars* the "best example" of a contemporary "managed fad":

> No American parent or child missed George Lucas's trilogy of *Star Wars* films between 1977 and 1983 or the merchandising mania that accompanied it.

By 1987, some 94 figures and 60 accessories had been manufactured by Kenner. While the first two *Star Wars* movies earned $870 million at the box office, by 1983 licensed products had pulled in $2 billion. The lessons learned through *Star Wars* were used again and again in highly orchestrated commercial festivals build around PLCs (program-length commercials) and Disney movies in the 1980s and 1990s.[94]

This vast production, however, is a consequence of the same kind of non-mass, popular impulses that brought back *Star Trek* and sanctified Mark McGwire; as George Sorensen is previously quoted, "the demand is already out there, and we're just meeting it—it would exist without us."[95] *Star Wars* has an enormous audience with significant power; it is likely that the second trilogy was made after a sixteen-year gap because continuing fan involvement kept the past alive. The demand that Sorenson responds to is fan desire, kept going from 1983 to 1999. Yet what is truly popular is essentially taken over by the merchandising impulse that seeks to control the phenomenon. Cross calls consumer culture "a more dynamic and popular, while less destructive ideology of public life than most political belief systems of the twentieth century";[96] popularity and dynamism are indeed the motivations for an active nonexclusive popular culture that echoes its medieval ancestors. The tension between this dynamism on the one hand and passivity on the other is the great contradiction of consumerist culture. Sorenson is correct to say that fan enthusiasm "would exist without us," yet he also acknowledges the need of the franchise itself to exert control over these popular phenomena with their potential for, if not disruption, a hijacking of the master narrative that would draw financial gains and narrative oversight away from the agents of mass culture and place them with the fans. Unlike the other examples explored in this work, in this case, popular expression on a broad scale is repressed so that the authorities (LucasArts) can take over its story.

Walter Benjamin suggests, "in the case of films, mechanical reproduction is not, as with literature and painting, an external condition for mass distribution. Mechanical reproduction is inherent in the very techniques of film production. This technique not only permits in the most direct way but virtually causes mass distribution."[97] Thus it may be the conditions of the medium that impose this top-down consumerist culture upon *Star Wars*' cult following. Even though the films that draw the ritualized and cultish reaction that Benjamin suggests are qualities of premodern culture, recast in the modern world, this medievalized product is ultimately less medieval. Rather than being original, they are, as Roland Barthes might call them, "a bastard form of mass culture" that is "humiliated repetition" in which "content, ideological schema, the blurring of contradictions—these are repeated, but the superficial forms are varied: always new books, new programs, new films, news items, but always the same meaning."[98] If in the other examples in this work, the medieval popular impulses of audience and genre revivify the past for the present, here they condemn it to a kind of repetitive circularity, one visible to anyone viewing the two newest *Star Wars* films and seeing the efflorescent merchandising of the same items all over again. Andreas Huyssen suggests that "modern mass culture is administered and imposed from above and the threat it represents resides not in the masses but in those who run the industry," showing the creation of homogeneity out of popular potential.[99] A look at objects (and the *Star Wars* franchise has produced vast quantities of objects, from films to figures to happy-meal toys) shows both the dovetailing of consumer and medievalized popular culture and reveals the ways the former may overwhelm the latter. Defining consumerism as "the belief that goods give meaning to individuals and their roles in society,"[100] Cross shows both how similar and different objects are from each other in these two schema. In both, things mean more than their utility or function; they suggest membership in a community and thus reflect back on their owners. But if the affectivity of things, particularly cultural things, in the medieval world was in their potential for transcendence, they provided a kind of consolation impossible in the modern world. Speaking of objects within contemporary society, Jean Baudrillard observes, "the systematic and limitless process of consumption arises from the disappointed demand for totality that underlies the project of life. In their ideality sign-objects are all equivalent and may multiply indefinitely; indeed, they *must multiply* at every moment to make up for a reality that is absent. Consumption is irrepressible, in the last reckoning, because it is founded upon a *lack*."[101] Because objects within mass culture can never fulfil desire, they must always increase, leading to Barthes's bastardized and humiliated repetition. Thus *Star Wars*, for all its pretension to religious significance and mythological importance, cannot, finally provide the kinds of consolation these impulses seek. Instead, it is destined, like the Arthurian romance that remains a popular source of book, film, and television mini-series, to return and return again.

Tipping its hand toward its modern commercial motive, *Star Wars* allows its audience to be a part of that romance world if they buy the stuff and learn the names of peripheral characters who are on screen for two seconds, and so forth. As with Eco's assessment of Disneyland, if the fan pays the price, "he can have not only 'the real thing' but the abundance of the reconstructed truth" that is "an immense and continuous 'found object.'"[102] John Seabrook asks, "What is it that makes people crave the Star Wars brand in so many different flavors?"[103] His answer suggests that in marketing itself, *Star Wars* found that "an alchemical transformation was taking place: dreams were being spun into desire, and desire forged into product."[104] The emphasis on the relationship between experience and things reflects T. J. Jackson Lears's sense that collecting (owning the stuff) is a desire to "create other realms of meaning, based on alternative relationships to objects, alongside throwaway culture."[105] It is the things that provide the entrée into the romance theme park here; by constructing a world of objects around itself, *Star Wars* creates for itself a "place in the cultural hierarchy," made out of its "materiality and history."[106] Thus desire for the objects becomes intertwined with a desire for the morals that the *Star Wars* project offers; because the objects "arouse powerful emotions," which they then seem to return, they stimulate a "need to gather more and more of the same kind."[107] Thus, in a capitalistic and materialistic manner, the *Star Wars* project perpetuates its own need, assuring its status as a "rex quondam rexque futurus." Seabrook projects an ironically resurrectionist image in his comment: "even if the story were to fade from the surface of the Earth it will remain buried underground in the form of Luke Skywalker pizza boxes and Obi-Wan sixteen-ounce beverage cups."[108] The subterranean lurking of *Star Wars* stuff under the earth, waiting for its resurrection (by future anthropologists, perhaps, thus turning it into Lucas's desired myth), suggests Arthur waiting patiently in Avalon. However, this disposable stuff is eclipsed by those things that endure; each addition to the *Star Wars* whole perpetuates the same desires for acquisition and repetitive experience; in an essentially modern, and thus commodified form, *Star Wars* offers up a debased version of the perpetuity of the Arthurian story for our own time.

NOTES

Introduction

* Geoffrey Moorhouse. "The Patron Saint of Greenies," *New York Times Book Review*. March 11, 2001. 7:13. Moorehouse's source for this quotation from Tuchman is unclear.

1. Jack (John Frank) Fournier (1889–1973) had a fifteen-year Major League baseball career (1912–27) with the Chicago White Sox, New York Yankees, St. Louis Browns, Brooklyn Dodgers, and Boston Braves.

2. Umberto Eco, *Baudolino*, trans. William Weaver (New York: Harcourt, 2002), pp. 520–21.

3. Eco, *Travels*, p. 62.

4. Umberto, Eco, *Travels* in Hyperreality, trans. William Weaver (New York: Harcourt, Brace, and Jovanovich, 1986), p. 62.

5. Eco, *Travels*, p. 63.

6. Eco, *Travels*, p. 74.

7. See, among numerous examples, Randy Boswell, "Medieval Crusades Revived in Terrorism-War Rhetoric," *Ottawa Citizen*, September 25, 2001, A2 and Susan Sachs, "Bin Laden's Images Mesmerize Muslims," *New York Times*, October 9, 2001 (www.nytimes.com).

8. Paul Zumthor, *Toward a Medieval Poetics*, trans. Phillip Bennett (Minneapolis: University of Minnesota Press, 1992), p. 3.

9. Catherine Brown, "In the Middle," *Journal Of Medieval and Early Modern Studies* 30.3 (2000), p. 548.

10. Brown, "In the Middle," p. 548.

11. In the middle of her own sentence, Brown inserts this apt quotation from Lee Patterson, "On the Margin: Postmodernism, Ironic History, and Medieval Studies," *Speculum* 65 (1990), p. 103.

12. Brown, "In the Middle," p. 567.

13. *A Knight's Tale*, 132 mins., Color, Columbia/TriStar Pictures, Burbank, CA, 2001.

14. Queen, "We Will Rock You," 1978.

15. Geoffrey Chaucer, *Troilus and Criseyde. The Riverside Chaucer*, 3rd edn., ed. Larry D. Benson (Boston: Houghton, Mifflin, 1987), 1. I: 109.

16. *Monty Python and the Holy Grail*, 91 mins., Color, Columbia/TriStar Pictures, UK, 1974. I am grateful to Joan M. Ferrante for this insight (and countless others) of which I have made great use in my own teaching.

17. Eco, *Travels*, p. 81–2.

18. Eco, *Travels*, p. 82.

19. As a contraction of "oral literature," orature defines the body of literary material not experienced in primarily textual ways; designed for oral performance, it may be ultimately preserved in textual forms (such as *Beowulf* manuscript preserved in Anglo-Saxon England), yet in its production and use it differed from works whose composition and transmission were primarily undertaken on paper.

20. Eco, *Travels*, p. 82.

21. Eco, *Travels*, p. 83

22. Andreas Huyssen, *After the Great Divide: Modernism, Mass Culture, Postmodernism* (Bloomington: Indiana University Press, 1986), p. vii.

23. Huyssen, *After the Great Divide*, p. vii.

24. Maud Hart Lovelace, *Carney's House Party* (New York: HarperCollins, 1949), p. 190.

25. Maud Hart Lovelace, *Emily of Deep Valley* (New York: HarperCollins, 1950).

26. Laura Ingalls Wilder, *Little Town on the Prairie* (New York: Harper & Row, 1941).

27. For a more detailed examination of Tennyson's sales figures, see Robert Bernard Martin, *Tennyson: The Unquiet Heart* (Oxford: Clarendon Press, 1893). See, in particular, p. 480.

28. These sales rankings are for August 10, 2002; they change daily. However, two other works from 1998, Don DeLillo's *Underworld* (New York: Scribners, 1998) and Stephen J. Sansweet and Timothy Zahn's *The Star Wars Encyclopedia* (New York: Ballantine, 1998) rank 12,382 and 11,582 respectively (www.amazon.com).

29. Huyssen, *After the Great Divide*, p. 18.

30. Hyussen, *After the Great Divide*, p. 21.

31. Huyssen, *After the Great Divide*, p. 21.

32. Ulf Boethius, "The History of High and Low Culture," in *Youth Culture in Late Modernity*, ed. Johan Fornäs and Göran Bolin (London: Sage, 1995), pp. 12–38, 24.

33. *Safe at Home*, 1962, United Artists, USA, Black and White, 84 mins.

34. Details on Marty Neff and the Marty Neff Fan Club can be found in Neal Karlen's *Slouching Towards Fargo* (New York: Avon, 1999). In 1996, Mary Neff hit .330 with 8 home runs and 41 runs batted in the first half but was nonetheless traded to the Sioux City Explorers because he drove his manager crazy, pp. 179–80. The trade caused an open rebellion in the Marty Neff fan club, who planned trips to see their idol play in Sioux City and harassed the owner and manager of the Saints at every game (Karlen, pp. 180–81).

35. Boethius, "The History of High and Low Culture," p. 12.

36. Aron Gurevich, *Medieval Popular Culture: Problems of Belief and Perception*, trans. János M. Bak and Paul A. Hollingsowrth (Cambridge: Cambridge University Press, 1988), p. 4.

37. Boethius, "The History of High and Low Culture," p. 13.

38. Huyssen, *After the Great Divide*, p. 17.

39. *Star Trek* and *Star Wars* do have conventions, yet these, such as the annual Creation Convention in Pasadena, California, feature talks by actors and animators rather than academics, and sell autographed photographs and replica phasers instead of scholarly books.

40. Walter Benjamin, "The Work of Art in the Age of Mechanical Reproduction," in *Illuminations*, ed. Hannah Arendt, trans. Harry Zohn (New York: Schocken Books, 1988), pp. 224–25.

41. Benjamin, "The Work of Art," p. 223.

42. Benjamin, "The Work of Art," p. 244, n. 7.

43. Abel Gance, "Le Temps de l'image est venu," *L'art Cinématographique* 2 (1927), p. 94; qtd. in Benjamin, "The Work of Art," p. 222.

44. Benjamin, "The Work of Art," p. 241.

45. For instance, the minor figure of Boba Fett, Bounty Hunter, has emerged as one of *Star Wars'* most popular characters, despite appearing in only one film for about five minutes. A series of Boba Fett novels, homemade Boba Fett costumes, and Boba Fett fan sites abound, and if they don't outdistance the more obvious Luke Skywalker and Han Solo devotions, they certainly challenge their expected supremacy.

46. Eco, *Travels*, p. 65.

47. Susan Stewart, *On Longing: Narratives of the Miniature, the Gigantic, the Souvenir, the Collection* (Durham, NC: Duke University Press, 1993), p. ix.

48. Stewart, *On Longing*, p. xi.

49. Susan Pearce, *Museums, Objects, and Collections* (Washington: Smithsonian Institution, 1992), p. 72.

50. Jean Baudrillard, *For a Critique of the Political Economy of the Sign*, trans. Charles Levin (St. Louis: Telos Press, 1981), p. 38.

51. Stewart, *On Longing*, p. xi.

52. Danielle Régnier-Bohler. "Imagining the Self. Part I: Exploring Literature," *A History of Private Life II: Revelations of the Medieval World*, ed. Georges Duby, trans. Arthur Goldhammer (Cambridge, MA: Belknap Press, 1988), p. 313.

53. Régnier-Bohler, "Imagining the Self," p. 313.

54. Régnier-Bohler, "Imagining the Self," p. 313.

55. Boethius, "The History of High and Low Culture," p. 36.

56. Will and Ariel Durant, *The Age of Faith: A History of Medieval Civilization*, in *The Story of Civilization*, vol. 2 (New York: Simon and Schuster, 1950).

57. Troy Soos, *Murder at Ebbets Field* (New York: Kensington Press, 1995), p. 1.

58. Michael A. Messer, *Power at Play: Sports and the Problem of Masculinity* (Boston: Beacon Press, 1992), p. 1.

59. Harlequin is the largest publisher in North America, producing more books per annum than any other commercial company and topped in volume only by the U.S. government (www.eharlequin.com).

60. *Star Trek: The Next Generation*, Paramount Pictures, Syndicated, 1987–94. The original series began with a slightly different version of the same speech: "to explore strange new worlds, to seek out new life and new civilizations, to boldly go where no man has gone before." Although this version ultimately reflects some of the repressive ideas inherent in medieval (and modern) romance, I have chosen to use the *Next Generation* as my example for the chapter. *Star Trek*, Desilu Productions, NBC, 1966–69.

61. Erich Auerbach, "The Knight Sets Forth," *Mimesis: The Representation of Reality in Western Literature*, trans. Willard R. Trask (Princeton: Princeton University Press, 1953), pp. 123–42.

62. Auerbach, *Mimesis*, p. 138.

63. Auerbach, *Mimesis*, p. 131.

64. *Star Trek* won the American Scene Award, presented by the Screen Actor's Guild, on February 24, 1996 for the "Outstanding Portrayal of the American Scene": "thirty years of diversity in casting and special efforts to accurately portray the American Scene" (www.sagawards.com).

65. Auerbach, *Mimesis*, p. 136.

66. David Gerold, *The World of Star Trek* (New York: Balantine Books, 1973), p. 17.

67. Geoffrey Moorhouse. "The Patron Saint of Greenies," p. 7:13.

68. Robertson Davies, *The Rebel Angels*, p. 29.

69. "Heroes and Demons," *Star Trek: Voyager*, episode #112, Paramount Pictures, first aired, April 4, 1995.

70. Carolyn Dinshaw, *Getting Medieval: Sexualities and Communities, Pre- and Post-Modern* (Durham, NC: Duke University Press, 1999), p. 2.

71. Dinshaw, *Getting Medieval*, p. 2.

Chapter 1   From Big Mac to Saint Mark: Saints, Relics, and the Pilgrimage to Cooperstown

1. The Cloisters is the Metropolitan Museum of Art in New York's medieval wing; located uptown in Fort Tryon Park, it is composed of pieces of actual cloisters imported from Europe by the Rockefeller family. The Cloisters provides access to a full spectrum of medieval art and architecture in a setting at once medieval and modern, as the old functional and devotional objects interact with contemporary ideas of observation and collection that inform the contemporary museum. Also, this patchwork medieval structure rises out of the hillside in a park that serves the city's diverse immigrant communities of Washington Heights and Inwood, and provides a disjunctive and sometimes incongruous pairing as the museum-goer walks up the hill from the subway station.

2. Although the development of women's professional basketball and soccer leagues may allow this to change, the construction of the athlete as hero is still a primarily masculine phenomenon. The exceptions tend to be based on a singular heroic event, such as the American gymnast Kerri Strug's vault in the 1996 Olympics which, despite the injured ankle that ended her career, solidified the U.S. team's victory in the all-around competition. Female athletes' overall presentation, on the other hand, is rarely drawn in this particular way.

3. *Medieval Popular Religion 1000–1500: A Reader*, ed. John Shinners (Peterborough, ON: Broadview Press, 1997), p. xvi.

4. *Medieval Popular Religion*, p. xvi.

5. *Medieval Popular Religion*, p. xvi.

6. *Medieval Popular Religion*, p. xvi.

7. *Medieval Popular Religion*, p. xvi.

8. *Medieval Popular Religion*, p. xvi.

9. *Medieval Popular Religion*, p. xvii.

10. *Medieval Popular Religion*, p. 274.

11. See, e.g., the Worldwide Church of Baseball (www.worldwidechurch.com).

12. Russell Hollander, "The Religion of Baseball: Psychological Perspectives," *Nine* 3.1 (1994), p. 1.

13. Hollander, "The Religion of Baseball," p. 2.

14. Philip Lowry, *Green Cathedrals* (New York: Addison Wesley, 1992) qtd. in Hollander, "The Religion of Baseball," p. 2.

15. *Green Cathedrals*, qtd. in Hollander, "The Religion of Baseball," p. 2.

16. Hollander, "The Religion of Baseball," p. 4.

17. Abraham Maslow, *Religions, Values and Peak Experiences* (New York: Viking, 1971) paraphrased in Hollander, "The Religion of Baseball," p. 6.

18. A. Bartlett Giamatti, *Take Time for Paradise: Americans and Their Games* (New York: Summit Books, 1989), p. 32.

19. Giamatti, *Take Time for Paradise*, p. 25.

20. Giamatti, *Take Time for Paradise*, p. 23.

21. Giamatti, *Take Time for Paradise*, p. 23.

22. Giamatti, *Take Time for Paradise*, p. 24.

23. Peter Brown, *The Cult of the Saints: Its Rise and Function in Latin Christianity* (Chicago: University of Chicago Press, 1981), p. 3.

24. Giamatti, *Take Time for Paradise*, p. 32.

25. Giamatti, *Take Time for Paradise*, p. 33.

26. Giamatti, *Take Time for Paradise*, p. 34.

27. Giamatti, *Take Time for Paradise*, p. 36.

28. Giamatti, *Take Time for Paradise*, p. 42.

29. These figures play the role of saints rather than that of Dante's Virgil, Beatrice, or Bernard because of the lack of any real, personal interaction between them and their followers; the closest most fans come to these figures is a brief moment in which an autograph is exchanged; this then becomes a reliquary object, available for private devotion. But the sustained

encounter between Dante and his guides, and the achievement of paradise, never actually takes place, except possibly in dreams.

30. Brown, *The Cult of the Saints*, p. 50.

31. Mark McGwire played for the Oakland As from 1987 to 1997; in his first season, he set the rookie home run record with forty-nine. In 1997, he was traded to the St. Louis Cardinals, and the following season hit seventy home runs to establish a new record. He retired after the 2001 season, following a series of injuries, the same season his home run record was broken by the San Francisco Giants's Barry Bonds, with seventy-three. McGwire retired with 584 home runs, keeping him from joining the elite group of players (Babe Ruth, Hank Aaron, Willie Mays, and in 2002, Barry Bonds) who have hit over 600 home runs; McGwire hit twenty-nine home runs in 2001 while only batting .187, so it is likely that had he recuperated from his injury over the winter, he would doubtless have hit the requisite 16+ required to become a member of the 600 club. His choice was thus questioned by fans and sportswriters, although it confirmed McGwire's oft repeated statement that he didn't play baseball for the records, but because he loved it.

32. Kenneth Woodward, *Making Saints* (New York: Touchstone, 1990), p. 19.

33. This is also a trait of medieval narrative, in which comic and debased forms are often used to treat serious matters; medieval narrative does not impose a rigid separation of church and state, thus the rhetoric of religion can describe the experience of love in a secular romance, while the rhetoric of romance, even in its most erotic forms, is used to describe devotion to Christ, Mary, and the Saints. The incongruity modern readers find in this metaphoric intertextual exchange seems ironic in light of the contemporary world's willingness to apply this same elevated language to sports.

34. Woodward, *Making Saints*, p. 18.

35. This hagiography is entirely my own creation, yet all the reflections of medieval ideology appear in the articles and websites dedicated to Mark McGwire's accomplishments. While they contain religious language that will be examined in detail in this chapter, this example is my fabrication, constructed by my imposition of the language and structures of the *Legenda Aurea* onto the attitudes toward and assumptions about McGwire revealed in the coverage of his career from his arrival in St. Louis in 1997 to his retirement in 2001.

36. While this chapter focuses primarily on Mark McGwire, his competitor in the home run race, Sammy Sosa, was also elevated. In the American national imagination, which claims baseball as its "national pastime," McGwire received greater press, at least in part because of his "all American boy" identity, and in part because he seemed predestined to break Maris's record since his impressive home run hitting feats in his rookie year. Sammy Sosa, however, captured the national imagination of the Dominican Republic from which he hails, as well as winning the hearts of Dominicans in the United States. Indeed, some of the salutary

rhetoric surrounding Sosa in the DR was as miraculous as that which McGwire received; after Hurricaine Georges wrought havoc on the Dominican in September of 1998, shoeshine boy Papi de la Rosa was noted as saying "Sammy Sosa is our only hope. Sammy will help us. He always does when he comes home" (qtd. in Peter Golenbock, *The Spirit of St. Louis: A History of the St. Louis Cardinals and Browns* [New York: Avon, 2000], p. 598). At one hotel in Santo Domingo, someone slipped a note under everyone's door, despite flooding and a total lack of electricity, to tell the guests of Sosa hitting his sixty-fourth and sixty-fifth home runs. According to Peter Golenbock, "More than 1,000 people filled Mercedes Church in downtown Santo Domingo to say prayers for their hero." "The nation has come to pray for the boy," said the Reverend Jose Arellano. "He helps us unite" (598). Sosa went on to contribute significantly to the country's relief efforts. The competing rhetorics of Saint Mark and Saint Sammy are worthy of further comparison, and indeed, their rivalry is susceptible to medievalizing interpretation. While their competition certainly galvanized interest in the home run race (indeed, in 2001 people were more interested in Barry Bonds when Luis Gonzalez of the Arizona Diamondbacks was matching him home run for home run until the All-Star Break), it is perhaps surprisingly, Sosa's continued success, coupled with his casually cheerful persona, that have prevented his sanctification. If McGwire always maintained a kind of superhuman distance from his fans, Sosa's presentation as a happy-go-lucky guy with enormous talent to match his enormous smile has made him incredibly popular in a different way. At some level, it may even keep him from the recognition he deserves (his overall career statistics are likely to outstrip McGwire's in many categories), although there's no doubt that Sosa will be inducted into the Hall of Fame on his first ballot as well. In 1998, it is worth noting, Sosa won the National League Most Valuable Player award, not McGwire.

37. Richard Kieckhefer, *Unquiet Souls* (Chicago: University of Chicago Press, 1984), p. 7.

38. Jacobus de Voragine, *Golden Legend*, vol. 2, trans. William Granger Ryan (Princeton: Princeton University Press, 1993), p. 10.

39. *New York Daily News*, September 9, 1998, pp. 52–53.

40. *New York Daily News*, September 9, 1998, pp. 60–61.

41. *Time*, December 28, 1998–January 4, 1999, p. 138.

42. *Time*, December 28, 1998– January 4, 1999, p. 147.

43. *Sports Illustrated* 89:11 September 14, 1998, p. 28

44. Rob Rains, *Mark McGwire: Home Run Hero* (New York: St. Martin's Press, 1998), p. 13.

45. Rains, *Mark McGwire*, p. 14.

46. Rains, *Mark McGwire*, p. 14.

47. Jacobus de Voragine, *Golden Legend*, vol. 2, p. 98.

48. Jacobus de Voragine, *Golden Legend*, vol. 2, p. 99.

49. Rains, *Mark McGwire*, p. 13.

50. Jacobus de Voragine, *Golden Legend*, p. 10.

51. Rains, *Mark McGwire*, p. 22.

52. Rains, *Mark McGwire*, p. 23.

53. Kieckhefer, *Unquiet Souls*, p. 10.

54. Rick Reilly, "The Good Father," *Sports Illustrated*, September 7, 1998, p. 38.

55. Jacobus de Voragine, *Golden Legend*, vol. 1, trans. William Granger Ryan (Princeton: Princeton University Press, 1993), p. 386.

56. Brown, *The Cult of the Saints*, p. 71.

57. It may be, in fact, the overdetermined nature of McGwire's presentation that points to what's different between him and his friendly rival for the home run record, Sammy Sosa. If McGwire led up to his record by hitting fifty-eight home runs in 1997, and having significant home run totals in several earlier seasons, Sosa, despite being a talented hitter, did not have the kind of record that made him an obvious candidate. Once he entered the race and showed himself a clear competitor for the title, the media was essentially playing a kind of catch up.

58. Rick Hummel, "Redbirds Make Their Mark," *St. Louis Post-Dispatch*, September 17, 1997, 1A.

59. Hummel, "Redbirds Make Their Mark," 1A.

60. Tom Timmermann, "McGwire's Stature Rose as Tears Fell: 'I Was Wanting So Much to Help Young Children,' " *St. Louis Post-Dispatch*, September 20, 1997, p. 14.

61. Timmermann, "McGwire's Stature Rose as Tears Fell," p. 14.

62. Jeff Gordon, "McGwire's Mark on Community One For the Ages," *St. Louis Post-Dispatch*, September 19, 1997, 1D.

63. The St. Louis Gateway Arch, the city's largest tourist attraction, provides a potentially comic counter-reading in which the Arch becomes McDonald's Golden Arches and "Big Mac" its saint even more overtly constructed for the postmodern world. Sosa and McGwire, in fact, did do commercials for McDonald's after the 1998 baseball season, Sosa willingly and McGwire apparently reluctantly.

64. All quotations in the paragraph are from Gordon, "McGwire's Mark on Community One for the Ages," 1D.

65. Brown, *The Cult of the Saints*, p. 6.

66. Kieckhefer, *Unquiet Souls*, p. 189.

67. As a female religious, Margery is not an ideal comparison; she is not canonized, and while her *Booke* reads very much like a hagiography, it also has many differences from the more abbreviated saints' legends. While female saints are sometimes heroic in the protection of their virginity, and Margery is certainly very interested in maintaining her chaste marriage at certain points in the autobiography, she is not particularly noted for the kinds of actions in which male saints engage. She does, however, provide an extended examination of the assumptions of religious selection, mixing socially acceptable and admirable characteristics with the eccentric and isolating activities that separate the religious, particularly saints, from the common populace and is thus a useful point of reference.

68. Jacobus de Voragine, *Golden Legend*, vol. 1, pp. 14–15. Prodigious weeping is a feature of many saints' lives and appears in many forms—the weeping of the Saint who longs for salvation or feels his own guilt, such as Augustine; the mysterious weeping of the mystic, most forcefully narrated in the *Book of Margery Kempe*; and the weeping with sorrow over the plight of the unfortunate, as in the Saint Andrew model. While the first two are essentially private acts (although often enacted in public), a dialogue between the saint and God, the latter, as an intercessionary act, is more public in its function; by working outside the saint, for others, it becomes an act of compassion that leads to charity.

69. It is certainly possible to read an athlete's training regimen as the functional equivalent of self-affliction and a form of self-denial, especially in players like Mark McGwire who are conditioning enthusiasts and spend a great deal of time on their off-field workouts. Since much of McGwire's training in recent years included rehabbing injuries, it is likely that a considerable amount of pain was involved as well.

70. Timmermann, "McGwire's Stature Rose as Tears Fell," p. 14.

71. Timmermann, "McGwire's Stature Rose as Tears Fell," p. 14.

72. "Series Ball aid sick Boy." *New York Times*, October 7, 1926, 21:2.

73. "Series Ball aid sick Boy." *New York Times*, October 7, 1926, 21:2.

74. "Boy Regains Health as Ruth Hits Homers." *New York Times*, October 8, 1926, 17:2.

75. "Boy Regains Health as Ruth Hits Homers." *New York Times*, October 8, 1926, 17:2

76. "Dr. Babe Ruth calls on His Boy Patient." *New York Times*, October 12, 1926, 1:2.

77. "Boy Regains Health as Ruth His Homers." *New York Times*, October 8, 1926, 17:2.

78. "Sick Boy Expecting Ruth Homers Today." *New York Times*, October 9, 1926, 19:3.

79. Robert Creamer, *Babe Ruth: The Legend Comes to Life* (New York: Simon and Schuster, 1974), p. 328.

80. *The Babe Ruth Story* 107 min., Black and White, Allied Artists, Hollywood, CA., 1948.

81. "The Basball Hero," *New York Times*, October 8, 1926, 22:5.

82. "The Baseball Hero," *New York Times*, October 8, 1926, 22:5.

83. Ellen Chase, "Mark and Sammy Captivate a Nation," *Star-Ledger*, September 6, 1998, p. 1.

84. Chase, "Mark and Sammy," p. 1.

85. Tom Verducci, "Making his Mark," *Sports Illustrated*, 89:11 September 14, 1998, p. 32.

86. Daniel Okrent, "A Mac for All Seasons," *Time*, December 28, 1998 January 4, 1999, p. 140.

87. Michael Kaufman, "Testing of a President," *New York Times*, September 17, 1998, p. 1.

88. John F. Harris, "Havel is Mystified by America's Latest Pastime," *Washington Post*, September 17, 1998, A14.

89. Kaufman, "Testing of a President," A1.

90. Chase, "Mark and Sammy," p. 1.

91. Peter Golenbock, *The Spirit of St. Louis: A History of the St. Louis Cardinals and Browns* (New York: Avon, 2000), pp. 591–600.

92. Luke Cyphers, "A Mark for the Ages," *New York Daily News*, September 9, 1998, p. 57.

93. Chase, "Mark and Sammy," p. 1.

94. Amy Ellis Nutt, "McGwire helps put baseball in the pink," *Newark Star-Ledger*, September 13, 1998, p. 1.

95. Chase, "Mark and Sammy," p. 1.

96. Golenbock, *Spirit of St. Louis*, p. 598.

97. Gumby's Mark McGwire Message Board (www.mcgwire.com), posted by Joyce, June 21, 2001.

98. Brown, *Cult of the Saints*, p. 39.

99. Tom Verducci, "48, 49, 50," *Sports Illustrated*, 89.9 (1998), p. 30.

100. Chase, "Mark and Sammy," p. 1.

101. Anthony Bianco, "A Grand-Slam Season," *Business Week*, November 2, 1998, p. 104.

102. Bianco, "Grand-Slam," p. 104.

103. "Seats out in Left," p. 67.

104. "Seats out in Left," p. 67.

105. The fate of most of these balls is discussed at length in Daniel Paisner's *The Ball: Mark McGwire's 70th Home Run Ball and the Marketing of the American Dream* (New York: Viking, 1999); some of these stories will be treated at length in the "Relics" section of this chapter; a long string of fans chose to give them back, a chain that was broken by someone asking for too much in exchange. After that, the precedent was set, which led to Philip Ozersky's auctioning of the seventieth home run ball for $3.05 million dollars.

106. Kieckhefer, *Unquiet Souls*, p. 4.

107. Sportswriters determine entry into the National Baseball Hall of Fame, which is not affiliated with Major League Baseball. The status of writers lies between organized baseball and its fans. However, to vote on Hall of Fame inductions, writers must be official, card-carrying members of the Baseball Writers Association of America, which requires ten years of service, and the tendency to use statistical criteria for election (such as 3,000 hits) rather than popularity, has often put writers at odds with the fans. For instance, Phil Rizzuto, New York Yankee shortstop of the 1940s and 1950s, never received enough votes to be inducted until the Veterans Committee, composed of living inducted players, voted for him in 1994.

108. Jerry Izenberg, "Big Mac takes over the city with the Arch," *Newark Star-Ledger*, September 2, 1998, p. 17.

109. Rick Riley, "The Good Father," *Sports Illustrated*, September 7, 1998, p. 36.

110. Joel Stein, "Long Live the King," *Time*, September 21, 1998, p. 93.

111. Jerry Izenberg, "The History," *Newark Star-Ledger*, September 7, 1998, p. 57.

112. Izenberg, "The History," p. 57.

113. Izenberg, "The History," p. 57.

114. Vic Ziegel, "You Can't Measure a Home Run This Big," *New York Daily News*, September 9, 1998, p. 52.

115. Mike Vaccaro, "As McGwire Hits Homer 62, Time Stands Still," *Newark Star-Ledger*, September 9, 1998, p. 1.

116. Vaccaro, "As McGwire Hits Homer 62," p. 1.

117. Stein, "Long Live the King," p. 93.

118. Benedicta Ward, *Miracles and the Medieval Mind: Theory, Record and Event 1000–1215*, 1982 (Philadelphia: University of Pennsylvania Press, 1987), p. 4; Augustine, *De Civitate Dei*, 22:8.

119. Stein, "Long Live the King," p. 93.

120. Gregorii episcopi Turonensis, *Miracula et opera minora. Liber Vitae Patrum*, ed. B. Krusch, Monumenta Geramniae Historica: Scriptores Rerum Merovingicarum, pp. 1, 2 (Hanover: Hahn, 1885). *VP* 7.3.328. qtd. in Brown, *Cult of the Saints*, p. 77.

121. I have taken a highly unscientific poll to test this theory, asking friends, students, and several fellow fans at Yankee and Shea stadiums in the 2000 and 2001 baseball seasons. No one has known for certain, including my longtime fan husband, my most baseball-devoted student, and a self-professed "baseball trivia maniac" at Yankee Stadium, although several have guessed correctly (with a 50–50 chance, this is to be expected). However, this poll is not representative, since I have encountered only one nonresident St. Louis fan whose interest is more theoretical than actual. She didn't know either. The Cardinals won, 6–3.

122. "Road to the Record" (Chart) *New York Daily News*, September 9, 1998, p. 56.

123. Qtd. in Golenbock, *Spirit of St. Louis*, p. 596.

124. See Allan Guttman, *From Ritual to Record* (New York: Columbia University Press, 1978), pp. 51–52 for a discussion of the time-altering qualities of sports records, which he calls "a stimulus to unimagined heights of achievement and a psychic barrier which thwarts our efforts, it is an occasion for frenzy, a form of rationalized madness, a symbol of our civilization." That this could equally describe the reaction of a cult to a popular saint is striking.

125. Woodward, *Making Saints*, p. 18.

126. Kieckhefer, *Unquiet Souls*, p. 13.

127. Kieckhefer, *Unquiet Souls*, p. 200.

128. Luke Cyphers, "A Mark of Excellence" *New York Daily News*, September 9, 1998, p. 57; Mark Hyman, "Holy Cow, was that a $25 Million Homer?" *Business Week*, September 21, 1998, p. 104.

129. Brown, *Cult of the Saints*, p. 50.

130. Woodward, *Making Saints*, p. 60.

131. Joel Stein, "Mark of Excellence," *Time*, December 28, 1998–January 4, 1999, p. 150.

132. "Our Tribute to Mark McGwire" (www.geocites.com/Colusseum/Sideline/5121/mcgwire.htm).

133. "The Mark McGwire Shrine" (www.geocities.com/Pentagon/Quarters/8861/McGwire.html).

134. "Mark McGwire Online" (members.aol.com/trigrhpykj/mcgwire.html).

135. While the site owner of "Mark McGwire Ate My Balls," the self-styled "PerplexedMacabre," is one fan vocally critical of McGwire's use of androstenedione, and indeed, to some extent of McGwire himself, he nonetheless links the Mark McGwire Foundation for Children website to his page and praises McGwire for his charitable works. Thus he impresses even his detractors (www.geocities.com/perplexedmacabre/mcgwire).

136. Kieckhefer, *Unquiet Souls*, p. 13.

137. Okrent, "A Mac for All Seasons," p. 140.

138. *The Newark Star-Ledger*, July 9, 1998, 1A.

139. *Baseball Weekly*, 10:39, 2000.

140. *Sports Illustrated*, 89:12, 1998.

141. Matthew, 19:21.

142. These public service announcements are available for viewing in slide form on the Mark McGwire Foundation for Children website (www.mcgwire.kids.yahoo.com).

143. *Medieval Saints: A Reader*, ed. Mary-Ann Stouck (Peterborough, ON: Broadview Press, 1999), p. 207.

144. *Medieval Saints: A Reader*, p. 284.

145. *Medieval Saints: A Reader*, p. 285.

146. Stein, "Mark of Excellence," p. 150.

147. Reilly, "The Good Father," p. 37.

148. Reilly, "The Good Father," p. 37.

149. Regarding José Canseco, a fellow member of the Oakland A's in the late 1980s and early 1990s, McGwire is noted to have said, "There's no one like Jose. I can't do what he does, but he can do what I do" (Raines, *Mark McGwire*, p. 129). While this seems ironic, given both players' fates (McGwire has enjoyed great fan loyalty and success, while Canseco, plagued by injury, has become a journeyman, forced to play for the unaffiliated Newark Bears in the 2001 season to regain a chance at returning to the Major Leagues), it seems likely, from McGwire's pronouncements, that he may still feel this way.

150. Cyphers, "A Mark for the Ages," p. 56.

151. Cyphers, "A Mark for the Ages," p. 56.

152. Cyphers, "A Mark for the Ages," p. 56.

153. *Medieval Saints: A Reader*, p. 140.

154. Reilly, "The Good Father," p. 45.

155. Cyphers, "A Mark for the Ages," p. 56.

156. Sammy Sosa, "Mi Amigo Mark," *Time*, December 28, 1998–January 4, 1999, p. 142.

157. *Medieval Saints: A Reader*, p. 141.

158. Reilly, "The Good Father," p. 45.

159. Raines, *Mark McGwire*, p. 218.

160. See the Picture Archive on Gumby's Mark McGwire Homepage (www.mcgwire.com) for numerous examples, most notably in the "Off the Field" section, that features McGwire tearing up at the 1998 Player's Choice Awards, and the "Press Conference" section that pictures several lachrymose interviews.

161. Gumby's Mark McGwire Message Board (www.mcgwire.com). Posted by Joyce June 21, 2001.

162. Fox Family Channel's "Family Baseball" games show little difference from any other games broadcast at any other time; for instance, the players are no less likely to spit and grab their crotches than on the Fox Game of the Week or on local broadcasts, and the commentary is not pitched to younger fans, although the announcers do tend to explain the game at a slightly lower level of complexity and sophistication. It has a slightly more positive air—fewer discourses on the state of baseball and more on the glory of the game—but the differences are essentially minimal. However, the crowd shots do tend to dwell on families and children.

163. *Who's Who in Baseball*, 86th edn., ed. Bill Shannon (New York: Who's Who in Baseball Magazine, Co., 2001), p. 121.

164. *Street and Smith's Baseball Annual*, February 2001, p. 134; *The Sporting News Baseball Annual*, February 2001, p. 75.

165. "The Official St. Louis Cardinals Website" (cardinals.mlb.com).

166. Reilly, "The Good Father," p. 34.

167. Okrent, "A Mac for All Seasons," p. 140.

168. Verducci, "48,49,50," p. 30.

169. Hyman, "Holy Cow, was that a $25 Million Homer?" p. 104.

170. Gumby's Mark McGwire Message Board (www.mcgwire.com). Posted by Melissa August 12, 2001.

171. Nennius, *Historia Brittonum*, "Arthur in the Latin Chronicles," *The Legend of Arthur*, ed. James J. Wilhelm and Laia Zamuelis Gross (New York: Garland, 1984), p. 7.

172. Jacobus de Voragine, *Golden Legend*, vol. 2, p. 11.

173. *Medieval Saints: A Reader*, p. 571.

174. "The Power of Caring: Mark McGwire is a Hero for More than Just His Homers." Advertising Feasture presented by Cigna, *Sports Illustrated*, 89:12, December 9, 1998, p. 22.

175. Okrent, "A Mac for All Seasons," p. 144.

176. Jeffrey Jerome Cohen, *On Giants* (Minneapolis: University of Minnesota Press, 1999), p. xii.

177. Susan Stewart, *On Longing* (Durham, NC: Duke University Press, 1993), p. 74.

178. David Gordon White, *Myths of the Dog-Man* (Chicago: University of Chicago Press, 1991), p. 35.

179. Cohen, *On Giants*, p. xi.

180. Edmund Burke, *Enquiry into the Sublime and Beautiful*, 157–58; qtd. in Cohen, p. xi.

181. See, e.g., one of the many Mike Piazza fan sites, such as The Mike Piazza Fan Page (www.piazza.com).

182. Cohen, *On Giants*, p. xii.

183. Cohen, *On Giants*, p. xii.

184. "Mark of Excellence," *Time*, December 2, 1998–January 4, 1999, pp. 147–48.

185. "Mark of Excellence," *Time*, December 2, 1998–January 4, 1999, pp. 147–48.

186. Cyphers, "A Mark for the Ages," p. 56.

187. Reilly, "The Good Father," p. 34.

188. Reilly, "The Good Father," p. 34.

189. Reilly, "The Good Father," p. 36.

190. Reilly, "The Good Father," p. 45.

191. Cohen, *On Giants*, p. xi.

192. Okrent, "A Mac for All Seasons," p. 144.

193. Woodward, *Making Saints*, p. 337.

194. Jacobus de Voragine, *The Golden Legend*, vol. 2, p. 13.

195. In another informal and unscientific poll, I asked everyone I could find if they found Mark McGwire sexually attractive. The poll included straight and gay men, as well as straight and gay women. Everyone, approximately twenty-five people, said no, some vehemently. I sent the several friends I asked over email a series of pictures, one half-naked, yet all of their responses remained the same.

196. An exploration of the two major Mark McGwire sites, "Gumby's Mark McGwire Message Board (www.mcgwire.com) and Markistheman (yahoo.groups.mcgwire) shows very little desirous language that is overtly—or even particularly covertly—sexual. While Gumby's board states the policy "No discussion of McGwire's private business, who he is dating and such," Markistheman purports to allow it; however, my perusal of the over 8,000 messages posted showed very little of this kind of speculation. Only one thread on Gumby's board really dealt with McGwire's off-field life, and while one or two posts seemed on the verge of sexual fantasy, even they were constructed in a rather domestic light. Indeed, one poster seemed annoyed at McGwire for mentioning his girlfriend in an interview, as if this asexual construction should necessarily be supported by McGwire's own private life. After McGwire's retirement and his subsequent marriage to a woman fourteen years his junior, however, the discussion on the sites became increasingly focused on his personal life, in particular his motivations for marrying a woman perceived as a trophy wife.

197. George Henn, "Mac Calls it Quits," New York Daily News, 12 November 2001, p. 64.

198. Henn, "Mac Calls it Quits," p. 64.

199. Henn, "Mac Calls it Quits," p. 64.

200. Henn, "Mac Calls it Quits," p. 64.

201. Paisner, *The Ball*, p. 192.

202. Kieckhefer, *Unquiet Souls*, p. 16.

203. Patrick Geary, *Living with the Dead in the Middle Ages* (Ithaca: Cornell University Press, 1994), p. 202.

204. *Medieval Saints: A Reader*, p. xvii.

205. *Medieval Saints: A Reader*, p. xviii; Woodward, *Making Saints*, p. 18; Kieckhefer, *Unquiet Souls*, p. 3.

206. Raines, *Mark McGwire*, pp. 138–39.

207. Raines, *Mark McGwire*, p. 140.

208. William Butler Yeats, "Crazy Jane Talks to the Bishop," *The Poems of W. B. Yeats*, ed. Richard J. Finnerman (New York: Macmillan, 1986), pp. 259–60.

209. William Butler Yeats, "Sailing to Byzantium," *The Poems of W. B. Yeats*, ed. Richard J. Finnerman (New York: Macmillan, 1986), pp. 193–94.

210. Gould, "How the New Sultan of Swat Measures Up," p. A22.

211. Gould, "How the New Sultan of Swat Measures Up," p. A22.

212. Patrick J. Geary, *Furta Sacra: Thefts of Relics in the Central Middle Ages*, 1978 (Princeton: Princeton University Press, 1990), p. 5.

213. Geary, *Living with the Dead*, p. 194.

214. Geary, *Living with the Dead*, p. 194.

215. Geary, *Furta Sacra*, p. 5.

216. Geary, *Furta Sacra*, p. 6.

217. Geary, *Living with the Dead*, pp. 200–01.

218. Geary, *Furta Sacra*, p. 22.

219. Geary, *Furta Sacra*, p. 22.

220. Igor Kopytoff, "The Cultural Biography of Things: Commoditization as Process," in *The Social Life of Things: Commodities in Cultural Perspective*, ed. Arjun Appadurai (New York: Cambridge University Press, 1986), p. 65.

221. Kopytoff, "The Cultural Biography of Things: Commoditization as Process," p. 68.

222. *The Barry Halper Collection of Baseball Memorabilia* Catalogue—Auction Results List (New York: Sotheby's, 1999). Auction date: September 23–29, 1999.

223. Geary, *Living with the Dead*, p. 200.

224. Geary, *Living with the Dead*, p. 200.

225. Mark Hyman, "Baseball's Biggest Auction Ever," *Business Week*, February 22, 1999, pp. 151–52.

226. Geary, *Living with the Dead*, p. 201.

227. Mike Lupica, *Summer of '98: When Homers Flew, Records Fell, and Baseball Reclaimed America* (New York: Putnam, 1999), p. 3.

228. Lupica, *Summer of '98*, p. 5.

229. Lupica, *Summer of '98*, p. 6.

230. Lupica, *Summer of '98*, p. 6.

231. Lupica, *Summer of '98*, p. 10.

232. Tsvetan Todorov, *Introduction to Poetics*, trans. Richard Howard (Minneapolis: University of Minnesota Press, 1981), p. 7.

233. Geary, *Furta Sacra*, p. 5.

234. Eugene A. Dooley, *Church Law on Sacred Relics* (Washington, D.C.: Catholic University Press, 1931), p. 3.

235. Brown, *Cult of the Saints*, p. 88.

236. Woodward, *Making Saints*, p. 59.

237. Woodward, *Making Saints*, p. 59.

238. Some Elvis fans feel that their relics do work miracles. For instance, John Strasbaugh relates the following story, told to him by a fan at a memorabilia auction: "During one of his seventies concerts Elvis removed his cape and belt buckle and handed them to a little seven-year-old fan. The kid kept them as he grew up and then traded them to Jimmy Velvet for a brand new Trans Am, which he proceeded accidentally to crash into a tree, killing himself" (*E: Reflections on the Birth of the Elvis Faith*, New York: Blast, 1995), p. 193.

239. Paisner, *The Ball*, p. 202.

240. Major League Baseball Authentication Program pamphlet; 2001.

241. Major League Baseball Authentication Program pamphlet; 2001.

242. Major League Baseball Authentication Program pamphlet; 2001.

243. Dooley, *Church Law on Sacred Relics*, pp. 75–76.

244. This irony of this statement, given Arthur Andersen's ignominious demise in the wake of the 2002 Enron scandal could not have been determined when Major League Baseball wrote their pamphlet, yet it seems that their "impeccable third party" may be a prelate with some bodily infirmity after all. The fallibility of Arthur Anderson emerged at the same time as the cover-up of sexual misconduct within the American Catholic Church suggesting that the public may be the best authenticator of relics after all.

245. Major League Baseball Authentication Program pamphlet; 2001.

246. Michael O'Keefe and Bill Madden, "Bidder Beware," *New York Daily News*, May 14, 2000, p. 67.

247. O'Keefe and Madden, "Bidder Beware," p. 67.

248. "Autograph Quiz," Gumby's Mark McGwire Online (www.mcgwire.com/authentication/index.html).

249. Geary, *Furta Sacra*, p. 53.

250. Geary, *Furta Sacra*, pp. 44–45.

251. Geary, *Furta Sacra*, p. 44.

252. Paisner, *The Ball*, p. 14.

253. Paisner, *The Ball*, p. 14.

254. Paisner, *The Ball*, p. 16.

255. Joshua Harris Prager, "Efforts to Track Historic Homer are Absolutely Out in Left Field," *Wall Street Journal*, September 8, 1998, A22.

256. Paisner, *The Ball*, p. 21.

257. Game balls do have one claim to a certain mystique. All major league balls are rubbed with a pinch of Lena Blackburne's Baseball Rubbing Mud, "the mysterious compound dredged from the shores of New Jersey's Pennsauken Creek, a tributary to the Delaware River. . .the mud is stuff of baseball legend. The precise location of the mud bank is a closely held secret. The mud is collected once a year, late at night, by the extended members of a single family working by flashlight, after which it's carted off in fifty-five-gallon drums, processed, and dispatched to big league clubhouses in nondescript coffee cans donated by neighbors" (Daniel Paisner, *The Ball*, p. 26).

258. Paisner, *The Ball*, p. 30.

259. Paisner, *The Ball*, p. 31.

260. See "Randall's Collection" at Gumby's Mark McGwire Online (www.mcgwire.com) for Randall Hahn's examples of falsified items, including those listed above. Hahn holds himself to be the most accurate authenticator of McGwire's autograph, the prelate without infirmity.

261. Yi-Wyn Yen, "In the Endorsement Game, No Power Display from McGwire," *Newark Star-Ledger*, September 7, 1998, p. 1.

262. Yen, "In the Endorsement Game," p. 1.

263. Yen, "In the Endorsement Game," p. 8.

264. Yen, "In the Endorsement Game," p. 8.

265. Yen, "In the Endorsement Game," p. 8.

266. Apparently forged items are as rampant among McGwire collectibles as the pardoner's false relics; according to Gary's post on "Gumby's Mark McGwire Message Board," one should "NEVER, and I mean NEEEEVER buy a Mac auto on any online auction or anyone you don't know. The fakes far out number the authentic Mac autos out there. Your best bet it to do as someone else said. Get a hold of Randall. It will cost you a bit, but at least you'll know its real." (All spelling errors are taken directly from the post.) (Posted by "Gary" on August 2, 2001.) Randall Hahn's "Mark McGwire Autograph Authentication Quiz" is available online at www.mcgwire.com, and Randall himself—and his sometimes purchasable, authentic collection—is also accessible through this extensive, albeit unofficial, website. Hahn himself offers the "Autograph Authentication Service," charging $50 for a certificate that guarantees the signed item's actual value. Claiming that he doesn't "like taking someone's money and telling them they bought fakes," he nontheless suggests that one's "best bet is to send one and see how it goes." Randall Hahn claims his authority because he is "an aggressive McGwire collector since the early '90s and have an extensive collection of his memorabilia" and because "over the years I have owned dozens of McGwire signed items and have grown very accustomed to his autograph style which has changed significantly over this time. I don't claim to be an expert on a lot of things, but rest assured when it comes to McGwire I am the most accurate in the business. If I am not 100% sure of authenticity I would not put my name on it." Hahn also lays claim to

having "done authentication work for several national auction houses" and to have "authenticated the only signed McGwire home run ball sold in the January '99 Guernsey's Home Run Ball auction (Where Mac's #70 sold for $3 million!)" (www.mcgwire.com/authentication/index.html).

267. Geary, *Furta Sacra*, p. 34.

268. Walter Benjamin, "The Work of Art in the Age of Mechanical Reproduction," *Illuminations*, 1968, ed. Hannah Arendt, trans. Harry Zohn (New York: Schocken Books, 1988), p. 220.

269. Paisner, *The Ball*, p. 33. It is worth noting that Sammy Sosa, perhaps with less sense of the value of Cooperstown as a pilgrimage site, autographed the balls that fans caught and gave them back (Paisner, *The Ball*, p. 33). He also cheerfully gave away bats, jerseys, and gloves, creating some controversy over who actually had the bats with which he hit his sixty-second and sixty-sixth home runs. The Hall of Fame claims to have the authentic ones, although that claim has been challenged by others vouching for the authenticity of their relics. Unlike the True Cross, which apparently generated enough pieces that had it been reassembled it would have reached the moon, the modern age believes value comes solely through uniqueness and the establishment of truth.

270. Mike Vaccaro, "Baseball Fans' Reaction to McGwire's Heroics is Simply Priceless," *Newark Star-Ledger*, September 9, 1998, p. 65.

271. Vaccaro, "Baseball Fans' Reaction," p. 65.

272. Verducci, "Making his Mark," p. 33.

273. Gary Smith, "The Mother of All Pearls," *Sports Illustrated*, September 21, 1998, p. 59.

274. Verducci, "Making his Mark," p. 30.

275. Verducci, "Making his Mark," p. 30.

276. Verducci, "Making his Mark," p. 30.

277. Verducci, "Making his Mark," p. 30.

278. Verducci, "Making his Mark," p. 32.

279. Verducci, "Making his Mark," p. 32.

280. While Roger Maris did not deal especially well with the press attention and indeed did start to lose his hair, he received a great deal of fan support in 1961 as well as significant praise in the media. Although the story is often told that the fans treated him badly because he broke the beloved Babe Ruth's record and was beating equally beloved Mickey Mantle for the title, actual media coverage does not support this opprobrium. Maris did receive significant derision in the following year for failing to live up to the standards he had set in 1961; because of his generally solid but not groundbreaking numbers in all but one year of his career, he has not been elected to the Hall of Fame. While McGwire's four consecutive seasons of 50+ home runs assures his place in Cooperstown, his injury-ridden, poor season in 2001 earned him fairly intense fan and media criticism as well.

281. Jerry Izenberg, *Newark Star Ledger*, September 9, 1998, p. 67.

282. Verducci, "Making his Mark," p. 33.
283. Richard Sandomir, "$1 Million Offering for Ball to Aid Human Rights Case," *New York Times*, September 5, 1998, D3:5.
284. Vaccaro, "As McGwire Hits Homer 62, Time Stands Still," p. 1. See note 115 for details.
285. Vaccaro, "Baseball Fans' Reaction," p. 65
286. Vaccaro, "Baseball Fans' Reaction," p. 65
287. Vaccaro, "Baseball Fans' Reaction," p. 65
288. Smith, "The Mother of all Pearls," p. 59.
289. Vaccaro, "Baseball Fans' Reaction," p. 65
290. Smith, "The Mother of all Pearls," p. 59.
291. Smith, "The Mother of all Pearls," p. 59.
292. Vaccaro, "Baseball Fans' Reaction," p. 65
293. Tom Wheatley, "Generosity Still Pays Dividends in Forneris Saga," *Saint Louis Post-Dispatch*, August 10, 1999, C1.
294. Wheatley, "Generosity Still Pays Dividends in Forneris Saga," C1.
295. Geary, *Living with the Dead*, p. 202.
296. Wheatley, "Generosity Still Pays Dividends in Forneris Saga," C1.
297. Jack McCallum and Richard O'Brien, "Keep your eye on the Balls," *Sports Illustrated*, September 28, 1998, p. 24.
298. McCallum and O'Brien, "Keep Your Eye on the Balls," p. 24.
299. Geary, *Furta Sacra*, p. xii.
300. Geary, *Living with the Dead*, p. 214.
301. Paisner, *The Ball*, p. 71.
302. Paisner, *The Ball*, p. 74.
303. Paisner, *The Ball*, p. 77.
304. Paisner, *The Ball*, p. 77.
305. A striking example of the contemporary need for relics came to my attention after the World Trade Center disaster, as the news showed many people taking away pieces of the destroyed buildings—bits of steel, concrete, and brick—keeping a piece of the thing so that they "would never forget"—as if they ever could. Not miraculous yet narrative, these pieces of mortar stand for the dead just as pieces of the saints bodies did in the Middle Ages, maintaining a link between the past (in which their loved ones, the Trade Towers, and a sense of peace prevailed) and the tenuous, sorrowful present (New York 1 News, September 11, 2001).
306. Alex Tresniowski and Mary M. Harrison, "Going, Going, Gone!" *People Weekly*, 51:4, February 1, 1999, p. 52.
307. Tresniowski and Harrison, "Going, Going, Gone!" p. 52.
308. Geary, *Furta Sacra*, p. xiii.
309. Michael Grunwald, "One Fan's $3 Million Catch," *Washington Post*, January 13, 1999, A01.
310. Douglas Martin, "No. 70 Goes after Another Record," *New York Times*, January 4, 1999, B1:2.
311. Paisner, *The Ball*, p. 82.
312. Grunwald, "One Fan's $3 Million Catch," A01.

313. Martin, "No. 70 Goes after Another Record," B1:2.

314. Paisner, *The Ball*, p. 87.

315. Paisner, *The Ball*, p. 87.

316. Paisner, *The Ball*, p. 87.

317. Paisner, *The Ball*, p. 111.

318. R. W. Southern, *Western Society and the Church in the Middle Ages* (Grand Rapids, MI: Eerdmans, 1970), p. 30.

319. Paisner, *The Ball*, p. 96.

320. Paisner, *The Ball*, p. 95.

321. Paisner, *The Ball*, p. 96.

322. Kieckhefer, *Unquiet Souls*, p. 63.

323. Paisner, *The Ball*, p. 92.

324. Paisner, *The Ball*, p. 92.

325. Benjamin, "The Work of Art," p. 220.

326. Geary, *Living with the Dead*, p. 116.

327. Grunwald, "One Fan's $3 Million Catch," A01.

328. Grunwald, "One Fan's $3 Million Catch," A01.

329. Bill Smith, "Fans Enjoy Fame after Retrieving McGwire's Home Run Balls," *St. Louis Post-Dispatch*, October 4, 1998, A14.

330. Smith, "The Mother of All Pearls," p. 59.

331. Smith, "The Mother of All Pearls," p. 59.

332. Smith, "Fans Enjoy Fame," A14.

333. Smith, "Fans Enjoy Fame," A14.

334. Smith, "Fans Enjoy Fame," A14.

335. Bill Egbert and Bill Hutchinson, "2.7M Buys Mac's 70th Home run History Fetches Record," *New York Daily News*, January 13, 1999, p. 5.

336. Paisner, *The Ball*, p. 196.

337. Paisner, *The Ball*, p. 197.

338. Brown, *The Cult of the Saints*, p. 89.

339. Paisner, *The Ball*, pp. 198–99.

340. Paisner, *The Ball*, p. 199.

341. Brown, *The Cult of the Saints*, pp. 94–95.

342. Paisner, *The Ball*, p. 202.

343. Southern, *Western Society and the Church in the Middle Ages*, p. 30.

344. Geary, *Living with the Dead*, p. 205.

345. Qtd. by Darren Rovell, The Official ESPN Website (www.espn.com).

346. Both Barry Bonds's 73rd home run ball from 2001 and his 600th career home run ball from 2002 are involved in legal disputes over their true ownership. One person claims that he caught #73 but had it wrestled away from him and is suing for its possession; the friends of the person who caught #600 are claiming that they had a group agreement to share any revenues produced by the ball, which the catcher now denies, while several others who gave them the game tickets in the first place are claiming their share of the ball's purchase price. These cases are likely to be tied up in California courts for some time.

347. Geary, *Living with the Dead*, p. 216.

348. Geary, *Furta Sacra*, p. 115.

349. Brown, *The Cult of the Saints*, p. 78.

350. Paisner, *The Ball*, p. 4.

351. Grunwald, "One Fan's $3 Million Catch," A01.

352. Paisner, *The Ball*, p.103.

353. Paisner, *The Ball*, p. 97.

354. Walter Benjamin, "Unpacking My Library," *Illuminations*, ed. Hannah Arendt trans. Harry Zohn (New York: Shocken, 1968), p. 67.

355. Martin, "No. 70 Goes after Another Record," B1:2.

356. Krysztof Pomian, *Collectors and Curiosities: Paris and Venice, 1500–1800*, 1987, trans. Elisabeth Wiles-Portier (Cambridge: Polity Press, 1990), p. 22.

357. Pomian, *Collectors and Curiosities*, p. 22.

358. Pomian, *Collectors and Curiosities*, p. 22.

359. Philip Fisher, *Making and Effacing Art: Modern American Art in a Culture of Museums* (New York: Oxford University Press, 1991), pp. 3–4.

360. Geoffrey Chaucer, "The General Prologue," *The Riverside Chaucer*, ed. Larry D. Benson (Boston: Houghton Mifflin, 1987), I ll. 12–18. This may be one of the most famous statements about the impulsive, seasonal nature of pilgrimages; The National Baseball Hall of Fame, open all year around, sees a marked increase in visitors in the spring and summer months.

361. Steve Rushin, *Road Swing* (New York: Doubleday, 1998), p. 9.

362. Huston Smith, "Foreward," *The Art of Pilgrimage: Seeker's Guide to Making Travel Sacred* by Phil Cousineau (Berkeley, CA: Conari Press, 1998), p. xi.

363. Cousineau, *The Art of Pilgrimage*, p. xxi.

364. Cousineau, *The Art of Pilgrimage*, p. xxiii.

365. Cousineau, *The Art of Pilgrimage*, p. xxiii.

366. Cousineau, *The Art of Pilgrimage*, p. xxv.

367. Cousineau, *The Art of Pilgrimage*, p. xxv.

368. Cousineau, *The Art of Pilgrimage*, p. xxvi.

369. Cousineau, *The Art of Pilgrimage*, p. xxvi.

370. Geary, *Living with the Dead*, p. 164.

371. Geary, *Living with the Dead*, p. 166.

372. Woodward, *Making Saints*, p. 18.

373. For a discussion of the Hall of Fame as pilgrimage site in a more modern context see Roberta Newman, "The American Church of Baseball and the National Baseball Hall of Fame," *Nine: A Journal of Baseball History and Culture*, 10, no. 1 (2001): 46–63. Newman and I drew our conclusions independently from each other's, yet their similarity show the profound ways in which Hall of Fame has developed as a secular site for sacred experience, shaped by medieval assumptions and influenced by modern concerns. I am grateful to Roberta Newman for sharing her work, and conversations, with me in advance of the publication of her article.

374. Other examples include Strawberry Fields in New York's Central Park, which has become a shrine to John Lennon, and the grave of Jim Morrison in the Pere LaChaise Cemetary in Paris. These, however,

possibly because of their locations in bustling urban areas, have not generated the same economic communities that Graceland and the National
Baseball Hall of Fame have.

375. Victor Turner and Edith Turner, *Image and Pilgrimage in Christian Culture:
     Anthropological Perspectives* (New York: Columbia University Press,
     1978), p. 7.

376. Diana Webb, *Pilgrims and Pilgrimage in the Medieval West* (London:
     I.B. Tauris, 1999), p. 15.

377. Jonathan Sumption, *Pilgrimage: An Image of Medieval Religion* (Totowa, NJ:
     Rowman and Littlefield, 1975), p. 169.

378. Sumption, *Pilgrimage*, p. 169.

379. Sumption, *Pilgrimage*, p. 171.

380. Sumption, *Pilgrimage*, p. 175.

381. Sumption, *Pilgrimage*, p. 175.

382. Qtd. in Sumption, *Pilgrimage*, p. 175.

383. Sumption, *Pilgrimage*, p. 177.

384. Sumption, *Pilgrimage*, p. 177.

385. Qtd. in Sumption, *Pilgrimage*, p. 180.

386. Sumption, *Pilgrimage*, p. 180.

387. Webb, *Pilgrims and Pilgrimage*, p. 19.

388. Webb, *Pilgrims and Pilgrimage*, p. 19.

389. Webb, *Pilgrims and Pilgrimage*, p. 20.

390. Webb, *Pilgrims and Pilgrimage*, p. 20.

391. Webb, *Pilgrims and Pilgrimage*, p. 20.

392. Geary, *Furta Sacra*, p. 61.

393. Geary, *Furta Sacra*, p. 58.

394. Geary, *Furta Sacra*, p. 61.

395. Jonathan Yardley, "Stealing Home to Cooperstown," *Washington Post*,
     October 21, 1985; qtd. in Charles Freuhling Springwood, *Cooperstown to
     Dyersville: A Geography of Baseball Nostalgia* (Boulder, CO: Westview
     Press, 1996), p. 65.

396. Springwood, *Cooperstown to Dyersville*, p. 66.

397. John Thorn, *The Treasures of the Hall of Fame* (New York: Villard,
     1998), p. 3.

398. Rushin, *Road Swing*, p. 9.

399. Rushin, *Road Swing*, p. 9.

400. Rushin, *Road Swing*, p. 20.

401. Rushin, *Road Swing*, p. 19.

402. Springwood, *Cooperstown to Dyersville*, p. 116.

403. Monika Otter, *Inventiones: Fiction and Referentiality in Twelfth-Century
     English Historical Writing* (Chapel Hill, NC: University of North Carolina
     Press, 1996), p. 21.

404. Otter, *Inventiones*, pp. 28–29.

405. Otter, *Inventiones*, p. 28.

406. Otter, *Inventiones*, p. 29.

407. Otter, *Inventiones*, p. 31.

408. Otter, *Inventiones*, p. 31.

409. Otter, *Inventiones*, p. 36.

410. Otter, *Inventiones*, p. 36.

411. Otter, *Inventiones*, p. 36.

412. Springwood, *Cooperstown to Dyersville*, p. 31.

413. Jane Austen writes, in *Northanger Abbey*: "It was not very wonderful that Catherine, who had nothing heroic about her, should prefer cricket, base ball, riding on horseback, and running about the country at the age of fourteen to books" (1818, ed. Anne Ehrenpries [New York: Penguin Books, 1972], p. 39). The baseball manuscript can be seen reproduced in the "Historical Baseball" exhibit at the Hall of Fame in Cooperstown; it is, however, displayed without identification.

414. Springwood, *Cooperstown to Dyersville*, p. 31.

415. Stephen Jay Gould, "The Creation Myths of Cooperstown," *Natural History*, November 19, 1989, pp. 10–14, 13.

416. Springwood, *Cooperstown to Dyersville*, p. 33.

417. An examination of two books that discuss Cooperstown's origin mythology provide different details, suggesting once again the fictionality of the story; John Thorn's *Treasures of the Hall of Fame* and Charles Fruehling Springwood's *Cooperstown to Dyersville* both present the essential story yet vary significantly in details. Springwood's volume has the authority of research; Thorn's the authority of place. While the former is a sociological study of geography and nostalgia, the latter is a publication of the Hall of Fame itself.

418. Ralph Birdsall, *The Story of Cooperstown* (New York: Arthur H. Crist Co, 1917), p. 254.

419. Thorn, *The Treasures of the Hall of Fame*, p. 5.

420. Thorn, *The Treasures of the Hall of Fame*, p. 5. The more likely story of baseball's origins posits that Alexander Cartwright developed the first coherent set of baseball rules and fielded the first organized team in 1845, called the New York Knickerbockers. Located in Manhattan, they played their first "official" game on June 19, 1846, in Hoboken, New Jersey on a Cricket Ground charmingly named the Elysian Fields (Springwood, *Cooperstown to Dyersville*, pp. 34–35). Although medieval and religious in its assumptions, the Elysian Fields are memorialized only by a plaque located on the grounds of the Maxwell House Coffee Factory.

421. Thorn, *The Treasures of the Hall of Fame*, p. 6.

422. Otter, *Inventiones*, p. 28.

423. Springwood, *Cooperstown to Dyersville*, p. 38.

424. Springwood, *Cooperstown to Dyersville*, p. 38.

425. Thorn, *Treasures*, p. 6.

426. There are sports *translationes* as well; after his death, Jim Thorpe's family essentially sold his body to a town in Pennsylvania on the condition that they build a monument and change the town's name to Jim Thorpe, PA. After the body was purchased, the citizens of the newly named Jim

Thorpe had it brought into town with great ceremony and interred by the monument. Unfortunately, Jim Thorpe, PA has never caught on as a pilgrimage site, realizing great profit for neither the town nor the family, and there is some pressure from Native American groups to recover Thorpe's body and rebury it at a tribal site.

427. Geary, *Living with the Dead*, p. 204.
428. Geary, *Living with the Dead*, p. 204.
429. Qtd. in Thorn, *The Treasures of the Hall of Fame*, p. 7.
430. Thorn, *The Treasures of the Hall of Fame*, p. 7.
431. Thorn, *The Treasures of the Hall of Fame*, p. 7.
432. Gould, "The Creation Myths of Cooperstown," p. 24.
433. National Baseball Hall of Fame, Doubleday Exhibit; also qtd. in Gould, "Creation Myths," p. 12.
434. Springwood, *Cooperstown to Dyersville*, p. 30.
435. Eric Hobsbawm "Inventing Traditions," in *The Invention of Tradtion*, ed. Eric Hobsbawm and Terrence Ranger (Cambridge: Cambridge University Press, 1983), p. 1.
436. Springwood, *Cooperstown to Dyersville*, p. 42.
437. In a strange act of balancing, the nominating committee decided to induct Alexander Cartwright, who is at the source of the "evolutionary" model of baseball's history because he created the first official set of baseball rules that differentiated the game from Town Ball while simultaneously understanding its long and complex origins, and mysteriously not Abner Doubleday. The fact that they seem to understand the mythological elements of the story they so strongly uphold raises questions about their motivations.
438. Gould, "The Creation Myths of Cooperstown," p. 12.
439. Otter, *Inventiones*, p. 35.
440. Ken Smith, *Baseball's Hall of Fame* (New York: Grosset and Dunlap, 1975), p. 32.
441. Smith, *Baseball's Hall of Fame*, p. 32.
442. Springwood, *Cooperstown to Dyersville*, p. 3.
443. Springwood, *Cooperstown to Dyersville*, p. 3.
444. Smith, *Baseball's Hall of Fame*, pp. 34–35.
445. Pamphlet, Cooperstown, NY: National Baseball Hall of Fame and Museum, no date; qtd. in Springwood, *Cooperstown to Dyersville*, p. 75.
446. Turner and Turner, *Image and Pilgrimage in Christian Culture*, p. 10.
447. Turner and Turner, *Image and Pilgrimage in Christian Culture*, p. 8.
448. Benjamin Rader, *American Sports: From the Age of Folk Games to the Age of Spectators* (Englewood Cliffs, NJ: Prentice Hall, 1983), p. 128.
449. Rader, *American Sports*, p. 128.
450. Clifford Geertz, *The Interpretation of Cultures* (New York: Basic Books, 1973), p. 90.
451. Springwood, *Cooperstown to Dyersville*, p. 63.
452. Turner and Turner, *Image and Pilgrimage in Christian Culture*, p. 9.
453. Webb, *Pilgrims and Pilgrimage*, p. 245.

454. Webb, *Pilgrims and Pilgrimage*, p. 244.

455. Webb, *Pilgrims and Pilgrimage*, p. 244.

456. Webb, *Pilgrims and Pilgrimage*, pp. 244–45.

457. Turner and Turner, *Image and Pilgrimage in Christian Culture*, p. 11.

458. In *Baseball: The Golden Age*, Harold Seymour notes, "What really saved baseball, legally at least [from the disaffection of the Black Sox Scandal in 1919], for the next half century was the protective canopy spread over it by the United States Supreme Court's decision in the Baltimore Federal League anti-trust suit against Organized Baseball in 1922. In it, Justice [Oliver Wendell] Holmes, speaking for a unanimous court, ruled that the business of giving baseball exhibitions for profit was not 'trade or commerce in the commonly-accepted use of those words' because 'personal effort, not related to production, is not the subject of commerce'; nor was it interstate, because the movement of ball clubs across state lines was merely 'incidental' to the business" (New York: Oxford University Press, 1991), p. 420. Seymour does point out that the popular mythology claiming that Holmes declared that baseball was not a business is strictly inaccurate; however, Holmes does distinguish it as a business unlike those others that would be affected by antitrust legislation. Seymour also quotes W. O. McGeehan, a sportswriter, as saying that it was the exploits of Babe Ruth that "shook the fans out of their shock and bewilderment over the scandal and enabled the baseball magnates to 'take heart and to talk about the immortality of the great American game' once more" (p. 420).

459. Roger Angel, *Once More Around the Park: A Baseball Reader* (New York: Ballantine, 1991), p. 27.

460. Woodward, *Making Saints*, p. 18.

461. Benjamin, "The Work of Art," pp. 224–25.

462. Geary, *Living with the Dead*, p. 165.

463. Thorn, *The Treasures of the Hall of Fame*, p. 10.

464. Thorn, *The Treasures of the Hall of Fame*, p. 10.

465. Thorn, *The Treasures of the Hall of Fame*, p. 12.

466. Thorn, *The Treasures of the Hall of Fame*, p. 12.

467. Thorn, *The Treasures of the Hall of Fame*, p. 12.

468. Thorn, *The Treasures of the Hall of Fame*, p. 14.

469. Thorn, *The Treasures of the Hall of Fame*, p. 14.

470. Thorn, *The Treasures of the Hall of Fame*, p. 14.

471. Geary, *Living with the Dead*, p. 164.

472. Rushin, *Road Swing*, p. 61.

473. Smith, *Baseball's Hall of Fame*, p. 21.

474. Smith, *Baseball's Hall of Fame*, p. 34.

475. Smith, *Baseball's Hall of Fame*, p. 35.

476. Alexander Cleland, the Hall of Fame's "moving spirit," qtd. in Smith, *Baseball's Hall of Fame*, p. 45.

477. Bill James, a noted member of the Society for American Baseball Research and creator of many methods of statistical analysis for baseball, is the author of *What Ever Happened to the Hall of Fame?* originally titled

The Politics of Glory (New York: Macmillan, 1994) which, in its front flap copy, claims to "take a hard look at the Hall—not only at the traditional questions of who is in and who is out and why, but at how the Hall of Fame operates, who operates it, how they make decisions, and why those decisions go awry." Focused on the various induction controversies, James rejects seeing the Hall of Fame as the bucolic, nostalgic, "spirit of baseball" that it chooses to present itself as. James is best known as a creator of interesting, intricate statistical analyses and for having strong, controversial opinions.

478. Springwood, *Cooperstown to Dyersville*, p. 63.

479. Springwood, e.g., quotes an article from the Hall of Fame Newsletter by Steve Rondinaro, who says that "To Dad and me, Cooperstown was sacred ground" ("In a League of His Own," *Memories and Dreams* (Hall of Fame Newsletter), 15:3 (1993), pp. 2–4, p. 2 qtd. in Springwood, *Cooperstown to Dyersville*, p. 65) among others, including a Japanese visitor who notes that the town "embodies a kind of splendor" and calls the Hall itself "the baseball sanctuary" located in "The Holy Land of baseball" (p. 67).

480. Brooke Hindle, "How Much is a Piece of the True Cross Worth?" *Material Culture and the Study of American Life*, ed. Uan M. G. Quimby (New York: W. W. Norton and Co., 1978), p. 5.

481. Hindle, "How Much is a Piece," pp. 6–7.

482. Turner and Turner, *Image and Pilgrimage in Christian Culture*, p. 23.

483. Tom Seaver letter qtd. in National Baseball Hall of Fame brochure.

484. National Baseball Hall of Fame brochure.

485. Springwood, *Cooperstown to Dyersville*, p. 79.

486. Indeed, baseball's origins are more likely urban.

487. Springwood, *Cooperstown to Dyersville*, p. 104.

488. Turner and Turner, *Image and Pilgrimage in Christian Culture*, pp. 25–26.

489. The Cooperstown Chamber of Commerce Website (www.cooperstown chamber.org).

490. Springwood, *Cooperstown to Dyersville*, p. 72.

491. Jesus Sports Statuettes, which feature a resin-cast Christ playing different sports with a group of children, are available from the Catholic Supply Company (www.catholicsupply.com). Also available are "Holy Sports Bears," Christian Sports Dog Tags, and St. Christopher Sports medallions on which the saint is engaged in active play. The St. Christopher/ Mark McGwire connection is further strengthened through these souvenirs.

492. Springwood, *Cooperstown to Dyersville*, p. 72.

493. This film has its own medieval content; essentially a retelling of the Arthur story, replete with Excalibur's modern equivalent, the bat named "Wonderboy"; the youthful Arthur's near-fatal run in with Morgan Le Fay later causes his eventual retirement from baseball, after a glorious ultimate game.

494. The inherent value of this shopping district for baseball fans is reflected in the Chamber of Commerce's sense that all visitors can be counted on to shop here; in a more personal sense, I was able to find several invaluable resources for this chapter in the several used bookstores with extensive sections devoted to baseball on Cooperstown's Main Street, and at the Hall of Fame Library's small gift shop, which peddled replica editions of Spalding's Baseball Rules.

495. Geary, *Living with the Dead*, p. 202.

496. Michael Hitchcock, "Introduction," *Souvenirs: The Material Culture of Tourism* ed. Michael Hitchcock and Ken Teague (Alderhshot, UK: Ashgate, 2000), p. 4.

497. Hitchcock, "Introduction," *Souvenirs*, p. 10.

498. Michael Houlihan, "Souvenirs with Soul: 800 Years of Pilgrimage to Santiago de Compostela," in Hitchcock and Teague, eds., *Souvenirs*, pp. 18–24, 20.

499. Houlihan, "Souvenirs with Soul," *Souvenirs*, p. 22.

500. Houlihan, "Souvenirs with Soul," *Souvenirs*, p. 22.

501. Houlihan, "Souvenirs with Soul," *Souvenirs*, p. 22.

502. Springwood, *Cooperstown to Dyersville*, p. 91.

503. Geary, *Living with the Dead*, p. 164.

504. Ward, *Miracles and the Medieval Mind*, p. 117.

505. Turner and Turner, *Image and Pilgrimage in Christian Culture*, p. 6.

506. Turner and Turner, *Image and Pilgrimage in Christian Culture*, p. 25.

507. P. A. Robinson, director and screenwriter, *Field of Dreams* (Universal City Studios, 1989); also qtd. in Springwood, *Cooperstown to Dyersville*, p. 204.

508. Springwood, *Cooperstown to Dyersville*, p. 7.

509. Stephen Mosher, "Fielding Our Dreams: Rounding Third in Dyersville," *Sociology of Sport Journal*, 8 (1991), p. 274.

510. Springwood, *Cooperstown to Dyersville*, p. 7.

511. Bobby Fong, "The Magic Cocktail: The Enduring Appeal of the Field of Dreams," *Aethlon*, 11:1 (1993), p. 29.

512. Rushin, *Road Swing*, p. 13.

513. Springwood, *Cooperstown to Dyersville*, p. 7.

514. Springwood, *Cooperstown to Dyersville*, p. 7.

515. Fong, "The Magic Cocktail," p. 29.

516. Springwood, *Cooperstown to Dyersville*, p. 13.

517. Springwood, *Cooperstown to Dyersville*, p. 112.

518. Springwood, *Cooperstown to Dyersville*, p. 113.

519. Springwood, *Cooperstown to Dyersville*, p. 113.

520. Qtd. in Springwood, *Cooperstown to Dyersville*, p. 113.

521. Springwood, *Cooperstown to Dyersville*, p. 114.

522. Springwood, *Cooperstown to Dyersville*, p. 116.

523. Springwood, *Cooperstown to Dyersville*, pp. 125, 166.

524. Jenanne Vielliard, ed., *Guide du Pèlerin de S. Jaques de Compostella 9.17* (Paris: Macon, 1969), p. 118; also qtd. in Ward, *Miracles and the Medieval Mind*, p. 111.

525. Sumption, *Pilgrimage*, p. 25.

526. Stewart, *On Longing*, p. 25.

527. Springwood, *Cooperstown to Dyersville*, p. 168.

528. Turner and Turner, *Image and Pilgrimage in Christian Culture*, p. 19.

529. The religion of Elvis is discussed at length by John Strassbaugh in *E: Reflections on the Birth of the Elvis Faith*; as a pilgrimage site, Graceland is marked by many of the same qualities that the Turners use to characterize a medieval site, and those that I have discussed in relation to Cooperstown. Annual pilgrimages to mark the dates of Elvis's birth and death culminate in candlelight vigils and rituals (p. 65) that create magic feelings for those who participate. In his book on Elvis, *the Magic Bus*, Douglas Brinkley employs similar language to Ken Smith's in his evocation of the Hall of Fame's power: "Graceland is truly a religious shrine and Elvis is a religious movement" (qtd. in Strassbaugh, p. 59). The Elvis Mall that surrounds Graceland, and the various lodging and eating places in the area, provide the economic basis for the site by selling Elvis relics and souvenirs as diverse as Elvis paintings and Elvis nail clippers. For a discussion of Christorama and Sainte Anne de Beauprey, see Cleo Paskal, "Pilgrimage to Christiorama," *Canadian Geographic*, 121:2 (March/April 2001), p. 98. In a review of Jeffrey F. Meyer's *Myths in Stone: Religious Dimensions of Washington, D.C.*, which considers Washington, DC as a pilgrimage site, Amy Schwartz suggests that the experience of viewing the "stone temples of the city's monumental core" is "fundamentally religious," with the architecture "playing the role of ritual" and Lincoln assuming "the aura of a Christlike figure who saved the Union by taking its sufferings on himself," *The Wilson Quarterly*, 25:2 (2001), pp. 120–21.

530. Sumption, *Pilgrimage*, p. 302.

531. Sumption, *Pilgrimage*, p. 302.

532. Nicholas Shrady, *Sacred Roads: Adventures from the Pilgrimage Trail* (San Francisco: HarperCollins, 1999), p. 3.

533. Daniel Knapp, "The Relyk of a Seint: A Gloss on Chaucer's Pilgrimage," *ELH*, 39:1 (1972), p. 21.

534. Geary, *Living with the Dead*, p. 216.

535. Geary, *Furta Sacra*, p. 59.

536. Andrea R. Harbin, "The Citizens of York and the Archetypal Christian Journey: Pilgrimage and Ritual in the York Cycle," *Medieval Perspectives* 14 (1999), p. 96.

Chapter 2   The Confessions of Wade Boggs; The Confessions of Saint Augustine: Sports, Sex Scandals, and Medieval Narrative Genres

1. Ethan Canin, "City of Broken Hearts," *The Palace Thief* (New York: Picador, 1994), p. 109.

2. Canin, "City of Broken Hearts," p. 130.

3. Jerry Klinkowitz, "Introduction," Writing Baseball (Urbana, IL: University of Illinois Press, 1991), p. 2. Sports are ripe with fictions put forward as realities; for instance, in, *Writing Baseball* Jerry Klinkowitz tells a story about Lou Piniella: after a bad pitch was called a strike, Piniella was purported to have said, "Where was that last one at?" to which the umpire is alleged to have responded that the ball was low and he shouldn't end a sentence with a preposition, to which Piniella replied, "Okay, where was that last one at, you asshole?" (Klinkowitz, p. 2). As anyone in the English business knows, this joke has much older origins, and is unlikely to have happened at all; the attachment of the myth to the sport is made by outside forces, in this case, probably Joe Garagiola, who is likely responsible for a good number of Yogi Berra's liveliest quotations.

4. Some, drawing on the novel's heritage in romance, even begin with the subject's parents.

5. Again, it is worth noting the novel's heritage in spiritual autobiography, a form that emerges in the Middle Ages with Augustine's *Confessions*: a work that will be vital for this discussion.

6. Michiko Kakutani, "Making Art of Sport," *New York Times Magazine*, December 15, 1996, p. 15.

7. Marie-Laure Ryan, "Narrative in Real Time: Chronicle, Mimesis, and Plot in the Baseball Broadcast," *Narrative*, 1:2 (1993), pp. 138–55.

8. Klinkowitz, *Writing Baseball*, p. 8.

9. Klinkowitz, *Writing Baseball*, p. 4.

10. Klinkowitz, *Writing Baseball*, p. 4.

11. Marie-Laure Ryan, "Narrative in Real Time: Chronicle, Mimesis, and Plot in the Baseball Broadcast," p. 144.

12. Some of the earliest team names seem rather unaware of the need to play out epic assumptions or at least to terrify the other team. Early organized baseball teams sported names like the Brooklyn Eckfords, the New York Highlanders (later the Yankees, another name absent of any fearful implications, at least when separated from the team's history), the Boston Bean Eaters, and the Brooklyn Trolley Dodgers. Some of the teams organized in the early twentieth century, such as the Boston Red Sox and the Chicago Cubs maintain unthreatening monikers; however, it is worth noting that most of the recent expansion teams in Major League Baseball have chosen to name themselves after dangerous sounding animals: the Tampa Bay Devil Rays, the Florida Marlins, and the Arizona Diamondbacks (a kind of snake). Only the Colorado Rockies have chosen another path.

13. An exception is A. Bartlett Giamatti's *Take Time for Paradise*, which in its final chapter, fittingly titled, "Baseball as Narrative," examines the game's connections to literature, both lyric and narrative. While Giamatti's focus is different than mine, his insights help to show how well baseball supports this kind of critical analysis.

14. Deeanne Westbrook, *Ground Rules: Baseball and Myth* (Urbana: University of Illinois Press, 1996), p. 1.

15. Peter Williams, *The Sports Immortals: Deifying the American Athlete*, (Bowling Green, OH: Bowling Green State University Popular Press, 1994), pp. 139–40.

16. While both Westbrook and Williams have essentially similar points to make, each presses the theory beyond its use, making more of sport as contemporary archetypal mythology than it probably deserves.

17. The prevalence of the heroic in individual sports is obvious; consider the 1996 Atlanta Summer Olympics, characterized by the chants of "USA, USA" that allegedly spurred American athletes to unexpected victories; or Kerri Strug's "heroic" vault in which she ignored an injured ankle, thus bringing victory to her team. That her score was ultimately unimportant will not remain a part of the narrative "fiction" of this event, and its enduring image is of her being carried, victorious, to the gold-medal podium.

18. When I began this chapter, Wade Boggs was still a member of the New York Yankees, my home team; as a result many of my examples are drawn from recent Yankee seasons. The essential journey here is Boggs's movement from Boston to New York. The rest of his career is secondary to this essay; Boggs left New York after the 1997 season to sign with the expansion Tampa Bay Devil Rays, where he recorded his 3,000th hit before retiring at the end of the 1999 season.

19. The Yankees repeat victories in 1998, 1999, and 2000 merely served to solidify the community sentiment that their 1996 win had created; the next three ticker-tape parades, while well attended, did not evoke the same enthusiasm as the first, and indeed, television coverage was also less extensive; fewer television stations carried the parades, and there were fewer feature stories on the local news in the days surrounding the event. These series were also without 1996s dramatic characters—the manager's near-death brother revived by a heart transplant the night before the final game, his sister the macarena-dancing nun, etc. Perhaps telling is the fact that a TV movie was made about the first series but not about the others; business as usual and a four-game sweep provide significantly less narrative potential than the stories of the first "come-from-behind" series. While the third series created character and pathos through three players who had recently lost their fathers, and while these events were used to show the "heroes'" intensity, the failure of any of the three to have an exceptional World Series kept these narratives from getting the same play they might have otherwise.

20. Umberto Eco, *Travels in Hyperreality*, trans. William Weaver (New York: Harcourt, Brace, and Co., 1983), p. 163.

21. Kakutani, "Making Art of Sport," p. 16.

22. The "humanness" of most athlete's bodies makes this superhuman quality difficult to sustain; indeed, the threat of age and its requisite reduction in status from hero to "formerly great" may well explain the seemingly "early" retirements of superstars like Michael Jordan and Barry Sanders, following the early example of Jim Brown, who left the NFL after nine great seasons to go make movies. To leave at the peak of one's career leaves

the image of greatness without the image of decline; the myth is preserved, and the athlete does not suffer Beowulf's or Roland's fate—to die in the last attempt, matched, if not overmatched, by the latest monster.

23. While Dwight Gooden has hung on, despite ineffective pitching and several trips to the minor leagues, Darryl Strawberry again returned at the end of the 1999 season from a suspension, levied by the Commissioner. While undergoing chemotheraphy for colon cancer and beginning his rehabilitation therapy, he was caught by Tampa, FL police soliciting a prostitute and carrying drugs. The exile and redemption process thus repeats itself.

24. Scandals have been much in the news lately, and it is easy to see the ways in which narrative expectations have governed their presentation. The Clinton/Lewinsky scandal follows the same essential patterns of character and plot. The *Starr Report*, e.g., includes far more fabliau-like detail about sexual escapades and alleged monetary compensation than is necessary for its political function; after all, sex—even kinky sex—is perfectly legal; the question at hand was perjury. But the scabrous nature of the document sold the copies and chained people to the Internet looking for the juiciest details. And the ensuing breast beating and apologies on the president's part followed the essential religious/confessional mode required for an effective redemption. The parts of fallen hero, long-suffering and patient wife, and dark lady were quickly assigned and fulfilled; Hillary Clinton received sympathy and Monica Lewinsky, opprobium. That the president continued to do perfectly well in approval ratings is a function of the effectiveness of his confession and redemption. Dick Morris and Marv Albert haven't entirely returned to their former prominence, they, too, followed the pattern epic–fabliau–confessional and have regained a place in the worlds they formerly inhabited.

25. These epics often complicate this duality; e.g., Vergil's portrait of Dido is sympathetic. However, the story is still governed by these conventions even when it seeks to challenge them; Dido ends up dead, and Aeneas marries Lavinia and founds Rome. So too, the portrait of Briseis in the *Iliad* is humanized, but she, too, finally ends up forgotten. In contemporary reporting, however, little energy is given to sympathizing with the "other woman," while much is devoted to reviling her.

26. Christopher Baswell, "Men in the *Roman D'Eneas*: the Construction of Empire," *Medieval Masculinities: Regarding Men in the Middle Ages*, ed. Clare A. Lees (Minneapolis: University of Minnesota Press, 1994), p. 150.

27. Baswell, "Men in the *Roman D'Eneas*: The Construction of Empire," p. 161.

28. A. Bartlett Giamatti, *Take Time for Paradise: Americans and Their Games* (New York: Summit Books, 1989), p. 15.

29. Giamatti, *Take Time for Paradise: Americans and Their Games*, p. 32.

30. Giamatti, *Take Time for Paradise: Americans and Their Games*, p. 25.

31. *Le Chanson de Roland*, ed. Pierre Jonin (Paris: Gallimard, 1979); the translation is from *The Song of Roland*, trans. Frederick Goldin (New York: W.W. Norton and Co, 1978). For one of numerous examples, see Laisse 79, l. 1015.

32. Eighty-four is not an exaggeration. Although his whole list of superstitions has not been specifically delineated, it included performing certain actions at certain specific times, never stepping on foul lines, drawing a "chai" in the dirt of the batter's box before every at-bat, and, of course, eating chicken before every game. Reporters periodically check in with Boggs to see if all his superstitions are still in place; they always are. See, e.g., Harper or "Boggs' Fowl Play. . ."

33. Doris Kearns Goodwin, "Batting Champ Wade Boggs Hits With a Cool Eye, A Hot Hand and a Resolve to Help his Sister Overcome Illness," *People Magazine*, April, 1986, p. 103.

34. Goodwin, "Batting Champ Wade Boggs Hits With a Cool Eye. . . ," p. 103.

35. Goodwin, "Batting Champ Wade Boggs Hits With a Cool Eye. . . ," p. 103.

36. Bob Croce, "Boggs at Home in Hall," *Albany Times-Union*, July 25, 1989, sec. D.

37. R. Howard Bloch, *The Scandal of the Fabliaux* (Chicago: University of Chicago Press, 1986), p. 127.

38. Bloch, *The Scandal of the Fabliaux*, p. 4.

39. Bloch, *The Scandal of the Fabliaux*, p. 39.

40. John W. Baldwin, *The Language of Sex* (Chicago: University of Chicago Press, 1994), p. 227.

41. Baldwin, *The Language of Sex*, p. 40.

42. Bloch, *The Scandal of the Fabliaux*, p. 127.

43. E. Talbot Donaldson, "The Idiom of Popular Poetry in the Miller's Tale," *Speaking of Chaucer* (New York: W. W. Norton and Company, 1970), p. 25.

44. Charles Muscatine, *The Old French Fabliaux* (New Haven: Yale University Press, 1986), p. 83.

45. Mike Shaughnessy, "The Low Down on the Boggs-Adams Saga," *Boston Globe*, February 11, 1989, p. 29. The similarity of some of these events to those in the earlier film *Bull Durham* serves to demonstrate the interconnectedness of life and art; the public details revealed in the papers are those that most reflect readers' narrative expectations.

46. Ted Sillary, "Hahn, Rice, and Adams? Palimony Suit against Boggs has Potential to get Messy," *Albany Times-Union*, July 15, 1988, sec. D.

47. A more comical association of sex and money came from a Toronto *Star* columnist, John Robertson, who seemed to feel that Margo Adams was asking for too little money: "Anyone who can prove she actually spent four seasons on the road watching nothing but Rex Sox games should be good for $12 million in damages for mental anguish, easily, even if she never went back to the hotel" (qtd. in Sillary, "Hahn, Rice, and. . . Adams?" D3).

48. David Margolick, "The Tantalizing Boggs Case: One Ballplayer, Two Women, and Three National Pastimes," *New York Times*, March 3, 1989, sec. B.

49. David D. Shumacher, "Designated Swinger," *Penthouse*, April 1989, p. 58.

50. Shumacher, "Designated Swinger," p. 58.

51. Bob Stanley and Steve Crawford are two of Boggs's Red Sox teammates.

52. Steve Fainaru, "Adams Article Set for March: Story on Boggs termed 'interesting, explosive,'" *Boston Globe*, February 2, 1989, p. 49. Bob Stanley and Steve Crawford were Boggs's teammates on the Red Sox, Stanley from 1977 to 1989 and Crawford from 1980 to 1987.

53. "Boggs Shirts Brisk Sellers," *USA Today*, April 11, 1989, sec. C.

54. Shumacher, "Designated Swinger," p. 46.

55. Charles Muscatine, *The Old French Fabliaux*, p. 76. For extended descriptions of fabliaux meals and their often erotic descriptions of eating, see Muscatine, pp. 75–83 plus Muscatine, p. 76.

56. Shumacher, "Designated Swinger," p. 96.

57. Bloch, *The Scandal of the Fabliaux*, p. 103.

58. Bloch, *The Scandal of the Fabliaux*, p. 103.

59. Again, for further examples of sex and violence in the fabliaux, see Muscatine, pp. 127–28.

60. Will McDonnough, "Boggs Runs Risk of Losing Fame," *Boston Globe*, February 9, 1989, 49.

61. McDonnough, "Boggs Runs Risk of Losing Fame," p. 49.

62. Michael Madden, "Battered Image Needs Restoring," *Boston Globe*, March 8, 1989, 73.

63. Michael Madden, "Battered Image Needs Restoring," p. 73.

64. "On TV Boggs Tells of 'Disease,'" *Boston Globe*, February 2, 1989, p. 50.

65. Susan Trausch, "Boggs' 'Addiction' is Off Base," *Boston Globe*, March 2, 1989, p. 12.

66. Aurelius Augustinus, *The Confessions of St. Augustine*, ed. John Gibb and William Montgomery (Cambridge: Cambridge University Press, 1927), VIII.v. 20–21. English translation from Augustine, *Confessions*, trans. R. S. Pine-Coffin (Harmondsworth: Penguin Books, 1961), p. 165.

67. In *Sex and the Penetentials* (Toronto: University of Toronto Press, 1986), Pierre J. Payer notes that all penetential manuals after 813 C.E. required a significant penance for adultery, ranging from six months to seven years (132–32); the penitent is also required to refrain from further sexual relations with his or her fellow adulterous partner (pp. 20–23).

68. Recent examples include Monica Lewinsky's television interview with Walters and Hillary Clinton's interview in *Talk* magazine, blaming her husband's philandering on child abuse. Indeed, the Boggses were also interviewed by Barbara Walters in March of 1989.

69. Michel Foucault, *The History of Sexuality: An Introduction*, vol. 1. 1976, trans. Robert Hurley, 1978 (New York: Vintage Press, 1990), p. 58.

70. Foucault, *The History of Sexuality: An Introduction*, p. 58.

71. Foucault, *The History of Sexuality: An Introduction*, p. 59.

72. Foucault, *The History of Sexuality: An Introduction*, p. 60.

73. Foucault, *The History of Sexuality: An Introduction*, p. 62.

74. Foucault, *The History of Sexuality: An Introduction*, p. 63.

75. Augustine, VIII.xi. 17–18; *Confessions*, 175.

76. Baldwin, *The Language of Sex*, p. 225.

77. Marilyn Desmond, *Reading Dido: Gender, Textuality, and the Medieval Aeneid, Medieval Cultures* 8 (Minneapolis: University of Minnesota Press, 1994), p.74.

78. Marilyn Desmond, *Reading Dido*, pp. 62–63.

79. Boggs's struggles are by no means equivalent to Augustine's sincere theological conflicts, represented by his turn to Manicheanism and the influence of several false mentors, although within Boggs's own narrow context, they may well have appeared very profound—to him, if not to the sports writers who documented them in both critical and comic terms. However, the central model of personal conflict and the fall from an idealized path into an attractive "wrong" remains from the Augustinian model. The perfect sports hero is supposed to put the team ahead of personal records, and it is just this selfish quality attributed to Boggs that led to the glee that writers seemed to feel in skewering him for his failures. Selfishness in a player, real or imagined, can often cost him fan and teammate popularity and reputation: Boggs, his teammate Roger Clemens, and Barry Bonds, current holder of the Home Run Record, all suffer from these accusations, while their equally talented counterparts, Cal Ripken, Jr., Tony Gwynn (both of whom got their 3,000th hit around the same time as Boggs), and Mark McGwire are all well loved because of the perception that they are team players. Even if trivial outside the world of sports, the struggle to maintain a reputation in the face of others' ideas can be challenging and difficult for talented players.

80. Joel Sherman, "Boggs gets 'Punchy' in Beantown," *New York Post*, June 30, 1994, p. 38.

81. Barnicle, "Needed at Third, A Cold Shower," p. 21.

82. E. M. Swift, "Facing the Music: Wade Boggs Stayed Cool Despite His Ex-Lover's Steamy Revelations," *Sports Illustrated*, March 6, 1989, p. 41.

83. E. M. Swift, "Facing the Music: Wade Boggs Stayed Cool Despite His Ex-Lover's Steamy Revelations," p. 41.

84. Kornheiser, "For Your Sins and Mine; Let Me Say I'm Sorry," sec. D.

85. Fainaru, "Adams Article Set for March: Story on Boggs termed interesting, explosive," p. 33.

86. Augustine, VIII.xii, 4 *Confessions*, p. 177.

87. Augustine, VIII.xii, 15–20, *Confessions*, p. 177.

88. Augustine, VII, *Confessions*, p. 178.

89. Tom Verducci, "A Quiet .300," *Sports Illustrated*, January 15, 1996, p. 70.

90. Bruce Jenkins, "Wade's Ways Just Boggle the Mind," *San Francisco Chronicle*, May 28, 1991, sec. D.

91. Jenkins, "Wade's Ways Just Boggle the Mind," sec. D.

92. Red Sox fans might say that leaving Boston to play for the Yankees is a kind of martyrdom; however, Boggs has never even suffered a metaphorical dismemberment since leaving Fenway Park. He was well received in New York (and still received ovations there when playing for the expansion Tampa Bay Devil Rays); still receives fanfare in Boston, and was popular enough in

Tampa that when he got close to 3,000 hits, the baseball milestone that would assure his ascension to the Hall of Fame, he considered not playing until the team returned home from a road trip to make sure his victory celebration took place in Tampa, in front of the home crowd. And when Boggs did get his 3,000th hit—a home run—on August 7, 1999 in Tampa, the fans exalted, while the "Wade Boggs Hit Counter" flashed "3,000" in red as he rounded the bases. Boggs then pointed to the sky in a gesture toward his dead mother and then fell on his knees and kissed the home plate, a gesture redolently symbolic of redemption and return.

93. *Sir Gawain and The Green Knight*, in *The Poems of the Pearl Manuscript*, ed. Malcolm Andrew and Ronald Waldron (London: Edwin Arnold, 1978); the translation is from *Sir Gawain and the Green Knight*, trans. Marie Boroff (New York: W. W. Norton and Co., 1967); ll. 2495–96; 2506–12.

94. Armando R. Favazza, *Bodies Under Siege: Self-Mutilation in Culture and Psychiatry* (Baltimore: John Hopkins University Press, 1987), p. 40; Kaplan pp. 483–84.

95. Pat Borzi, "The Machine: A Slave to his Routine, Wade Boggs Doggedly Pursues Two More Goals," *The Star-Ledger*, September 29, 1996, p. 14.

96. Murcer, Bobby, Phil Rizutto, and Suzyn Waldman, "New York Yankees vs. Cleveland Indians," WPIX Television, July 26, 1996.

97. "Bomber Bulletin," *New York Daily News*, June 24, 1998, p. 64.

98. Robert Squillace brought this advertisement to my attention; I am grateful to him telling me the whole Wade Boggs story in the first place.

99. The image is available on microfilm from several newspapers from Sunday, October 27, 1996; a color version, e.g., can be found on page C-1 of the *San Francisco Examiner*; a black and white version on the first page of the *New York Times'* sports section. For an image of Boggs's supplication before the home plate after his 3,000th hit, see *San Francisco Examiner*, August 6, 1999, B-1.

100. Fred Goodall, "Boggs Jumps onto the Milestone Bus," *San Francisco Examiner*, August 8, 1999, sec. B.

101. Goodall, "Boggs Jumps onto the Milestone Bus," sec. B.

102. Goodall, "Boggs Jumps onto the Milestone Bus," sec. B.

103. Goodall, "Boggs Jumps onto the Milestone Bus," sec. B.

104. Paul Ricoeur, *Temps et Regit*, vol. I (Paris: Seuil, 1983) qtd. in Ryan, p. 144.

105. Ryan, "Narrative in Real Time," p. 138.

Chapter 3   Where Many Have Gone Before:
Gender and Genre in *Star Trek*

★ *Star Trek* is an ambiguous term; it refers both to the "*Star Trek* franchise" and to the shows itself. Only the first series was simply called *Star Trek*, the subsequent four carried subtitles: "The Animated Series" (TAS); "The Next Generation" (TNG); "Deep Space Nine"(DS9); and

"Voyager" (VOY). What was once just called *Star Trek* is now called "The Original Series" (TOS). The most recent edition of the series, which premiered in September 2001, has dropped the "Star Trek" prefix and is simply called *Enterprise*.

1. Originally, the term "romance" referred to the vernacular; by association, it comes to mean a form of literary translation from Latin to "romance," which Marie de France, e.g., suggests she might do before realizing that it would not bring her fame. Composing lais in "romance," Marie is the first to associate vernacular language and courtly narrative. By the time Chaucer writes *Troilus and Criseyde*, the term "romance" has come to mean a literary genre that encompasses both the *Romans Antiques* that many read as the courtly romance's narrative ancestors and the courtly form itself.

2. One might note that while other sorts of romances, such as the *romans antiques* have their "strange new worlds" as well, these are constituted differently from that in the courtly and Celtic traditions. This difference lies, in part, in the *romans'* relationship to history, narrative and real.

3. Erich Auerbach, *Mimesis: The Representation of Reality in Western Literature*, trans. Willard Trask (Princeton: Princeton University Press, 1953), p. 134.

4. Frederic Jameson, *The Political Unconscious: Narrative as a Socially Symbolic Act* (Ithaca: Cornell University Press, 1981), p. 106.

5. Jameson, *Political Unconscious*, p. 107.

6. "Lay le Freine," *Middle English Verse Romances*, ed. Donald B. Sands (Exeter: University of Exeter Press, 1986) pp. 1, 12.

7. Eugene Vance, "Chrétien's *Yvain* and the Ideologies of Change and Exchange," *Yale French Studies*, 70 (1986), p. 47.

8. Auerbach, *Mimesis*, p. 128.

9. Patricia Parker, *Inescapable Romance* (Princeton: Princeton University Press, 1979), pp. 4–5. Looking at romances medieval and postmedieval, Parker notes the persistence of romance phenomena within certain different tendencies. For instance, she considers that Mallarmé's "deferral of revelation in the prose poem 'Le Nénuphar blanc' falls as much within the sphere of romance as the period before the unmaking of the 'Other' in the *Erec et Enide*," p. 5.

10. Parker, *Inescapable Romance*, p. 5.

11. *Sir Gawain and the Green Knight*, in *The Poems of The Pearl Manuscript*, ed. Malcolm Andrew and Ronald Waldron (London: Arnold, 1978). The translation is from *Sir Gawain and the Green Knight*, trans. Marie Boroff (New York: W. W. Norton, and Co., 1967) ll. 713–34.

12. Auerbach, *Mimesis*, p. 134.

13. Auerbach, *Mimesis*, pp. 134–35.

14. Auerbach, *Mimesis*, p. 135.

15. See, e.g., Susan Crane, *Gender and Romance in Chaucer's Canterbury Tales* (Princeton: Princeton University Press, 1994); Crane calls Chaucer's society one in which literary ideals were assimilated into practice (p. 181) by a higher strata of commoners in professional and mercantile circles (p. 180), thus extending court values well beyond the courts themselves.

While Lee Ramsay, in *Chivalric Romances: Popular Literature in Medieval England* (Bloomington: Indiana University Press, 1983) shows romance to remain a primarily courtly genre in the fourteenth century (p. 83), social mobility, increased literacy, and a desire to imitate upper class behaviors and values provided it a more broadly constituted audience. Thus the later romance puts forward "a straightforward set of teachable values" in which "courtliness is imitatable rather than exclusive" (Crane, p. 221).

16. Chrétien de Troyes, *Yvain*, ed. Mario Roques (Paris: Champions, 1982) Translation from *Yvain*, trans. Burton Raffel (New Haven: Yale University Press, 1987), pp. 1, 3. Raffel opens his able translation of the poem with the first three lines in the old French, exemplifying Chrétien's focus on the often conflicting but equally vital values of prowess and courtesy, two values that also define the world of Starfleet in the *Star Trek* series. All further quotations from *Yvain* are from Roques's edition and Raffel's translation.

17. Chrétien de Troyes, Yvain, ll. 6799–808.

18. Auerbach, *Mimesis*, p. 139.

19. Auerbach, *Mimesis*, p. 139.

20. Vance, "Chrétien's Yvain," p. 47.

21. Angela Jane Weisl, *Conquering the Reign of Femeny: Gender and Genre in Chaucer's Romance* (Cambridge: D. S. Brewer, 1995), p. 11.

22. Weisl, *Conquering*, p. 3.

23. Carolyn Dinshaw, *Chaucer's Sexual Poetics* (Madison: University of Wisconsin Press, 1989), p. 128. Dinshaw also notes that the knight "is not up to the challenge of this text, even after his year-long tutelage in feminine desire" (p. 138); thus the Loathly Lady becomes enormously powerful and authoritative, taking that role away from the masculine power structures of the medieval world, if only for a few fleeting pages.

24. Geoffrey Chaucer, "The Wife of Bath's Tale," *The Riverside Chaucer*, 3rd ed., ed. Larry D. Benson (Boston: Houghton, Mifflin, 1987), III, pp. 1255–56.

25. Chaucer, "Wife of Bath's Tale," III, pp. 1038–40.

26. Chrétien de Troyes, *Yvain*, ll. 1921–25.

27. Chrétien de Troyes, *Yvain*, ll. 1990–91.

28. Chrétien de Troyes, *Yvain*, ll. 2051–52.

29. Chrétien de Troyes, *Yvain*, ll. 1623–25.

30. *Star Trek V: The Final Frontier*, 107 min., Technicolor, Paramount Pictures, Los Angeles, CA, 1989. In this installment of the *Star Trek* film series, Captain Kirk goes in search of a legendary planet said to be inhabited by God. In its most memorable moment, Kirk asks the superbeing found on the planet, "What would God need with a starship?"

31. Frederick Goldin, "Introduction," *The Song of Roland*, ed. and trans. Frederick Goldin (New York: W. W. Norton and Co, 1978), pp. 16–17.

32. In this the film follows a preoccupation of both *Star Trek: The Original Series* and *Star Trek: The Next Generation* that share a fascination with Shakespeare and quote him frequently. *The Next Generation* often featured characters enacting Shakespearian scenes, no doubt taking advantage of Patrick Stewart's background and membership in the Royal Shakespeare

Company. No series, for all their reenactment of old movie plots and myths, has ever transposed one of Shakespeare's plots into space.

33. *Star Trek VI: The Undiscovered Country*, 110 min., Technicolor, Paramount Pictures, Los Angeles, CA, 1991. This film essentially provided a conclusion to *Star Trek: The Original Series*, ending the long-standing feud between the Federation and the Klingons and the reign of Kirk. Janet Maslin in the *New York Times* described the crew as "looking ever more ready for inter-galactic rocking chairs" (quoted in *Haliwell's Film Guide*, ed. John Walker [New York: Harper Collins, 1995], p. 1015). Although Captain Kirk appeared in the eighth film, along with two other characters from the original series, *Star Trek VIII: Generations*, (117 min., Technicolor, Paramount Pictures, Los Angeles, CA, 1994) served as a transitional narrative, passing the cinematic torch to Captain Jean-Luc Picard (Patrick Stewart) and the cast of *Star Trek: The Next Generation*. Kirk's death in the film cements the end of the original *Star Trek* era.

34. Auerbach, *Mimesis*, p. 130.

35. Auerbach, *Mimesis*, p. 131.

36. Michael Okuda, Denise Okuda, and Debbie Mirek. *The Star Trek Encyclopedia: A Reference Guide to the Future* (New York: Pocket Books, 1994), p. 361.

37. Okuda, Okuda, and Mirek, *Star Trek Encyclopedia*, p. 261.

38. M-Class planets are those supporting humanoid life, generally with an atmosphere sufficiently similar to Earth's to allow the cast not to have to wear space suits. This designation apparently comes from a Vulcan term, "Minchara-Class," although this was revealed only recently in the most current series, *Enterprise* (the first to forego the *Star Trek* prefix).

39. Although the Space Station on *Star Trek: Deep Space Nine* (DS9) certainly represents Starfleet and the Federation in many of the same ways the star-ships in the other four series do, because it is a static location, the stories told about it more strongly resemble the novel than the romance. Its fixed nature lent itself to more extended narrative arcs, taking up several episodes and often much of a season; in the final season, most stories were either a part of or played out against the background of a war with the ominous shapeshifters of the Dominion, an anti-Federation that enslaved other peoples for its own use and desired the complete annihilation of all "solids." The novelistic nature of this series also allowed a more complex exploration of race and gender, producing *Star Trek*'s most complex and interesting female and alien characters, for which it is rarely given credit. Overshadowed by both *The Next Generation* and *Voyager*, *Deep Space Nine* never received the same critical attention and audience enthusiasm, suggesting that for all fans' claimed desire to see new possibilities, what they really want is the same old thing.

40. Sarah Hardy and Rebecca Kulka, "A Paramount Narrative: Exploring Space on the Starship Enterprise," *Journal of Aesthetics and Art Criticism*, 57:2 (1999), pp. 177–91.

41. Hardy and Kulka, "Paramount," p. 180.

42. Hardy and Kulka, "Paramount," p. 184.

43. Michael Bakhtin, *Crisis in Dostoyevsky's Poetics*, trans. Caryl Emerson (Minneapolis: University of Minnesota Press, 1984), p. 169.

44. Hardy and Kulka, "Paramount," p. 191.

45. "The Inner Light," *Star Trek:The Next Generation*, episode #225, Paramount Pictures; first aired week of June 1, 1992.

46. This raises a recurrent ecological motif within *Star Trek*, in which various kinds of environmental dangers such as the extinction of whales and nuclear disaster preoccupy the narrative. More modern threats, certainly, yet they provide quests (such as in *Star Trek IV: The Voyage Home* in which the Enterprise Crew has to travel into the past to bring back a pair of humpback whales) and oppositions, as well as raising more contemporary questions.

47. *Sir Gawain and the Green Knight*, ll. 2514, 2518.

48. *Sir Gawain and the Green Knight*, ll. 2506–10.

49. Such transformations have a way of happening to Picard—he becomes Locutus of Borg, Mott the barber, a down-at-the–heels Shakespearean, a dangerous smuggler, and so forth—further establishing him as the Captain, the chief romance figure, the questing knight. Indeed, Captains Kirk and Sisko underwent arguably even more extreme changes of identity.

50. *Sir Gawain and the Green Knight*, ll. 2522–25.

51. Lynne Joyrich, "Feminist Enterprise?: *Star Trek: The Next Generation* and the Occupation of Femininity," *Cinema Journal*, 35:2 (1996), p. 65.

52. "Lessons," *StarTrek: The Next Generation*, episode #245, Paramount Pictures; first aired week of April 5, 1993.

53. Victor Turner and Edith Turner, *Image and Pilgrimage in Christian Culture: Anthropological Perspecitves* (New York: Columbia University Press, 1978), p. 3. Although the Turners are actually discussing the "out of the ordinary" experience of pilgrimage here, this description of liminality functions effectively as a description of romance, since the "going out" defines both the literal and narrative spaces that determine these genres. If pilgrimage puts the pilgrim in a threshold between the ordinary and the transcendent, romance puts both its characters and the reader in a space between the public world of social responsibility and courtly duty and the private world of interior change, played out in the exterior passages of adventure.

54. "Darmok," *Star Trek: The Next Generation*, episode #202, Paramount Pictures; first aired week of September 30, 1991.

55. Jameson, *Political Unconscious*, p. 112.

56. Jameson, *Political Unconscious*, pp. 118–19.

57. Ilsa J. Bick. "Boys in Space: *Star Trek*, Latency, and the Neverending Story," *Enterprise Zones: Critical Positions on Star Trek*, ed. Taylor Harrison et al. (Boulder, CO: Westview Press, 1996), pp. 189–210, 190.

58. For a discussion of these rescue missions, see Sarah Projansky, "When the Body Speaks: Deanna Troi's Tenuous Authority and the Rationalization of Federation Superiority in *Star Trek: The Next Generation Rape Narratives*,"

Enterprise Zones: Critical Positions on Star Trek, ed. Taylor Harrison et al. (Boulder, CO: Westview Press, 1996), pp. 33–50, 33–34.

59. Projansky, "When the Body Speaks," p. 35.

60. Frederick Goldin, *The Mirror of Narcissus in the Courtly Love Lyric* (Ithaca: Cornell University Press, 1967), p. vii.

61. Goldin, *Mirror*, p. 2.

62. "The Naked Now," *Star Trek: The Next Generation*, episode #103, Paramount Pictures; first aired, week of October 5, 1987.

63. Steven F. Collins. "For the Greater Good: Trilateralism and Hegemony in *Star Trek: The Next Generation*," *Enterprise Zones: Critical Positions on Star Trek*, ed. Taylor Harrison et al. (Boulder, CO: Westview Press, 1996), pp. 137–56, 145.

64. Hardy and Kulka, "A Paramount Narrative," p. 181.

65. "Code of Honor," *Star Trek: The Next Generation*, episode #104, Paramount Pictures; first aired, week of October 12, 1987.

66. Many readers see an equation between species and race, Starfleet representing white America repressing all others. However, this formula is too simple; an alien species can stand for race, in its postmedieval sense, drawn from ideas of nationalism and colonialism, but aliens can also stand for various kinds of "otherness," utopic or distopic. For instance, the half-human, half-mechanical Borg clearly represent an anxiety about our lives being taken over by machines and our place in an increasingly mechanized culture. Supernatural figures along the Grendel or Dragon line, that which is both outside the "real" world as liminal, and that which is outside but comments "in" are also represented by alien species. Reducing the portrayal of aliens on *Star Trek* to a univalent racial conflict misses the way that these figures are used to deal with separation on multiple levels. That said, the portrayal of the inhabitants of Ligon is profoundly racist, as is the depiction of the neo-Irish Bringloidi in "Up the Long Ladder" (*Star Trek: The Next Generation*, episode #144, Paramount Pictures; first aired, week of May 22, 1989.). Critics examining race in *Star Trek* include Daniel Leonard Bernardi, *Star Trek and History: Race-ing Toward a White Future* (New Brunswick, NJ: Rutgers University Press, 1998.); Denise Alessandria Hurd, "The Monster Inside: Nineteenth Century Racial Constructs in the Twenty-Fourth Century Mythos of Star Trek," *Journal of Popular Culture*, 31.1 (1997), pp. 23–35; and articles by Hastie, Wilcox, and Vande Berg in *Enterprise Zones*.

67. "The Last Outpost," *Star Trek: The Next Generation*, episode #107, Paramount Pictures; first aired, week of October 19, 1987.

68. "Justice," *Star Trek: The Next Generation*, episode #109, Paramount Pictures; first aired, week of November 9, 1987.

69. Lee E. Heller, "The Persistence of Difference: Post-Feminism, Popular Discourse, and Heterosexuality in *Star Trek: The Next Generation*," *Science Fiction Studies*, 24:2 (1997), pp. 226–44, 230.

70. Jeffrey A. Weinstock, "Freaks in Space: 'Extraterrestrialism' and 'Deep Space Multiculturalism,'" *Freakery: Cultural Spectacles of the Extraordinary Body*,

ed. Rosemarie Garland Thompson (New York: New York University Press, 1996), pp. 327–37, 335.

71. Chrétien de Troyes, *Erec and Enide*, trans. Burton Raffel (New Haven: Yale University Press, 1997), ll. 1014–25.

72. *Chrétien, Erec and Enide*, l. 1191.

73. *Chrétien, Erec and Enide*, ll. 3631–35.

74. Weinstock, "Freaks in Space," p. 335.

75. *Chrétien, Erec and Enide*, ll. 4456–65, 4467–70.

76. It is worth noting that rank is very different from status in medieval society, conferred not by birth but by work. Starfleet is the home of a variety of misfits and half-breeds; in the *Next Generation* alone, the audience is offered the half-human, half-betazoid empath Deanna Troi; the unique android Data who wishes to be human but lacks emotion and attempts to build a daughter to assuage his loneliness; Ensign Ro, whose Bajoran people are in the midst of a devastating war, and who eventually becomes a vigilante freedom fighter; Worf, the only Klingon in Starfleet, adopted by humans after the destruction of his home planet; and his predecessor Tasha Yar, who brought her troubled childhood and revolutionary past to the Enterprise Bridge. I would like to thank Sharon Kinoshita for bringing this distinction to my attention.

77. Crane, *Gender*, pp. 3–4.

78. Weisl, *Conquering*, p. 3.

79. Marleen S. Barr, *Alien to Femininity: Speculative Fiction and Feminity Theory* (New York: Greenwood Press, 1987), p. xi.

80. Donna Reid-Jeffrey, "*Star Trek*: The Last Frontier in Modern American Myth," *Folklore and Mythology Studies*, 6 (1982) pp. 34–41, 37–38.

81. Susan C. Hines, "What's Academic about *Trek*," *Extrapolations*, 3:61 (1995) pp. 5–9, 7.

82. "Liasons," *Star Trek: The Next Generation*, episode #253, Paramount Pictures; first aired, week of September 20, 1993.

83. *Sir Gawain and the Green Knight*, ll. 2459–60.

84. Larry Nemecek, *The Star Trek: The Next Generation Companion* (New York: Pocket Books, 1995), p. 179.

85. "Devil's Due," *Star Trek: The Next Generation*, episode #187, Paramount Pictures; first aired, week of February 4, 1991. This was the highest-rated episode of the series' six-year run.

86. "The Drumhead," *Star Trek: The Next Generation*, episode #195, Paramount Pictures; first aired, week of April 29, 1991.

87. Lee Patterson, "'For the Wyves Love of Bathe': Feminine Rhetoric and Poetic Resolution in the *Roman de La Rose* and the *Canterbury Tales*," *Speculum*, 58:3 (1983), pp. 656–95, 660–61.

88. "The Perfect Mate," *Star Trek: The Next Generation*, episode # 221, Paramount Pictures; first aired, week of April 27, 1992.

89. Chaucer, "The Wife of Bath's Tale," ll. III, pp. 1232–33.

90. Chaucer, "The Wife of Bath's Tale," ll. III, pp. 1255–56.

91. See, e.g., Peggy Knapp, "Alisoun of Bath and the Re-appropriation of Tradition," *Chaucer Review*, 24 (1989), pp. 45–52 and *Chaucer and the Social Contest* (New York: Routledge, 1990), and H. Marshall Leicester, Jr., *The Disappointed Self: Representing the Subject in the Canterbury Tales* (Berkeley: University of California Press, 1990) and "Of a fire in the dark: Public and Private Feminist in the *Wife of Bath's Tale*," *Women's Studies*, 11 (1984), pp. 157–78.

92. "The Perfect Mate,'" *Star Trek: The Next Generation*, episode #221.

93. Heller, "The Persistence of Difference," p. 233.

94. Haller, "The Persistence of Difference," p. 234.

95. Susan C. Hines, "What's Academic about *Trek*," *Extrapolations*, 36:0 (1995), pp. 5–9, 9.

96. "The Perfect Mate," *Star Trek: The Next Generation*, episode #122.

97. Emily Hegarty, "Some Suspect of Ill: Shakespeare's Sonnets and the 'Perfect Mate,' " *Extrapolation*, 36:1 (1995), pp. 55–64, 61.

98. Hegarty, "Some Suspect of Ill," p. 63.

99. Goldin, *Mirror*, p. 77.

100. Goldin, *Mirror*, p. 78.

101. Goldin, *Mirror*, p. 105.

102. "The Perfect Mate," *Star Trek: The Next Generation*, episode #122.

103. Goldin, *Mirror*, p. vii.

104. "Sub Rosa," *Star Trek: The Next Generation*, episode #266, Paramount Pictures; first aired, week of January 31, 1994.

105. Nemecek, *The Star Trek: The Next Generation Companion*, p. 280.

106. "Lessons," *Star Trek: The Next Generation*, episode #245, Paramount Pictures, first aired, week of April 5, 1993. On a side note, one of the things that attracts Picard to Nella Darren is her musical talent, and their romance develops as they play duets, she on the piano and he on his wooden flute from the planet Kataan, from "The Inner Light."

107. "The Host," *Star Trek: The Next Generation*, episode #197, Paramount Pictures; first aired, week of May 12, 1991.

108. "All Good Things. . . ." *Star Trek: The Next Generation*, episode #277, Paramount Pictures; first aired, week of May 23, 1994.

109. Marleen S. Barr, " 'All Good Things. . .': The *End of Star Trek: The Next Generation*, the End of Camelot—The End of the Tale about Women as Handmaid to Patriarchy as Superman," *Enterprise Zones: Critical Positions on Star Trek*, ed. Taylor Harrison et al. (Boulder, CO: Westview Press, 1996), pp. 231–43, 238.

110. Lynne Joyrich, "Feminist Enterprise?: *Star Trek: The Next Generation* and the Occupation of Femininity," pp. 61–84, 64.

111. Amelie Hastie, "A Fabricated Space: Assimilating the Individual on *Star Trek: The Next Generation*," *Enterprise Zones: Critical Positions on Star Trek*, ed. Taylor Harrison et al. (Boulder, CO: Westview Press, 1996), pp. 115–36, 122.

112. Projansky, "When the Body Speaks," p. 35.

113. "The Child," *Star Trek: The Next Generation*, episode #127, Paramount Pictures; first aired, week of November 21, 1988.

114. "Violations," *Star Trek: The Next Generation*, episode #212, Paramount Pictures; first aired, week of February 3, 1992.

115. "Man of the People," *Star Trek: The Next Generation*, episode #229, Paramount Pictures; first aired, week of October 5, 1992.

116. Projansky, "When the Body Speaks," p. 38.

117. "Chain of Command, I," *Star Trek: The Next Generation*, episode #236, Paramount Pictures; first aired, week of December 14, 1992.

118. Hastie, "Fabricated Space," p. 127.

119. "Thine Own Self," *Star Trek: The Next Generation*, episode #268, Paramount Pictures; first aired, week of February 14, 1994.

120. "Face of the Enemy," *Star Trek: The Next Generation*, episode #240, Paramount Pictures; first aired, week of February 8, 1993.

121. Nemecek, *The Star Trek: The Next Generation Companion*, p. 234.

122. Michael Logan, "The Magnificent Seven," *TV Guide*, May 14, 1994, p. 14.

123. "Second Chances," *Star Trek: The Next Generation*, episode #250, Paramount Pictures; first aired, week of May 24, 1993.

124. "Parallels," *Star Trek: The Next Generation*, episode #263, Paramount Pictures; first aired, week of November 29, 1993.

125. "Eye of the Beholder," *Star Trek: The Next Generation*, episode #270, Paramount Pictures; first aired, week of February 28, 1994.

126. Hastie, "Fabricated Space," pp. 128–29.

127. Hastie, "Fabricated Space," p. 129.

128. Hastie, "Fabricated Space," p. 130.

129. Hastie, "Fabricated Space," p. 130.

130. The *Star Trek* industry attempted to address this situation in its subsequent series. While the more novel-like nature of *Star Trek: Deep Space Nine*, whose primary plot followed a more sustained narrative arc than any of the other *Star Trek* series, released some of the constrictions of the romance, allowing for the significantly more complex and autonomous characters Kira Nerys (the station's Bajoran First Officer and former Resistance Fighter) and Jadzia Dax (a Trill Science Officer whose parasite was previously several different men and women), the fact that both of them were aliens may have also freed them from certain restraints. While the show had its share of dangerous women, it also provided more opportunities for its various recurring female characters. Returning to the romance genre with *Star Trek: Voyager*, Paramount enlisted a female captain; because the genre provided no models for stories of women in power, the show never found its stride nor garnered critical success or equal fan enthusiasm. The latest series, *Enterprise*, has returned to formula; its two female characters fulfill traditional roles. Ensign Hoshii Sato, the Communications Officer, is cute, wimpy, and often uncertain about what she's doing in space. To date, the one story focused on her dealt with her trying to find out (at the Captain's orders) the Tactical

Officer's favorite food. T'Pol, the Vulcan Science Officer, appears dressed in a skin-tight jump suit; slightly mysterious and dangerous because of her emotionless demeanor, she has no sexual desires of her own, yet those of others are projected onto her. The process of taming her has already begun; not only has she failed in a mission that got one of her people's sacred monasteries destroyed, she has also shown her feminine side by secretly trying pecan pie, a food she publicly declared "illogical."

131. Matilda Tomaryn Bruckner, *Shaping Romance: Interpretation, Truth, and Closure in Twelfth-Century French Fictions* (Philadelphia: University of Pennsylvania Press, 1993), p. 3.

132. Bruckner, *Shaping Romance*, p. 228, n. 7.

133. Frederic Jameson. "Reification and Utopia in Mass Culture," *Social Text*, 1 (1979) pp. 130–48, 144.

134. Jameson, "Reification and Utopia," p. 141.

Chapter 4   Rexque Quondam [the foreseeable] Futurus: *Star Wars* and the Commerce of Arthurian Romance

1. John Seabrook, "Why is the Force Still with Us?" *The New Yorker*, January 6, 1997, pp. 40–53, 44.

2. Tom Dupree, editor of the Bantam *Star Wars* series of novels, qtd. in Seabrook, "Why is the Force Still with Us?" p. 44.

3. Seabrook, "Why is the Force Still with Us?" p. 40.

4. Jack Sorensen, president of LucasArts, qtd. in Seabrook, "Why is the Force Still with Us?" p. 45.

5. Bill Moyers, "Of Myth and Men: An Interview with George Lucas," *Time*, April 26, 1999, p. 60.

6. Moyers, "Of Myth and Men," p. 60.

7. Moyers, "Of Myth and Men," p. 60, 64.

8. Daniel McKay, "*Star Wars*: The Magic of the Anti-Myth," *Foundation*, 76 (1999), pp. 63–75, 65.

9. Andrew Gordon, "*Star Wars:* A Myth for our Time," *Literature/Film Quarterly*, 6 (1976), pp. 314–26, 315; qtd. in MacKay, pp. 65–66.

10. Armand Singer and Michael Lastinger, "Themes and Sources of *Star Wars*: John Carter and Flash Gordon Enlist in the First Crusade," *Popular Culture Review*, 9:2 (1998), pp. 65–77, 66.

11. Singer and Lastinger, "Themes and Sources," p. 65.

12. Singer and Lastinger, "Themes and Sources," p. 67.

13. Orville Schell, "George Lucas: A Galaxy of Myth, Money, and Kids," *New York Times*, March 21, 1991 (www.nytimes.com/library/film/032199lucas-wars-profile.html).

14. Schell, "George Lucas" (www.nytimes.com/library/film/032199 lucas-wars-profile.html).

15. Schell, "George Lucas" (www.nytimes.com/library/film/032199 lucas-wars-profile.html).

16. MacKay, "*Star Wars*," p. 67.

17. MacKay, "*Star Wars*," p. 72.

18. Thomas Bulfinch, *Bulfinch's Mythology*, 1867 (New York: Avenel, 1978), p. v.

19. Bulfinch, *Mythology*, p. v.

20. Edward Donald Kennedy, "Introduction," *King Arthur: A Casebook* (New York: Garland Publishing, 1996), p. xiii.

21. Kennedy, "Introduction," *King Arthur: A Casebook*, p. xiv.

22. Christopher Baswell and William Sharpe, "Introduction: Rex Quondam Rexque Futurus," *The Passing of Arthur: New Essays in Arthurian Tradition*, ed. Christopher Baswell and William Sharpe (New York: Garland, 1986), p. xi.

23. Baswell and Sharpe, "Introduction: Rex Quondam Rexque Futurus," p. xii.

24. *Star Wars* receives no mention, for instance, in Kevin J. Harty's *Cinema Arthuriana: Essays on Arthurian Film* (New York: Garland Publishing, 1991). Although Harty says that the essays in the book "are meant to suggest the wealth of the Arthurian cinematic tradition" (p. xiii), *Star Wars* is not considered in any of them. Noting that there have been "more than forty cinematic transpositions of the legend of King Arthur," and that "the major names in the film industry both before and behind the camera have been associated with Arthurian film" (p. xvii), Harty consistently leaves out the major names of George Lucas, Alec Guinness, Carrie Fisher, and Harrison Ford in his overview, even though many of the films included in the collection have "more in common with. . .contemporary non-Arthurian films' than they do with other strictly Arthurian examples" (p. xvii).

25. Norris J. Lacy, "Preface," *The Arthurian Encyclopedia*, ed. Norris J. Lacy (New York: Garland Publishing, 1986), p. xvi.

26. Lacy, "Preface," p. xvi.

27. Umberto Eco, *Travels in Hyperreality*, trans. William Weaver (New York: Harcourt Brace, 1983), p. 67.

28. Eco, *Travels*, pp. 67–68.

29. Eco, *Travels*, p. 72.

30. Moyers, "Of Myth and Men," p. 60.

31. Jessica Tiffin, "Digitally Remythicized: *Star Wars*, Modern Popular Mythology, and *Madam and Eve*," *Journal of Literary Studies*, 15:1–2 (1999), pp. 66–80, 67.

32. Moyers, "Myth and Man," p. 62.

33. Arthur, too, comes of age (pulling the sword from the stone and becoming king), acquires knowledge of his family as well as real and symbolic relations (Morgan, Mordred, Guenevere, Merlin), and finds his future, for better or worse, as king of Logres.

34. Tiffin, "Digitally Remythicized," p. 70.

35. Seabrook, "Why is the Force Still with Us?" p. 40.

36. Jeffrey Weinstock, "Freaks in Space: 'Extraterrestrialism' and 'Deep Space Multiculturalism,'" *Freakery: Cultural Spectacles of the Extraordinary Body*,

ed. Rosemarie Garland Thomson (New York: New York University Press, 1996), pp. 327–37, 331.

37. Weinstock, "Freaks in Space," pp. 232–33.

38. John Rieder, "Embracing the Alien: Science Fiction in Mass Culture," *Science Fiction Studies*, 9 (1982), p. 34.

39. Tiffin, "Digitally Remythicized," pp. 68–69.

40. Kevin Kelly and Paula Parisi, "*Star Wars*: What's Next for George Lucas?" *Wired*, February 1997, pp. 160–66, 210–17, 160; also qtd. in Tiffin, "Digitally Remythicized," p. 68.

41. Northrup Frye, *The Anatomy of Criticism* (Princeton: Princeton University Press, 1957), p. 33.

42. Moyers, "Myth and Man," p. 63.

43. John Rieder, "Embracing the Alien," p. 33.

44. Geoffrey Chaucer, "The Wife of Bath's Tale," *The Riverside Chaucer*, ed. Larry D. Benson (Boston: Houghton, Mifflin, 1987), ll. III, pp. 857–58.

45. Chaucer, "Wife of Bath's Tale," ll. III, p. 859–61.

46. Chaucer, "Wife of Bath's Tale," l. III, p. 863.

47. David Wyatt, "*Star Wars* and the Productions of Time," *Virginia Quarterly Review*, 58:4 (1982), p. 609.

48. Rieder, "Embracing the Alien," p. 34.

49. Roberta L. Krueger, "Desire, Meaning, and the Female Reader: The Problem in Chrétien's *Charette*," *The Passing of Arthur: New Essays in Arthurian Tradition*, ed. Christopher Baswell and William Sharpe (New York: Garland, 1986), p. 34.

50. Krueger, "Desire, Meaning, and the Female Reader," p. 34.

51. Lucas, *StarWars: A New Hope*, facsimile script, p. 151.

52. Dan Ruby, "*Star Wars*: Not So Far Away," *Jump Cut*, 18 (1978): 11, qtd. in Gordon, "The Power of the Force," p. 196.

53. Sheila Fisher, "Leaving Morgan Aside: Women, History, and Revisionism in *Sir Gawain and the Green Knight*," *The Passing of Arthur: New Essays in Arthurian Tradition*, ed. Christopher Baswell and William Sharpe (New York: Garland, 1986), pp. 129–51, 130.

54. Fisher, "Leaving Morgan Aside," p. 146.

55. Madeline Pelner Cosman, *The Education of the Hero in Arthurian Romance* (Chapel Hill: University of North Carolina Press, 1965), p. 50.

56. Cosman, "The Education of the Hero," p. 150.

57. Cosman, "The Education of the Hero," p. 150.

58. Marilyn R. Sherman. "*Star Wars*: New Worlds and Ancient Myths," *Kentucky Folklore Record*, 25 (1979), pp. 6–10, 7.

59. Sara Boyle, "A long time ago in a kingdom far, far away. . .," *Avalon to Camelot*, 1.1 (1983), pp. 6–8, 6.

60. Boyle, "A Long Time Ago," p. 6.

61. Sir Thomas Malory, *Works*, ed. Eugene Vinaver (Oxford: Oxford University Press, 1971), p. 9.

62. *The Empire Strikes Back*, 124 mins., Eastman Color/Panavision, TCF/ Lucasfilm, Los Angeles, CA, 1980.

63. Boyle, "A Long Time Ago," p. 7.

64. David Wyatt, "*Star Wars* and the Productions of Time," *Virginia Quarterly Review*, 58:4 (1982), pp. 600–15, 602.

65. Malory, *Works*, p. 35.

66. *Star Wars: A New Hope*, 121 mins., Technicolor/Panavision, TCF/Lucasfilm, Los Angeles, CA, 1977.

67. Malory, *Works*, p. 19.

68. Boyle, "A Long Time Ago," p. 7.

69. Boyle, "A Long Time Ago," p. 7.

70. Boyle, "A Long Time Ago," p. 7.

71. Malory, *Works*, p. 60.

72. *Star Wars: A New Hope*.

73. George Lucas, *Star Wars: A New Hope*, facsimile script (New York: Ballantine Books, 1998), pp. 35–36. I am grateful to Cristina Ramundo for lending me her copies of these scripts, which have proved invaluable in interpreting Lucas's understanding of the film's directions. Far more than providing the film's words in accessible fashion, they offer "stage directions," which reveal much of the film's emotional content.

74. Malory, *Works*, p. 340.

75. Andrew Gordon, "The Power of the Force: Sex in the *Star Wars* Trilogy," *Eros in the Mind's Eye: Sexuality and the Fantastic in Art and Film*, ed. Donald Palumbo (New York: Greenwood, 1986), pp. 193–207, 199.

76. Gordon, "The Power of the Force," p. 201.

77. Gordon, "The Power of the Force," p. 197.

78. This scene echoes Luke's orgasmic moment at the end of *Star Wars IV: A New Hope* when he penetrates the Death Star in his x-wing fighter, using only the force as a navigational tool, shoots his weapon into its core, and then cheers as the death star blows up in a vast shower of sparks.

79. *The Return of the Jedi*, 132 mins, DeLuxe/Panavision, TCF/Lucasfilm, Los Angeles, CA, 1983.

80. George Lucas, *Return of the Jedi*, facsimile script (New York: Ballantine Books, 1998), p. 83.

81. Malory, *Works*, p. 713.

82. Malory, *Works*, pp. 713–14.

83. Malory, *Works*, p. 718.

84. Malory, *Works*, p. 717.

85. Comics Plus is located at 302 Seventh Avenue in Park Slope, Brooklyn. The proprietor (who requested not to be named) noted that "*Star Wars* toys do well even when a movie hasn't just come out." Personal interview, January 12, 2002. Forbidden Planet, located at 840 Broadway, offers a wide selection of *Star Wars* items in all price ranges, from small plastic action figures to larger, resin-cast decorative ones, life-sized cardboard cut outs, comic books, novels, post cards, buttons, magnets, t-shirts, and toys. They also indicated that these had sold well since the release of the first sets of movie-related paraphernalia in the late 1970s.

86. Malory, *Works*, p. 27.

87. Sherman, "*Star Wars*: New Worlds," p. 9.

88. Sherman, "*Star Wars*: New Worlds," p. 6.

89. Steven A. Galipeau, The *Journey of Luke Skywalker: An Analysis of Modern Myth and Symbol* (Chicago: Open Court, 2001), p. 1. Galipeau reads the whole *Star Wars* enterprise as a Jungian analyst; for him, the films proceed as a series of archetypes of the unconscious. In this reading, he follows Maurice Phipps, "The Myth and Magic of 'Star Wars': A Jungian Interpretation," *Viewpoints*, 120 (1983), pp. 1–13. Phipps sees *Star Wars* as "a fairly tale projected into the future which exemplifies in a clear-cut manner many of the archetypes of Jungian psychology. These films are modern retelling of ancient myths" (abstract).

90. Moyers, "Of Myths and Men," p. 62.

91. Moyers, "Of Myths and Men," p. 63.

92. Eco, *Travels*, p. 83.

93. Seabrook, "Why is the Force Still With Us?" p. 43.

94. Gary Cross, *The All-Consuming Century: Why Commercialism Won in Modern America* (New York: Columbia University Press, 2000), p. 210.

95. Sorensen, qtd. in Seabrook "Why is the Force Still With Us," p. 44; see also n. 7 to this chapter.

96. Cross, *All-Consuming Century*, p. viii.

97. Walter Benjamin, "Art in the Age of Mechanical Reproduction," *Illuminations*, 1968, ed. Hannah Arendt, trans. Harry Zohn (New York: Schocken Books, 1988), p. 244, n. 7.

98. Roland Barthes, *The Pleasure of the Text* (New York: Hill and Lang, 1975), p. 41, qtd. in Huyssen, p. 211.

99. Andreas Huyssen, *After the Great Divide: Modernism, Mass Culture, Postmodernism* (Bloomington: Indiana University Press, 1986), p. 48.

100. Cross, *The All-Consuming Century*, p. 1.

101. Jean Baudrillard, *System of Objects*, 1968, trans. James Benedict (London: Verso, 1996), p. 205.

102. Eco, *Travels*, p. 48.

103. Seabrook, "Why is the Force Still With Us?" p. 40.

104. Seabrook, "Why is the Force Still With Us?" p. 40.

105. T. J. Jackson Lears, *Fables of Abundance: A Cultural History of Advertising in America* (New York: Basic Books, 1994), p. 6. I am very grateful to Mary Balkun for sharing this insight with me.

106. Lears, *Fables of Abundance*, p. 7.

107. Susan M. Pearce, *Museums, Objects, and Collections: A Cultural Study* (Washington: Smithsonian Institution Press, 1992), p. 83. For this information, too, I am indebted to Mary Balkun.

108. Seabrook, "Why is the Force Still With Us?" p. 41.

BIBLIOGRAPHY

"All Good Things. . . ." *Star Trek: The Next Generation*. Episode 277. Paramount Pictures. May 23, 1994.

Angel, Roger. *Once More Around the Park: A Baseball Reader*. New York: Ballantine, 1991.

Auerbach, Erich. "The Knight Sets Forth." In *Mimesis: The Representation of Reality in Western Literature*. Translated by Willard R. Trask. Princeton: Princeton University Press, 1953.

Augustine. *Confessions*. Translated by R. S. Pine-Coffin. Harmondsworth: Penguin Books, 1961.

Austen, Jane. *Northanger Abbey*. 1818. Edited by Anne Ehrenpries. New York: Penguin Books, 1972.

The Babe Ruth Story. 107 mins. Allied Artists. 1948.

Bakhtin, Michael. *Crisis in Dostoyevsky's Poetics*. Translated by Caryl Emmerson. Minneapolis: University of Minnesota Press, 1984.

Baldwin, John W. *The Language of Sex*. Chicago: University of Chicago Press, 1994.

Barr, Marleen S. *Alien to Femininity: Speculative Fiction and Femininity Theory*. New York: Greenwood Press, 1987.

Barr, Marleen S. " 'All Good Things. . .': The End of *Star Trek: The Next Generation*, the End of Camelot—The End of the Tale about Women as Handmaid to Patriarchy as Superman." In *Enterprise Zones: Critical Positions on* Star Trek, edited by Taylor Harrison et al. Boulder, Colorado: Westview Press, 1996.

The Barry Halper Collection of Baseball Memorabilia Catalogue. New York: Sotheby's, 1999. Auction date: September 23–29, 1999.

Baseball Weekly 10, no. 39 (2000).

Baswell, Christopher. "Men in the *Roman D'Eneas*: The Construction of Empire." In *Medieval Masculinities: Regarding Men in the Middle Ages*, edited by Clare A. Lees. Minneapolis: University of Minnesota Press, 1994.

Baswell, Christopher and William Sharpe. "Introduction: Rex Quondam Rexque Futurus." In *The Passing of Arthur: New Essays in Arthurian Tradition*, edited by Christopher Baswell and William Sharpe. New York: Garland, 1986.

Baudrillard, Jean. *For a Critique of the Political Economy of the Sign*. Translated by Charles Levin. St. Louis: Telos Press, 1981.

Baudrillard, Jean. *The System of Objects*. Translated by James Benedict. New York: Verso, 1996.

Benjamin, Walter. "Unpacking My Library." In *Illuminations*, translated by Harry Zohn. New York: Shocken, 1968.

Benjamin, Walter. "The Work of Art in the Age of Mechanical Reproduction." In *Illuminations*, translated by Harry Zohn. New York: Shocken, 1968.

Bennett, James. "Testing of a President." *New York Times*, September 17, 1998. Sec. A1.

Bernardi, Daniel Leonard. *Star Trek and History: Race-ing Toward a White Future*. New Brunswick, New Jersey: Rutgers University Press, 1998.

Bianco, Anthony. "A Grand-Slam Season." *Business Week*, November 2, 1998, 104.

Bick, Ilsa J. "Boys in Space: *Star Trek*, Latency, and the Neverending Story." In *Enterprise Zones: Critical Positions on Star Trek*, edited by Taylor Harrison et al. Boulder, Colorado: Westview Press, 1996.

Birdsall, Ralph. *The Story of Cooperstown*. New York: Arthur H. Crist Co., 1917.

Bloch, R. Howard. *The Scandal of the Fabliaux*. Chicago: University of Chicago Press, 1994.

Boethius, Ulf. "The History of High and Low Culture." In *Youth Culture in Late Modernity*, edited by Johan Förnas and Göran Bolin. London: Sage, 1995.

"Bomber Bulletin." *New York Daily News*, June 24, 1998, 64.

Borzi, Pat. "The Machine: A Slave to his Routine, Wade Boggs Doggedly Pursues Two More Goals." *The Star-Ledger*, September 29, 1996, 14.

Boswell, Randy. "Medieval Crusades Revived in Terrorism-War Rhetoric." *Ottawa Citizen*, September 25, 2001, A2.

Boyle, Sara. "A long time ago in a kingdom far, far away. . ." *Avalon to Camelot* 1:1 (1983): 6–8.

Brown, Catherine. "In the Middle." *Journal of Medieval and Early Modern Studies* 30:3 (2000): 548–67.

Brown, Peter. The *Cult of the Saints: Its Rise and Function in Latin Christianity*. Chicago: University of Chicago Press, 1981.

Bruckner, Matilda Tomaryn. *Shaping Romance: Interpretation, Truth and Closure in Twelfth-Century French Fictions*. Philadelphia: University of Pennsylvania Press, 1993.

Bulfinch, Thomas. *Bulfinch's Mythology*. 1867. New York: Avenel, 1978.

Burke, Edmund. *Enquiry into the Sublime and Beautiful*. 1796. New York: Columbia University Press, 1958.

Canin, Ethan. "City of Broken Hearts." In *The Palace Thief*. New York: Picador, 1994.

"Chain of Command, I." *Star Trek: The Next Generation*. Episode 236. Paramount Pictures. December 14, 1992.

Chase, Ellen. "Mark and Sammy Captivate a Nation." *Star-Ledger*, September 6, 1998. Sec. 1.

Chaucer, Geoffrey. *The Riverside Chaucer*, 3rd ed., edited by Larry D. Benson. Boston: Houghton, Mifflin, 1987.

"The Child." *Star Trek: The Next Generation*. Episode 127. Paramount Pictures. November 21, 1988.

Chrétien de Troyes. *Erec et Enide*. Edited by Mario Roques. Paris: Champions, 1982.

Chrétien de Troyes. *Erec and Enide*. Translated by Burton Raffel. New Haven: Yale University Press, 1987.

Chrétien de Troyes. *Yvain*. Edited by Mario Roques. Paris: Champions, 1982.

Chrétien de Troyes. *Yvain*. Translated by Burton Rafael. New Haven: Yale University Press, 1987.

"Code of Honor." *Star Trek: The Next Generation*. Episode 104. Paramount Pictures. October 12, 1987.

Coffey, Wayne. "Baseball Lifts his Spirit: Fireman's Find Finds Hall Home." *New York Daily News*, November 8, 2001, 92.

Cohen, Jeffrey Jerome. *On Giants*. Minneapolis: University of Minnesota Press, 1999.

Collins, Steven F. "For the Greater Good: Trilateralism and Hegemony in *Star Trek: The Next Generation*." In *Enterprise Zones: Critical Positions on Star Trek*, edited by Taylor Harrison et al. Boulder, Colorado: Westview Press, 1996.

Cosman, Madeline Pelner. *The Education of the Hero in Arthurian Romance*. Chapel Hill: University of North Carolina Press, 1965.

Cousineau, Phil. *The Art of Pilgrimage*. Berkeley, California: Conari Press, 1998.

Crane, Susan. *Gender and Romance in Chaucer's Canterbury Tales*. Princeton: Princeton University Press, 1994.

Croce, Bob. "Boggs at Home in Hall." *Albany Times-Union*, July 25, 1989. Sec. D.

Cross, Gary. *The All-Consuming Century: Why Commercialism Won in Modern America*. New York: Columbia University Press, 2000.

Cyphers, Luke. "A Mark for the Ages." *New York Daily News*, September 9, 1998, 57.

"Darmok." *Star Trek: The Next Generation*. Episode 202. Paramount Pictures. September 30, 1991.

Davies, Robertson. *The Rebel Angels*. New York: Penguin, 1980.

Desmond, Marilyn. *Reading Dido: Gender, Textuality, and the Medieval Aeneid. Medieval Cultures*, vol. 8. Minneapolis: University of Minnesota Press, 1994.

de Voraigne, Jacobus. *Golden Legend*. Vols. 1 and 2. Translated by William Granger Ryan. Princeton: Princeton University Press, 1993.

"Devil's Due." *Star Trek: The Next Generation*. Episode 187. Paramount Pictures. February 4, 1991.

Dinshaw, Carolyn. *Chaucer's Sexual Poetics*. Madison: University of Wisconsin Press, 1989.

Dinshaw, Carolyn. *Getting Medieval: Sexualities and Communities, Pre-and Post-Modern*. Durham, North Carolina: Duke University Press, 1999.

Donaldson, E. Talbot. "The Idiom of Popular Poetry in the Miller's Tale." In *Speaking of Chaucer*. New York: W. W. Norton and Company, 1970.

Dooley, Eugene A. *Church Law on Sacred Relics*. Washington, D.C.: Catholic University Press, 1931.

"The Drumhead." *Star Trek: The Next Generation*. Episode 195. Paramount Pictures. April 29, 1991.

Durant, Will and Ariel. *The Age of Faith: A History of Medieval Civilization*. Vol. 2 of *The Story of Civilization*. New York: Simon and Schuster, 1950.

Eco, Umberto. *Travels in Hyperreality*. New York: Harcourt, Brace, and Jovanovich, 1986.

Egbert, Bill and Bill Hutchinson. "2.7M Buys Mac's 70th Home Run History Fetches Record." *New York Daily News*, January 13, 1999, 5.

The Empire Strikes Back. 124 mins. Eastman Color/Panavision. TCF/Lucasfilm, Los Angeles, California, 1980.

"Eye of the Beholder." *Star Trek: The Next Generation*. Episode 270. Paramount
    Pictures. February 28, 1994.
"Face of the Enemy." *Star Trek: The Next Generation*. Episode 240. Paramount
    Pictures. February 8, 1993.
Fainaru, Steve. "Adams Article Set for March: Story on Boggs termed 'interesting,
    explosive.'" Boston Globe, February 2, 1989, 49.
Favazza, Armando R. *Bodies Under Siege: Self-Mutilation in Culture and Psychiatry*.
    Baltimore: Johns Hopkins University Press, 1987.
Field of Dreams. Directed and screenwritten by P. A. Robinson. Universal City
    Studios, 1989.
Fisher, Philip. *Making and Effacing Art: Modern American Art in a Culture of Museums*.
    New York: Oxford University Press, 1991.
Fisher, Sheila. "Leaving Morgan Aside: Women, History, and Revisionism in *Sir
    Gawain and the Green Knight*." In *The Passing of Arthur: New Essays in Arthurian
    Tradition*, edited by Christopher Baswell and William Sharpe. New York:
    Garland, 1986.
Fong, Bobby. "The Magic Cocktail: The Enduring Appeal of the Field of Dreams."
    Aethlon 11, no. 1 (1993): 29–35.
Förnas, Johan. "Youth, Culture, and Modernity." In *Youth Culture in Late Modernity*,
    edited by Johan Förnas and Göran Bolin. London: Sage, 1995.
Förnas, Johan and Göran Bolin, eds. *Youth Culture in Late Modernity*. London: Sage,
    1995.
Foucault, Michel. *The History of Sexuality: An Introduction*. Vol. 1. Translated by
    Robert Hurley, 1978. New York: Vintage Press, 1990.
Frye, Northrop. *The Anatomy of Criticism*. Princeton: Princeton University Press, 1957.
Galipeau, Steven A. *The Journey of Luke Skywalker: An Analysis of Modern Myth and
    Symbol*. Chicago: Open Court, 2001.
Geary, Patrick. *Living with the Dead in the Middle Ages*. Ithaca: Cornell University
    Press, 1994.
Geary, Patrick J. *Furta Sacra: Thefts of Relics in the Central Middle Ages*. 1978.
    Princeton: Princeton University Press, 1990.
Geertz, Clifford. *The Interpretation of Cultures*. New York: Basic Books, 1973.
Gerold, David. The *World of Star Trek*. New York: Balantine Books, 1973.
Giamatti, A. Bartlett. *Take Time for Paradise: Americans and Their Games*. New York:
    Summit Books, 1989.
Goldin, Frederick. "Introduction." *The Song of Roland*. Edited and translated by
    Frederick Goldin. New York: W. W. Norton and Co., 1978.
Goldin, Frederick. *The Mirror of Narcissus in the Courtly Love Lyric*. Ithaca: Cornell
    University Press, 1967.
Golenblock, Peter. *The Spirit of St. Louis: A History of the St. Louis Cardinals and
    Browns*. New York: Avon, 2000.
Goodall, Fred. "Boggs Jumps onto the Milestone Bus." *San Francisco Examiner*,
    August 8, 1999. Sec. B.
Goodwin, Doris Kearns. "Batting Champ Wade Boggs Hits With a Cool Eye,
    A Hot Hand and a Resolve to Help his Sister Overcome Illness." *People
    Magazine*, April 1986, 103.

Gordon, Andrew. "The Power of the Force: Sex in the *Star Wars* Trilogy." In *Eros in the Mind's Eye: Sexuality and the Fantastic in Art and Film*, edited by Donald Palumbo. New York: Greenwood, 1986.

Gordon, Andrew. "*Star Wars*: A Myth for our Time." *Literature/Film Quarterly* 6 (1999): 63–75.

Gordon, Jeff. "McGwire's Mark on Community One for the Ages." *St. Louis Post-Dispatch*, September 19, 1997. Sec. 01D.

Gould, Stephen Jay. "The Creation Myths of Cooperstown." *Natural History*, November 19, 1989: 10–14.

Gould, Stephen Jay. "How the New Sultan of Swat Measures Up." *Wall Street Journal*, September 10, 1998. Sec. A22.

Gregorii episcopi Turonensis, *Miracula et opera minora. Liber Vitae Patrum*. Edited by B. Krusch, Monumenta Geramniae Historica: Scriptores Rerum Merovingicarum. Vols. 1 and 2. Hanover: Hahn, 1885.

Grunwald, Michael. "One Fan's $3 Million Catch." *Washington Post*, January 13, 1999. Sec. A01.

Gurevich, Aron. *Medieval Popular Culture: Problems of Belief and Perception*. Translated by János M. Bak and Paul A. Hollingsworth. Cambridge: Cambridge University Press, 1988.

Guttman, Allan. *From Ritual to Record*. New York: Columbia University Press, 1978.

Harbin, Andrea R. "The Citizens of York and the Archetypal Christian Journey: Pilgrimage and Ritual in the York Cycle." *Medieval Perspectives* 14 (1999): 84–97.

Hastie, Amelie. "A Fabricated Space: Assimilating the Individual on *Star Trek: The Next Generation*." *Enterprise Zones: Critical Positions on Star Trek*. Edited by Taylor Harrison et al. Boulder, Colorado: Westview Press, 1996.

Hardy, Sarah and Rebecca Kulka. "A Paramount Narrative: Exploring Space on the Starship Enterprise." *Journal of Aesthetics and Art Criticism* 57, no. 2 (1999): 177–91.

Harris, John F. "Havel is Mystified by America's Latest Pastime." *Washington Post*, September 17, 1998. Sec. A14.

Harty, Kevin J. *Cinema Arthuriana: Essays on Arthurian Film*. New York: Garland Publishing, 1996.

Hegarty, Emily. "Some Suspect of Ill: Shakespeare's Sonnets and the 'Perfect Mate.' " *Extrapolations* 36, no. 1 (1995): 55–64.

Heller, Lee E. "The Persistence of Difference: Post-Feminism, Popular Discourse, and Heterosexuality in *Star Trek: The Next Generation*." *Science Fiction Studies* 24, no. 2 (1997): 226–44.

Henn, George. "Mac Calls it Quits." *New York Daily News*, November 12, 2001, 64.

"Heroes and Demons." *Star Trek: The Next Generation*. Episode 112. Paramount Pictures. April 4, 1995.

Hindle, Brooke. "How Much is a Piece of the True Cross Worth?" In *Material Culture and the Study of American Life*, edited by Ian M. G. Quimby. New York: W. W. Norton and Co., 1978.

Hines, Susan C. "What's Academic about *Trek*." *Extrapolations* 3, no. 61 (1995): 5–9.

Hitchcock, Michael. "Introduction." In *Souvenirs: The Material Culture of Tourism*, edited by Michael Hitchcock and Ken Teague. Aldershot, United Kingdom: Ashgate, 2000.

Hobsbawm, Eric. "Inventing Traditions." In *The Invention of Tradition*, edited by Eric Hobsbawm and Terrence Ranger. Cambridge: Cambridge University Press, 1983.

Hollander, Russell. "The Religion of Baseball: Psychological Perspectives." *Nine* 3, no. 1 (1994): 1–11.

Houlihan, Michael. "Souvenirs with Soul: 800 Years of Pilgrimage to Santiago de Compostela." In *Souvenirs: The Material Culture of Tourism*, edited by Michael Hitchcock and Ken Teague. Aldershot, United Kingdom: Ashgate, 2000.

"The Host." *Star Trek: The Next Generation*. Episode 197. Paramount Pictures. May 12, 1991.

Hummel, Rick. "Redbirds Make their Mark." *St. Louis Post-Dispatch*. September 17, 1997. Sec. 1A.

Hurd, Denise Alessandria. "The Monster Inside: Nineteenth Century Racial Constructs in the Twenty-Fourth Century Mythos of *Star Trek*." *Journal of Popular Culture* 31, no. 1 (1997): 23–35.

Huyssen, Andreas. *After the Great Divide: Modernism, Mass Culture, Postmodernism*. Bloomington: Indiana University Press, 1986.

Hyman, Mark. "Baseball's Biggest Auction Ever." *Business Week*, February 22, 1999, 151.

Hyman, Mark. "Holy Cow, Was that a $25 Million Homer?" *Business Week*, September 21, 1998, 104.

"The Inner Light." *Star Trek: The Next Generation*. Episode 225. Paramount Pictures. June 1, 1992.

Izenberg, Jerry. *Newark Star-Ledger*, September 9, 1998, 67.

Izenberg, Jerry. "Big Mac Takes Over the City with the Arch." *Newark Star-Ledger*, September 2, 1998, 17.

Izenberg, Jerry. "The History." *Newark Star-Ledger*, September 7, 1998, 57.

James, Bill. *What Ever Happened to the Hall of Fame?* New York: Macmillan, 1994.

Jameson, Frederic. *The Political Unconscious: Narrative as a Socially Symbolic Act*. Ithaca: Cornell University Press, 1981.

Jameson, Frederic. "Reification and Utopia in Mass Culture." *Social Text* 1 (1979): 130–48.

Jenkins, Bruce. "Wade's Ways Just Boggle the Mind." *San Francisco Chronicle*, May 28, 1991. Sec. D.

Joyce. "Gumby's Mark McGwire Message Board." June 21, 2001. www.mcgwire.com.

Joyrich, Lynne. "Feminist Enterprise?: *Star Trek: The Next Generation* and the Occupation of Femininity." *Cinema Journal* 35, no. 2 (1996): 61–84.

"Justice." *Star Trek: The Next Generation*. Episode 109. Paramount Pictures. November 9, 1987.

Kakutani, Michiko. "Making Art of Sport." *New York Times Magazine*, December 15, 1996, 15.

Kaufman, Michael. "Testing of a President." *New York Times*, September 17, 1998. Sec. 1.

Kelly, Kevin and Paula Parisi. "*Star Wars*: What's Next for George Lucas?" *Wired*, February 1997, 160–66, 210–17.

Kennedy, Edward Donald. "Introduction." In *King Arthur: A Casebook*. New York: Garland Publishing, 1996.

Kieckhefer, Richard. *Unquiet Souls*. Chicago: University of Chicago Press, 1984.

Klinkowitz, Jerry. "Introduction." In *Writing Baseball*. Urbana, Illinois: University of Illinois Press, 1991.

Knapp, Daniel. "The Relyk of a Seint: A Gloss on Chaucer's Pilgrimage." *ELH* 39, no. 1 (1972): 1–26.

Knapp, Peggy. "Alisoun of Bath and the Re-appropriation of Tradition." *Chaucer Review* 24 (1989): 45–52.

Knapp, Peggy. *Chaucer and the Social Contest*. New York: Routledge, 1990.

A Knight's Tale. 132 mins. Columbia/TriStar Pictures. 2001.

Kopytoff, Igor. "The Cultural Biography of Things: Commoditization as Process." In *The Social Life of Things: Commoditization as Process*, edited by Arjun Appadurai. New York: Cambridge University Press, 1986.

Kornheiser, Tony. "For Your Sins and Mine; Let Me Say I'm Sorry." *Washington Post*, February 24, 1989. Sec. D1.

Krueger, Roberta L. "Desire, Meaning, and the Female Reader: The Problem in Chrétien's Charette." In *The Passing of Arthur: New Essays in Arthurian Tradition*, edited by Christopher Baswell and William Sharpe. New York: Garland, 1986.

Lacy, Norris J. "Preface." In *The Arthurian Encyclopedia*, edited by Norris J. Lacy. New York: Garland Publishing, 1986.

"The Last Outpost." *Star Trek: The Next Generation*. Episode 107. Paramount Pictures. October 19, 1987.

"Lay le Freine." *Middle English Verse Romances*, edited by Donald B. Sands. Exeter: University of Exeter Press, 1986.

Lears, T. J. Jackson. *Fables of Abundance: A Cultural History of Advertising in America*. New York: Basic Books, 1994.

Leicester, Jr., H. Marshall. *The Disappointed Self: Representing the Subject in the Canterbury Tales*. Berkeley: University of California Press, 1990.

Leicester, Jr., H. Marshall. "Of a fire in the dark: Public and Private Feminism in the *Wife of Bath's Tale*." *Women's Studies* 11 (1984): 157–78.

"Lessons." *Star Trek: The Next Generation*. Episode 245. Paramount Pictures. April 5, 1993.

"Liaisons." *Star Trek: The Next Generation*. Episode 245. Paramount Pictures. September 20, 1993.

Logan, Michael. "The Magnificent Seven." *TV Guide*, May 14, 1994, 14.

Lovelace, Maud Hart. *Carney's House Party*. New York: HarperCollins, 1949.

Lovelace, Maud Hart. *Emily of Deep Valley*. New York: HarperCollins, 1950.

Lowry, Philip. *Green Cathedrals*. New York: Addison Wesley, 1992.

Lucas, George. *Return of the Jedi*. Facsimilie Script. New York: Ballantine Books, 1998.

Lucas, George. *Star Wars: A New Hope*. Facsimilie Script. New York: Ballantine Books, 1998.

Lupica, Mike. *Summer of '98: When Homers Flew, Records Fell, and Baseball Reclaimed America*. New York: Putnam, 1999.

"A Mac for All Seasons." *Time*, December 28, 1998–January 4, 1999, 138.

"Mac Sets the Mark." *New York Daily News*, September 9, 1998, 52–53.

Madden, Michael. "Battered Image Needs Restoring." *Boston Globe*, March 8, 1989, 73.

Major League Baseball Authentication Program pamphlet. 2001.

"Making His Mark." *Sports Illustrated*, September 14, 1998, 28.

Malory, Sir Thomas. *Works*, edited by Eugene Vinaver. Oxford: Oxford University Press, 1971.

Margolick, David. "The Tantalizing Boggs Case: One Ballplayer, Two Women, and Three National Pastimes." *New York Times*, March 3, 1989. Sec. B.

Martin, Robert. *Tennyson: The Unquiet Heart*. Oxford: Clarendon Press, 1983.

"Man of the People." *Star Trek: The Next Generation*. Episode 229. Paramount Pictures. October 5, 1992.

"A Mark for the Ages." *New York Daily News*, September 9, 1998, 60–61.

"The Mark of Excellence." *Time*, December 28, 1998–January 4, 1999, 147.

Martin, Douglas. "No. 70 Goes After Another Record." *New York Times*, January 4, 1999. Sec. B1:2.

Maslow, Abraham. *Religions, Values and Peak Experiences*. New York: Viking, 1971.

McCallum, Jack and Richard O'Brien. "Keep your eye on the Balls." *Sports Illustrated*, September 28, 1998, 24.

McDonough, Will. "Boggs Runs Risk of Losing Fame." *Boston Globe*, February 9, 1989, 49.

MacKay, Daniel. "*Star Wars*: The Magic of the Anti-Myth." *Foundation* 76 (1999): 63–75.

Messer, Michael A. *Power at Play: Sports and the Problem of Masculinity*. Boston: Beacon Press, 1992.

Monty Python and the Holy Grail. 91 mins. Columbia/TriStar Pictures. 1974.

Moorehouse, Geoffrey. "The Patron Saint of Greenies." *New York Times Book Review* 7, no. 13 (March 11, 2001).

Mosher, Stephen. "Fielding Our Dreams: Rounding Third in Dyersville." *Sociology of Sport Journal* 8 (1991): 272–80.

Moyers, Bill. "Of Myth and Men: An Interview with George Lucas." *Time*, April 26, 1999, 60.

Murcer, Bobby, Phil Rizutto, and Suzyn Waldman. "New York Yankees vs. Cleveland Indians." WPIX Television, July 26, 1996.

Muscatine, Charles. *The Old French Fabliaux*. New Haven: Yale University Press, 1986.

"The Naked Now." *Star Trek: The Next Generation*. Episode 103. Paramount Pictures. October 5, 1987.

The Natural. 137 mins. Tristar/Delphi. United States, 1984.

The Newark Star-Ledger, July 9, 1998. Sec. 1A.

Nemecek, Larry. *The Star Trek: The Next Generation Companion*. New York: Pocket Books, 1995.

Nennius. *Historia Brittonum*. "Arthur in the Latin Chronicles." *The Legend of Arthur*. Edited by James J. Wilhelm and Laia Zammuelis Gross. New York: Garland, 1984.

"Newman, Roberta." "The American Church of Baseball and The National Baseball Hall of Fame." *Nine: A Journal of Baseball History and Culture* 10, no. 1 (2001): 46–63.

"Dr. Babe Ruth Calls on his Boy Patient." *New York Times*, October 12, 1926. Sec. 1.

"The Baseball Hero." *New York Times*, October 8, 1926. Sec. 22.

"Boy Regains Health as Ruth Hits Homers." *New York Times*, October 8, 1926. Sec. 17.

"Series Balls Aid Sick Boy." *New York Times*, October 7, 1926. Sec. 21.

"Sick Boy Expecting Ruth 'Homer' Today." *New York Times*, October 9, 1926. Sec. 19.

Nutt, Amy Ellis. "McGwire helps put baseball in the pink." *Newark Star-Ledger*, September 13, 1998. Sec. 1.

O'Keefe, Michael and Bill Madden. "Bidder Beware." *New York Daily News*, May 14, 2000, 67.

Okrent, David. "A Mac for All Seasons." *Time*, December 28, 1998–January 4, 1999, 140.

Okuda, Michael, Denise Okuda, and Debbie Mirek. *The Star Trek Encyclopedia: A Reference Guide to the Future.* New York: Pocket Books, 1994.

"On TV Boggs Tells of 'Disease.' " *Boston Globe*, February 2, 1989, 50.

Otter, Monika. *Inventiones: Fiction and Referentiality in Twelfth-Century English Historical Writing.* Chapel Hill, North Carolina: University of North Carolina Press, 1996.

Paisner, Daniel. *The Ball: Mark McGwire's 70th Home Run Ball and the Marketing of the American Dream.* New York: Viking, 1999.

Pamphlet. Cooperstown, New York: National Baseball Hall of Fame and Museum, no date. Quoted in Charles Freuhling Springwood. *Cooperstown to Dyersville: A Geography of Baseball Nostalgia.* Boulder, Colorado: Westview Press, 1996.

Parker, Patricia. *Inescapable Romance.* Princeton: Princeton University Press, 1979.

Paskal, Cleo. "Pilgrimage to Christorama." *Canadian Geographic* 121, no. 2 (March/April 2001): 98.

Patterson, Lee. " 'For the Wyves Love of Bathe': Feminine Rhetoric and Poetic Resolution in the *Roman de la Rose* and the *Canterbury Tales*." *Speculum* 58, no. 3 (1983): 656–95.

Patterson, Lee. "On the Margin: Postmodernism, Ironic History, and Medieval Studies." *Speculum* 65, no. 1 (1990): 87–108.

Payer, Pierre J. *Sex and the Penetentials.* Toronto: University of Toronto Press, 1984.

Pearce, Susan. *Museums, Objects, and Collections.* Washington, D.C.: Smithsonian Institution, 1992.

"The Perfect Mate." *Star Trek: The Next Generation.* Episode 221. Paramount Pictures. April 27, 1992.

Phipps, Maurice. "The Myth and Magic of 'Star Wars': A Jungian Interpretation." *Viewpoints* 120 (1983): 1–13.

Pomian, Krysztof. *Collectors and Curiosities: Paris and Venice, 1500–1800.* 1987. Translated by Elisabeth Wiles-Portier. Cambridge: Polity Press, 1990.

"The Power of Caring: Mark McGwire is a Hero for More than Just His Homers." Advertising Feature presented by Cigna. *Sports Illustrated*, December 9, 1998, 22.

Projansky, Sarah. "When the Body Speaks: Deanna Troi's Tenuous Authority on the Rationalization of Federation Superiority in *Star Trek: The Next Generation* Rape Narratives." In *Enterprise Zones: Critical Positions on Star Trek*, edited by Taylor Harrison et al. Boulder, Colorado: Westview Press, 1996.

Queen. "We Will Rock You." 1978.

Rader, Benjamin. *American Sports: From the Age of Folk Games to the Age of Spectators*. Englewood Cliffs, New Jersey: Prentice Hall, 1983.

Rains, Rob. *Mark McGwire: Home Run Hero*. New York: St. Martin's Press, 1998.

Ramsay, Lee. *Chivalric Romances: Popular Literature in Medieval England*. Bloomington: Indiana University Press, 1983.

Régnier-Bohler, Danielle. "Imagining the Self. Part I: Exploring Literature." In *A History of Private Life II: Revelations of the Medieval World*, edited by Georges Duby, translated by Arthur Goldhammer. Cambridge, Massachussets: Belknap Press, 1988.

Reid-Jeffrey, Donna. "*Star Trek*: The Last Frontier in Modern American Myth." *Folklore and Mythology Studies* 6 (1982): 34–41.

The Return of the Jedi. 132 mins. DeLuxe/Panavision, TCF/Lucasfilm, Los Angeles, California, 1983.

Rieder, John. "Embracing the Alien: Science Fiction in Mass Culture." *Science Fiction Studies* 9 (1982): 26–37.

Riley, Rick. "The Good Father." *Sports Illustrated*, September 7, 1998, 38.

"Road to the Record." *New York Daily News*, September 9, 1998, 56.

Rondinaro, Steve. "In a League of His Own." *Memories and Dreams* 15, no. 3 (1993): 2. Quoted in Charles Freuhling Springwood. *Cooperstown to Dyersville: A Geography of Baseball Nostalgia*. Boulder, Colorado: Westview Press, 1996.

Ruby, Dan. "*Star Wars*: Not So Far Away." *Jump Cut* 18 (1978): 11.

Rushin, Steve. *Road Swing*. New York: Doubleday, 1998.

Ryan, Marie-Laure. "Narrative in Real Time: Chronicle, Mimesis, and Plot in the Baseball Broadcast." *Narrative* 1, no. 2 (1993): 138–55.

Sachs, Susan. "Bin Laden's Images Mesmerize Muslims." *New York Times*, October 9, 2001 (www.nytimes.com).

Sandomir, Richard. "$1 Million Offering for Ball to Aid Human Rights Case." *New York Times*, September 5, 1998, Sec. D3:5.

Schwartz, Amy. *The Wilson Quarterly* 25, no. 2 (2001): 120–21.

Seabrook, John. "Why is the Force Still with Us?" *The New Yorker*, January 6, 1997, 40.

"Seats out in Left Catching on at Busch." *Newark Star-Ledger*, September 9, 1998, 67.

"Second Chances." *Star Trek: The Next Generation*. Episode 250. Paramount Pictures. May 24, 1993.

Seymour, Harold. *Baseball: The Golden Age*. New York: Oxford University Press, 1991.

Shannon, Bill, ed. *Who's Who in Baseball*. 8th ed. New York: Who's Who in Baseball Magazine Co., 2001.

Shaughnessy, Mike. "The Low Down on the Boggs-Adams Saga." *Boston Globe*, February 11, 1989, 29.

Sherman, Joel. "Boggs gets 'Punchy' in Beantown." New York Post, June 30, 1994, 38.

Sherman, Marilyn R. "*Star Wars*: New Worlds and Ancient Myths." *Kentucky Folklore Record* 25 (1979): 6–10.

Shrady, Nicholas. *Sacred Roads: Adventures From the Pilgrimage Trail.* San Francisco: HarperCollins, 1999.

Shinners, John, ed. *Medieval Popular Religion 1000–1500: A Reader.* Peterborough, Ontario: Broadview Press, 1997.

Shumacher, David D. "Designated Swinger." *Penthouse*, April 1989, 58.

Sillary, Ted. "Hahn, Rice, and. . .Adams? Palimony Suit against Boggs has potential to get messy." *Albany Times-Union*, July 15, 1988, Sec. D.

Singer, Armand and Michael Lastinger. "Themes and Sources of *Star Wars*: John Carter and Flash Gordon Enlist in the First Crusade." *Popular Culture Review* 9, no. 2 (1998): 65–77.

Sir Gawain and the Green Knight. In *The Poems of the Pearl Manuscript*, edited by. Malcolm Andrew and Ronald Waldron. London: Arnold, 1978.

Sir Gawain and the Green Knight. Translated by Marie Boroff. New York: W. W. Norton and Co., 1967.

Smith, Bill. "Fans Enjoy Fame after Retrieving McGwire's Home Run Balls." *St. Louis Post-Dispatch*, October 4, 1998, Sec. A14.

Smith, Gary. "The Mother of All Pearls." *Sports Illustrated*, September 21, 1998, 59.

Smith, Huston. "Foreword." In *The Art of Pilgrimage: Seeker's Guide to Making Travel Sacred.* By Phil Cousineau. Berkeley, California: Conari Press, 1998.

Smith, Ken. *Baseball's Hall of Fame.* New York: Grosset and Dunlap, 1975.

The Song of Roland. Translated by Frederick Goldin. New York: W. W. Norton and Co., 1978.

Soos, Troy. *Murder at Ebbets Field.* New York: Kensington Press, 1995.

Sosa, Sammy. "Mi Amigo Mark." *Time*, December 28, 1998–January 4, 1999, 142.

Southern, R. W. *Western Society and the Church in the Middle Ages.* Grand Rapids, Michigan: Eerdmans, 1970.

"The Spirit of Giving." *Baseball Weekly* 10, no. 35 (2000): 1, 6–7.

The Sporting News Baseball Annual (February 2001).

Springwood, Charles Freuhling. *Cooperstown to Dyersville: A Geography of Baseball Nostalgia.* Boulder, Colorado: Westview Press, 1996.

Star Trek. Desilu Productions. NBC. 1966–69.

Star Trek V: The Final Frontier. 197 mins. Technicolor. Paramont Pictures, Los Angeles, California, 1989.

Star Trek VI: The Undiscovered Country. 110 mins. Technicolor. Paramount Pictures, Los Angeles, California, 1991.

Star Trek VIII: Generations. 117 mins. Technicolor. Paramount Pictures, Los Angeles, California, 1994.

Star Trek: The Next Generation. Paramount Pictures. Syndicated. 1987–94.

Star Wars: A New Hope. 121 mins. Technicolor/Panavision. TCF Lucasfilm, Los Angeles, California, 1977.

Stein, Joel. "Long Live the King." *Time*, September 21, 1998, 57.

Stein, Joel. "Mark of Excellence." *Time*, December 28, 1998–4 January 1999, 150.

Stewart, Susan. *On Longing: Narratives of the Miniature, the Gigantic, the Souvenir, the Collection*. Durham, North Carolina: Duke University Press, 1993.

Stouck, Mary-Ann, ed. *Medieval Saints: A Reader*. Peterborough, Ontania: Broadview, 1999.

Strasbaugh, John. *E: Reflections on the Birth of the Elvis Faith*. New York: Blast, 1995.

Street and Smith's Baseball Annual (February 2001).

"Sub Rosa." *Star Trek: The Next Generation*. Episode 266. Paramount Pictures. January 31, 1994.

Sumption, Jonathan. *Pilgrimage: An Image of Medieval Religion*. Totowa, New Jersey: Rowmann and Littlefield, 1975.

Swift, E. M. "Facing the Music: Wade Boggs Stayed Cool Despite His Ex-Lover's Steamy Revelations." *Sports Illustrated*, March 6, 1989, 41.

"Thine Own Self." *Star Trek: The Next Generation*. Episode 268. Paramount Pictures. February 14, 1994.

Thorn, John. *The Treasures of the Hall of Fame*. New York: Villard, 1998.

Tiffin, Jessica. "Digitally Remythicized: *Star Wars*, Modern Popular Mythology, and *Madam and Eve*." *Journal of Literary Studies* 15, nos. 1–2 (1999): 66–80.

Timmerman, Tom. "McGwire's Stature Rose as Tears Fell: 'I Was Wanting So Much to Help Young Children.'" *St. Louis Post-Dispatch*, September 17, 1997, Sec. 1A.

Todorov, Tsvetan. *Introduction to Poetics*. Translated by Richard Howard. Minneapolis: University of Minnesota Press, 1981.

Trausch, Susan. "Boggs' 'Addiction' is Off Base." *Boston Globe*, March 2, 1989, 12.

Tresniowski, Alex and Mary M. Harrison. "Going, Going, Gone!" *People Weekly* 51, no. 4 (February 1, 1999): 52.

Turner, Victor and Edith Turner. *Image and Pilgrimage in Christian Culture: Anthropological Perspectives*. New York: Columbia University Press, 1978.

"Up the Long Ladder." *Star Trek: The Next Generation.* Episode 144. Paramount Pictures. May 22, 1989.

Vaccaro, Mike. "As McGwire Hits Homer 62, Time Stands Still." *Newark Star-Ledger*, September 9, 1998, 1.

Vaccaro, Mike. "Baseball Fans' Reaction to McGwire's Heroics is Simply Priceless." *Newark Star-Ledger*, September 9, 1998, 65.

Vance, Eugene. "Chrétien's *Yvain* and the Ideologies of Change and Exchange." *Yale French Studies* 70 (1986): 42–62.

Vance, Eugene. *Mervelous Signals: Poetics and Sign Theory in the Middle Ages*. Lincoln: University of Nebraska Press, 1986.

Verducci, Tom. "48, 49, 50." *Sports Illustrated* 89, no. 9 (1998): 30.

Verducci, Tom. "Making his Mark." *Sports Illustrated*, September 14, 1998, 32.

Verducci, Tom. "A Quiet. 300." *Sports Illustrated*, January 15, 1996, 70.

Vielliard, Jenanne, ed. *Guide du Pelerin de S. Jacques de Compostella* 9.17. Paris: Macon, 1969.

"Violations." *Star Trek: The Next Generation*. Episode 212. Paramount Pictures. February 3, 1992.

Walker, John, ed. *Halliwell's Film Guide*. New York: HarperCollins, 1995.

Ward, Benedicta. *Miracles and the Medieval Mind: Theory, Record and Event 1000–1215*. Philadelphia: University of Pennsylvania Press, 1987.

Webb, Diana. *Pilgrims and Pilgrimage in the Medieval West*. London: I. B. Tauris, 1999.

Weinstock, Jeffrey. "Freaks in Space: 'Extraterrestrialism' and 'Deep Space Multiculturalism.'" In *Freakery: Cultural Spectacles of the Extraordinary Body*, edited by Rosemarie Garland Thomason. New York: New York University Press, 1996.

Weisl, Angela Jane. *Conquering the Reign of Femeny: Gender and Genre in Chaucer's Romance*. Cambridge: D. S. Brewer, 1995.

Westbrook, Deanne. *Ground Rules: Baseball and Myth*. Urbana: University of Illinois Press, 1996.

Williams, Peter. *The Sports Immortals: Deifying the American Athlete*. Bowling Green, Ohio: Bowling Green State University Popular Press, 1994.

Wheatley, Tom. "Generosity Still Pays Dividends in Forneris Saga." *Saint Louis Post-Dispatch*, August 10, 1999, Sec. C1.

White, David Gordon. *Myths of the Dog-Man*. Chicago: University of Chicago Press, 1991.

Wilder, Laura Ingalls. *Little Town on the Prairie*. New York: Harper & Row, 1941.

Woodward, Kenneth. *Making Saints*. New York: Touchstone, 1990.

Wyatt, David. "*Star Wars* and the Productions of Time." *Virginia Quarterly Review* 58, no. 4 (1982): 600–15.

Yardley, Jonathan. "Stealing Home to Cooperstown." *Washington Post*, October 21, 1985. Quoted in Charles Freuhling Springwood. *Cooperstown to Dyersville: A Geography of Baseball Nostalgia*. Boulder, Colorado: Westview Press, 1996.

Yeats, William Butler. "Crazy Jane Talks to the Bishop." In *The Poems of W. B. Yeats*, edited by Richard J. Finnerman. New York: Macmillan, 1986.

Yeats, William Butler. "Sailing to Byzantium." In *The Poems of W. B. Yeats*, edited by Richard J. Finnerman. New York: Macmillan, 1986.

Ziegel, Vic. "You Can't Measure a Home Run This Big." *New York Daily News*, September 9, 1998, 52.

Zumthor, Paul. *Towards a Medievalist Poetics*. Translated by Phillip Bennett. Minneapolis: University of Minnesota Press, 1992.

INDEX